VERNACULAR EDENS

Tropes of Translation in Medieval European Fictions

SIMONE MARCHESI

Vernacular Edens

Tropes of Translation in Medieval European Fictions

UNIVERSITY OF TORONTO PRESS
Toronto Buffalo London

© University of Toronto Press 2025
Toronto Buffalo London
utorontopress.com
Printed in the USA

ISBN 978-1-4875-5830-7 (cloth)   ISBN 978-1-4875-5832-1 (EPUB)
                                  ISBN 978-1-4875-5831-4 (PDF)

Library and Archives Canada Cataloguing in Publication

Title: Vernacular edens : tropes of translation in medieval European fictions /
    Simone Marchesi.
Names: Marchesi, Simone, author.
Description: Includes bibliographical references and index.
Identifiers: Canadiana (print) 20240413369 | Canadiana (ebook) 20240413377 |
    ISBN 9781487558307 (cloth) | ISBN 9781487558314 (PDF) |
    ISBN 9781487558321 (EPUB)
Subjects: LCSH: Fiction, Medieval – Translations – History and criticism. |
    LCSH: Gardens in literature.
Classification: LCC PN692 .M37 2025 | DDC 809.3/9364–dc23

Cover design: John Beadle
Cover image: Albrecht Durer, *Adam and Eve (The Fall of Man)*, copperplate engraving,
1504. Alamy Stock Photo.

We wish to acknowledge the land on which the University of Toronto Press
operates. This land is the traditional territory of the Wendat, the Anishnaabeg, the
Haudenosaunee, the Métis, and the Mississaugas of the Credit First Nation.

University of Toronto Press acknowledges the financial support of the Government of
Canada, the Canada Council for the Arts, and the Ontario Arts Council, an agency of
the Government of Ontario, for its publishing activities.

For John V. Fleming of Princeton

Contents

Preface

Beyond Babel: The Tower and the Garden

This book is about a widespread trope, the literary representation of gardens, and an equally widespread activity, the redeployment of classical material via vertical translation from Latin into a vernacular language, as they appear in late medieval vernacular fictions. Living and operating in a state of diglossia, the authors of such works often discussed their most engaging novelty, their use of the vernacular, in terms of tradition and translation. Given the Christian system of religious symbolism and ethical imagination in which they moved, they also appeared ready to associate the natural and human space of the garden with the biblical model of the place in the East where God planted a garden and placed Adam and Eve before the fall. Neither statement is particularly surprising, and both make sense independently. This book attempts to bring them together.[1]

Simply stated, the main contention of this book is that the recurrence of the garden setting in conjunction with passages that establish a deep and clear relation between a new text and an "original" one, explicitly presented as drafted in an "original" language, is significant, and it may be used to understand how translation was understood in a specific segment of medieval literary culture. The connection of gardens, when presented as allusive new instantiations of the Garden of Eden with self-consciously staged scenes of translation, as moments of heightened metahistorical awareness, sheds light on how a segment of medieval culture conceptualized the act of transmission and reception involving classical textual culture. The vernacular fiction writers whose texts are studied here participated in the formation and deployment of a trope, which in part depended on their work and through which in part they, in turn, produced meaning. In a cultural sense, when these writers conceived of their work as translators of previous literature, they did so by thinking about their activity within the trope of Eden. In a philological sense, each text helps – through the recurrence of elements across distinct, identifiable contexts and traditions – to reconstruct the trope in all its complexity. Ideally, philology helps to establish the connection between the cultural construct of Eden and the issue of translation, while the larger cultural perspective helps to conceptualize what acts of translation have to do with Eden.

It is perhaps paradoxical that medieval writers of vernacular fiction translated frequently but did not often talk about their activity as translators. With some notable and well-studied exceptions, which offer a starting point for most of the following chapters in this book, it seems that translational practice and conceptualization did not automatically go together, and many central texts in medieval vernacular literature match the intense practice of translating with a systematic undertheorizing of its guiding principles.[2] This book suggests that, rather than using a shared theory of translation or conflicting versions of one, medieval vernacular fiction writers created a figural set of associations between an element in the narrative, the visit to a garden, and an act, the translative reuse of past cultural material, to show rather than tell on what principles they were operating.

Seen in this light, the central role that gardens perform in literary works, openly engaging with translation, balances the relative scarcity of statements containing the metalanguage we commonly associate with theoretical reflections on the act of producing new linguistic versions of old material. When we look at medieval literary gardens, in other words, we may redress the apparent imbalance between the predominance of the practice *of* translation and the lack of metaliterary reflection *on* it. While their authors do not problematize the act of translating itself, they do consider their dialogue with ancient works integral to the value and identity of their projects. Thanks to a precise set of cultural connotations established in patristic texts, which forms the object of the initial chapter in this book, medieval writers and their audience felt authorized to use the figure of the garden in lieu of abstract and formalized discussions of their motives for translating, the advantages they derived from the process, and the actual modalities adopted while producing literature in new and current language. In an attempt to bring together literary practice and theoretical speculation in a historical vein, this book proposes to study the way medieval fictional texts used a recurring figure as a viable equivalent of formal theorizations.

Since it looks at the trope of the Edenic garden active in selected medieval fictional texts as a figural surrogate of formalized theory statements, this book discusses both medieval gardens and translation theories as a matter of course, but it is concerned with neither of these subjects per se. It focuses rather on one of the ways in which medieval fiction established itself as the latest link – most specifically *not* "the last" one – in a literary tradition that envisions past and present as strongly connected. Accordingly, its critical contribution is mainly historical-critical or perhaps even cultural-anthropological.[3] From today's perspective, a primary motivation for the literary analysis and cultural reconstruction at the core of this book is the need to dispel a contemporary popular bias about translation that may misguide readers when they approach such a distant and multiform textual tradition. Unlike some of their counterparts today, who often associate translation with loss, readers of medieval vernacular fiction were offered works conceived as both fully contemporary and also in harmony with their antecedents, in a cultural framework that accepted – even welcomed – translation.[4] As a body of texts that was at once current and historical, medieval fictions freely acknowledged both the multiplicity of languages in which texts were produced and the process that transposed some of them across different ages, localities, and idioms. The modern conceit that translation is at best a necessary evil, a process that produces an unavoidable and potentially deadly loss, though it existed in certain patristic circles, is not the dominant trope in the tradition this book studies. The corpus of texts presented instead reveals an insistence on the potential fruitfulness of linguistic transmutation, a cultural notion that is entrusted not so much to theoretical discussion, but is present, rather, in the evocation of the garden setting, an element that accompanies particularly self-aware moments of translation.

Thinking about Eden as a trope, as a space culturally associated with translation, offers a possible reason for why medieval fictional writers were vindicating their use of the vernacular while visiting narrative gardens – why they were doing one thing in the framework of the other. The theological frame of reference for this cultural practice is not difficult to delineate. In general, cultural terms, medieval thinking never considered the loss of Eden, and of the unity of language developed there by and with Adam, as the last of the vicissitudes befalling human language. According to Christian world-historical thinking, the linguistic fall embodied in the Tower of Babel, a tragic event which many saw as replicating the original fall in Eden, was not final. The advent of Christ and his sacrifice inaugurated a new temporal dispensation, one in which the effects of Adam's original sin were – at least potentially – undone, and Christ's sacrifice restored the grace that counterbalanced them to humankind. In this new dispensation, Christ the "New Adam" gave humanity access to a New Eden: the paradise that had been lost by their forefathers could be regained – this time, in an updated and better form. Heaven was the new and better garden, figurally foreshadowed by the old, earthly, and provisional one of which the Scriptures – now conceptualized as the old and now fulfilled Old Testament – spoke.

Christian thinking about matters of historical providential development relied on a compact series of culturally charged binaries. The old and the new dispensations came to be associated with the historical supersession of Judaism by the Christian religion, the ethical displacement of law by grace, the hermeneutic overcoming of the letter by the spirit, and the metaphysical preeminence of Paradise over Eden. The new dispensation also had a clear and essential linguistic dimension. In conceptualizing Christ as the Logos, the *Verbum*, Christian theologized historical thinking was responsible for developing this linguistic dimension from the start. In a rewriting of the incipit of Genesis, the Gospel of John opens with a statement asserting the theological primacy of the Word as essence of, and as agent being before, the act of creation: "In principio erat Verbum, et Verbum

erat apud Deum, et Deus erat Verbum" (Ioa 1:1). The same primacy of the Word
is reasserted in full force, in just a few verses, in the articulation of incarnation:
"Verbum caro factum est et habitavit in nobis" (Ioa 1:14). In dwelling among us,
the Word made flesh entered not only precise coordinates of space and time but
also a mutable linguistic sphere. Following Paul's lead, whose theological work
had moved Christianity from the status of a local Jewish cult into an international
intellectual arena, cultural powerhouses such as Augustine and Jerome were keenly
interested in coding the cultural tension at the core of the Christian message as
intergenerational progress. After all, the new religion was multifarious, appealing
to the Greek-speaking and -reading communities of a Latin-speaking empire that
was the source of law, while also emanating from a compact corpus of writings
originally composed (in its vast majority) in Hebrew.

The same set of radical oppositions between the old and the new that was at
the centre of their supersessionist theology spawned the dichotomy between a discounted monolingualism (coded as Jewish) and a favoured multilingualism (coded
as Christian). This multilingualism, at its most ideal level, had been rescued from
the status of Babelic confusion by the coming of Christ and, at its most practical level, consisted in the essentially Christian practice of translation. As active
interpreters and translators themselves, Christian Fathers were responsible in no
small part for putting a positive spin on the intercultural process of translation, a
process which they made coterminous with Christianity as a doctrine addressing
all people, with the multicultural and multilingual figure of Paul, *doctor gentium*,
as its ecumenical core – and thus eliding the cultural and often social violence
historically associated with the process of supersession. The watershed between the
two periods of history was, again, Incarnation, this time perceived, most specifically, as a linguistic event.

This vital modernism (a term I use to indicate the strategic cultural privileging
of what is "new" over what is treated as "old"), which is at the core of Christian
humanistic culture, permeates the texts that make up the body of this book. Medieval culture never perceived the banishment from the garden or the dissension of
languages as negative or final. What it did, rather, was to polarize their representation. While the punishment issued at Babel and the ensuing historical linguistic differentiation acted as a negative reminder of the act of trespass, the garden
became a prospective token of the redemptive coming of Christ. The trope of
the garden could be marked, that is, by the conditional promise that Incarnation
(the Word being made flesh) will recover and even surpass the linguistic felicity
depicted as both a potential and a promised state in Eden. As Ambrose put it in
his *De paradiso*, in Adam man exists in a shadowy condition ("siue in umbra uitae
erat propter figuram") which also essentially is a promise of a different one ("siue in
quodam pignore uitae erat," *De paradiso* 5, 29), and the same is true for the garden
of delights.[5] The analytical sections that make up the bulk of this book attempt to
isolate the optimistic strains of this figural linguistics, in which the tower and the

garden act as opposite typological markers, as well as some of the conditions that need to be in place for the promise of the garden to be fulfilled and not turn into an attempt to recapture the original status which had been possible in it. But what does the regaining of paradise entail? The medieval fiction writers studied here did not choose to retrogress toward either a lost and ultimately irrecoverable origin of language or an inessential, because artificial, unity of language, as was either considered or even proposed in some pre-utopian or pre-humanistic quarters of their culture. In keeping with the culture in which and for which they were producing their texts, they opted for progression through multiplicity. The antidote to Babel that they chose in their reflections on and practices of multilingualism was the practice of translation, framed optimistically as an ever-productive rewriting of the "ancient" authors by their "modern" counterparts.

A crucial caveat is in order here, to account for the significant categorial shift that took place when writers of medieval fictions adopted conceptualizations developed in biblical (and sacred) textuality in their secular (and classicizing) works. While the model of productive translatability that was found in Christian religious culture appeared suitable to negotiate the divide between authoritative texts from the past and evolving vernacular literacy, the special field in which it was developed – that of assumed "inspired" writing – also recommended that a corrective system of checks and balances be put in place in the new literary situation. In establishing the place and value of their works within the same Christian writing culture from which they drew their literary strategies, different writers behaved differently, adopting a wide compass of solutions to indicate the relative distance from or proximity to sacred texts. These solutions ranged from the subtly but powerfully articulated claim to prophetic authority advanced by the *theologus poeta* of the *Commedia*, a text that on occasion does not hesitate to put itself on par with canonical visionary literature, to the disengaged attitude of Chaucer's pilgrims, who at times explicitly request purely recreational narratives, "som myrie tale," to entertain them on their journey – as in the Prologue to the Clerk's Tale. Between these extremes, one may find the insistence on the oneiric and yet significant quality of the lover's experience in the *Roman de la Rose*, or the vindication of Boccaccio's *Decameron* that it will provide readers both pleasure and profit in equal proportions – both declinations of the traditional claim that literary fictions may ultimately be understood as falling within the bounds of ethics. These attitudes, through which writers signposted for their audiences and negotiated the sacred/secular divide, are at once too well known and too problematic to be discussed here in depth. It is important, however, to keep them in mind as they are co-implicated in the formation of the translation trope, a new secular literary adaptation of originally biblical hermeneutical practices.

What follows is a preliminary overview of the work carried out in the body of this book and may serve to orient readers through a variety of literary texts and cultural traditions. In the Introduction, I present the essential components of the interconnection of questions of multilingualism and biblical translation, as established in patristic, specifically Augustinian, discourse. I argue that the negative view of the Babel episode in Genesis is balanced by a consideration of the advantages that multilingualism, when imbricated with a positive attitude toward the work of translators, may afford to the ecumenic dimension of Christianity. In particular, I insist on the structural and visual connection that Augustine constructs between the quadriform directionality of the flow of translated biblical textuality, spreading far and wide through the circle of Earth, and the image of the garden of Eden as a place from which four cardinally directional rivers issue forth. Found in this association, which originates in Christian neo-testamentary identity and spawns a series of subsequent connections between the four Gospels and the spiritual message of the religion, is the inception and grounding of the trope of translation, which gives structure to similar connections in early Old French texts and eventually in the Italian and English literary tradition of vernacular fictions. To ground this argument, my analysis considers first Marie de France's prologues to her *Lais* and *Fables*, addressing her metapoetic statements, in light of the positive connotations she attributes to the work of modern interpreter-translators as willing and fruitful contributors to the meaning embedded in their texts by ancient authors. It then considers Chrétien de Troyes' formal and seminal treatment of the topos of *translatio studii et imperii* in the prologue of the *Cligès*, suggesting its alignment with the same optimism incarnate in Marie's prologues. The Introduction concludes with a brief treatment of two garden scenes, from Marie's *Guigemar* and Chrétien's *Érec et Énide*, which involve a programmatic connection with Latin classical antecedents paired with their productive redeployment (and reinterpretation) in the modern vernacular of the new texts.

In chapter 1, building upon the "modern-favouring" framework afforded by Marie de France's and Chrétien de Troyes' texts, I look at the overlapping of literary and theological questions shaping two sections of the *Roman de la Rose*. I concentrate on the poetic genealogy scene that appears midway through the poem, and on the discussion of the so-called *Evangile pardurable*, the object of doctrinal debate and some academic-political controversy in Jean de Meun's days. The interconnectedness of literary and scriptural issues of tradition and translation in a vernacular text is, in my view, inseparable from the precise garden setting that the authors of the *Rose* establish for the fictional narrative they develop throughout the work. The clear determination to present a pseudo-Eden that marks Guillaume's portion of the *Rose*, and the equally stark limitations that Jean imposes in his reprisal of the same material in his counterpointing continuation, point to the crucial status of the garden as a space open to redescription and interpretation.

In my reading, I highlight three elements that will be reactivated at different junctures in the tradition of garden-visit narratives. First, the garden of the *Rose* is the space in which, with a high degree of self-awareness, the text establishes a connection with a tradition that it translates, at once redeploying and reinterpreting it. Echoing the initial self-definition of Guillaume's *Rose* as containing subject matter triumphantly labelled "good and new," Jean's catalogue of the dead Latin poets that the God of Love evokes, as he introduces the two authors of the *Rose* as his vassals, defines the romance as the product of systematic reinterpretation and linguistic vernacularization. Secondly, the garden in Guillaume's *Rose* is described through a precise set of incompossible traits, the main one being that it is both round and square. The quadriform quality of Deduit's garden is both an echo of its Edenic quality and, in particular, a collateral signal of the evangelic aspirations of the text containing it. In light of this connection, it is significant that the second half of the poem juxtaposes these features of Guillaume's garden with another place, the Park of the Lamb, in Genius's speech. This new, metaphysically stable place systematically targets the original interpretive ambiguities embedded in the first garden, framing it as a provisional sign, one that essentially points beyond itself. Finally, the reinterpretation of the garden space that the *Rose* invites in its second half, predicated upon a hermeneutic that takes advantage of the openness of a narrative to new translations, dovetails with the discussion of the *Evangile pardurable*, in False-Seeming's speech. The affair is not simply of some consequence for the historical and theological background of the *Rose*; as the romance presents it, the divinely inspired new Gospel by Joachim of Flora becomes a case of pathological hermeneutic that signals the limits of the kind of interpretation that the text advocates for itself. By proposing what the text treats as an *avant-le-temps* evacuation of all Scripture, the advocates of a "new" New Testament brought to the fore the notion that scriptural interpretations could not only produce new meaning but also, paradoxically, fully exhaust the text's potential for signification.

These three elements, the chapter finally argues, leave a distinctive trace in two early Italian texts, Brunetto Latini's *Tesoretto* and the *Fiore*, a translation of the *Rose* attributable to Dante. Readers of the *Rose* are invited to evaluate descriptive ambiguities, negotiate topographical continuities and discontinuities between the garden and the park, and interrogate themselves about sacred and secular hermeneutic paradigms. Accordingly, in the *Tesoretto*, the realm of Love, not a garden per se but a meadow that like the garden is both "square and round," is presented as a self-contradictory space, a region of unlikeness in which the phenomenology of passions is displayed in its extremes, and also a translational space. It is no coincidence that the Latin poet Ovid appears here to instruct the protagonist, speaking both "openly" and in the latter's "modern" vernacular. Brunetto's characterization of Ovid's teaching confirms that for the *Tesoretto*, too, translation has a double valence, being at once a new linguistic version and an explicative commentary, and that to vernacularization is associated a tradition-forming power. While it is even more deeply involved with the *Rose* than the *Tesoretto*, the *Fiore* chooses a different path to negotiate the ambiguities of the garden: it simply skips the ample description present in its model. In place of a description of an Eden-like space containing allusions to the same cardinal directionality of its rivers, readers of the *Fiore* find a straight evocation of the four Gospels. Introduced as the specific object of the Amante's (the *Rose* Lover's Italian counterpart) abjuration in favour of a new set of commandments, this mention of "Luke, Matthew, Marc and John" suggests that an insightful and engaged reader of the poem had perceived this element in the text. In both cases, I argue, what the *Rose* left in its Italian vernacular descendants is a contextual signature rather than a textual one, which existed and should be read with a view to uniting garden visits and translational texts.

In chapter 2, devoted to Dante's "other works" as they relate to the *Commedia*, I begin by drawing attention to the peculiar disappearance of the figure of the parrot, which gets lost in the course of an act of self-translation in which Dante engaged, by moving one of his arguments across two parallel and practically contemporaneous passages drafted in the early years of his exile. To balance the smallness of the sample, and intimate its non-arbitrary quality, I frame my readings within a larger survey of Dante's reflection on issues of linguistics and literary history drawn from his pre-comedic works. In this section, I argue that Dante's most innovative discovery in the field of linguistics (namely, the mutability intrinsic to natural languages, the vernaculars), when combined with his similarly strong commitment to the notion that stability (which grammatical languages are designed to ensure) is a positive marker in a language of culture, brought him to a theoretical deadlock. Dante's impasse in matters of linguistics may be counted among the causes of the eventual failure and incompleteness of the treatises in which he articulates it. A consequence of this same crisis in linguistic postulates, which paved the way for the writing of the *Commedia* (and precipitated some of its principles), was the overcoming of his most explicit, and most sceptical, pronouncement on the inadvisability, for the modern writer, of producing translations of poetic texts. This sentiment is articulated in a *Convivio* passage that, as I show in the concluding section of the chapter, should be considered a provisional as well as partial statement, in no way indicative of Dante's overall and final position on matters of translation. As has been noted recently and will emerge from the reading of this chapter, Dante's poetry is not simply permeable but systematically and programmatically open to translation. In what I hope is a virtuous hermeneutic circularity, my argument moves from text to context to text again, shuttling between Dante's Latin and vernacular works, their cultural underpinnings, and the narrative of his poem.

My analysis of the eventual (and new) linguistics that Dante practises in the *Commedia*, without explicitly theorizing it, targets a cross-section of Dante's epics – three cantos numerologically connected in a vertical reading – and a short block of tercets in *Paradiso* 5. By looking at the larger linguistic framing of episodes contained in the coda segments of the three Cantos 26 in the *Commedia*, I argue that a common pattern emerges, in which issues of translation as transhistorical or transcultural communication clearly connect with an evocation of the garden of Eden. The combined effect of these cantos, especially as they are retrospectively framed by the last of the co-numerary segments devoted to Adam, the first speaker and first inhabitant of the original Garden, establishes a new linguistic ecology for the *Commedia*. Similarly, by focusing on the technical language Dante deploys in his sole theoretical (and idiosyncratic) reflection on the limits of translation, and contrasting it with his most daring (and revolutionary) act of poetic transmutation (the acrostic *Pesce* as a vernacularization of the sacred Christological acrostic *Ichthus* in *Paradiso* 5), I suggest that, once he moves into the *Commedia*, Dante's initial and limited scepticism about the possibility of translating poetry turns into the deep conviction that no particle of language can or should be subtracted from the natural flow of language in time, and that translation across time and space is the vehicle for that intrinsic, essential agility.

Following and building upon a discussion of the Dantean material, chapter 3 is devoted to a series of explorations of Boccaccio's *Decameron*, in two related steps. First, in discussing the Second Garden in the *Decameron*, the setting in which the narrative in Days 3 to 6 unfolds uninterrupted, the chapter highlights its nature as a deeply literary garden. It surveys the intertextual relationship between Boccaccio's description of this pleasant narrative setting and two of its antecedents: the garden of the *Roman de la Rose*, already discussed in the first chapter, but now analysed in its literary afterlife, and a possible earlier, complementary Latin intertext, the description of his Tuscan villa that appears in Pliny the Younger's *Epistle* 4.26, a text that might have been within Boccaccio's philological reach. While the first part of my argument is unsurprising, since it brings together two traditionally celebrated and traditionally related garden descriptions, the second part is more novel. As such, it is offered more tentatively and in coordination with the first. It is my contention that, when considered in its entirety, Pliny's letter appears more than just casually related to Boccaccio's text. In particular, the epistle provides some specific and unprecedented antecedents for the other framing narrative space that bookends this section of the *Decameron*: the Valley of the Women, with whose description Day 6 concludes. Consequently, two distinctively translated literary texts about gardens frame Boccaccio's main garden of literary narration. Unsurprisingly at this point in the book, my argument also re-evaluates the Edenic quality of Boccaccio's imaginary garden, which is asserted both implicitly through the description of the place and explicitly in some remarks made by the members of the *brigata*, relayed by the narrator. With an essential provision in place, namely that Eden may, but perhaps should not, be made on earth, the *Decameron* attributes an indirect but pointed assessment to its narrators: the place they enter at the beginning of their third day of storytelling is the closest possible equivalent of earthly paradise.

The second section of the chapter moves from the *cornice* to a reading of two tales. My aim here is to show how the storytelling frame resonates with the theme of the stories that are told within it: *Decameron* 3.1, the tale of Masetto, a resourceful young man who enters into the service of a convent as a gardener and ends up sleeping with all of the nuns, and 6.10, the story of Frate Cipolla, a wandering preacher of Saint Anthony's order, who is tricked by some friends by way of a fake relic exchange (they replace a parrot feather he carries with burnt coals) and is thus forced to improvise a sermon for Certaldo's lay congregation, a sermon that proves just as effective as the one he originally planned to deliver. At first sight these stories have little in common beyond their interest in depicting the interactions between the religious and secular worlds. However, they also share structural and symbolic elements. Bookending the first stretch of narrative that takes place in the garden, the tales of Masetto, the feigned mute, and of Frate Cipolla, the brilliant orator, are both deeply concerned with exploring the nature and limits of language. Though going in opposite directions, they speak of characters that either instrumentally and provisionally renounce speech or deceivingly, as well as brilliantly, practise what the Middle Ages considered a rather problematic *multiloquium*.

In focusing on the linguistic aspect of the tales, my argument suggests that both stories maintain a special relation to the extradiegetic setting in which they are told. By providing contrastive examples of what is entailed in the regression into or the divergence from the Garden of Eden, they also confirm the linguistic nature of that garden. What is more, by detailing the risks inherent in trying too hard to make paradise on earth, or to renounce it altogether, the stories point to what the *Decameron* suggests is the appropriate cultural behaviour in the Christian dispensation, a behaviour that is emblematized in the frame-tale garden to which they allude. Aligning himself with the other literary representatives of the garden trope, Boccaccio seems to practise the same vernacular optimism, based on the positive effects attributed to acts of translation, which characterized their approach to tradition and translation. Looking at the verbal fabric of the text reveals his sense of what writing in the vernacular ultimately means.

In chapter 4, the final segment in the book focusing on medieval material, I follow a subtle thread in the narrative fabric of one of Chaucer's *Canterbury Tales*: the Merchant's Tale. In my reading, I contrast Chaucer's text with a pertinent intra- and an extratextual antecedent: the Clerk's Tale that immediately precedes the text in question and is presented as a new version of Petrarch's *Griselda*, a Latin rendering of *Decameron* 10.10. The diptych thus formed emerges as a particularly polarized nexus of translations and retranslations, in which the trope of the garden visit plays an essential role. While in Petrarch garden imagery is absent but symbolically evoked in the reading scenes that frame the text, in Chaucer it is overwhelmingly present, both as an active backdrop for salient episodes in the tale and as a cultural reference point for their ethical assessment. I argue that this polarization is ultimately not gratuitous but matches the different underlying linguistic attitudes of the two authors and their diverging assessments of the power of translation to produce new meanings in and through new texts.

In my analysis of Petrarch's *Seniles* 17.3 and 4, I concentrate on the framing sections of the letters, highlighting the tensions at work in the metalanguage

Petrarch uses to qualify his activity as an *interpres* of Boccaccio's story – that is, both its interpretive "reader" and its translational "writer." Designed to respond to the intentional hermeneutic instability of Dioneo's final tale with a single interpretation for the story, Petrarch's work on the *Griselda* is based on a theoretical framework marked by deep, unsettling fractures. The first element to emerge is Petrarch's claim that his rewriting is technically a translation: it is triggered, that is, by the realization that the story would be inaccessible to readers unfamiliar with the vernacular he shares with Boccaccio. As such, Petrarch-the-translator claims he did not proceed word-by-word but took liberties by occasionally adding and replacing some of the original language. Petrarch has obtained this strategy on good authority: namely, Horace's precept in the *Ars poetica* that characterizes the true (as opposed to the *fidus*) *interpres* as free from the fetters of translating verbatim. The epistle coordinates this assertion with a second, equally compelling element: a strategic abdication of hermeneutic responsibility. The story Petrarch has translated, both in its dubious truth-value as *historia* or *fabula* (as relation of actual events or fabrication) and in its ultimate significance as an example not of unattainable marital patience but of ethical steadfastness, has firmly remained the sole property of its original author. The epistle's language is both clear and insistent: Petrarch addresses Boccaccio as the sole "auctor" of the tale, then repeatedly tells him that the story is "tuam historiam"; it is uncompromisingly one among "rerum tuarum."

This double set of corresponding oppositions is crucial for the chapter's argument. Petrarch's insistence on the paramount authority of the original author and his simultaneous and clear vindication of his own role as interpreter is, in fact, paradoxical for two reasons. First, although it moves within the same cultural coordinates, Petrarch's operation seems to diverge from the tradition of vernacular fiction writers who, as this book has shown, apparently relish the idea that translation endows original texts with new meanings by redeploying them in new temporal, linguistic, and cultural settings. Petrarch's studious eschewal of his own authorial responsibility in favour of Boccaccio's is, in other words, singular. In "dis-owning" his work, he refuses to perform the traditional task of the translator. Second, his abdication of interpretive responsibility also clashes with his own practice as interpreter of Boccaccio's text: by providing a new framework for reading Boccaccio's story – as he does at the end of the epistle to respond to the original openness of Dioneo's tale in the *Decameron* – Petrarch is engaging in an aggressive interpretation of the text he is translating, while claiming that this is precisely what he is not doing.

In sum, although he provides a crucial link in the translative chain uniting Boccaccio and Chaucer, Petrarch is unlike all other authors we have encountered in this book. While he is undoubtedly (and admittedly as an exception) working as a translator, he matches the translative optimism that has been seen to animate such work with an originalist attitude. Petrarch's theoretical singularity matches his singular practice. I also argue that the retrograde direction of his translation, from vernacular to Latin, is not insignificant here but reverberates on a narrative element as well. The pointed details Petrarch adds to Boccaccio's portrait of the story's protagonists are equally relevant: independently of any signal in his source-text, he associates their biographical youth with an exceptional ethical maturity, a feature more proper to old age.

A matching originalist take on translation and a corresponding praise of the old are not unmarked and occasional traits peculiar to the case of *Seniles* 17.3–4 that might be left unchallenged. At least, they may not have been perceived as such by Chaucer. As I show by surveying two important moments in his retranslation of Petrarch's translation of Boccaccio's story, the Clerk's Tale intentionally upsets the axiological system foregrounded in its Latin antecedent. Whereas Petrarch's version affirms a moral "senility" in both the tale's protagonists that may in part justify their behaviour (rendering, for his readership's expectations, the husband's "testing" of his wife less obsessively gratuitous and the wife's obdurate and virile "constancy" less improbable in a young woman), Chaucer's text strategically elimi-nates that trait from their portraits. Interestingly, oldness is not completely banned from the lexical landscape of the Clerk's narrative; rather it is systematically shifted from the characters to Grisildis' "original," pre-marital situation. In the Clerk's Tale, Janicula is understandably but insistently old (as well as utterly poor), but "old" is also used to describe the dress that Grisildis leaves behind when she moves into her "new" (and reclothed) status as Marchioness of Saluzzo, and with which her father unsuccessfully tries to cover her body as she makes her way back home, ostensibly repudiated and literally spoliated by her husband. This attributive shift has metaliterary connotations: Petrarch's own account of his work as translator was phrased as a mere "re-clothing" of Boccaccio's text, an operation that simply involved providing the original with "new stylistic garb," whereas the protagonist's change in status in Chaucer is specifically labelled a translation, Griseldes having been "translated … in swich richesse" (The Clerk's Tale, l. 385).

While absent from the immediate horizon of Petrarch's translation but, as I have noted, evoked in the reading scene staged in the accompanying epistle, in Chaucer's Merchant's Tale the visit to a garden is crucial. In the deftly interwoven narrative strands of this interpretively challenging story, the garden of delights that the protagonist has had made next to his house is reached only at the end of the story. Its relevance for the tale as a whole is, however, anticipated in earlier sections, especially as a stand-in (at once a symbol for and a result of) the institution of marriage, which is perhaps its central concern. Marriage, the joining together of "white" Januarie with "fresshe" Mayus, comes under cultural and narrative scru-tiny, especially in its variant as mismatched contract. As a misalliance of old and young age, the tale insists, this marriage is not the Eden-like joyful state that its protagonist wishes it to be. Similarly, the grotesque sexual exploits of the husband, consummated first in the wedding chamber and then in his garden of delights, are cause for little celebration – to the point that the garden itself eventually becomes the setting for the trick that his wife plays on him.

After the story of the steadfast Grisildis, a tale whose plot is intended to point, through Petrarch's Latin, back to Boccaccio's original vernacular, there is little surprise in the tenor of the tale Chaucer's Merchant tells. The strong continuity between the two stories is also reinforced in the author's own epilogue to the Clerk's Tale, where the lament for the paradigm of constancy that has forever disappeared with Petrarch's stoically immutable heroine (and Boccaccio's highly controversial character) is yoked to an exploration of feminine rhetorical mobility and verbal versatility. *Copia*, the ability never to run out of words, never to be at a loss in a dialogue or dispute, is, after all, *both* what the author invites his contemporary un-Grisildis-like wives, whom he addresses in the epilogue, to achieve *and* the gift that Proserpina will bestow on the female protagonist of the Clerk's Tale and, through her, to all women. Questions of cultural representation come to the fore when the literary and metaliterary elements interspersed in the tale are isolated and connected to one another. At stake in Chaucer's tale, which tells the foreseeable consequences of a marriage in which "tendre youth hath wedded stoupyng age" (l. 1378), are questions not only of old age and youth but also, more essentially, of cultural decay and renewal. Thus, the narrative joins issues of tradition and cultural inheritance, as well as childbearing and marriage contracts, to acts of translation and creation of new poetic texts, precipitated in instances of ridiculous singing by the protagonist.

In the end, I argue that Chaucer's relationship to the vernacular with respect to its involvement with translation is part of the counter-misogynistic leaning in both his and Boccaccio's texts. Choosing to write literature about women, and showing them in a positive light, is for Chaucer and his Italian antecedent both a choice of audience and language and a choice of rhetorical cultural trend. In other words, the vernacular is coded as an alternative to the learned Latin tradition, and the dialogue engaged by and through translation is supposed never to stop, always to have a *replica*. The interplay of these final texts reveals that vernacular literature is by definition philogynist as well as bent in favour of the "moderns." These aspects are two sides of the very same coin.

Seen in the framework of this book, Chaucer's Januarie embodies the two monolingual options that Dante outlined as potential responses to Babel's multilingualism: artificial Grammar or regressive Hebrew. Both options, once tested in the story, are found lacking. Just as there should be no going back to Jerusalem in the new Christian dispensation, only *going to*, so too there is no return from the diaspora, only pilgrimage to a place that is not sufficient *per se*, but essential as a sign of a better one. Correspondingly, in the Merchant's Tale no remaking of paradise on earth may exist for the old man, no Genesis-like playful innocence, no recapturing of original wholeness, only self-deception and silence. In Christian discourse, a better ethical and cultural response than the one Januarie attempts does exist: to accept the movement away from the garden, the profluence and dissemination connected to the new dispensation. Following the model of the Gospels, which, in their translational essence, anticipate the new vernacular textuality, is exactly what Januarie is depicted as incapable of doing, given the aggressive web of associations in which he is caught in Chaucer's tale. On the contrary, Mayus, whose fertile womb Januarie caresses as they leave the garden at the end of the tale, represents not only a stark, if parodic, reminder of the generative power associated with the age of the Son in Christian culture, but also a linguistic equivalent of Proserpina's gift. Narrative philogyny, textual vernacularity, and translative "modernism" are connected in her. Depicted in her ability to always have something to reply to any authoritative discourse is not only what the Renaissance would codify as *copia*, but also something perfectly medieval: the acceptance of the instability of any meaning articulated in language and the articulation of truth in interlinguistic and inter-age negotiations.

In my conclusion, I take momentary leave from direct readings of ancient and medieval texts to concentrate on a twentieth-century work: Primo Levi's chapter "The Canto of Ulysses," the centrepiece of his memoir *If This Is a Man*. I do so in order to address a set of cultural and political questions surrounding the core intervention of this book, as they are mobilized in Levi's text and made to resonate in a specific medieval antecedent. I read this episode in Levi's account of his survival in Auschwitz as a time temporarily imbued with the same translational optimism that marks the tradition studied in this book. Primo and Jean use a moment of respite and Dante's text as opportunities to practise an ethic of translation that breaks away from the linguistic hellscape of the Lager, where Babelic plurilingualism is part of the oppressive and dehumanizing violence inflicted upon the prisoners. In doing so, they actively resist the camp's machinery of dehumanization.

As Primo and Jean break free of the time- and place-boundedness of language in the camp to reach for a text that does not resist but invites translation, the successful experiment of teaching the rudiments of a language through a literary text evolves into a shared experience of what Walter Benjamin deemed the most valuable potentiality of translation: the ability to unite human beings across any divisive, nationalistically inflected identity. In the successful crossing of temporal, linguistic, and politically imposed borders, the lesson in Levi's "Canto of Ulysses" proves that the openness of medieval text to supporting constant reinterpretation could be used as an effective antidote to a nationalist weaponizing of national identities. Siding with Benjamin's and Augustine's core ideas that translation is the vehicle for, not a hindrance to, truth, this book suggests that these same elements may be effectively used as an antidote to contemporary appropriations of medieval literature.

VERNACULAR EDENS

Introduction

The garden scene is a commonplace in late medieval vernacular fictions. Heavily influenced by the model of the biblical Eden, literary gardens are a charged and utterly familiar topos for modern readers of vernacular texts. There are many examples of the literary treatment of this object, such as at least one of Chrétien de Troyes' romances, *Érec et Énide*, which includes an adventure in a magical or quasi-magical garden. The action in the *Roman de la Rose* is similarly and crucially staged for almost its entirety in such a fantastic setting. The protagonist-narrator in Brunetto Latini's *Tesoretto* visits the garden of love under the guidance of Ovid, and the section of Dante's *Commedia* in which the protagonist is admitted into the earthly paradise under the waning leadership of Virgil and meets his second guide, Beatrice, unfolds in such a charged space. Three full days of storytelling in Boccaccio's *Decameron* are explicitly located in a carefully described villa garden on the hills outside of Florence, while the Merchant's Tale in the *Canterbury Tales* revolves around the erotic use of a garden built by the old protagonist, Januarie, a paradise-like enclosure which is reminiscent of both Boccaccio's and Guillaume de Lorris's green spaces. The examples provided here are not chosen randomly but offer a quick preview of this book's content. My work will focus on these specific literary gardens as representative of larger cultural habits that they both embody and exemplify, also incorporating a few "other" texts which devote passing attention to the trope of the garden visit and thus help reinforce or qualify my central argument.

Similarly topical in the texts that contain singularly extended treatments of the garden motif is the keen attention they devote to situating themselves in a tradition. Constructing their value as modern vernacular counterparts to classical Latin models, these texts inscribe themselves in a larger conceptual framework where past and present interact in fruitful continuity. From the *translatio studii*, a cultural construct activated in the romances of the late twelfth century, to the evocation of biblical paradigms of poetics in Chaucer two hundred years later, passing through the Ovidian and Virgilian presences prominent both in the plots and in the metapoetic setup of the late thirteenth- and early fourteenth-century Italian section of this corpus, medieval vernacular fictions distinguish themselves as the continuation in a new idiom of a cultural discourse begun in the past. These texts formulate a crucial cultural connection established between different times, spaces, and idioms, both in terms of the subject matter they treat and of the language they use to do so.

The concurrence of topos and topic is not coincidental. Rather, this book argues, it is the effect of a broad understanding of Eden as related to the act of translation. The translation-garden connection is a trope that has its origins in Patristic literature, particularly in Augustine, and was reactivated between the twelfth and fourteenth centuries by vernacular writers. Because of the way they were constructed and narrated, the fictional gardens of these vernacular texts became a central space for radically optimistic acts of literary translation and cultural negotiation that were rooted in a Christian understanding of textual culture. When we look at them through the lens of their interest in staging acts of vernacularization in an Eden-like setting, we discover that the pervasive anxiety of loss associated with translation in popular modern discourse is an alien concern to writers who had a strong belief in the hermeneutical gain that the present offers to the reading of canonical texts.

1. Frameworks

There may be two ways to conceptualize and describe the phenomenon this book studies. It appears that the traces of the connection between topos and topic – that is, between the literary description of gardens and the awareness of the process of cultural translation – can be interpreted in two interdependent levels.

For one thing, it is conceivable that the corpus of vernacular fiction of the later European Middle Ages contained a cultural trope – a cluster of images or, perhaps better, a structured constellation of ideas – which associated the *topos* of garden description with the *topic* of the necessary connection between tradition and translation. This argument concerns and is admittedly based on wide-ranging and general evidence, but it is not vague. It does emerge from a real set of phenomena, a philologically tangible recurrence of literary objects (plots, settings, characters, descriptors) that are observable across texts, but one that exists in patterns that are unspecific to any individual work-to-work transmission, any distinct cross-pollination within literary genres, or any cohesion based on linguistic or national tradition. While general in formulation, this argument is grounded in, and related to, objects which emerge in the framework of a cultural-historical approach to literature. Though moving from literary studies and insisting on openly literary texts, my argument reaches out toward the limit-discipline and discourse of cultural history. In studying the trope of the Garden as a space for the staging of acts of translation, I attempt to define the parameters of a culturally central and, as such, widespread idea in a segment of European vernacular literary history.

On the other hand, while formulated in most general terms and given an all-encompassing field of application, the perspective adopted here is intended for the service of specific analyses. The work of this book hinges on individual texts and develops a series of pointed observations for precise passages in which these literary works present themselves as links in a chain of cultural transmission. While the ocean of medieval literature is undoubtedly vast, the specific subset of vernacular fictional narratives studied here is also rounded by a contiguous continent of intercultural, when not even intertextual, connections. From the prologue to Marie de France's *Lais* to the narrative opening of Chretien de Troyes' *Cligès*, from the metapoetic sections in Guillaume de Lorris's and Jan de Meun's *Rose* to Brunetto Latini's vision of the Kingdom of Love, from Dante's linguistic theories to his understanding of Eden as a limit condition for human language, from Boccaccio's description of the second garden in the *Decameron* to the interplay between the Merchant's and the Clerk's tales in Chaucer, medieval vernacular fictional writers keep returning to the same topics and topoi of tradition and translation both because "it is the thing to do" and because they are familiar with each other.

Accordingly, the local glosses which my work produces, and which attempt an interpretation of the peculiar features of these texts, may be read as a series of interpretive flashcards for individual passages. Insofar as they are local, the explanatory notes fall quite naturally under the heading of Philology, in its dynamic chronological instantiation as Literary History. In this sense, and for these reasons, my study is philological in nature, being interested in part in providing "readings" (ideally "new" ones) of a precise subset of canonical texts. At the same time, the consistent way in which these texts flag their intention to reactivate the memory of their literary antecedents makes them a distinct and coherent corpus. When they stage their awareness (with various degrees of explicitness) that they are directly translating and radically transposing their "sources" through the same tropes, these texts invite a cultural analysis that dispenses with as much as relies upon direct connections.

Both approaches, if pursued independently, have significant potential drawbacks. Though they do indeed produce hermeneutic results from (and for) the local evidence on which they are based, individual philological readings of precise textual spaces do not seem to address the full import of the texts to which they are applied. In other words, while it may outline the dynamics of a tradition, philology does little to account for the narrative localization of the translation acts in (or in the narrative proximity of) gardens, and for the recurrence of ostensibly unrelated elements across the plurality of individual texts. Inversely, interpretive categorizations developed through general cultural-historical analysis produce, for the same texts, an explanatory communal framework that reaches back to authoritative and pervasive, but ultimately unspecific, paradigms. The notion that Eden is a prototype for gardens on the one hand, and the idea that the interwoven status of tradition and translation is the model for the relationship of modern texts to their past on the other, emerge from the survey of the texts but remain somewhat abstract. General considerations elide, or at least defuse, the peculiarity of the intersections – the historical dynamics of the variegated traditions upon which they insist and without which they would not exist. In so doing, they risk underplaying the interpretative skills that characterize the work of medieval vernacular writers of fiction.

Studying the ways in which an individual text defines itself by projecting, even creating, its own literary past, and the intellectual milieu with which it interacts to do so, should mean bringing together both macro- and micro-observations. Each of the texts listed above contains an exploration of Eden-like narrative spaces and is involved in an intensely self-aware process of translation, both of which invite a common reading hypothesis and a framework for understanding their common semiotic strategies. To provide a potentially unitary interpretive framework for the plurality of texts at hand, an analysis that takes into account the contribution of both philology and cultural history is required. The philological and cultural approach that I propose in this book attempts to capture both the micro- and macroscopic continuities marking the corpus, the integrated quality of local figures and general configurations, and the necessary interplay of culture and texts that at once support and rely on it.

The coming together of garden descriptions and acts of translation that recurs throughout the body of work just outlined is neither an accident of philology nor a feature of this corpus's generic identity. Rather, it is the effect of a common cultural frame of reference for its texts. The eventual success or failure of this book in advancing its central notion – namely, that medieval writers of vernacular fictions unite in treating Eden as a space associated to their acts of translation – ultimately rests on the virtuous circularity at the core of this hermeneutic wager.

2. At the Origins of the Trope: Eden and the New Testament

The origin of this book is an accidental one. My interest in the trope of the translative garden was triggered by a problem of translation. While working on Dante's literary relation to Augustine's thinking on matters of linguistics, poetics, and hermeneutics, I came across a passage on translation that I could not, at first, fully and convincingly translate. In addition to being arguably the single most important authority on the issues of semantics for the Middle Ages (or at least, as we shall see, for Dante), Augustine was also responsible for a short but essential examination of the question of the multifarious quality of biblical texts. In a cursory yet dense treatment of the origins and effects of linguistic differentiation, as they are narrated in Genesis, Augustine issued a statement that I could not initially reconcile with what I thought was the received wisdom about the anxiety-ridden field of translation theory. Augustine appeared to say that the multilingual condition in which the sacred text was to be found after Babel was merely an accident of history, not an essential trait of humanity's post-lapsarian condition. What the passage appeared to imply, in other words, was that Nimrod's act of pride, which God had punished by confusing human languages and visiting linguistic dissension upon humankind, was not a problem but an opportunity. A stumbling block of text in Augustine's treatment of these questions, and in particular of the linguistic aftermath of Babel, gave me pause. Speaking of Babel, Augustine noted:

> Ex quo factum est ut etiam scriptura divina, qua tantis morbis humanarum voluntatium subvenitur, ab una lingua profecta, qua opportune potuit per orbem terrarum disseminari, per varias interpretum linguas longe lateque diffusa innotesceret gentibus ad salutem.

> Wherefrom it happened that even the divine scripture, by which are healed so many ailments of the human will, having left one language, by which it had been able to be disseminated throughout the world at first, came to instruct many nations toward salvation, having been poured out far and wide through the various languages of its translators. (*De doctrina Christiana* II, v, 6)[1]

My difficulty in reading the passage stemmed from the axiological equivalence that Augustine seemingly established between the times before and after Babel, from Adamic monolingualism, which ceased to be a viable option of biblical dissemination at Babel, to the post-Babel world, dominated by a lapsed multilingualism that produced the need for translation. What I knew about the theological approach to the history of language, admittedly based on Dante's account of its drama in his *De vulgari eloquentia*, appeared to militate against this serene picture. Was I reading Augustine poorly or had I misunderstood the cultural context of his work?

After all, I thought, the second chapter of Genesis had set up the issue of linguistics in what appeared to be a linear and clear fashion. The earliest history of humankind, as it unfolded in the Garden of Eden, included some essential and essentially linguistic episodes. In the garden, Adam was given the privilege of performing one of the critical tasks of language: the imposition of names. In naming the animals, Adam founded language in an absolute sense, as a means for ordering the world of nature and establishing his own privileged status in it. Significantly, I reflected, the act of naming is the first active part Adam takes in the ordering of creation:

[19] formatis igitur Dominus Deus de humo cunctis animantibus terrae et universis volatilibus caeli adduxit ea ad Adam ut videret quid vocaret ea omne enim quod vocavit

Adam animae viventis ipsum est nomen eius [20] appellavitque Adam nominibus suis cuncta animantia et universa volatilia caeli et omnes bestias terrae.

The Lord God having formed from the earth all animals of the earth and the birds of the sky, brought them before Adam, so that he might see what to call them. For indeed whatsoever Adam called it was the name of each living creature. So Adam named all the living creatures with their proper names and all the birds of the sky and all the beasts of the earth. (Gen. 2:19–20)[2]

According to the biblical narrative, the act of nomination was as much a foundational act as it was felicitous in its outcome. While today we may be tempted to discern in it the traces of a solipsistic exercise of power, the presiding presence of the Creator next to the nomenclator guaranteed its unimpeachable quality from a theological point of view. It mattered little, in other words, that there was no one else in the garden with whom the names of the animals could be agreed upon, negotiated, and exchanged – all conditions that today we may tend to think a language must fulfil to be considered a real language. Of course, without God, the Being whose language creates Nature (rather than solely describing it), Adam's naming of all creatures would merely be the first, misguided, gratuitous, and groundless act of linguistic prevarication at the root of western metaphysics. But the biblical text made sure to frame the situation otherwise. God was there during Adam's naming. The original language, created by the father of humankind, acquired the special status of that original, perfect, and at least theoretically unchangeable pre-lapsarian language that writers such as Dante granted it. From this status as vouched-for-by-God, Adamic language derived its exceptionality and the wide array of privileges that made it unique. It was a language that told the truth about reality, one that possessed an essential ability to accurately represent the cosmos, as mentioned in the Bible, also embodying thoughts with no residual unclarity and expressing all internal states with full transparency. The reasoning went as follows: since God only creates what is best, and Adam was God's best creature, the God-sanctioned language that Adam made before the fall must have been the best possible language.

Of course, soon there was a problem – or actually, two – in humankind's linguistic history. The first problem was original sin, which brought about the expulsion of humankind from the space of Eden. The Bible says nothing about how the loss of paradise affected the language that was spoken during the first human diaspora away from the Garden, though some traditions do speak of a first linguistic fall, which included the loss of interspecies communication (in the beginning, all creatures shared one "language"). As a matter of fact, the Book of Genesis openly confirms the *longue durée* of this initial state. Up until Babel, the earth had one language and a common speech: "Erat autem terra labii unius, et sermonum eorumdem" (Gen. 11:1). On the other hand, the biblical narrative has a lot to say about the second problem, Babel. At Babel, as a punishment for their pride in wanting to make a name for themselves, humans received their just desert: the confusion of languages. The reaction to the reawakening of human pride is described as follows:

> [7] venite igitur descendamus et confundamus ibi linguam eorum ut non audiat unusquisque vocem proximi sui [8] atque ita divisit eos Dominus ex illo loco in universas terras, et cessaverunt aedificare civitatem [9] et idcirco vocatum est nomen ejus Babel quia ibi confusum est labium universae terrae.

> So, let us descend and there confuse their tongues, to that no one may understand the voice of his neighbour. The Lord thus scattered them from that place throughout the earth, and they ceased to build the city. This is the reason why it bears the name Babel: it was here that the language of all the earth was confused. (Gen. 11:7–9)

With the preemptive punishment of confusion that God visited upon its unitary speech, humankind's linguistic state was radically altered. Rather than unity of language, a multiplicity of idioms arose; rather than the absolute ontological foundation or the highest axiological status of the original language, interlinguistic misunderstanding came about. There seemed to be no positives in this account of the state in which humanity was to exist. But despite this dire start, I could detect no particularly sorrowful accent in Augustine's text. I could not hear, that is, the tone of lamentation to which I had grown accustomed, again mainly from reading Dante. On the contrary, Augustine seemed to insist that the mission of Scripture, which consisted in providing humans with teachings useful for their spiritual health, had not only understandably continued from the monolingual to the polyglot world unchallenged, but also justified the varied idioms in which it was to be converted by its translators. This was, at least, what Augustine appeared to be saying.

To make sense of this apparent contradiction between the position Augustine took and the biblical context with which it resonated, I continued to read *De doctrina Christiana*. I did not have to look much further to begin seeing that the problem was not with Augustine's text, but with my cultural bias. Some theological reasons for the radical neutrality Augustine maintained on the issue of language emerged from the passage immediately preceding his discussion of biblical mono- and pluri-lingualism. In the context of a discussion of the birth of writing culture, Augustine added a revealing consideration on the nature of human multilingualism. In talking about the origin of the biblical text as written text, he noted how the ephemerality of sound brought about the need for letters. This graphic equivalent of words could not be common to all, but *not*, as we may expect, because of the accident of Nimrod's tower, but on account of something that runs deeper in human nature and in a way logically, if not chronologically, precedes the confusion of languages at Babel. Augustine described the situation in linear terms:

> Ista signa igitur non potuerunt communia esse omnibus gentibus peccato quodam dissensionis humanae, cum ad se quisque principatum rapit. Cuius superbiae signum

est erecta illa turris in caelum, ubi homines impii non solum animos, sed etiam voces
dissonas habere meruerunt.

> These signs, however, could not be common to all nations, because of the sinful con-
> flictual quality of humankind, since each man desires to snatch power for himself.
> As a sign of this pride stands the famous tower erected to reach the heavens, where
> ungodly men merited to have not only discord in their souls, but also dissonance in
> their voices. (*De doctrina Christiana* II, iv, 5)

The multifarious condition in which humankind is destined to live after Babel is,
thus, not at the root of any sin – the opposite, rather, appears to be true. Pride,
the root of all sins and the inherent human vice, ignited the violent discord that
caused the multiplicity of languages to embody everyone's desire for preeminence
in linguistic form. The tower is the "sign" of human pride, the desire to excel above
all others, and embodies the potential violence of every ungodly enterprise in this
world. The problem of multilingualism is, in sum, connected to the endemic
conflictual quality of the human condition, and the variety of languages existing
in the world is the consequence, not the cause, of human dissension. The different
languages mirror the state of spiritual dissension; they do not determine it.

But there is more. When I reread the passage that I could not translate, I realized that the paradigm Augustine created for biblical translation was not simply
neutral, but actually (though allusively) positive in the progress it suggested. In
summarizing the troubled linguistic history of humankind, Augustine delineated
two connected but heterogenous stages in the development of the transmission
of the word of God. In the first stage, which he attributes to the old, pre-Babel
dispensation, identical monolingual texts were disseminated from one central
place of authority. This stage had existed in time, and was valid in itself. There
was a time for that dissemination: a time that Augustine nonetheless deemed no
longer current, given the combined effect of the aoristic *potuit* (it could, but no
longer can) and of the adverb *opportune* (which seems to imply time rather than
method) he uses in his text. There is now a second stage in the history of biblical
transmission, continues Augustine, one that his text represents as a profluence
of plurilingual material along two co-planar axes, that is, into the four cardinal
directions. Again, Augustine's lexicon is suggestive of the difference between the
first and second stage of biblical history: *diffusa* is the past participle of *diffundere*,
etymologically linked to the idea of pouring a liquid (*fundere*); the adverbs *longe
lateque* have a transparent longitudinal and latitudinal quality, signalling the four
corners of the world. While in Augustine's passage both ways appear as timely,
valid ways of disseminating and diffusing the Word of God, they are not completely superimposed: his prose introduces a qualitative difference between them.
By juxtaposing dissemination and profluence, Augustine's paradigm correlates
two understandings of biblical textual circulation in supersession to each other. I
would argue that it does so thanks to a specific connotation of the directionality

to which it alludes. The quadriform directionality Augustine attributes to post-Babel biblical diffusion is indirectly linked to the image of Eden and, in particular, to the allegorical interpretation of its four rivers as the four Gospels at the core of the New Testament.

What began to emerge from my rereading is that, in a two-stage format, Augustine subordinated a model of monogenesis and dissemination, the one connected to the original monolingualism of Scripture, to a polydirectional, if still monocentric, effluence into the four spatial directions. In both cases, the horizon of dissemination and flow is the same: the wide circle of the earth, the *orbis terrarum*. As we shall see in a moment, this double system of circular and quadriform shape is mapped on, and in turn constructs, the schematic image of Eden, as it emerges from late antique imagination and is carried over into the topographical and allegorical imagination of medieval fictions. According to the biblical narrative, Eden is a charged space: it is a garden, from which all seeds proceed (hence the dissemination metaphor), and it is an irrigated space, marked by one central stream eventually forming four rivers (hence the flowing in four different directions). The text of Genesis clarifies both points: in verse 5, it states that no shrub or plant had yet appeared on the surface of the earth, because God had not sent rain over the land, nor created man to tend the garden: "et omne virgultum agri antequam oriretur in terra, omnemque herbam regionis priusquam germinaret" (Gen. 2:5). Correspondingly, the fourfold derivation of the rivers from the Garden is immediately and openly stated:

> [8] plantaverat autem Dominus Deus paradisum voluptatis a principio in quo posuit hominem quem formaverat …[10] et fluvius egrediebatur de loco voluptatis ad inrigandum paradisum, qui inde dividitur in quattuor capita.

> And the Lord God had planted a garden of delight from the start, in which he placed the man he had formed … And a river flowed from the place of delight and irrigated the garden, a river which then divided into four streams. (Gen. 2:8 and 10)

The complex identity of Eden established in the text, which is seemingly at the root of the metaphorical language Augustine adopted to discuss the translational quality of biblical reception, has a peculiar exegetical history. In biblical commentaries, the flowing of the four rivers out of Eden is explicitly associated with a particular section of the scriptural corpus: the New Testament, organized in the fourfold system of the Gospels. As Augustine himself (but he is not alone) glosses in his *City of God*, discussing potential allegorical interpretations of Genesis, the four rivers *are* the four Gospels.

> Possunt haec etiam in ecclesia intellegi, ut ea melius accipiamus tamquam prophetica indicia praecedentia futurorum: paradisum scilicet ipsam ecclesiam, sicut de illa legitur in *Cantico canticorum*; quattuor autem paradisi flumina quattuor evangelia etc …

All these elements can also be seen as indicating the Church and considered as prophetic and proleptic indications of what was to come: the garden, that is, would be the Church itself, as it is said about it in the *Song of songs*; the four rivers of the garden are the four Gospels … (*De civitate Dei* 13.21)[3]

Augustine's is only one of several voices that mention the four rivers of Eden in connection with the Gospels and in the context of translation. Jerome too, in the Preface of his *Commentary on the Gospel of Matthew*, combines the fourfold flowing of Eden's rivers with the image of the four-cornered Ark of the Covenant to form the figure of the Church. Throughout the Prologue, Jerome insists on the necessary limitation in number of the Gospels that the Church should accept as canonical. The number chosen is four, of course, and Jerome provides his addressee with a review of the long series of allegorical hints pointing to that number as the right one:

Ecclesia autem … quatuor flumina paradisi instar eructans, quatur et angulos et annulos habet, per quos quasi arca Testamenti et custos Legis Domini, lignis immobilibus vehitur.

Like the Paradise from which four rivers flow (Gen. 2:10), the Church has four corners and rings (Ex. 25:10), through which, as the Ark of the Covenant and the guardian of the Law of the Lord, she is conveyed by inflexible wooden poles. (Jerome, *Commentari in Matthaeum*, Prologus 4)[4]

The first of these "inflexible poles" that his work as translator has proceeded to move from one idiom into the next is Matthew, the tax collector – that is, the text of the first Gospel. Jerome extends his review of fourfold scriptural elements that anticipate and determine the number of canonical Gospels to include the correspondence between the four animals seen by Ezekiel in his first vision (Ez. 1:5 and 10) and those in John's apocalyptic new vision (Rev. 4:7):

Haec igitur quatuor Evangelia multo ante praedicta, Ezechielis quoque volumen probat, in quo prima visio ita contexitur: Et in medio sicut similitudo quatuor animalium: et vultus eorum facies hominis, et facies leonis, et facies vituli, et facies aquilae … Unde et Apocalypsis Ioannis, post expositionem viginti quatuor seniorum qui tenentes citharas et phialas, adorabant Agnum Dei, introducit fulgura, et tonitrua, et septem spiritus discurrentes, et mare vitreum et quatuor animalia plena oculis, dicens: Animal primum simile leoni, et secundum simile vitulo, et tertium simile homini, et quartum simile aquilae volanti.

The four Gospels were indeed foretold long before, as Ezekiel's book proves, a text in which this first vision is presented as follows: And in the centre there were the figures of four animals, and their appearance was like a human face, that of a lion, of a calf, and of an eagle ... Accordingly also John's Revelation, after having presented the twenty-four elders who, holding the harps and vials, fell in adoration of the Lamb of God, introduces lightning and thunder and seven spirits spreading through, and the vitreous sea, and the four animals filled with eyes, saying: The first animal was like a lion, and the second like a calf, and the third like a human, and the fourth like a soaring eagle. (Prologus 9–10)

Confirmed, in appearance and number, by the consistency across the Old and New Testaments, we find the four Evangelists, Matthew, Mark, Luke, and John, and their texts, seen in their iconographic attributes: the Man, the Lion, the Calf, and the Eagle. The conclusion readers may draw from such a neat correspondence may only be one, at least for Jerome:

Quibus cunctis perspicue ostenditur, quatuor tantum Evangelia debere suscipi, et omnes apocryphorum naenias mortuis magis haereticis, quam Ecclesiasticis vivis canendas.

All evidence points to the fact that we have to accept only four Gospels. All the other apocryphal texts are like childish incantations to be sung to the dead heretics rather than to the living members of the Church. (Prologus 11)

In the same way, and while similarly interested in connecting typology and visuality, Hrabanus Maurus, in his *De laudibus Sanctae Crucis*, spells out the numerical relationship we have seen in Augustine and Jerome, adding a crucial Christological element, the Lamb, at the centre:

Quattuor ergo Euangelia a quattuor euangelistis conscripta, quattuor flumina paradisi de uno fonte procedentia significant, quia sicut ipsa ex una matrice fontis procedentia totam terram rigauerunt, ita ab uno uero fonte, hoc est, Christo, a quo qui semel bibit, non sitiet in aeternum, quattuor Euangelia emanantia et per praedicatorum ora diffluentia, totum mundum ad uirtutum fructus germinandum irrigant.

The four rivers issuing from one single source in paradise signify the four Gospels written by the four evangelists. Those rivers, moving out from one and the same central source, marked the whole earth. Similarly, the four Gospels emanating from one single true source, which is Christ (a source that quenches a drinker's thirst forever), and flowing through the mouths of those who preach, irrigate the whole world, so that it may produce the fruit of virtues. (*In honorem sanctae Crucis* – Declaratio figurae C 15, 68–74)[5]

As we see with Hrabanus's *declaratio*, the pervasive quality of this interpretation extends beyond the realm of the written word. There are abundant iconographic examples of objects that capture the stratification of meaning triggered in mentioning a quadriform structure. Here it may suffice to look at one, a twelfth-century illumination from a breviary originating from the Abbey of Zwiefalten, which, in its spatial conciseness, offers a neat delineation of the system (figure 1).

Figure 1 Illumination of quadriform structure. Stuttgart Württembergische Landesbibliothek Libellus capitulorum Cod. Brev. 128 fol. 10r.

As is the case with Hrabanus's text and image, at the centre of the cross we see the Lamb, encircled in a round space, a single source from which (or, alternatively, a single point of reference to which) the four rivers of Eden flow. The four quadrants thus created are occupied by the four Evangelists, each of them looking up from the text he is drafting to his symbolic animal, in a clear visual transcription of the mechanism of inspiration as a fully human scribal act bridging the physical (textual) destination of a message and its metaphysical (mystical) origin. That the cultural space represented in the illumination partakes of both the earthly and the metaphysical realm is suggested by the figures in its outermost frame. The four cardinal virtues, with their traditional iconographic attributes, occupy the four corners of the quadrangular structure, thus allowing, together with the rivers and the four Gospels, the temporal and the eternal dimensions of the biblical text to interact with one another.

The complex system of spatial and iconic relations generated in the illumination responds well to the verbal diagram that the syntax in Augustine's passage quite carefully constructs. In Augustine's words, the division of space is the same as is present in the Zwiefalten cross, one that brings together the circle of the *orbis terrarum* and the lists of the quadrants, the four perpendicular radii that structure Augustine's directional indications *longe lateque*. However subtly and verbally constructed in his passage, the resulting figure is a circle that is also squared – that is directionally partitioned by longitude and latitude. This form resonates with the topography of the Garden of Eden.

What is absent from Augustine's text – but nonetheless an essential tacit component of his reasoning – is the Lamb, featured at the centre of the cross. In the Zwiefalten illumination, the coming of Christ into the world permeates the space via the directional force of the cruciform model it imposes on it. At the same time, as the gravitational centre of the textuality embodied in the Gospels that issue from and converge on the figure of the Lamb, Incarnation is what defines the transition from the old dispensation to the new one, from an old way to a new way of communicating God's word. Similarly, in Augustine's passage, the New Testament quality of the translational diffusion of Scripture is as eerily subsumed as it is inescapable. The new method of diffusion for biblical texts through translation is not simply post-Babel, as openly stated in the text; it is allusively post-Incarnational as well. If Incarnation has come to atone for Adam's transgression and heal its effects on humankind, it has also paved a new way for the word of God to reach humankind, the directional effluence embodied in the Gospels, thus shedding a positive light on post-Babel practices of textual transmission and interlinguistic translation.

The direction that the rivers of Eden (turned Gospels) take is the same one Augustine most allusively, but with perfect cultural coherence, associates with the act of translation. As the adverbs *longe lateque* suggest, the action of salvific instruction that translated Scripture performed also points to the four cardinal directions in which such action developed. By way of the four-directional, quadripartite association, they evoke the Gospels, the four textual rivers flowing into the four corners of a round world. The final association is meaningful, because it brings together the act of translation, the geography of Eden, and the role of the New Testament as a text that, for Augustine and his Christian readers, has superseded the Old.

It is worth noting that the coordination of the cultural associations in Augustine is not inclusive: firstly, Augustine only connects the second stage of biblical divulgation with translation; secondly, it is translation alone that he associates with the quadri-directional flowing of the word of God; finally, it is only the Gospels that are depicted in the flowing rivers of Eden. This symbolic system rests, that is, on the supersessionist specificity attributed to the New Testament. This kind of cultural construct, which projects the textuality of the pre-Christian Bible as "old," is not surprising. It is in tune with Augustine's general understanding of biblical exegesis and the cultural dynamics that he sees at work in the transition from the old (and biblical) dispensation to the new (and Christian) one. In the cultural system in which and for which he writes, the second movement is to be perceived as axiologically superior to the first. All this does not mean, of course, that *one may say* that the New Testament is superior to the Old Testament, because such phrasing would border on, if not cross into, heresy. The difference, however, is inscribed at the core of Christianity as a culture that relies on theological and interpretive supersession, no matter how meekly filial it frames its work of canonization and reinterpretation of the older texts.

It may suffice to read the sentence immediately following the account of the post-Babel dynamics of scriptural diffusion, to gather a sense of Augustine's "modernism," his penchant for privileging the new over the old. Readers of the translated scriptures, Augustine notes, are responsible for activating their meaning: they are their new and, it can be surmised, better interpreters:

> Quam [scil. scriptura divina] legentes nihil aliud appetunt quam cogitationes voluntatemque illorum, a quibus conscripta est, invenire et per illas voluntatem Dei, secundum quam tales homines locutos credimus.

> In reading divine Scripture, readers desire nothing else than to find the thoughts and intention of those by which it has been drafted and through these the will of God, according to which those men, we believe, have spoken. (*De doctrina Christiana* II, v, 6)

Interpreting the Bible is an activity that emerges from the passage with a dual role. The first level of interpretation consists in what modern vocabulary conceptualizes as "translation." As we have seen, the various tongues of the interpreters are the medium by which Scripture flows through the world. Reading the Bible, however, is in turn an active task for the reader, one that consists in the interpretive discovery of the human writers' will and, through that provisional and intermediate stage, of God's will. In what is a perhaps confusing semantic reversal, *interpres* is for Augustine the modern translator, while his *legentes* are the modern interpreters. Those who have the task of reconstructing the authorial and inspirational intention of the text they are reading move through the field of interpretation. Just as translation appears to have a hermeneutic side, reading is also, in essence, a translative act. The emergence of meaning from the text relies on a reading that is interpretive in the same way as it relies on an interpretive translation.

The semantic ambiguity of the term *interpres* in medieval culture is well known. At once translator and exegete, the figure of the "interpreter" is assigned the role of mediating difference, be it in time or space, between the meaning that a text contained in its original setting and the one that it may acquire in the new context of its reception. Augustine's passage goes one step further in orienting the process axiologically. In his reasoning, the nexus of translation and interpretation becomes a part of the new and richer dispensation, the one figured in the garden of Eden, an Eden that includes the tokens of redemption. This move is, in a way, foundational. The corpus of medieval fictional texts I consider in this book share that general positive outlook on translation so prominent in Augustine. The new work, drafted in a new language, understands itself as coming to supersede an old one. No matter how originally prestigious the old language and the old text happened to be, or how provisional in time and space the new language and the new text are thought to be, newer is also better. Working in a cultural climate permeable to, if not saturated with, the same notions we find in Augustine's passage, medieval writers also make Eden, as refracted into the many gardens they construct, a central trope.

Marie de France and Chrétien de Troyes, Brunetto and Dante, Boccaccio, and Chaucer all appear to consider Eden as having the potential to become a productive space for multilingual translation because they write new, Christian humanistic texts. They and their readers assume they are working in the age of the Son, that is, of the Word made flesh dwelling in the world. For them, as for Augustine, Incarnation, as the coming of the *Verbum* into the world of space and time, is the condition without which Eden is an uninhabited and sterile place, and any attempt to regain it is doomed to become a potentially idolatrous negation of Christ. In literary historical terms, the progressive arising of this second strain of thought would bring about the end of the trope this book sets out to map. The creeping doubt that the productive, ever-changing multilingualism of vernacular literature could be threatened by, and eventually succumb to, a regressive return to the classicizing monolingualism of humanistic Latin is the ultimate horizon of the imaginary gardens from which new texts in new vernaculars are disseminated and pour forth. As such, that doubt, which was also a possibility, prescribed if not fully actualized in a key text by Petrarch, his epistle on the ascent to Mont Ventoux, is likewise the horizon of my work.

3. Neighbouring Tropes: Tradition and Translation

Augustine's authoritative, technical considerations may be used to frame the following literary and narrative examples, which appear to practise what patristic thought established as a potentiality. I begin with two relatively early, but not peripheral, texts that embody what I call the French wave of vernacular optimism. In my reading, I combine the two prologues to Marie de France's *Lais* and *Fables*, and then move on to an examination of two celebrated passages from two romances by Chrétien de Troyes in which metapoetics and narrative imbrications are central. I have chosen to lead with two texts that are only tangentially pertinent to the garden-visit trope because they help us perceive how writers in the vernacular invited their readers to conceptualize the acts of interpretation, translation, and tradition-formation that they performed as an active process of semiotic enrichment. The optimistic outlook on the passing of time and the movement through different cultures that is at the core of these texts is coherent with Augustine's own modern-favouring stance.[6]

Let us begin with the parallel reading of two of Marie's authorially self-aware prologues:

Lais – **Prologue**	*Fables* – **Prologue**
Custume fu as anciëns,	Cil, ki sevent de letreüre,
Ceo testimonie Preciëns,	Devreient bien metre lur cure
Es livres que jadis feseient	Es bons livres e es escriz,
Assez oscurement diseient	E es essamples, e es diz,
Pur ceus ki a venir esteient	Que li philosophe troverent
E ki apendre les deveient,	E escristrent e remembrerent.
Ki puessent gloser la letre	Par moralité escriveient
E de lur sen le surplus metre.	Les bons proverbes qu'il oeient,
Li philesophe le saveient,	Que cil amender se poïssent
E par els meme entendeient,	Ki lur entente en bien meïssent.
Cum plus trespasserunt le tens,	Xo firent li encien père. (ll. 1–11)
E plus serreient sutil de sens	
E plus se savereient garder	Esopes escrist a sun mestre
De ceo ki ert a trespasser.	Ki bien kunut lui e sun estre,
Ki de vice se volt defendre,	Unes fables qu'il ot trovees
Estudier deit e entendre	De Griu en Latin translatees;
E grevos overe comencier;	Merveille en orent li plusur
Par ceo se puet plus esloignier	Qu'il mist sun sens en tel labur;
E de grant dolur delivrer. (ll. 9–22)	Mes n'i a fables de folie,
	U il nen ait philosophie
	Es essamples ki sunt après,
	U des cuntes est tuz li fes.
	A mei, ki la rime en dei faire
	N'avenist niënt à retraire
	Plusurs paroles ki i sunt,
	mes nepuruec (ll. 17–30)

Prologue to the Lais: The ancients had the habit, as Priscian attests, to speak quite obscurely in their books, so that those who were to come and needed to learn from them had a chance to gloss the letter and thus add their additional meaning. The philosophers knew and had ascertained by themselves that the passing of time would bring an increased subtlety of understanding and an ability to keep away from what constitutes a transgression. He who wants to fend off vice should study and develop an understanding and undertake a difficult task. Through this, he may leave behind all that, and free himself from great suffering.

Prologue to the Fables: Whoever is learned and well-read should truly care for good books and writings as well as for moral stories and sayings that the philosophers composed, wrote and transmitted. They wrote the good pronouncements they heard with morality in mind, so that those who set their mind to good would be able to amend their ways. So did the ancient fathers ... Aesop wrote for his master, whose knowledge and personality he knew well, some fables that he had composed translating from Greek to Latin. Many marveled that he had put his wisdom in that work. Yet, there are no fables so fantastic where philosophy has no part, as in the moral tales that follow, which are the essence of the stories. It was not becoming to me, whose task was to translate them into rhymes, to repeat quite a few words that are there, but nonetheless ...[7]

In these passages, four related elements are noteworthy. The first is the sense that the work of the vernacular writer, who consciously and explicitly sets herself up as such, is located at the end of a cross-linguistic and cross-cultural chain of translations, stretching from the works of the *anciëns* to the modern text. The ancients are the origin of the matter that the *Lais* bring into the present, their distance immediately reinforced by the adverb "jadis" (once, in the past, back then). The gap between past and present is bridged by a combined effort of rereading and rewriting that was originally foreseen by the initial authors and took place as the tradition unfolded. While the prologue to the *Lais* presents the chain of transmission and transference of texts as a hermeneutic process, the quoted passage from the *Fables* treats the handing over of subject matter from one age to the next as a transmutation of the linguistic garb. In putting Aesop's text into rhyme (a keyword for translation into the vernacular), Marie points to its origin as a work in turn *translatee* (transposed, transmitted, and translated) from Greek into Latin. The building of the literary and textual tradition into which Marie inscribes her texts consists in the movement of cultural material from Greece to Rome and from there to France.[8] This idea will reappear at several other junctures in the form of the topos of *translatio studii*, one example of which we will soon consider by reading the Prologue to Chrétien's *Cligès*. Here it may suffice to isolate the notion that this movement from time past to time present takes place through subsequent translations and interpretations, each adding meaning to the previous one. If textual instability does indeed derive from interlinguistic shifts, that is, Marie's text insists it is hermeneutically fruitful. Any classicism on Marie's part thus acquires a characteristically multilingual quality and a strongly positive bent.

Marie also insistently returns to the conceptual and ethical goal with which she tasks the writer's intellectual enterprise, a work she frames as a process of interfacing different historical and cultural times. Some keywords in the first passage point in this direction. First, "li philosophe" act as ethical guides to avoid "vices." They set an example of how to lead an intellectual life: they are guides on how "estudier" and "entendre" (existentially "to tend," but also, hermeneutically, "to interpret"), and how to compose works on weighty subjects. The task of the modern writer responds to this aspect of ancient lore: picking the good books, isolating and developing their moralities and *auctoritates* (what Marie calls "proverbes"), and treating texts as repositories of examples. By zeroing in on the ethical dimension of literature, however, modern writers like Marie do not simply follow the ancients' suit. By focusing on ethics, the branch of philosophy most directly connected to action in the present, the moderns are also adopting and adapting the ancients to make them new. The classicism Marie delineates is thus a modernizing one, in both its nature and ultimate goals. The process of sense-making unfolds not only through time, but also in an axiologically determined direction.

Thirdly, Marie's texts suggest that the content that modern writers activate in the texts, with which they dialogue, is not static. The passing of time and the progress of scholarly traditions contribute new and better (that is, deeper, more articulate, and more complex) meanings to the hermeneutic potential of the texts. In glossing the letter of the received text, posterity brings its surplus of meaning to the original it reworks. The readership that the ancients foresaw and for whom they adopted an obscure style of composition is, Marie insists, a better-equipped and more productive one. As Priscian, who is cited as an authority, would perhaps have granted, "Cum plus trespassereit de tens, / Plus serreient sutil de sens" (ll. 14–15). The statement Marie attributes to Priscian is an effective, if out of context, rendering of his comment on the competence of grammarians, who "quanto sunt iuniores tanto perspicaciores" (*Prisciani ad Iulianum epistula* 1), which the new author, somewhat ironically but also perfectly appropriately, endows with a wider than originally intended scope. According to Marie's modern version of old Priscian's dictum, new readers will be able to make the text "mean" better and more. They will position it in a way that conveys meanings that were in part strategically hidden and are in part simply dormant in the original version. Those who are to come, from the perspective of the ancients, are bearers of a subtler sense, she unambiguously writes: they possess a deeper understanding and a deeper power of interpretation.[9] It should be noted that when the relationship between text and gloss becomes the model for the relationship between original and translation, Marie's text makes a move that defuses any potential anxiety concerning the subalternity of the translator or the semiotic loss endemic to translation. Both concerns seem totally absent from these programmatic passages. Unlike in modern philological and archaeological understandings of what any recovery and reuse of the past entails, in Marie's classicism there is hardly a trace of pessimism. Her approach and disposition are, in sum, radically progressive.

Notably, such optimism is not native to the vernacular tradition; the reverse is sometimes true. The first stanza of the *Vie de Saint Alexis*, for instance, articulates exactly the opposite tenet:

> Bons fut li secles al tens ancienur,
> quer feit i eret e iustisie et amour;
> Si ert creance, dunt or n'i at nul prut;
> Tut est muez, perdud ad sa colur:
> ia mais n'iert tels cum fut as anceisurs.

> Good was humanity in the time of the ancients, since then there used to be faith, justice, and love; there also was trust then, of which there now is none at all. Everything has changed and lost its colour: nothing will ever be as in time past. (*Vie da Saint Alexis* ll. 1–5)[10]

The sense of the ever-increasing semiotic potentiality of ancient texts is, instead, the essence of the historical dynamics laid out in Marie's first prologue, but the notion is also echoed in the second one. When she notes that readers and writers of the modern age should follow their predecessors in turning "lur entente en bien" – that is, in turning their intentions to good (desiring to act, but also reading, technically, *in bono*) – Marie ethically declines a hermeneutic notion. The mobilizing of hermeneutic lexicon in a context of translation and interpretation acts is not a neutral choice. In Marie's prologues, the envisioned relation of the gloss to the original text is the same that exists between translation and original. Here too, as in Augustine's passage, the translator (in the modern sense) is essentially an interpreter (in the hermeneutic sense). The new text is a gloss to the old in the same breath as it is a translation. As a new translator-writer who is also an interpreter-reader, the author of the two prologues reflects the same productive conflation as Augustine, the theorist of Christian culture. In Marie's sense of her activity, the two professional figures of the commentator and the translator that we now distinguish are one, just as they were in Augustine's profiling of the "interpreter" of the biblical text.

To sum up, Marie's optimism is predicated on two related notions, which are both essentially medieval and essential for the medieval understanding of literary culture. The first is that the passage of time does not detract from the cultural capital of a literary object. On the contrary, every new age endows texts with better, clearer, more abundant, and subtler understandings. The obscurity of the ancient texts is not only a challenge for readers and writers to exercise their hermeneutic skills and gain a better appreciation for the meaning elicited from the text. Any difficulty in reading is also, and above all else, the opportunity for new generations of thinkers to add their meaning to the text. The second and related notion mobilized in Marie's prologue is that entering a chain of cultural transmission by reproposing old material in new linguistic garb is as much an act of translation as it is an interpretive commentary. Translating is the equivalent of glossing the text. The keyword Marie uses in her passage is technical: "gloser la letre." Once again, the hermeneutic act is not framed in terms of the discovery of something hidden in the text, but rather as the "activation" of a latent potential or, more radically, the "addition" of a valuable *surplus* of meaning. However strange and distant it may sound to our modern ears, trained by philology as readers and animated as translators by "archaeological" concerns, it bears repeating that this conceptual constellation is perfectly aligned with the more generally Christian humanistic frame of reference in which an *old* text is good whenever a *new* one has come to reframe it. "Reframing" is certainly the most neutral term available, at least to me, for describing what Marie's prologue asserts as the task of the translator. The term has a technical significance when applied to Marie's text, but it may also be used to characterize a larger and more crucial cultural phenomenon in the textual field, one that extends outside of literature. In Christian culture, reframing – as fulfilling without discounting or overcoming without forgetting – is what the New Testament does to the Old, Grace to the Law, and Christ to Adam.

To suggest how the notions teased out of Marie's text may resonate with widespread trends of thought, we may look at another example from the Old French literary canon, in which the dynamics of tradition-forming through translation are similarly theorized. While in Marie's prologue the hermeneutic gain intrinsic to approaching a text from a later perspective was connected to her activity as translator, in the programmatic statement contained in the prologue of Chrétien de Troyes' *Cligès*, the task of the writer as translator appears to follow the silence of the old texts out of necessity. For Chrétien, the new text reactivates the old by recreating its meaning in a new context that is not simply linguistic, but more widely hermeneutical. Accordingly, the author of what is considered Chrétien's most classicizing romance introduces himself at once as a maker and a translator:

> Cil qui fist d'Erec et d'Enide
> Et les Comandemanz d'Ovide
> Et l'Art d'Amors an romanz mist
> Et le Mors de l'Espaule fist,
> Del roi Marc e d'Iseut la blonde,
> Et de la Hupe et de l'Aronde
> Et del Rossignol la Muance,
> Un novel conte recomance
> D'un vaslet, qui an Grece fu
> De lignage le roi Artu. (ll. 1–10)

I, the one who composed the *Érec et Énide*, who set the *Laws* of Ovid as well as his *Art of Love* to a Romance language, who composed *The Shoulder's Bite* and the story

of king Marc and *Iseult the Blonde*, and the *Metamorphosis* of the hoopoe, the swallow,
and the nightingale, here start a new tale about a young knight who lived in Greece,
of the lineage of Arthur the king.[11]

The catalogue of published works through which Chrétien defines his profile
as writer of a new work includes several different types of texts. According to
the author's own terminology, there are some explicitly translated ones, such
as Ovid's *Ars amatoria* and *Remedia amoris*, which are set *an romans*. There are
also some "original" narratives like the *Érec et Énide*, which he is said to have
"made." These are in their turn followed by some other texts of intermediate
status, like the mythological story of Paelops, which is classical in origin, but
is still listed, again, as "made." Finally, there are some (at least for our terminological standards) clearly translated texts, such as the triple metamorphosis
("la muance") of the Philomela-Procne-Tereus myth, also taken from Book 6
of Ovid's *Metamorphoses*, or some others, most likely of a different status, such
as the story of Marc and Iseult, with no verb attached that could indicate the
process of their production more precisely. In sum, the range of activity that
defines Chrétien is laid out on a continuum. Different degrees of proximity
to his activity as either "maker" (seemingly expressed in the verb "fist") or as
"translator" (seemingly associated with the verb "mist") may be perceived at the
extremes of the range, but there is a wide grey area at its centre. Here, Chrétien
is possibly conceivable as a "re-maker" (i.e., a maker within a strong tradition)
of traditional material.[12]

There is something in these lines, however, that the elusive semantics of the
verbs associated with each specific work may not obscure: Chrétien's clearly classicizing posture, articulated within an all-encompassing authorial and biographical
frame. As has long been noted, the passage that registers the central homage to the
Latin *magister amoris*, the Ovid of which Chrétien has been both translator and
maker, is also designed to evoke a textual model, which is just as markedly classical.
Chrétien patterns the opening of his new story, that is, on four (spurious) Virgilian lines, traditionally found before the acknowledged and official *incipit* of the
Aeneid: "arma virumque cano." The lines in questions read as follows:

A Ille ego qui quondam gracili modulatus auena
B carmen et egressus siluis uicina coegi
C ut quamuis avido parerent arua colono,
D gratum opus agricolis, at nunc horrentia Martis
1. Arma uirumque cano   (*Aeneid* I.A-1)

I am the one who, long time ago, composed a poem, tuning it on a slender reed; then,
having left the woods, forced the fields nearby to yield to the greedy labourer, a work
the farmers appreciate, but now of the bristling weapons of Mars and the hero I sing.[13]

Just as the incipit of Chrétien's romance does, the spurious Virgilian proem also used a thin veil of periphrases to give an overview of his published works, from the early *Bucolics* (the pastoral "carmen" modulated on a tenuous reed), through the *Georgics* (the "opus" appreciated by the farmers for its agricultural subject matter), to his culminating epic, the war-filled *Aeneid*. At first sight, one may read this game of allusion as Chrétien's way of balancing the martial Virgil and the erotic Ovid through their reverse matrix of presence in the proem. In this reading, Virgil would be the object of only a proemial allusion, embedded in a work that is mostly martial in quality (traces of the Virgilian model have been detected in many of the poem's battle scenes). Ovid, on the contrary, would be expressly indicated as an authority who had provided previous inspiration and poetic material for Chrétien, but whose teachings on erotic subjects are carefully and subtly interspersed (in fully "translated" form) throughout the romance. As at least one section of Chrétien's audience knew, however, the turn of phrase "Ille ego qui" also existed elsewhere in the Latin tradition, featuring prominently in the first elegy of the fourth book of Ovid's *Tristia*, his poetry from exile. The Ovidian antecedent is even more pertinent for the prologue to the *Cligès* than its Virgilian counterpart, since it engages the author in an even more open game of identification with, and distancing from, old works he had composed. In his poetry from exile, the disgraced Ovid vindicated, before present and future audiences, both his innocence and the authorship of a work he acknowledges as the source of his geopolitical displacement and present predicament:

> Ille ego qui fuerim, tenerorum lusor amorum,
> quem legis, ut noris, accipe posteritas.
> Sulmo mihi patria est, gelidis uberrimus undis,
> milia qui novies distat ab Vrbe decem.   (*Tristia* IV.i.1–4)

> I am the one who once was the playful poet of tender loves: hear me, posterity, so that you may know who it is you are reading. My homeland is Sulmo, rich for its cold waters, ninety miles from Rome.[14]

The balanced Virgilian (epic) and Ovidian (pseudo-epic and erotic) incipit of the *Cligès* is complex because of its stratified strategy of allusion, but it is certainly a clear and self-aware marker of authorial allegiance to the classical tradition. The classicism of the *Cligès* does not rely, however, solely on authorial awareness. In the same breath as Chrétien articulates this paradigm on personal terms, he also evokes the cultural counterpart of the self-portrait as alter-Virgil or alter-Ovid, one which unfolds at world-historical level.

In addition to these clear traces of classicizing authorial self-fashioning as a reincorporation of authoritative ancient models, the opening gambit of the *Cligès* contains one of the most distinct vernacular articulations of another widespread late antique and medieval cultural trope, that of the *translatio studii et imperii*. According to this understanding of the patterns of cultural and political domination, history is perceived as a precise and linear narrative, in which the centre of knowledge and power moves from one civilization to the next on the world stage. The movement has some stable itinerary checkpoints: from the distant past, marked by the flourishing of eastern civilizations, to the present glory of the Christian world, centred on the Franco-German imperial court, through the intermediary step of Rome's civilization. Evidently, this trope of world-historical transmission of power and knowledge is also a trope of translation.

This predominantly literary construct is inspired by the biblical and patristic model of the four kingdoms of Daniel 2 and 7, each defining, in the prophet's interpretation of the king's dream, a specific era in ancient history; the trope of *translatio* maps the shift of both political and cultural preeminence as the passing of a cultural torch. The unfolding of history along such a linear axis conforms well to ideas of history as divinely ordained, as the biblical passage in question proclaims, by giving God the ability to "transfer" power through time and space: "Et ipse mutat tempora, et aetates: transfert regna, atque constituit" (The Lord makes seasons and ages change; He moves kingdoms and creates them, Dn. 2:11). In an act of self-promotion as latecomer, Chrétien's prologue contains one of the most elaborate and triumphant instantiations of the translation trope, in which the terms *chivalrie* (the disciplines of active life) and *clergie* (their equivalent for contemplative life) translate the Latin concepts of *imperium* and *studium*, respectively, while mapping their *translatio* from Greece to Rome and from Rome to France:

> Ce nos ont nostre livre apris,
> Qu Grece ot de chevalerie
> Le premier los et de clergie.
> Puis vint chevalerie a Rome
> Et de la clergie la some,
> Qui ore est an France venue.
> Des doint qu'ele i soit retenue.
>
> (ll. 29–36)

This have taught us our books: that once the highest fame of chivalry and clergy was in Greece. Then power came to Rome and the sum of all knowledge too, those that now have arrived to France. May God grant that they are kept there.

Just as it is integral to the patristic understanding of the supersession that the new Christian dispensation operated on old traditions, a notion that accompanied the phenomenon of interlinguistic and intercultural translation, so too Chrétien's romance establishes itself as a new instantiation of an old tradition that it updates for the present.

When Chrétien speaks of the transference of power and knowledge from east to west and from antiquity to the present, he insists on the necessary thinning out of both political and cultural might that characterizes human history. Both *imperium* and *fama* are subject to the subsequent action of time, which determines their initial increase and eventual erosion. As earthly phenomena, they come into being and die out, so that transference is not so much the passing of something like a baton, in a socio-cultural world-historical relay race, as Hegel would put it. Rather, it is the emergence in different circumstances of time, space, and language of an always new and always better understanding.

The notion that there is a *thing* at the core of what is made the object of such transference may actually be more the product of a modern projection than an original thought in the conceptualization of what "translating" means in the trope of the "transference" of knowledge and power. Chrétien, in other words, does not articulate a process in which something that used to be in Greece and in Greek (let's say Homer's Trojan cycle) was brought to Rome and into Latin by a strain of writers of the ilk of Naevius, Livius Andronicus, and Ennius, until it became something else (let's call it Virgil's *Aeneid*). Accordingly, he would probably not subscribe to the idea that writers in the *langue d'oïl* took up this now Latin "thing" and made it into *romans* (*de Troie* or *d'Eneàs*), which eventually gave us something (let's call it the *Cligès*) that is still – only in part, but an essential part – what it used to be back in Greece and Greek. From Chrétien's passage *translatio* appears to consist, rather, in the progressive "happening" (as in "taking place") of an increasingly deeper meaning in a subject matter. Interpretation and translation, as the movement of a *matière* through ever-changing circumstances and different languages, coincide essentially and axiologically. The term that indicates the practitioner of both, *interpres*, is the same, and Chrétien's text also predicates a positive hermeneutic accrual on both.

Most specifically, and most interestingly for the argument of this book, Chrétien conceives of *translatio* as a process that involves language not only in its last stage or in its articulation on the page. The new text comes to lend a new voice to the ancient writer, thus correcting the cultural silence into which the past has fallen. Thus, translation is framed as the necessary representation of the past:

Mes des Grezois ne des Romains
Ne dit an mes ne plus ne mains;
D'aus est la parole remese
Et estainte la vive brese. (ll. 41–4)

But of the Greeks and Romans no one speaks anymore; of them the language is muted, and the live embers extinguished.

Chrétien presents the setting of the ancient *fama* in both its passive and active verbal aspects: no one speaks of the ancient Greeks and Romans anymore, and the ancients themselves cannot speak. Their "parole," their "fame" but also their capacity to speak, is gone. The work of the new poet is to give new matters a new voice: no archaeological approach seems to be possible, only one that complies with the flow of history and moves through the different age-defining languages of culture.

The incipit of the *Cligès* contains a retrospective gaze at another of Chretien's romances, the conjugal story of *Érec et Énide*, in which the practice of poetic imitation and literal translation is just as strong, albeit articulated in a less programmatically prominent place. One moment in that earlier romance is, however, particularly worth looking at in detail, because it brings together in one single episode the issues of tradition-forming translation and an allusively Edenic garden setting. A little context will help us get our bearings in the wide-ranging and complex system of adventures that makes up the bulk of the romance. Two-thirds into the narrative, in the close of the episode of Érec's healing, Énide receives a noble palfrey as a gift. Chrétien's narrative stops and launches into a brief ekphrasis, detailing the carvings on the ivory of the *arçon*, a part of the lavishly decorated saddle Énide was given by the generous host. On that piece of equestrian equipment an exceptional craftsman had depicted the "translation" parable of Aeneas from Troy to Carthage to Latium, and, in particular, the failed love story between the Trojan hero and Dido, recounted according to the Ovidian pro-heroine perspective, which speaks of Dido's joyous amorous reception and her eventual betrayal by Aeneas:

> La sele fu d'autre meniere,
> Coverte d'une porpre chiere;
> Li arçon estoient d'ivoire,
> S'i fu antailliee l'estoire
> Comant Eneas vint de Troye,
> Comant a Cartaige a grant joie
> Dido an son leu le reçut,
> Comant Eneas la deçut,
> Comant ele por lui s'ocist,
> Comant Eneas puis conquist
> Laurente et tote Lonbardie,
> Dom il fui rois tote sa vie.   (ll. 5287–98)

The saddle was made differently, covered by a rich purple. The gullet was ivory, and the history carved there included how Eneas came from Troy, how he was received with great joy in Carthage by Dido in her home, how Eneas betrayed her, how she killed herself for him, and how Eneas eventually conquered Latium and the whole of Italy, over which he ruled throughout his life.

This moment of blatant retrospective classicism opens a cavalcade that, in a relatively short span of lines, leads into Érec's next adventure. The new episode goes by the name *Joi de la court* and takes place in an enchanted space: a garden of eternal spring-summer, filled with the pleasant song of birds and all useful medicinal plants imaginable. Two passages from this long adventure deserve quotation in full, since they have several elements in common with other gardens of this book and the narratives that unfold in them. Both the delimitation of the garden, in this romance a magical one, and the complex ecosystem of flora and fauna it encloses are topical:

> El vergier n'avoit an viron
> Mur ne paliz, se de l'air non;
> Mes de l'air est de totes parz
> Par nigromance clos li jarz,
> Si que riens antrer n'i pooit,
> Se par un seul leu n'i antroit,
> Ne que s'il fust toz clos de fer.
> Et tot esté et tot yver
> Y avoit flors et fruit maür;
> Et li fruiz avoit tel eür
> Que leanz se lessoit mangier
> Mes au porter hors fet dongier ... (ll. 5693–9)

The garden had around it neither wall nor palisade, just air. It was by dark magic that the air enclosed the garden from all sides, so that nothing might enter, except through one place, as if walled-off with iron. Inside, both in summer and in winter, there were flowers and ripe fruit. These fruits had the special quality that they might be eaten in the garden, but they would imperil those who tried to carry them out.

As an unseasonably fruitful garden of eternal spring, the magic "vergier" in which Érec will face the crucial adventure of the *Joi de la court* certainly evokes Eden. Both the inaccessible nature of the place and the prohibition on carrying out the fruit clearly point in the same, biblical direction. So, too, does the insistence on the complete coverage of all possible (pleasant and positive) species of birds and plants present in this particular space:

> Ne soz ciel n'a oisel volant,
> Tant pleise a home par son chant,
> Por lui deduire et resjoïr,
> Qu'iluec ne poïst l'an oïr
> Plusors de chascune nature.
> Et terre, tant com ele dure,
> Ne porte espice ne mecine,

Qui vaille a nule medicine,
Que iluec n'i eüst planté,
S'an i avoit a grant planté.   (ll. 5709–18)

There is no bird flying under the heavens that delights man with its song, to bring
him joy and delight, that one could not hear there – and many of each kind. The
earth, for all it is wide, has no spice nor herb that may work as medicine that is not
planted there, and one could get it in great abundance.

While the garden is allusively Eden-like, it is also openly classicizing. It is in
this magical and yet Eden-like setting that Érec will find his adventure, defeat-
ing a knight imprisoned by a mysterious lady, who had bound him never to
leave the garden unless overpowered by a worthier knight. In the course of the
adventure, Érec sees this beautiful woman at the centre of the garden, seated on
a bed under a sycamore tree. To literally measure the beauty of this lady, the text
turns again to a classical example, evoking Lavinia, the wife for whom Aeneas
will wage his wars in Italy, after having left behind both (almost blamelessly)
the dead Creusa in Troy and (somewhat more culpably) the equally dead Dido
in Carthage:

De li ne vuel plus deviser,
Mes qui bien seüst raviser
Et son ator et sa biauté,
Dire poïst por verité
C'onques Lavine de Laurente
Qui tant par fu et bele et gente,
N'en ot de sa biauté le quart.   (ll. 5841–7)

About her I will write no more, but those who may have a chance to observe well
both her beauty and her grace would be able to say truly that Lavinia of Laurentum,
who was such a model of beauty and elegance, had not a quarter of her charm.

While the first classicizing passage in the romance recapitulated the whole parable
of Aeneas' journey from the East of Troy to the West of Rome via Carthage in the
carvings of Énide's saddle, here only the last woman in the life of the ancient hero
appears, symbolic of his destination reached. Just as the prologue of the romance
established, in presenting former civilizations as extinguished and mute, here too
the present of adventure outdoes every past model. In keeping with the general
attitude of the story, the beauty of the mysterious lady of the garden is said to surpass fourfold that of the heroine in the ancient poem. The new outdoes the old in
the same breath as it recovers it, and it does so in the setting of a unique garden, at
once exceptionally beautiful and inaccessible, fruitful and forbidden.

Whereas in the *Cligès* the translation moment was used as foundational incipit for a classicizing narrative, in the *Érec et Énide* the theme of translation is connected to a garden setting, which is at the same time Edenic and explicitly reminiscent of (and measured against) a classical counterpart. The topos of the garden intersects with a moment of optimistic cultural translation, which extends from the macro-figure of the romance (marked by recurrent actualizations of ancient narrative material) to the micro-figure of the lady in the garden. The seamless combination and transfer of traditional and classical material into the new narrative organism is part of what Chrétien could have called, as he does in his prologue, an effective thematic and narrative imbrication, "une molt bele conjointure" (l. 14). In a doubly engaging act of translation, by mobilizing a classical model in his new text, Chrétien transposes the Horatian *callida iunctura* of the *Ars poetica* from the level of diction to that of storytelling, and he does so in a garden setting.

In conclusion, it may not be coincidental that a similarly translative garden is also present in the first of Marie's *Lais*, the song of *Guigemar*. Though its layout is mentioned in passing, the garden space is a crucial element of the plot. An enclosed garden next to a tower is in fact the place where the once love-averse protagonist, who has been wounded by a ricocheting arrow he shot at a supernatural creature (a hind with stag's antlers on her head) and magically abducted by a self-steering ship, encounters the woman who will cure him through reciprocal love. The description of this natural and cultural setting for the story is minimal, but the role the place plays in the *lai* is significant:

> En un vergier suz le dongun,
> La out un clos tut environ;
> De vert marbre fu li muralz,
> Mult par esteit espés e halz;
> N'i out fors une sule entrée,
> Cele fu not e jur guardee.　　　　　　　　　　　　　(*Guigemar* 218–24)

[She was kept] in a garden under the tower, a space walled all around, with a wall of green marble, thick and tall, which had just one entrance, watched over day and night.

The lady with whom Guigemar will fall in love, and who will reciprocate his affection, finds herself inhabiting this garden because she is married to an old and, therefore, jealous husband (so the story doctrinally asserts). The old man has taken every precaution to remain unchallenged in his control of the wife – to the point that he has hired a eunuch priest to feed her, bodily and spiritually – while ensuring that her life has all possible material amenities. To that end – namely, to safeguard his wife, as the text glosses – he has had a magnificent chamber built within the walled garden. The chamber has a chapel and a bedroom, which is richly decorated with paintings that cover all the walls. These paintings depict Venus, the goddess of love, along with all the information, in graphic format, necessary to perform the appropriate behaviours of committed and refined lovers:

> Venus, la deuesse d'amur,
> Fu tresbien mise en la peinture,
> Le traiz mustrez e la nature
> Cument hom deit amur tenir
> E lëalmen e bien servir.
> Le livre Ovide, ou il enseine
> Coment chascun s'amur estreine,
> En un fu ardant le gettout
> E tuz iceus escumengout
> Ki ja mais cel libre lirreient
> Ne sun enseignement nient fereient.   (*Guigemar* 234–44)

Venus, the goddess of love, was beautifully set in the painting, which also showed the actions and qualities necessary to be in love and perform good and loyal service. She was depicted in the act of casting into a burning fire the book of Ovid, the one in which he teaches how to constrict one's love, and of excommunicating all those who ever read that book and would not follow her own teachings.

The irony of furnishing a space he intended for the sexual containment of his wife with an iconographic scheme that points to the venereal discipline is seemingly lost to the potential *auctor intellectualis* of the frescos, the jealous old man, who is literally out of the picture in this part of the story. More than for any jarring effect that may be produced by the interplay of intended and achieved effects in the maladroitly chosen iconography (if the husband did indeed commission the frescos), or by the juxtaposition of sacred and erotic elements in the architecture of the place, the paintings of the lady's chamber are relevant because of their reference to Ovid.[15] Appearing in the form of a specific text (most likely the *Remedia amoris*), Ovid-the-book is consigned to the flames because it contains teachings contrary to those that Venus herself imparts.[16] The excommunication of those who refuse to do the goddess's bidding involves them as "readers" of the *Remedia*, a text condemned to what appears an unappealable destiny: a silencing burning. However, by having Venus define her faithful as those who do not read that book and are hence ready to heed her teachings, the text also suggests that burning one book, however closely associated with the name of its author, does not mean silencing and excision from the tradition. By framing her own teachings ("sun enseignement") as opposite to those that the book contained ("il enseiñ"), Venus evokes and accedes to an alternative textuality, one that undoes the alleged, originally ironic, anti-erotic and palinodic turn Ovid took in the *Remedia*. By imposing a one-eighty turn on a one-eighty conversion, that is, the painted Venus recommends another no less Ovidian and no less magisterial body of texts. Her gesture of breaking with (one branch of) the classical tradition of *artes amandi* opens up a space for (another branch of) that same tradition to reassert itself.

What the book-burning scene stages for Marie's readers is, in other words, a paradigm of reuse that does not coincide with consumption. Not unlike the translational Greek and Roman textuality that Chrétien evoked in his *translatio* trope, the book-burning scene in *Guigemar*, depicted at the centre of a built environment surrounded by an enclosed garden, evokes the possibility of a new voice.[17] As this sally into Old French classicizing narrative texts suggests, and as the exploration of what comes after in the tradition of the garden trope will confirm, the garden and the act of translation are more than occasionally connected.

Chapter One

Encompassing Imperfection:
The Garden of the *Rose*

The image of the earthly paradise haunts the *Roman de la Rose*, and the *Roman* haunts the literature of succeeding centuries.

(Bart Giamatti [1966, 66], quoted by John Fleming [1969, 57 & 1986, 201])

Because of its complicated origin, early reception, and immediate critical fortune, the allegorical narrative of the *Romance of the Rose* has always displayed multiple literary and hermeneutic identities. Penned by two different authors in the span of almost half a century, between the 1230s and 1270s, it was a divided and self-reflective work from the start. Its early fortune outside of the French language made it the object of various reworkings and translations as different as the Italian *Fiore* and Chaucer's *Romaunt*. The poem also found itself at the centre of a harshly fought and polarized hermeneutic confrontation, in which such disparate intellectuals as Christine de Pizan and Jean Gerson took part – a *querelle* about the possible meanings and uses of the poem, which has accompanied the scholarly debate into the present.[1] The protean fortune of their text would not have disappointed its authors, who certainly fostered the most pressing question of the long literary-historical reception of the *Rose*: how should we read this poem? In this chapter, conceived as an extended gloss to this question, I argue that, among other things, the *Rose* is a culminating (if internally fraught) example of the same French wave of optimism that was at the core of the literary operations we have seen performed by Marie de France and Chrétien de Troyes. As is the case with their works, the *Rose* also vindicates its own status as a translation; that is, as a fruitful recasting of traditional material. Similarly, the poem predicates its hermeneutic potential on its own availability to interpretation.

A hermeneutically challenging and ultimately open text, and the latest link in the transition of a subject matter that it translates and transforms, the *Rose* intends to be at once definitive and provisional. In its dialogue with literary and prophetic antecedents, the text projects the necessity it deems inherent in any tradition of writing, beginning with the scriptural one, to invite readings that constantly destabilize their provisional meaning. As I argue in this chapter, Guillaume and Jean's poem casts itself as the rewriting of a classical *Ars amandi*, while also gesturing toward the ambiguous possibility of having a new and final Gospel, an *Evangile pardurable*, a text and a paradigm of final supersessional writing that is at once evoked and stigmatized. In consciously locating itself at the ever-tilting point in which tradition is made present, the *Rose* embodies the same nexus of hermeneutic and translative availability which characterizes the corpus of fictional texts under scrutiny. Incidentally, but not coincidentally, it does so by staging all its action within the confines of an allusively and literarily overcharged garden.

As the motto adopted for this chapter suggests, reading the *Roman de la Rose* while investigating the literary fortune and value of the garden trope is an inescapable act for at least two reasons. First, and quite literally, the *Rose* contains the trope of the garden visit as a privileged opportunity to stage acts of translation, in its almost pure form. The garden and text of the *Rose* are not simply the locus for the protagonist's story of falling in love, the vicissitudes of his romantic captivation, and finally his erotic initiation. They also offer themselves as the locus for the writing of an "Art of Love" that transmits and translates its literary past. A monument of medieval "classicism," the *Romance of the Rose* is also rich in descriptive details of its luscious setting, representing a literary culmination of the topos of garden description. In particular, the poem includes several specific elements that later texts reactivate, pointing with different degrees of explicitness to this work as their authoritative literary antecedent, and to its garden as the narrative model for their own. In the following pages, there will not be an opportunity to comment on the list of all the pleasant elements in the garden (be they delightfully singing birds or trees of every possible variety) or to map onto their (largely classical) models the "doctrinal" points articulated in the didactic interventions on erotic matters entrusted to various characters. Both tasks have been not only masterfully carried out in the scholarly literature about the poem, but also addressed at a distance in chapters 3 and 4, dedicated to Boccaccio's and Chaucer's "rewritings" of the *Rose*. As we will see, however, the insistence on and recurrence of specific descriptive details or metaliterary statements are not simply a matter of rhetorical ornamentation or cultural authorization, but get to the heart of understanding what a medieval literary garden is and how it works as a translative space.

1. A Literary Space for Translation: The Authorities of the *Rose*

The *Roman de la Rose* is a poem deeply concerned with the question of translation and tradition. This sentence reads almost as a truism: starting from the liminal act of self-nomination in the poem's prologue, Guillaume's text at once evokes its dependence on a literary tradition and vindicates its own privileged position in it. As a dream fiction seeking cultural legitimacy among serious works of literature, the poem opens with a preliminary defence of the possibility that dreams may contain more than just fabrications and lies ("fables et mençonges"):

> Aucunes genz dient qu'en songe
> N'a se fables non et mençonges.
> Mes l'en puet tex songes songier
> Qui ne sont mie mençongier,
> Ainz sont aprés bien aparant.
> Si en puis bien traire a garant
> Un auctor qui ot non Macrobes,
> Qui ne tint pas songes a lobes. (ll. 1–8)

Some people say that in dreams there is nothing but fables and lies. One may, however, dream such dreams that are not mendacious, but turn out in the end to be evident. One may call as witness the authority of Macrobius, who does not deem dreams false at all.[2]

Guillaume's claim of narrative and cultural validity has simple content and a local context. The content is that truth-bearing dreams exist, and that, accordingly, this poem's fiction is that it is not a fiction. The context is similarly inflected by metaliterary questions. The truth of the *Rose* is made to rest on the authority of Macrobius as commentator of Cicero's *Somnium Scipionis*, a work which was in its turn a reworking in Latin of Plato's myth of Er from the *Republic*.[3] The programmatic vindication of such an authoritative pedigree is at once courageous and revealing of the transhistorical self-positioning of the poem as the latest link in a multilingual and transhistorical chain of reworkings that comprises both interlingual translations and commentary-based interpretations.

Once it is clarified which side of oneirocritics and fictionality the text supports (there can be truth-bearing dreams, and this poem's fiction is that it is not a fiction), the author-narrator-protagonist moves on to the executive and narrative part of his work, but he still engages with metaliterary questions. In claiming that, when he was twenty years old, he had a dream that proved prophetic of what would eventually happen to him, and declaring his intent to narrate it in full, he also introduces his work in a specific light:

> Or veil cel songe rimeer
> Pour vos cuers plus feire agueer,
> Qu'Amors le me prie et commande. (ll. 31–3)

Now I intend to put this dream in verse to bring more joy to your hearts, since Love entreats and commands me to do so.

Following the traditional *accessus* model, these three programmatic lines detail the origin (in a dream), the goal (the recreation of the audience and author's hearts), and the authority (the God or passion of Love) for the narrative that the author is about to produce. They also establish the specific linguistic register of this narrative: the vernacular fictional poetic form conveyed by the term "rimeer." Immediately following this introduction, and still in self-analytical mode, the author-narrator-protagonist turns to his audience, in a hypothetical gesture patterned on a classical rhetorical move. Taking up Propertius' strategy of coopting readers into the production and definition of the text, by presenting it as a response to a request enclosed in the formula *quaeritis* (you, readers, ask me), Guillaume provides a key definition of the content of his work: the *romanz* begun here, the title of which is *The Romance of the Rose*, "encompasses" (or encloses) "in its entirety the art of love." But this is not all: the classicizing move also triggers a concomitant modern-favouring response, with the narrator stating that the subject *matière* presented by the narrative is both "good and new":

> Et se nule ne nus demande
> Comant je veil que li romanz
> Soit apelez que je comanz,
> Ce est li Romanz de la Rose
> Ou l'art d'Amors est tote enclose.
> La matire est et bone et nueve.   (ll. 34–9)

> And if anyone was to ask what I want the romance I begin here to be called, this is the *Romance of the Rose*, where the art of love is contained in full. Its subject matter is both good and new.

Notably, the writer's reference to a tradition in which his work intends to be inscribed passes through two distinct but related stages. First, the text claims, this *romanz* contains in full (encloses) the art of love. The word "art" is a technical term, alluding to the practical aspects of a craft, which guarantees an ethical dimension for the text (its applicability in the present). It also contains a transparent reference to Ovid's Latin poem on the instruction of lovers, the *Ars amatoria*. In quoting its title, the text presents its readers with a culturally charged, authoritative anteced-ent from the classical world, which should contribute to the metacritical framing of their reading. The second element in the self-definition of the work, which positions it as the most recent instalment in an orderly sequence, is the coupling of two specific adjectives which define its *matière*. Unmistakably "modernist" in spirit, the phrase "et bone et nueve" contrasts the poem with a textual background which is at once "old" (not "new") and "inadequate" (not "good"). I believe that the alleged ability to contain all that it is possible to say (and has been said) about the art of love is not unrelated to the text's claim that its subject matter is both good and new. The deliberately non-classical language in which it is drafted comes to play an important role in the "newness" and coordinated "goodness" that the text vindicates here.

On first reading, the qualification of the subject matter as "good and new" seems to have little to do with the transitional relation between vernacular and Latin, which is established in the evocation of Ovid's *Ars amatoria* tradition, and with the combined import of the terms *Romanz* and *rimeer*, both alluding to a movement away from classical culture into modern vernacular format. The lexicon and the cultural paradigms mobilized, however, distinctly (though allusively) profile this text as related to another one, that of the Gospels, which is most foundationally a *new* text that is also *good*. After all, the central text in the canon of the "New" Testament, the Gospel is also, as *eu-angelion*, the conveyor of an etymologically "good" message. The status of the *Rose*, in other words, seems to be that of a work which bears a *good* message of (and into) a *new* temporal and linguistic dispensation. Like the Gospels before it, the *Rose* does so in a *new* language.

The precision with which the text defines itself as a romance that treats a good and new subject matter makes it quite difficult to underestimate the neo-testamentary quality of the *Rose*'s claim. Not only does the self-definition suggest that the text contains *Good News*; the relationship of dependence on and replacement of the classical antecedent, which the poem's definition also implies, points to the mechanism of neo-testamentary translation, which we have seen at work before. The *Rose* is not only potentially alluding to itself as a Gospel; it does so as a translating text. Concomitantly and vice versa, the poem not only declares that its subject matter is of a novelty and goodness that resonate with neo-testamentary attitudes, but also it does so specifically as a translative text. We will revisit this point in due course, by exploring the text's strategic return to the Gospel model in later sections and its reception in the most direct Italian reworking of the poem, the *Fiore*. Thus far, it is enough to note the foundational force of this resonance, and to address a potential modern bias in our reading of this facet, the claim to novelty, in the text's proemial self-presentation.

When the poet in the *Rose* states that the poem's subject matter is "new," he does not mean that it is "unprecedented." Inventiveness is not, of course, a feature one would easily ascribe to the encyclopedic rehashing of traditional material that constitutes the bulk of the work as a whole. The "novelty" of the *Rose* consists, more technically, in the new declination of traditional cultural material, according to the same ambivalent paradigm of continuity and re-presentation on which a large section of medieval literary culture also relies. This relationship is similarly present at the level of invention: the garden of the *Rose* is a "double" of its model, Eden. In two alternative yet coordinated ways, it appears at once as a "sign" and a "replica" of its antecedent. The difference between these two co-implicated statuses is one of hermeneutic emphasis. When continuities between the old and new object are perceived and emphasized, the "new" garden of the *Rose* functions as a sign of the former garden. The Eden-like garden of the *Rose* is, in this sense, an Eden made available so that a new narrative may unfold. In other words, the new place is not intended to replace the old one, but rather to point to it. When, instead, the perception of and emphasis on difference prevail, the new garden functions as a distant, provisional, and failing replica of the original one. In this sense, the garden in the *Rose* is an alternative Eden, an "other" garden that asks to be measured against the reality of its antecedent. Insisting on the "otherness" of the space it uses, the text of the romance engages in a process which, quite literally, puts a place in place of a place.

In reproducing and representing their models through a new instantiation, both garden and text converge and eventually coincide. Their cohesion extends from the narrative to the metaliterary level. In the same breath as it articulates its position in a tradition encompassing works about the art of love, the romance alludes to a key feature of that very Edenic garden which it is about to incorporate into the narrative, by projecting on it a metaliterary dimension. In specifying that the new text contains a complete course on the art of love ("ou l'art d'Amors est tote *enclose*"), the *Rose* defines itself as a literary-spatial enclosure, a container that separates an inside, where the whole of the matter is found, and an outside, where none of it is left. In precisely this sense, enclosure is one of the prominent features of both the dream-garden and its scriptural model, the *hortus conclusus*. A walled-off space created for humankind and now forbidden, Eden encloses both the narrative space and the subject matter of the poem. Guillaume de Lorris's preliminary definition of his poem goes this far. But it is a culturally advanced point. The continuator of his work takes the reasoning even further.

In the section devoted to the eventual suturing of the two parts of the *Rose*, about twenty thousand lines into the narrative, Jean de Meun's rehashing of this inaugural motif develops along the same, albeit less cryptically allusive, lines. The text's inscription into a clearly delineated tradition, spanning classical Latin models and a new culminating vernacular work, is an element that the new section of the poem strategically confirms. In his rallying speech in front of the allegorical army assembled to provide the protagonist with help in securing his desired "rose," the God of Love constructs a canon of lover-writers who have fought in his camp. In the short span of just about twenty lines, the list stretches from Tibullus to Guillaume de Lorris, and eventually includes Jean de Meun (as the two subsequent authors of the text), mentioning a few other significant Latin erotic poets in between. Except for the last champion (who is yet to be born at the fictional time of the narrative), all authorities on love's games whom the God of Love mentions are dead. As was the case in Chrétien's *translatio* prologue, the *Rose* passage contains more than just a coyly phrased catalogue of antecedents for the poem: the God of Love's construction of the tradition passes through a clear series of acts of translation.[4]

The first champion whose loss the God of Love laments is Tibullus, for whom he adopts and adapts Ovid's funeral eulogy, to all effects translating a significant section of it:

Puis que Tibullus m'est failliz,
Qui connoisset si bien mes teiches,
Pour cui mort je brisai mes fleiches,
Quassai mes ars, et meis cuiriees
Traïnai toutes desciriees …   (ll. 10478–82)

Gallus, Catillus et Ovides,
Qui bien sorent d'amors trestier,
Nous reüssent or bien mestier
Mais chascuns d'aus gist mort porriz!   (ll. 10492–5)

After I have been deserted by Tibullus, who knew so well my nature, and on account of whose death I broke my arrows, snapped my bows, and dragged my quivers behind me all torn … Gallus, Catullus, and Ovid, who could treat love so well, would really be handy now, but they are every one of them dead and gone.

Tradition and translation converge in this passage. In the language Jean uses, and in the turns of phrase he imports from Ovid's *Amores* III.9, the God of Love transparently evokes an established Latin text, which he translates into the present by grafting it into the new narrative organism of the vernacular poem:

Ille tui vates operis, tua fama, Tibullus
ardet in extructo, corpus inane, rogo.
ecce, puer Veneris fert eversamque pharetram
et fractos arcus et sine luce facem;
adspice, demissis ut eat miserabilis alis
pectoraque infesta tundat aperta manu!   (*Amores* III.9.5–10)

He, the singer of your work, your fame-giver, Tibullus, now an empty corpse, burns on his funeral pyre. Behold, the child of Venus drags his quiver upside down; his bow is broken, and the torch flameless. Look how he walks with his wings downcast, how he beats his naked chest with a cruel hand.[5]

Recontextualization and vernacularization go hand in hand here. What is more, they establish a semiotic connection between translated and translating text. The new vernacular poem takes the old one not only as its antecedent but also as its own sign. By giving a new account of the same mourning process Ovid had described, Jean's God of Love replaces his predecessor. In the same way, the new vernacular text starring Love translates its ancient Latin model. The same comprehensive displacement of ancient material takes place in the following lines. The God of Love now quotes the acts of mourning that Ovid attributes to him in the elegy written for the death of Tibullus, thus moving them from Latin into French; he also does the same with the catalogue of erotic poets he summons as his authorities on matters of erotic conquest, a list he models on a later passage in that same Ovidian elegy. In its concluding epitaph-like section, Ovid's poem depicted an underworld meet-and-greet scene, in which the recently dead elegist is welcomed to a serene portion of the afterlife by his colleagues and predecessors in the art of love poetry, Catullus and Calvus, and perhaps also Gallus. Here is Ovid's lament for Tibullus:

> Si tamen e nobis aliquid nisi nomen et umbra
> restat, in Elysia valle Tibullus erit.
> obvius huic venias hedera iuvenalia cinctus
> tempora cum Calvo, docte Catulle, tuo.
> tu quoque, si falsum est temerati crimen amici,
> sanguinis atque animae prodige Galle tuae.   (*Amores* III.9.59–63)

If anything of us beyond a name and a shade remains, Tibullus will be in the Elysian valley. And you, learned Catullus, will meet him there – with your youthful temples adorned with ivy – alongside Calvus. And you, as well, Gallus, who gave away too freely your blood and soul, if the crime of having betrayed your fearful friend is false.

In the corresponding passage of *Rose*, the God of Love's prophecy immediately creates an impossible narrative situation. Another aid to the God of Love, Guillaume de Lorris, the poet who is credited with penning the first section of the poem we are reading, is invoked and listed, only to have his death registered and lamented as well. After declaring Guillaume dead and retrospectively marking the textual place in which he stopped drafting the poem, the intermediate metanarrator of the *Rose* also introduces the new author, Jean Chopinel, who has continued his antecedent's work thus far in the narrative and is destined to complete the rest of the poem:

> Vez ci Guillaume de Lorriz
> ...
> Car por ma grace deservir
> Doit il conmancier le romant
> Ou seront mis tuit mi conmant.
> Puis vendra Johans Chopinel,
> ...

Cist avra le romanz si chier
Qu'il le voudra tout parfenir
Se tens et leus l'en puet venir *etc.*   (ll. 10496; 10517–19; 10535; 10554–6)

But *voilà,* here is Guillaume de Lorris ... who is destined to begin the romance where all my orders will be gathered ... Then Jean Chopinel will come ... He will hold the romance so dear that he will want to complete it – if he has the time and opportunity to do so.

In this dense, heavily metaliterary passage, readers are asked to process a significant amount of information, not all of which makes immediate sense. First, while the protagonist of the narrative is asleep and still dreaming (not awake and writing, as promised at the start of the work), the author-narrator, who has thus far been identified with him, is actually dead. Correspondingly, since Guillaume (the author whose mouthpiece the narrator-protagonist has been thus far) is dead, there is a new author, Jean. He has been drafting the poem readers have been enjoying (starting from a certain point and until now), but he is no longer the same as the protagonist, since this is still the old author. To make things worse, the new author, this Jean, is yet to be born. At the fictional date of the work, which includes the forty years intervening between the initial literary record of the fictional beginning of the dream and the current time within the narrative that has registered no hiatus, the new writer has replaced the old one and continued his work. Apparently, he has also replaced his antecedent as the protagonist of the poem, since he is the one who will complete the adventure in the garden, says the God of Love. He – that is, Jean (who both has and hasn't replaced Guillaume) – will pluck the rose, wake up, and expound upon the meaning of the whole dream.[6]

The chain of references to imbricated (and incompossible) narratives is dizzying. Beyond the passage's absurd mechanics, and its quite possibly comical quality, one element of the book's renewed self-presentation remains strong: its totalizing aspiration. The God of Love states again, as Guillaume did in the beginning of the work, that the *romant* contains the whole of the art of love. This time, the formulation he uses addresses a more specific point, but still with totalizing aspirations: all of the "conmant" issuing from him are now its content. The collapsing of time that the text forces upon readers is symptomatic of a tension in the relationship the poem establishes with the authorities it incorporates. It speaks, that is, to the troubling double nature of the canon, which is at once *a lineage* of dead poets and texts, recapitulated in their new translated form, as well as a *corpus* of texts, all coexisting and available in the present in their specific linguistic garb. Accordingly, the Art of Love that the *Rose* "fully encircles" is a body of texts and a lineage of writers onto which both sections of the poem are grafted and of which they are also conceived as containers.

Neither aspect of the canon may exist without the other, of course, but both depend on translation. The self-proclaimed lord and master of this tradition, the God of Love himself, specifically frames translation as an act of both linguistic shift and semantic interpretation. In the tongue-in-cheek description of his tutelage of Jean, the God of Love insists on his plan to act as a teacher for his protégé and on the ability that his pupil will, in his turn, possess to teach others. Both points are made in the most technical terms:

> Je l'afubleré de mes eles
> Et li chanteré notes teles
> Que, puis qu'il sera hors d'enfance,
> Endoctrinez de ma sciance,
> Si fleütera noz paroles
> Par carrefors et par escoles
> Selonc le langage de France,
> Par tout le regne, en audiance,
> …
> Car tant en lira proprement
> Que tretuit cil qui ont a vivre
> Devroient apeler ce livre
> Le Miroër aus Amoreus.   (ll. 10607–55)

> I will cover him with my wings and sing him such songs that, once out of childhood, filled with the doctrine of my learning, he will proclaim our words at crossroads and in schools, in the language of France, throughout the kingdom, publicly … He will expound my teachings so well that all who live in the future will have to call this book *The Mirror for the Lovers.*

The "lire" (reading) which, as the text foretells, Jean is supposed to do in the future is a work performed on behalf of the God of Love, based on the "sciance" (doctrine) that emanates from him. Jean's language also directly relates the process of instruction that it imagines to a specific kind of "reading": the scholastic *lectio*. Conflating the act of "reading" with that of magisterial "glossing," the scholastic *lectio* brought together textual explication and interpretation. The passage in the *Rose* jokingly projects this traditional "reading method" adopted in institutions of higher learning onto a new language (the language of the specific kingdom of France), and into a wider range of places than one would expect (schools, naturally, but also crossroads). In doing so – and here there is perhaps a greater degree of seriousness in the operation – it also frames the work of its author as one of both re-interpretation and re-presentation of the tradition that the poem contains and conveys. The movement of the ancient "matter of love" into the *romance* is the crucial element connecting the two spheres of interpretation, "romance" being, after all, both the narrative form and the chosen language of the *Rose*.

2. A Curious Literary Garden: Squaring the Circle

In the same vein, returning from linguistics to horticulture, very little elaboration is needed to support the idea that the garden at the centre of the *Roman de la Rose* is a crucial narrative space for the work's narrative dynamics and semiotic strategies: almost the entirety of the poem's action unfolds there. Similarly, the literary garden's connection with Eden established in the plot is made evident from the start.[7] The garden of the *Rose* is (like) the Garden of Eden. The protagonist and narrator (the lover-dreamer) says so, as soon as he gains admission to that extraordinary space. While he is seized by a threefold synonymic jouissance, being "liez," "bauz," "joienz," he clarifies that delight is the essence of the place ("leus delitable"), not simply his reaction to it:

> Lors entrai, sanz plus dire mot
> Par l'uis que Oiseuse overt m'ot,
> El vergier; et quant je fui enz
> Je fui liez et bauz et joienz.
> Et sachez que je cuidai estre
> Por voir em paradis terrestre;
> Tant estoit li leus delitable
> Qu'i sembloit estre esperitables.
> Car, si com lors m'ert avis,
> Il ne fet en nul paradis
> Si bon estre com il fessoit
> El vergier, qui tant me plesoit.   (ll. 629–40)

Thus, I entered without saying another word, through the door Idleness opened for me, into the garden. I became happy, spirited, and joyous when I was inside. Believe me, I thought I was truly in the earthly paradise: so pleasurable was the place that it appeared to belong to the spiritual realm. Indeed, as I thought, there could not be such a good life in any paradise as there was in that garden that so delighted me.

With great etymological care, the narrator glosses his appreciation of the new environment with terms that reach back from French to Latin and from Latin to biblical Hebrew. By insisting on the "delitable" quality of the place, the text activates the Latin root *delicia*, which is the etymological link to the very word that signifies Eden in Latin, *locus deliciarum* being the translation of the biblical term. One has simply to look at Augustine to find this connection spelled out:

> In Eden, id est in deliciis … Nam deliciae, vel voluptates, vel epulum hoc verbo significari dicitur, si ex hebraeo in latinum interpretatur. (*De genesi contra manichaeos*, II.ix.12)

> In Eden, that is, in delights. Since delight or pleasure or feast this word is said to mean, if it is translated from Hebrew to Latin.[8]

Isidore gives basically the same explanation as Augustine, likewise insisting on the translation chain involved in the naming of the place:

> Paradisus est locus in orientis partibus constitutus, cuius vocabulum ex Graeco in Latinum vertitur hortus: porro Hebraice Eden dicitur, quod in nostra lingua deliciae interpretatur. Quod utcumque iunctum facit hortum deliciarum … E cuius medio fons prorumpens totum nemus inrigat, dividiturque in quattuor nascentia flumina. Cuius loci post peccatum hominis aditus interclusus est. (*Etymologiae* XIV.iii.2–3)

> Paradise is a place located in the East. The word translates from Greek into Latin as *hortus*. Furthermore, in Hebrew, one calls *Eden* what our language translates as *deliciae*. Put together, these two terms form the expression *hortus deliciarum*, the garden of pleasure … From its centre a spring issues that irrigates the whole wood; it divides into four rivers issuing forth from there. Access to this place was forbidden to humans after the fall.[9]

It may be interesting to note the careful temporal staging of Guillaume's passage, in which all tropological associations with the Eden of the Bible of the locality described in the plot are carefully framed as belonging to the past of the dream. While the adverbial phrase "por voir" (truly, for real) certainly points to an actual experience, the retelling of this experience is done through phrasings skewed toward the dreamer's subjectivity: "cuidai," "sembloit," "m'ert avis" (I thought, it seemed, I deemed). Readers are given a temporal intranarrative perspective, one through which the narrator makes room for a potential divergence between how the character conceptualizes reality and the actual nature of the place, a nature to be determined in a deferred present. The tension between verbs and adverbs conveys the same oblique, potential distancing. In "cuidai," the semantics of the verb open up a space for deception (I believed something, but that wasn't the case), which is immediately contrasted with the force of "por voir," which insists on the feeling of reality that came with the impression. The next few lines reinforce the notion, carefully framing the experience of this "leus … esperitables" (spiritual place) within the sphere of appearance and belief, intrinsically and implicitly opposed to the reality and certainty of evidence. The first consecutive nexus "tant estoit li leus delitables … que" (so pleasure-filled was the place … that) extends its force to the expression that closes the passage: "tant me plesoit" (so delighted was I). The reasoning, thus, goes as follows: so great is the pleasure the protagonist derives from his experience, so pleasurable was the place in which he found himself, that he considered it an Eden. But was it?

The potential error in conceptualization, based on the perhaps fallacious mechanism of consequential identification at work in the protagonist's perception of the garden (if x feels so good, it must be y, which is the epitome of good), will be made explicit in a distant, recapitulative episode to which we will turn in due course. Entrusted to the voice of Genius in the second part of the *Rose*, a retrospectively correcting gloss more clearly spells out the provisional nature of the earthly garden that the Lover accessed in the beginning. No matter how strongly the narrative connects, by way of etymological implication, the owner and ruler of this garden *Deduit* (pleasure), with Eden as a garden of *deliciae* (again, pleasures), a difference remains for the readers to appreciate. However, this difference is thus far only subtly suggested.

In such a richly descriptive text, not only etymology connects the garden of the *Rose* with Eden. The paradisal quality of the space that the text heralded at the opening of the garden's door is confirmed shortly thereafter, in the description of the general form of the place. The game of correspondences between the garden of the *Rose* and its biblical "sources" is neither simply generic nor vague. It actually relies on a series of specific topographic and hydrographic features that point to the garden in Eden as a central and original natural space, starting from the curious shape the text constructs for it. The Garden of Deduit in the *Rose* is both a square and a circle, partaking at once of a quadriform and round nature. Square on the outside, but paradoxically also rounded out – since visitors must walk along an encompassing path to inspect it all – the garden is also rounded out and square on the inside.

Philology and hermeneutics collaborate in the reconstruction of what increasingly appears as a curious gestalt image, and this analysis should now note some of the finer details of the text. The first element that gives pause is the contrasting value of the terms "compasseüre" and "querré," which appeared in the first descriptive passage in lines 511–12 and is taken up again, more explicitly, in the opposing rhyme words "compasseüre" and "quarreüre" in lines 1321–2. These two passages, one registering the first impression from outside the wall and the other devoted to a summative perception from the inside, converge to portray the garden as an ambivalent object. First, the protagonist performs a reconnaissance of the enclosed space encountered in his dream:

Lors m'en alai grant aleüre
Acernant la compasseüre
Et la cloison dou mur quarré
Tant c'un huisset mout bien serré
Trovai, petitet et estroit.   (ll. 513–17)

Then I started off with great haste, following the contour and the enclosure of the square wall, until I found a postern, well shut and locked, which was rather narrow and small.

Square on the outside, and yet also round, the internal elements and proportions of the Garden of Deduit are thus marked by the square and circle:

> Le vergier par compasseüre
> Fu toz de droite quarreüre,
> S'ot autant de lonc con de large.   (ll. 1320–2)

The green space all around was in a perfect square, being as long as it was wide.

The lexical choices repeated in these preliminary phrases produce an instability of vision and conceptualization of the place, which oscillates between two different forms. At first the text insists on the rectangular form of the wall ("mur quarré," "droite quarreüre"); the second passage adds a detail that is not adiaphoric: the garden is not simply a rectangle, but in fact a square – it possesses, that is, the same length and width. In specifying the geometry of the space, the text also calls to mind the technical instrument designed to take measurements and draw circles, the compass, with the abstract noun "compasseüre." This evocation has deep textual and cultural resonances.

The literary oscillopsia that governs the dual description of the garden is neither intrinsically neutral nor left without an eventual corrective in the text. The compass is the instrument of perfect design, as suggested by both the widespread iconographic motif of the Sapiential Christ actively "measuring" creation with a compass (a visual commonplace in medieval culture), and a specific later passage in the *Rose*. In introducing the character of Raison, who enters the narrative to offer herself to the protagonist as both an unheeded guide and a valid erotic alternative to the rose he desires, the text notes that her origin is technically supernatural. The vocabulary used is precise, especially because of the marked oppositions it constructs between physics and metaphysics, natural generation and unmediated creation:

> A son semblant et a son vis
> Part qu'el fu fete ou paravis
> Car Nature ne seüst pas
> Ovre fere de tel compas.
> Sachiez, se la letre ne ment,
> Que Dex la fist ou firmament
> A sa semblance et a s'image.   (ll. 2969–75)

In her demeanour and her face, it seemed that she [Reason] was made in paradise. For indeed nature would not have known how to produce a work of such harmony ("compas"). Know that, if Scripture tells the truth, God made her in the heavens, in his image and likeness.

The "compas" that Nature does not have at her disposal is at once a measure of harmony and regularity and the instrument that allows the most perfect geometrical figure to be drawn. In the account of the direct creation of Reason, God's compass precedes the building tools available to *Natura naturata*, which is bound to produce only provisional forms of harmony and regularity in this world, the design of which human art is then constrained to imitate. The peculiarly unstable nature of the garden as an object that is at once definitely square but also evoking a round model correlates both to the divide between the sphere of appearance and belief, in which this initial visionary garden is inscribed, and to the much more ontologically solid reality and certainty of a different, prospective garden. The Garden of Deduit is, in fact, not the only topographically charged space in the *Rose*.

As anticipated above, the narrative of the *Rose* eventually deconstructs the intrinsic ambiguity of the first garden, by contrasting the earthly and visionary setting it adopted with a second, alternative, transcendent, and more spiritually sound supernatural space: the Park of the Lamb. Designed as an anagogically final place of delight in the speech of Genius, this literal re-vision and contrastive revisitation of Guillaume's garden come to "correct" the readers' perspective on the first space precisely by stabilizing the initial ambiguity of its shape into a distinctive polarization.[10] Almost twenty thousand lines after the narrator has described the setting for his adventure, another intermediate (and somewhat more reliably orthodox) narrator launches into a contrastive evocation of the Garden of Deduit, pitting it against another, truer and better locale. By establishing a system of relationships that links the former to fable and this new park to truth (l. 20292), Genius explains that there is another space, as mystical as it is real, which is transparently heavenly. Into this "other" natural and cultivated place, he adds, the sheep will be shepherded once separated from the goats, following the lamb down the narrow path. The systematic syncrisis of the two gardens, in which the second author of the *Rose* rewrites, point by point, the opening phases of the action as narrated by the first, extends for about four hundred lines. Of interest here is its first contrastive element: unlike the Garden of Deduit, which was ambiguously square and round, the Park of the Lamb is specifically *not* square, but perfectly round:

Car qui dedanz ce parc soroit,
Asseür jurer oseroit,
Ou meïst san plus l'ueill leanz,
Que li jardins seroit neanz

> Au regart de ceste closture,
> Qui n'est pas fete en quarreüre,
> Ainz est si ronde et si soutille
> C'onques ne fu berill ne bille
> De forme si bien arondie.   (ll. 20259–67)

For those who are admitted into that [the Lamb's] park certainly would dare to swear that the [other] garden is nothing compared to this enclosure, which is not shaped as a square, but rather is so round and so subtly designed that there was never a beryl or a bead of such a perfectly rounded form.

This mystical rather than fictional garden, into which Genius invites all who follow the Christological Lamb, is in all respects a superior site, beginning with its form. The insistence on the superiority of the anagogical over the earthly is coded as an intrinsic superiority of the round over the square and the threefold over the fourfold. There is little theological ambiguity in the form and numerological features with which the text chooses to characterize the new "closture." Extending his review from its general arrangement to the system of water features, Genius continues to contrast earthly elements with more specifically theological ones. Whereas two conduits issuing from a central, eternally flowing spring watered the garden of the first *Rose*, Genius makes clear that the Park of the Lamb has a better source and form of irrigation. The new site is self-sufficient in its hydrology (as spelled out in ll. 20357ff.), while the former depended on external support:

> El sourt, ce dit il, a granz ondes
> Par deus doiz creuses et parfondes;
> Mes el n'a mie, bien le sai,
> Ses doiz ne ses eves de sai;
> N'est nule chose qu'ele tiegne
> Qui tretout d'ailleurs ne li viegne.   (ll. 20395–400)

That fountain springs forth, he said, in great gushes through two deeply carved channels. But I know for sure that neither the conduits nor the waters are its own. There is nothing at all that it contains that does not come to it from somewhere else.

Other features in both settings seem to confirm the utter dependency of the allegedly self-sustaining spring of the earthly garden, revealed through its contrast with the new heavenly space. Genius's point-by-point recantation continues in its counter-catalogue of permanent beauties: he first dismisses the virtue of the two crystals at the bottom of the pool (each able to offer only a partial vision, unlike the resplendent carbuncle of the new location), then moves to point out the sterile pride of the pine tree at the fountain of Narcissus, against which he measures the fruitful humility of an olive tree (a signifier of the incarnation and passion of the Christ) rooted in the other soil. The passage culminates with the description of the new spring, whose flow of waters is regulated by a distinctively ternary rather than quaternary principle:

> Cele fonteine que j'ai dite,
> Qui tant est bele et tant profite
> Pour guerir, tant sunt savourees,
> Toutes bestes anlangorees,
> Rant tourjorz par .iij. doiz soutives
> Eves douces, cleres et vives;
> Si sunt si pres a pres chascune
> Que toute s'assamblent a une,
> Si que, quant toutes les verroiz,
> Et une et .iij. en trouverroiz,
> S'ous voulez au conter esbatre,
> Ne ja n'an i trouveroz .iiij.,
> Mes tourjorz .iij. et tourjorz une:
> C'est leur proprieté commune. (ll. 20435–48)

That other fountain that I mentioned, which is beautiful and helpful in healing, so flavourful it is, all languishing animals, pours forth waters that are sweet, clear, and life-giving through three thin spouts. And these spouts are so close to one another that they gather up in one, so that, when you have seen all of them, you will discover that they are three and one. If, in sport, you set yourself to number them, you will never find that they are four, but always three and always one. This is their common property.

The Trinitarian quality of this fountain is evident, and no gloss would be required here, except perhaps to point to the retrospective clarification these lines offer to a detail in the description of the earthly *Rose* garden. Jean's text's insistence on the triune nature of this spring turns into a curious, retrospective *emendatio non petita* of the earlier portion in the text. This passage's insistence on the impossibility for the one-in-three and three-in-one-ness of this spring ever to yield a four casts an eerie shadow on the number used for the conduits sustaining the spring of Narcissus. While the earlier portion of the text stated that there was a certain number of such spouts, organized binarily, Genius's present warning that it is impossible to count the new fountain as having four sources suggests that such a result was at least possible for the former. In a way, now that readers have been given a retrospective correction, the earlier narrator's inability to provide a precise number for his accounts of the many fountains and rivulets irrigating the first garden of the *Rose* appears somewhat coyly professed. The corrective attention of Genius, insisting on the "never-four" quality of the better mystical spring, makes readers suspicious that a base-four hydrologic system did indeed lurk beneath the earthly garden's countless streams:

> Il ot par leus cleres fontaines
> Sanz barberotes et sanz raines
> Cui l'arbre fessoient ombre,
> Mes n'en sai pas dire le nombre.
> Par petiz ruisiaus, que Deduiz
> I ot fet fere par conduiz,
> Si en aloit l'eve fesant
> une noise douce et plesant.   (ll. 1381–8)

All about the place were clear springs of water, free from insects and frogs, in the shade of the trees – how many I cannot tell. The water moved, flowing through creeks and small streams, which lord *Deduit* had ordered made there, producing a soft, pleasant sound.

In reexamining Guillaume's garden and finding it lacking, Jean's section of the *Rose* polarizes its system of allusive reference, thus deconstructing an ambiguous feature present in the original text. While the first section of the *Rose* staged the action in a garden that was clearly reminiscent of, and allusively distancing itself from, the Garden of Eden, the second section of the poem insists on the potential dangers entailed in both moves. By spelling out the provisional nature of that initial setting, Jean's *Rose* creates a twofold contrast. First, the earthly space was not the Garden of Eden – something already hinted at in Guillaume's text, but evidently without sufficient clarity. Secondly, even if it were in some way related to the Garden of Eden, that space was nothing but an earthly place, a pale imitation of a better, anagogical garden: the Park of the Lamb.

Several considerations may be developed in light of the radical revisitation and pointed correction in the *Rose*. In the context of the present argument, one is perhaps most relevant. What may be interrupting the flow of the two sections of the poem is a crisis in the trust each author is ready to extend to his readership. In other words, Jean appears unwilling or unable to rely completely on his readers' ability to navigate the ambiguity of meanings in the first section of the *Rose*. Thus, he returns to that portion of the *Rose* narrative and forcefully disambiguates its signs. In claiming that the park is *not* square, the text of the romance draws our attention to the lexical ambivalence attached from the start to the garden at the centre of the poem; in professing the ternary rather than quaternary quality of its source, it redresses any possible misconception about its nature. Beyond this specific move, which is perhaps coherent with the pattern of larger retrospective interventions that mark the interaction of the two halves of the *Rose*, another element is worth noting for its potential prospective and retrospective relevance. The quadrangular shape of the garden and its paradoxically concomitant roundedness, together with its binary and perhaps fourfold system of irrigation, are doubly significant details. Not only are they integral to the trope of Eden suggested by Augustine in his account of biblical translation; but also they play a role in the intertextual tradition of the literary gardens depending on it, most notably in Brunetto Latini's *Tesoretto*, which it is now time to examine.

Perhaps the closest Italian vernacular antecedent of Dante's *Commedia*, both in terms of narrative pretexts and geographical and linguistic provenance, Brunetto Latini's *Tesoretto* is an unfinished visionary poem in couplets of seven-syllable verses of vast encyclopedic ambitions and eventually limited audience. Even from a cursory review of the plot and the characters involved, the text emerges as penned by a writer deeply interested, even "entangled," in the practice of vernacularization and cross-vernacular dialogue. This is in keeping with what we know of Brunetto Latini's work as prolific multilingual writer (he was the author of an encyclopedic treatise in *langue d'oïl*, the *Tresor*, in which his renderings of a wide variety of philosophical sources converge) and direct translator from classical texts (he also penned a vernacular version of Cicero's *De inventione*, known as his *Rettorica*).[11] As we are about to see, even his vernacular fiction combines narrative invention and rehashing of classical material. The premise of Latini's poem is that the narrator-protagonist, Ser Brunetto, while returning to Florence from a diplomatic mission in Spain, loses his way in a dark forest upon hearing the news of the rout of the Guelph army at Montaperti. Not unlike what happens in Dante's own voyage through an imaginary afterlife, the chronotope of the adventurous journey structures the rest of Brunetto's text. Moving through a progressively less confusing imaginary landscape, the namesake author-protagonist observes various natural and allegorical spectacles. He also receives instruction from an ample range of characters. First, Nature herself describes for him the order of the universe from creation on; then, after a visit to the four dwelling places of the cardinal virtues, the protagonist falls prey to the God of Love while wandering a pleasant meadow.[12] It is at this point that the character of the poet Ovid is made to intervene in the narrative. Introduced by the moniker *Ovidio maggiore* (and thus identified as both the author of the *Metamorphoses* and the authority on the "acts of love," a title connecting him to his authorship of "minor" erotic texts), the Latin poet comes as a remedial authority on how to free oneself from the bonds of love, a task that he fulfils by offering the immediate if unspecific deliverance of the protagonist from Love's fetters. Finally, after a penitential pilgrimage to Montpellier, culminating with a confession, and a highly condensed trip on horseback that brings Ser Brunetto to Mount Olympus, Ptolemy, the ancient authority on the natural world, appears. He is about to educate the protagonist on questions related to the four elements and their combinations, when the poem abruptly stops.

In what is now the central section of the poem, readers find the last fully developed adventure of the poet protagonist, the journey into the kingdom of Love. This is the point of interest for my argument. While absorbed in meditation on the spectacle he has just witnessed (a disquisition, held among transparent personifications, about what courtesy and courtly behaviour should consist in, in an urban setting), Ser Brunetto loses his way again, this time in a constantly changing space – technically, a region of unlikeness:

> Or si ne va il maestro Per lo camino a destro,
> Pensando duramente Intorno al convenente
> De le cose vedute: E son maggiore essute
> Ch'io non so divisare …
>
> Io giunsi in un bel prato Fiorito d'ogne lato,
> Lo più ricco del mondo. Ma or parea ritondo,
> Ora avea quadratura; Ora avea l'aria scura,
> Ora e chiara e lucente; Or veggio molta gente,
> Or non veggio persone; Or veggio padiglione,
> Or veggio casa e torre; L'un giace e l'altro corre,
> L'un fugge e l'altro caccia, Chi sta e chi procaccia,
> L'un gode e l'altro impazza, Chi piange e chi sollazza.   (ll. 2181–2207)

Now the teacher turns to the right, thinking hard about the meaning of the things he saw, which were greater that I can portray here … There I reached a beautiful meadow, with flowers everywhere. It was the most luscious in the world, but it looked round at times, at others, it was a perfect square; at times, it looked dark, at others, bright and shiny. Sometimes I see many a person, sometimes nobody. And I see pavilions, sometimes, houses and towers at others. Some people are stretched on the ground, others run around; some flee, and some chase; some are idle, and some are busy; some are happy, and some are furious; some cry, and some rejoice.[13]

Brunetto's *locus amoenus* is, evidently, as unstable as the garden of love that was portrayed in Guillaume's and Jean's texts. Like that garden, this Italian vernacular space is both round and square, drenched in light and sombre in darkness. As the first feature included in a long series of contradictions, the geometric ambiguity is as central in this passage as it was in the *Rose*. Given these premises and in this context, the double nature of Love – what the text will call, technically, the *bene* and *male* that the winged boy produces – is certainly responsible for the alternate presence of light and darkness in the meadow, as well as the frenzied polarization of behaviours observed in its inhabitants. Its concomitant circular and square nature, however, is as surprising as it is integral to the other transactions of hermeneutic and translative nature which take place there. Philological connection is not the only factor coming into play in this apparent return of the same motif of indistinction. The alternation of the meadow's circular and quadriform appearance is not only (and not so much) a passive reflex of the *Romance of the Rose* – that is, of a model-text. It is also (and, perhaps, rather) a refraction of the wider cultural context of which both texts partake, in which the peculiar nature of a space that is square and round has something to do with the Edenic setting of translation acts.

In this interpretive framework, the very fact that the protagonist's encounter with Ovid takes place here serves a double purpose.[14] It clarifies that this section of the narrative concerns disorientation in erotic matters as much as it stages, once again, a moment of tradition-formation in terms of translation. The same duplicity of vision affects the authority of Ovid as classical and vernacular author, as it does the space in which he manifests himself. As noted above, the Latin poet is introduced as, at once, the author of the *Metamorphoses* (this is what being "Ovid *maior*" means in the traditional literary nomenclature the poem uses) and apparently also the supreme authority about all the acts of love and the strategies to be adopted to free oneself from it – which is the role he is assigned, as author of the *Ars amatoria* and the *Remedia amoris*.

> Poi mi tornai da canto, E in un ricco manto
> Vidi Ovidio maggiore, Che gli atti dell'amore
> Che son così diversi, rasembra 'n motti e versi.
> E io mi trassi apresso E domandai lu' stesso
> Ched elli apertamente Mi dica il convenente
> E lo bene e lo male De lo fante dell'ale
> C'ha le saette e l'arco E onde tale incarco
> Li venne, che non vede. Ed elli in buona fede
> Mi rispose 'n volgare Che la forza d'amare
> Non sa chi no.lla prova.   (ll. 2357–75)

I then turned and, dressed in a rich cloak, I saw the greater Ovid, the one who treats the immensely varied acts of love in his poetry. I drew near and pleaded with him that he himself tell me openly what one needs to know about the good and evil deeds of the winged young boy, who bears arrows and bow, and wherefrom comes the hindrance that makes him blind. Thus he, in earnest, answered in the vernacular that no one can know the power of love who has not felt it first.

In the passage, Ovid's presence becomes the catalyst for an intratextual explanation for the varied phenomenology of love, which the text describes from the start as both negative and positive. The lexicon used in the *Tesoretto* to describe Ovid's teachings is technical. Ovid is the author who transcribes ("rasembra") the varied phenomenology of love in poetic form ("versi") and, as such, is a suitable authority to provide an explicatory account of what is good and bad about the individual allegorical attributes of Love: a blindfolded, winged young boy, bearing bow and arrows. There is little to surprise readers in this qualification, since medieval writers quite universally accept Ovid as *magister amoris*, a teacher in matters of love. However, the text introduces two notable details, one hermeneutic and one related to the linguistic garb of Ovid's teachings. First, the protagonist asks his *Ovidio maggiore* to give an "open" answer, thus endowing the new text that will register his answer with a specific hermeneutic quality. In this explicit phrasing, readers are invited to appreciate how reading the *Tesoretto* will amount to reading Ovid, but "apertamente" – that is, with interpretive clarity. The second notable and, I would argue, connected detail is that Ovid decides to answer in the vernacular ("'n volgare"). This element of the dialogue between the old and new *maestro* draws their exchange into the dynamics not only of tradition but also, more specifically, of translation. The authority of the Latin texts on matters of love authorizes the new text in its attempt to expound on the same topics, but it does so only while granting the new text a hermeneutic advantage and accepting translation into a new language. For the reader of Brunetto's poem, which interrogates an ancient author in the vernacular, the new idiom and the hermeneutic "gain" depend on each other.

3. Deferring Meaning: False Seeming and the *Evangile pardurable*

But let us return to the *Roman de la Rose* to explore a final feature of its poetics. One notable element in the semiotic system it constructs is that the text declares itself a fiction – an allegorical dream-fiction, to be precise – that programmatically announces its own dénouement but without ever fulfilling this promise. As noted, the author of the *Rose* declared from the start a staunch allegiance to the theory of dreams that Macrobius had developed in the prologue of his commentary on the *Dream of Scipio*. The ancient commentator's authority was invoked as vouching for the existence of some kinds of oneiric activity that are in fact meaningful. The narrator of the *Rose* had also added that the specific dream that he was about to recount was one of the prophetic dreams of which Macrobius wrote. The *Rose* did not choose, however, to clarify to what species of meaningful dreams its own dream belonged. According to the traditional typology of possible prophetic dreams, there exist three different kinds of possible truth-telling dreams: *visio*, *oraculum*, and *somnium*. Of the three possible types of meaningful dreams, Cicero's text is for Macrobius an example of the middle one, the *oraculum*. This kind of dream-event includes the appearance of an authoritative figure who expounds on some metaphysical truth for the dreamer. In the *Somnium Scipionis*, the truth at stake consisted in a review of the rewards that awaited those who had spent their lives in the service of the State in the afterlife. The dream of the *Rose* does not, of course, belong to this category of dreams. Scipio's *avision*, duly mentioned in line 9 with its technical label, is a reference text for the romance, but not a model. No authoritative character of the kind Cicero had enlisted in his work appears in the

Rose to expound metaphysical, revealed truths. Its quality as literary "transcription" of an oneiric experience thus remains undetermined. The problem is not confined to the opening gambit of the work. As a matter of fact, when readers try and attribute one specific status to the narrative before them, they encounter difficulties. Within its fiction, the *Rose* appears to claim an ambiguous condition, almost suspended between the other two possible categories that Macrobius listed, the *visio* and the *somnium*.

We might say that the dream of the *Rose* partakes of the prophetic *visio*, since the fiction of the dream is said to foretell something about to happen to the dreamer in real life. The text insists on this element of correspondence between the oneiric (and fictional) and the biographic (and "actual") realms: "Mes en ce songe onques riens n'ot / qui tretot avenu ne soit / si con li songes recensoit" (In that dream nothing ever took place that then did not come to pass exactly as the dream announced, ll. 28–30). One may just as well define this same dream, however, as an obscure *somnium*, one that announces truths under the guise of enigmatic images ("covertement," l. 19). The narrator specifies that the dream has (or, better, is) its "senefiance" – it is a sign of things and, accordingly, it has a meaning. A meaning it conveys through a system of obscure signs. The dream does not only "signify" by itself, however. In highlighting the obscurity of its means of communication, it also invites (as in both "requires" and "allows") a hermeneutic act, an "unveiling" of sorts. Confirming that the nature of the dream fiction is the same as Macrobius' *somnium*, the narrator pledges that he will provide readers with a full interpretation of the work in due course. The renewal of this hermeneutic promise comes in a later passage, in the context of the direct instruction that the protagonist receives from the God of Love in matters of erotic behaviour: the episode containing the "commandements" of Love.

Here, in a retrospective glance to the proemial self-definition, the text again specifies the poem's subject matter, or "matière," as "novele" (l. 2064). It also attempts to capture the readers' benevolent attention by promising that the register of the work is about to rise, given the weighty matter at hand. The teachings that the poem contains, the author promises, are not just important for the fictional vessel that conveys them, but in themselves. If the conclusion of the dream fiction is "bele" (l. 2063), it is also at that point that its meaning will be revealed in full. When the end of the dream has come, the teachings contained in the work will allow the audience to learn all about the games of love. The passage concludes by once again mobilizing the technical terminology of hermeneutics. Readers will benefit from the instruction they receive, provided they wait patiently for the narrator to reveal the dream's meaning:

> … puis que il veille tant atendre
> Que je die et que j'encomance
> Dou songe la senefiance.

> La verité, qui est coverte,
> Vos sera lores toute overte,
> Quant espondre m'oroiz le songe,
> Car il n'i a mot de mensonge.   (ll. 2068–74)

… as long as the reader waits a little while longer, that I begin to tell the meaning of the dream. The truth that is covered will then be fully open for you, when you hear me explain the dream, for there is not a single lie in it.

No matter how explicitly or repeatedly this dénouement is promised, however, readers receive nothing of the sort from the poem they are reading. It is possible, of course, that the incomplete state in which Guillaume left the first section of the *Rose* is responsible for this unmet promise. However, no redactional incompleteness or narrative difficulty may be blamed for this situation: Guillaume's vow is not only his, but also Jean's. In the second section of the poem, the second author of the *Rose* reiterates the same pledge that the meaning of the dream fiction will be available to its readers, expounded in full.

This time the statement is not authorial, but it is entrusted to an authoritative figure within the work. The God of Love, in the programmatic and metapoetic rallying of his troops before the final assault on the castle, promises that a similarly all-encompassing and all-clarifying gloss is about to come right after the narrative has concluded. And the dream fiction of Jean's *Rose* does indeed, for all purposes, conclude. According to his patron deity, Jean will not only resume writing where Guillaume leaves off, bringing the narrative to its erotic consummation and the dream to the moment that daylight arrives and the protagonist wakes up. He also will provide the best possible commentary of the text: "Puis vodra si la chose espondre / Que riens ne s'i porra repondre" (He will then want to explain the matter so that nothing remains hidden there, ll. 10573–4). Curiously enough, no such gloss is ever provided in the text after these repeated pledges, the last line of the poem being the simplest and most baffling declaration that daylight has come and the dream has ended. I believe that the repeated and frustrated intimations that an interpretation should follow the poem (though it never does) are not the product of an accident in philology, but have crucial internal justification.

The text of the *Rose* repeatedly invokes, and then always defers, an authorial interpretation for two interrelated reasons, which are at the core of the way its fiction works. There is a reason why the text promises its final gloss, and a reason why it does not deliver on the promise. First, such intimations intend to convey more an invitation to the readers than a commitment of the authors. They act as intratextual and metanarrative reminders that all texts (especially this one) require active readers to interpret them. By envisioning the necessity and possibility of an interpretation as part of the work's narrative horizon, the authorial voice coopts readers in the mechanisms of its sense-production. The absence of any authorial interpretive final act invites the readers to engage in interpretation, compelling them to provide an interpretation themselves, not so much after the fact, but during their reading. In sum, the *Rose* asks its readers to read actively: in this sense, the text of the *Rose*, its letter, *is* its meaning. This is the reason why the exposition is *invoked*. The second reason the text may have for frustrating an expectation of the reader it has systematically created is the idea that no text should (or may) receive a final exposition, of the kind the text gestures toward but never actually reaches.[15]

Both the invitation the text extends to its readers to interpret its letter and the limit set to such an interpretation are integral parts of the trope of translation as active interpretation that this book studies. The notion that the potential meaning of a text may be exhausted runs counter to the medieval interpretive optimism we have seen at the root of the vernacular translative texts preceding the *Rose*. Thus, it is surprising that in both Guillaume's and Jean's formulation (more explicitly and insistently in Jean's) the text qualifies the interpretation as exhaustive. Paradoxically, performing such an act would mean the death of the text as fiction. It is not difficult to see the reasons why providing internal and explicit interpretation of the dream in (and as) the text of the *Rose* would result in a hermeneutic stalemate. Providing a gloss that fully removed the narrative veil and completely solved the narrative's fictional ambiguities would both undermine the text's authority and, more radically, remove its reason for being. If ever provided, such an exhaustive gloss would de facto subject the text to the basic scholastic criticism that argued against the need for serious writing to proceed by way of figures and tropes. Since these accretions to the text's meaning only stand in the way of a clear perception of its truth-content, the argument ran, why use them in the first place? Why keep the chaff of fiction (the *integumentum* of allegory), once the text is provided with an exhaustive gloss, since all readers really need and eventually receive through commentaries is the wheat of its meaning (the *sensus*)? This potential attack on fiction from the philosophical analytical front is a latent danger for all fictional experiments in the age of scholasticism. It may also be the reason why in the *Rose* the exposition that both authors initially promise is then, in practice, constantly *deferred*.

The systematic and systematically frustrated pledge that a totalizing explanation of its contents will come may be more than a matter of expediency and defensive metaliterary self-positioning for the *Roman*. The notion that a commentary should, or even may, exhaust the meaning of a text extends well beyond the sphere of the lighthearted, fictional, erotic adventures narrated in the dream of the romance. The same possibility is also a core, burning issue for any approach readers may take to Scripture. While biblical exegetes are always concerned with producing always new, constantly more insightful, and ever deeper commentaries to the texts they gloss, the idea that the sacred text may have its potential for meaning exhausted by any given act of reading is simply blasphemous. A complex but significant episode included in the second section of the *Rose* may help show

how the cultural context from which it stems – and to which, in turn, it refers – casts the "exhausting" hermeneutic option in a negative light. In Faux Semblant's digressive account of the university banning of the so-called *Eternal Gospel*, which he includes in his self-presentation to the God of Love, readers find a treatment of the same theological problem, articulated from the point of view of the fictional writer of the *Rose*.[16]

As is to be expected in a highly self-aware moment in which a self-professed, systemically pathological liar is given the privilege of giving a true (that is, somewhat false) confession of his true (that is, utterly deceitful) nature, there have been several diverging interpretations of the episode. The semiotic instability of the character and his speech is perhaps so essential to the text that it is better left unchallenged and untouched here. Rather than reaching a fixed interpretation of the passage, that is, it may be useful to isolate some crucial strains within it and possibly connect them to the position the *Rose* takes on matters of hermeneutics. As a prominent work within the corpus of medieval fictions invested in reworking tradition through translation, the *Rose* appears to match its promise of, and resistance to, an exhaustive interpretation with Faux Semblant's comments on a book that claimed to be the final interpretive act of all Scripture: the *Evangile pardurable*.

Let us turn to the text of Faux Semblant's speech and his digression on the eternal gospel. A central figure in the host of champions that make up the God of Love's army, the character of False Seeming is eventually a determinant actor in the action. His swift and treacherous dispatching of Male Bouche (Slander) brings about the fall of the castle that defends the rose from the protagonist's desire. In his long confessional sermon of self-dénouement, which amounts to a lively and cogently argued attack of his own hypocrisy, the two-faced character reports an incident that took place in 1255 in Paris, when the university reacted against the publication of a radical book, the *Introductorius in Evangelium aeternum* or, as the *Rose* calls it, the "Evangile pardurable." The arch-deceiver turned socio-cultural chronicler gives the following reason for the banishing of this text:

> Et se ne fust la bone garde
> De l'Université, qui garde
> La clef de la crestienté,
> Tout eüst esté tourmenté,
> Quant par mauvese entencion,
> En l'an de l'incarnacion
> Mil et .II.C. V. et L,
> N'est hom vivanz qui m'en desmante,
> Fu bailliez, c'est bien chose voire,
> Por prendre commun exemplaire,
> Un livre de par le deable:

C'est l'Esvangile pardurable –
Que li Sainz Esperiz menistre
Si con il aparoit ou tistre,
Aisinc est il entitulez;
Bien est dignes d'estre brulez.   (ll. 11761–76)

What torments would have come to you, were it not for the watchful attitude of the
university, the guardian of the key to Christianity, when with wicked intent, in the
year of the Incarnation 1255 (there is no one alive who may contradict me) there
was released, to be copied from, a truly diabolical book! I mean the Eternal Gospel,
given by the Holy Spirit, as the title reads. This is, indeed, its title: it is well worthy
of being burned.

Some contextually relevant, contemporary texts help us see what is at stake in the
attention and the textual space the *Rose* devotes to the *Evangile pardurable*. First,
some points of doctrine. The book at the centre of the university's (and avowedly
False Seeming's) condemnation is a tract based on the doctrines of the abbot
Joachim of Flora (who had died in 1202), penned by a certain Brother Gerardo
da Borgo san Donnino, a Franciscan. The book has not survived, but, as witnessed
in documents containing its condemnation, it rehashed some radical ideas issuing
from Joachim's teachings, which had come under ecclesiastical suspicion in the
meantime. Among the original teachings of Joachim was the idea that the Church
had, in its present state, reached a level of profound corruption and was in need of
a radical reform. This is, of course, a common and periodically resurfacing notion
in the history of Christianity, and hardly one deserving a treatment as heresy. The
Introductorius book, however, added an apocalyptic urgency that made Joachim's
ideas both politically sensitive and a relatively easy target in the quarrel between
secular and regular teachers which was unfolding at the university of Paris in the
mid-1250s. In fact, the call issuing from the Spiritual Franciscan milieu active in
Paris at the time was not for reform but for the abolition of the secular Church
altogether. According to that specific and perhaps tendentious reading of Joachim,
the Church was not simply corrupt; it was obsolete.

This notion was, in turn, based on a point of theologically inflected world-
historiography. With the passing of time and the progress of salvation history,
Joachim maintained, humankind had actually reached the third and final dispensation, the Age of the Spirit, in which a higher calling toward contemplative life
had superseded the work of the intermediate body of the secular Church. This
passage in Joachim's corpus of prophetic writings summarizes this position:

Aliud tempus fuit, in quo vivebant homines secundum carnem, hoc est usque ad
Christum, cuius initiatio fuit in Adam; aliud in quo vivebant inter utrumque, hoc
est inter carne et spiritum, usque ad praesens tempus; aliud, in quo vivitur secundum

spiritum usque scilicet ad finem mundi, cuius initiatio a diebus b. Benedicti. (*De Concordia utriusque Testamenti* II.1.5)

There once was a time, in which humankind lived according to the flesh, a time that began with Adam and lasted until Christ. There then was another time, in which humankind lived between two states – that is, between flesh and spirit, and it lasted until now. There is also another time in which one lives according to the spirit, which began from the days of Saint Benedict and will stretch until the end of the world.[17]

The *Liber introductorius*, which the *Rose* says was made available for anyone to copy in 1255, apparently took up these thoughts and offered them as the core of a spiritual revolution, which included a replacement of what it deemed outdated canonical texts with the new, inspired ones produced by Joachim. Moving beyond Joachim, in other words, the *Introductorius* correlated the world-historical events in the history of salvation with specific bodies of texts issuing from them. The yoking of history and textuality had a deep implication. According to the Joachimite revivalists, both the Old and New Testaments, as texts corresponding to the ages of the Father and the Son, respectively, had become obsolete in the new spiritual dispensation into which humankind had entered. And therein lay the problem.

The reasoning, which the *Rose* defines as based on analogy ("comparoisons"), ran as follows: just as the age of Grace had replaced the age of Law with the coming of Christ, so too the age of spiritual illumination had come to replace Christian dispensation. The *Rose* provides some specific commentary precisely on this point, as a measure of that book's damnable unorthodoxy. The first point from which reader of the romance should derive a sense of the book's diabolical nature, False Seeming notes, relates to the boast at the centre of the *Evangile pardurable* that it had *de facto* superseded all Gospels:

> La trouvast par granz mespraisons
> Maintes teles comparaisons:
> Autant con par sa grant valeur
> Soit de clarté soit de chaleur,
> Serumonte li soleuz la lune,
> Qui trop est plus trouble et plus brune,
> …
> Tant seurmonte ceste evangile
> Ceus que li .iiij. evangelistre
> Jhesucrist firent a leur tistre.   (ll. 11781–92)

In that book, one might find several comparisons of this sort: just as, on account of its great power – in terms both of light and heat – the sun surpasses the moon, which is exceedingly dimmer and darker … so too this gospel surpasses those that the four evangelists of Jesus Christ produced, those that bear their names.

Thus, as the *Rose* reports the issue, the condemnation of the Newest Gospel of the Spiritual Franciscan did not only hinge on the denial of the theological tenets at the core of Joachim's teachings as the *Introductorius* had radicalized and politicized them. The problems with the book were also of a textual-hermeneutic nature. In other words, Joachimite advocates of the new gospel maintained that, because of the subsequent coming of the three ages, three different sacred texts were to be produced, one corresponding to each of the three Godheads. As William of Saint Amour (the same theologian who stars as a character in the *Rose* passage where we have started) wrote in his *De periculis*, Joachimite ideas about Scripture were problematic precisely for the reasons indicated in the *Rose*:

> Jam sunt anni LV quod aliqui laborant ad mutandum Evangelium quod dicunt fore perfectius, melius et dignius, quod appellant Evangelium spiritus sancti, scilicet Evangelium aeternum; quo adveniente evacuabitur, ut dicunt, Evangelium Christi: ut parati sumus ostendere in illo Evangelio maledicto. (*De periculis,* caput viii).

> It has by now been fifty-five years since some have begun toiling to change the Gospel, which they say will become more perfect and better and more dignified. They call it the Gospel of the Holy Spirit, or Eternal Gospel. With his coming, they say, the Gospel of Christ will become obsolete. These ideas we are ready to show are in that damnable Gospel.

One of the issues at the centre of the Paris incident is, thus, of strictly scriptural nature, consisting in the notion that history had brought about the emptying out of the Scriptures and that their replacement by the new, perpetual gospel penned by Joachim was in order. We find a trace of this notion also in the acts of the trials, in which the threefold succession of the Scriptures features among the "chief heresies" in the articles condemned:

> Quod alia est scriptura divina, quae data est fidelibus eo tempore, quo Deus Pater dictus est operari; et alia, quae data est Christianis eo tempore, quo Deus Filius dictus est operari; et alia, quae danda erit eo tempore, quo Spritus Sanctus proprietates Mysterii Trinitatis operabitur ... Quod tertius status mundi, qui proprie est Sancti Spiritus, erit sine aenigmate et sine figuris.

> One thing is the Holy Scripture given to the faithful at the time in which God the Father is said to be active. Another thing is the Scripture given to Christians at the time in which God the Son is said to be active. Yet another thing is the Scripture, which should be given at the time in which the Holy Ghost produces the essence of the mystery of Trinity ... The third age of the world, which belongs to the Holy Ghost, will be without any obscurity or figure.

That the issue at stake was of a textual and hermeneutic nature is an important detail for the point of view of the *Rose*, which we have seen is concerned with its own textuality and with the systematic deferring of interpretation. Indeed, the poem thoroughly stresses this element. A text based on conveying meaning through enigmatic figures in a dream, the *Rose* obliquely but sternly condemns the notion that humanity has reached an age in which it may proceed "sine aenigmate et sine figuris," in the full illumination of the Spirit. The attack on the book was, of course, as much political as it was theological. As the *Rose* does not fail to report, the theological notions Joachim of Flora had advanced in his writings half a century earlier were at the core of the swift and stern reaction of the university for the progressively anti-establishment spin they had recently received. The crucial point was not only that, in reading the signs of the end or days, the two parties diverged, with the secular teachers insisting on the mendicant orders being the false prophets of the Antichrist, and the spiritual Franciscans insisting on the Church being the Whore of Babylon of Revelation. The point was, more essentially, whether or not all signs that may be read in the present did indeed announce an impending apocalypse. False Seeming mentions how these questions not only had immediate political consequences but also were looking ahead to a fullness of times in which the present dispute would be adjudicated (and not in favour of the radical spiritual side) by an all-out war:

> Ainsint Antecrist atendrons,
> Tuit ensamble a lui nos tendrons.
>
> …
>
> Qu'il est escrit ainsint ou livre
> Qui ce raconte et senefie:
> Tant con Pierres ai seigneurie,
> Ne puet Jehan moutrer sa force.   (ll. 11815–16; 11824–7)

Thus, we will expect the Antichrist, drawing all together and striving toward him …
This [turn of events] is written in the book, which narrates it, phrasing it as follows:
When Peter reigns, John cannot show his strength.

By foreshadowing a struggle for power between secular clergy, which the text figures as Peter, and the most radical fringes of apocalyptic, spiritual Franciscans, identified with John, the speaker revisits a clearly political point that he projects on an end-of-days scenario. Even in this case, however, the textual aspect of the question is essential for his formulation. In the juxtaposition of Peter and John, the text bridges issues of canon and hermeneutics: the former party follows "la loi Jhesucrist" (the law of Jesus Christ, l. 11833), the latter argues that "n'est lois tenable / fors l'*Evangile pardurable*" (there is no other law to observe than the *Eternal Gospel*, ll. 11837–8). With this move, the text isolates a crucial hermeneutic tension.

The mentioning of John in this apocalyptic context points to his position as author of the concluding book of the scriptural canon, in a way that works counter to the pro-John hermeneutic camp. The party of the spiritual activists, notes False Seeming in one of his paradoxical condemnations of a text he also deems extremely useful for the systematic hypocrisy of his own ilk, is destined to succumb. Their defeat is, however, not merely a fact in history. In their appeal to John, spiritualist readers seem to activate a principle that goes against their whole project of completely replacing what they considered to be the obsolete scriptural canon. In the spiritual post-Joachim movement, all of the Scriptures appeared obsolete – not only the Old Testament, which had been fulfilled and superseded by the New Testament, but this latter one as well. In making their point, however, those who argued in favour of spiritual textual supersession also essentially relied on a text that was an integral part of the very textual complex they wished to forego: the Book of Revelation.

Two coordinated reasons make the idea of composing a new section of the canon, out of any source, simply wrong. The first is that there is no real need for the operation: there are glosses for that. Interpretation is what determines the life of the canonical text through time. Glosses have a crucial advantage over any "new" text that intends to add itself to the canon of sacred books. It is the work of commentators, in fact, that allows the text to respond to the spiritual conditions in the present. However, thinking that a gloss may exhaust the meaning of a text and thus be its final reading is an utter misunderstanding of what a gloss is. Precisely because it is timely, a gloss always provides readers with a provisional version of the text's meaning, apt to respond to present-day concerns and, as such, contingent on it. The second reason why the *Evangile pardurable* and any other aspiring "new" sacred text have no claim to existence is that the canon is not only constitutionally open to interpretation, but also definitely complete in membership. The presence of John, the author of Revelation, a text that contains the always-deferred meaning of its own letter, is what guarantees the corpus of the Christian Bible from ever having to face the need of a new textual supplement. In the orthodox understanding of Scripture, the final meaning of Revelation will take place at the end of earthly and textual time. At that point – and at that point only – all Scripture will be voided. The finality of the meaning of all Scripture will not be its endpoint, but rather its eschatological fullness. The notion that, instead, the nearing end of time may allow a bypassing of the openness of John, thus calling for a new text and a new canon, is what condemns the Joachimite's *Evangelium aeternum* to sterility.

In the *Rose*, these theological hermeneutic debates are not simply a matter of doctrinal background. The idea that this newest testament is not simply the latest but also the last possible one, a notion that the *Rose* makes every effort to show is radically untenable, certainly lurks among the theological problems with the Joachimite theses. The resistance we may detect in the romance is, however, not coincidental: finality in meaning is a notion that appears utterly alien to the *modus operandi* not only of the Christian Church but also of the *Rose* as fictional text, which insists on the systematic reinterpretation and retranslation of a received

subject matter. The text defers the final meaning of its subject in the same way
as it treats his own text as provisional: never part of a canon, but, like the canon,
always subject to an enlivening and interpreting translation. The translational
texts, with which the fictional garden-adventure of the *Rose* shares both its narrative setting and its positioning in relation to tradition, also share this core idea. It
is by way of translation qua interpretation, in the subsequent redeployments of
a sacred text across time and space, that the vitality of such texts – even possibly
of any text – is ensured. And indeed, one of the ways in which the *Rose* finally
accesses the mutable durability of translative text that it fostered by deferring its
own final interpretation is through a reworking. I am referring to what is known as
the *Fiore*, a poem famously "attributable" and often "attributed" to Dante, which
"translates" the *Romance of the Rose* into the Tuscan vernacular of the late thirteenth century. A brief look at one of the perhaps most extremist and enigmatic
statements contained in the Italian poem may provide us an indirect confirmation
of the analyses developed in this chapter, suggesting that the question of biblical
interpretation that subtends the interpretive model adopted in the *Rose* was perceived by a reader-translator of that text.

Drafted in an Italian strongly marked by French influences, the *Fiore* unfolds
as a close-knit series of sonnets that translate the bulk of the second section of
the *Rose*, sharply summarizing the action of Guillaume's part. In particular, the
Fiore glosses over the description of both the dream- and garden-setting of the
original and begins with the moment in which the God of Love pierces the protagonist's heart with his arrows.[18] By the end of Sonnet 5, the action of the *Fiore*
has reached the point in the plot of the *Rose* where "Amante" (as the text labels the
protagonist) pledges his allegiance to "Amore" (the God of Love), who provisionally vanishes from the plot – a development that happens around line 2750 of
the original narrative. The God of Love responds to the protagonist's profession
of absolute and unflinching observance by confirming the essential nature of this
pledge, which extends beyond any legally regulated contract. He also adds that his
service excludes that of any other god:

> E quelli allor mi disse: "Amico meo
> I' ò da·tte miglior pegno che carte:
>
> Fa che m'adori, ched i' son tu' deo;
> Ed ogn' altra credenza metti a parte,
> Né non creder né Luca né Matteo
> Né Marco né Giovanni". Allor si parte.   (*Fiore* 5.9–14)

At that point, he said to me: "My friend, I have received from you a pledge better
than any paper. So worship me, since I am your god. Set aside any other belief: don't
believe in Luke or Matthew, Mark or John." With this, he disappears.[19]

At first glance, the meaning of the passage is clear. This idolatrous commandment has the immediate effect of polarizing the reading of the *Fiore* as a counter-Gospel, and thus a text in which the actions of the protagonist are hardly readable in a positive light. Aligning itself with the procedures of the second section of its model, the Italian poem disambiguates the more careful system of cultural ambiguities that Guillaume's text established by setting his work in an Eden-like garden, a tropological space designed for the recitation and evaluation of ethical (or unethical) acts projected on a fictional character. Replacing Guillaume's balanced ethical ambiguities with a blatant call to apostasy, in other words, the *Fiore* appropriates Jean's explicitly paradoxical and contrastive procedures for its own communicative strategies.

But there is more. In quoting the God of Love's final words to the protagonist, the Italian text adds a detail that not only connects elements and themes developed in this chapter but also stands out in its gratuitousness. It is a detail that calls into question the role of the new text as a substitute for scriptural authorities and recovers, in strongly allusive fashion, the extended treatment of the garden in the *Rose*. By evoking the four Gospels and immediately dismissing them, the *Fiore* accomplishes more than a simple heretical self-positioning. For a reader coming to the *Fiore* after the *Rose*, the mention of the Gospels at this point also signals that the tropological garden of Eden of the model is pointedly absent from the narrative. Instead of translating the *Rose* description of the garden, the *Fiore* points to the departure from the original text by evoking a sign of the missing element and bypassing an account of the location where the action unfolds. Amore's mentioning the four authors by name activates the trope of the Gospel-like garden that was elided during the process of "translating" its model text, thus confirming that, although it is a secular and erotic text, the poem still explores and exploits the tropes of Christian writing. As will be the case with Chaucer's Merchant's Tale, where the *Fiore* will again offer an intriguing convergence, the pointed absence of a garden description is here accompanied by a marker of allusion.

In spite of their differences, the interplay of Brunetto Latini's and Dante's (or pseudo-Dante's) texts confirms – in passing but also significantly – that *both* the quadriform/round shape of the *Rose* garden, which the *Tesoretto* reproduced, *and* the attending insistence on scriptural hermeneutic fertility, which is registered through a conspicuous absence in the *Fiore*, are indeed related to the traditionally acknowledged fourfold nature of the Gospels as *both* multilingual texts *and* superseding pre-Christian biblical monlingualism. From the distant perspective of the Italian vernacular tradition, the visited garden and the translated canon distinctly blur into one another.

Chapter Two

Animal Instability: Dante's Theories of Language before and in the *Commedia*

For the parrot occupied a special place, in the traditional imagery of paradise.

Jean Delumeau, *History of Paradise*, p. 112.

In a book that surveys the corpus of texts in which acts of translation and textual transmission are staged within a tropological Garden or in proximity to one, Dante's presence is crucial. The *Commedia* is a work that makes no secret of its complex and fraught relation to classical culture in general, and Latin poetry in particular, a heritage it enthusiastically picks up and intentionally redeploys at all levels. From the scenes of canon formation that are staged in *Inferno* 4, when the protagonist, the poet Dante, in the company of Virgil, is made to meet and greet Homer, Horace, Ovid, and Lucan, to the long stretch of lines in which Statius, a historically Latin but fictionally Christian poet, accompanies Dante and Virgil through the upper ledges of *Purgatorio*, all the way to the scores of lines translated, episodes imitated, and expressions borrowed from the *Aeneid* and other authoritative classical texts, Dante's poem develops a mediated and meditated classicism that is one of its most distinctive markers. What an intertextual and intercultural reader faces in approaching the poem is, thus, an embarrassment of riches, a situation that calls for a carefully selected sampling.[1]

In the body of this chapter, I advance my argument through close readings of particular sections of text and some of their finer details. I shall begin with the strange case of a missing parrot, a bird that has been acknowledged as especially connected to the imagery of Eden. It is a curious literary mystery, affecting a word that disappears in a moment of under- (and self-) translation in Dante's corpus of theoretical texts, a disappearance that takes place in the movement between two coeval and coterminous passages in *De vulgari eloquentia* and *Convivio*. Though a minutia, an apparent slip of the pen, the marked absence of the parrot from the prose of the Latin treatise produces a significant differential detail in two works that today only attract a specialized audience and that must have had a rather scant readership from the start, having originally been left unfinished and uncirculated by their author. Its factors of marginality, however, do not hinder the semiotic potential of the variance at stake in the text. On the contrary, I believe that the divergent treatment of the parrot as talking animal in these two treatises illuminates larger issues in Dante's thought. In the interplay of the two passages in question, there are traces of the inception of Dante's evolving theories about the origin and function of human language: a set of compact, if multiform, reflections developed throughout his literary production. Moving beyond a strict "philological" line of interpretation for the demonstrably related treatment that the figure of the parrot receives in the two pre-comedic passages, my argument mobilizes "semiological" data, evoking the culture in which and for which Dante's works were produced. The common culture he shared with his audience is the context that allows an interpretation of the apparent textual accident in Dante's body of work. Unsurprisingly, the same polarities that define the scope of this book – the Tower of Babel as the origin of linguistic multiplicity and the Garden of Eden as a site of its overcoming – feature prominently in these texts.

This chapter has two principal parts, each divided into two headings. The first of these larger explorations takes Dante's texts and contexts as its starting point and addresses his linguistic theories and writing practices in the pre-comedic works. The leitmotiv in this section is the discontinuous fortune of the figure of the parrot within the systematic, but not untroubled, outline of the history of language and literary culture Dante drew in the works he composed in the early years of his exile. The chapter first establishes that, far from being an oversight or the result of a technical difficulty of translation, Dante's under-translation of the example of "magpies and parrots" into magpies and "other birds" across *Convivio* and *De vulgari eloquentia* is in no way accidental. To show why Dante's behaviour is meaningful, it then reconstructs the cultural foundations of Dante's linguistic and poetic thought by exploring some of his cultural sources, including Isidore of Seville's discussion of talking animals in his *Etymologiae*. A second block of analyses, centring on the *Commedia*, follows. It is similarly divided into two sections. First, in a vertical reading of three episodes in the poem, my argument suggests their convergence on the trope of the Edenic garden, which Dante appears to use as a setting for an exploration of multilingualism as well as inter-age translation. This part concludes with an exploration of Dante's tropological approach to the most technical aspects of the art of translation in *Paradiso*, set in contrast with one of his pre-comedic statements. The final section of the chapter is devoted to the new linguistic ecology of the *Commedia*, and targets two passages in which, by specifically poetic means – an ichthyologic reverse acrostic, spelling the word *pesce* (fish), hidden in the text, and a set of vegetative metaphors prominently displayed across several cantos – Dante provides his readers with a novel articulation of his theory and practice of translation, ultimately moving away from the cautionary discounting of the power of interlinguistic dialogue, which had marked his initial reflection on the topic, and moving to embrace a translative poetics. The conceptual hinge of this whole chapter is the varied use Dante makes of the idea of instability. This is a notion that progressively takes on different valences in his reflection on the linguistic dimension of literary work. It appears at first as the quintessential but most problematic trait in vernacular languages, which are deemed perpetually in need of reparation after Babel. It then returns as the still fundamental, but eventually fully accepted, feature of the idiom chosen for the poem, a place- and time-bound vernacular which opens itself to Edenic translatability. Dante's language of poetry ultimately is, to use his own terminology, "transmutabile ... per tutte guise": by nature open to all translations (*Paradiso* 5.98–9).

1. *Instabilissima avis*: Ornithology and Dante's Self-Translation

Dante's reflection on the interplay of languages, which characterized his culture and work as a poet, began early in his career, when in the *Vita nuova* he vindicated the right of new vernacular "rhymers" to use the same rhetorical figures as ancient authoritative "poets" such as Ovid, Virgil, and Horace. His famous statement that "dire per rima in volgare tanto è quanto dire per versi in latino, secondo alcuna proporzione" (writing rhymed poetry in the vernacular is tantamount to writing metrical poetry in Latin), placed at the centre of an engaged and polemical metapoetic stretch of the booklet, came as an early and radical profession of classicism, which involved not only a negotiation of the Latin/vernacular divide but also the profiling of a new professional figure, since, as he states, "questi dicitori per rima non siano altro che poete volgari" (these rhymers are nothing but poets in the vernacular, *Vita nuova* 25.4 and 7).[2] His most extended treatment of the linguistic dimension of vernacular poetics may be found, however, in his post-exilic treatise *De vulgari eloquentia*. This is a useful place to start, albeit with a local observation about an apparent inconsistency in two of Dante's texts that are in seemingly perfect conceptual alignment.[3] An initial intimation of the questions at stake manifests itself here, through a first case of animal instability: a missing parrot. While glossing the second of his treatise's *canzone*, *Amor che ne la mente mi ragiona*, Dante devotes an incidental aside to questions of linguistics and human ethology. In advocating for the necessary ethical coherence and cohesive treatment of human language ("che ... l'uomo parla") along with human habits ("ha reggimenti e portamenti"), he notes that only humans, since they are the sole rational creatures in the cosmos, are endowed with a social, communicative use of signs – linguistic signs in particular. Here is Dante:

(8) Onde è da sapere che solamente l'uomo intra li animali parla, ed ha reggimenti ed atti che si dicono razionali, però che solo elli ha in sé ragione.

(8) Therefore, one should know that only man among animals speaks and has habits and acts that are called rational, since he alone has reason in himself.

(9) E se alcuno volesse dire contra, dicendo che alcuno uccello parli, sì come pare di certi, massimamente della gazza e del pappagallo, e che alcuna bestia fa atti o vero reggimenti, sì come pare della scimia e d'alcuna altra, rispondo che non è vero che parlino né che abbiano reggimenti, però che non hanno ragione, dalla quale queste cose convegnono procedere; né è in loro lo principio di queste operazioni, né conoscono che sia ciò, né intendono per quello alcuna cosa significare, ma solo quello che veggiono e odono ripresentare.

(9) And should anyone object, saying that some birds do speak, as appears true of certain birds, such as in particular the magpie and the parrot, and that some animals perform acts or behaviours, as appears true of the ape and some others, I reply that it is not true that they speak or that they possess habits, since they do not have reason, from which these things must proceed. They do not have the principle of these operations within them, nor do they know what that is, nor do they intend to signify anything by it. Rather, they only strive to reproduce what they see and hear. (*Convivio* III, vii, 8–9)[4]

Significantly, the same matter and the same language Dante uses here recur, within a short chronological span, in the less incidental exposition of linguistic theory that he develops in the first book of *De vulgari eloquentia*. In the frame of a discussion of the primary (vernacular) and secondary (grammatical) languages that he sees being used in various linguistic communities, Dante crucially repeats that it is only to human beings, as opposed to all other living creatures, that language is given.

(1) Hec est nostra vera prima locutio. Non dico autem "nostra", ut et aliam sit esse locutionem quam hominis; nam eorum que sunt omnium soli homini datum est loqui, cum solum sibi necessarium fuerit.
(7) Si vero contra argumentetur quis de eo quod Ovidius dicit in quinto Metamorfoseos de picis loquentibus, dicimus quod hoc figurate dicit, aliud intelligens. Et si dicatur quod pice adhuc et alie aves locuntur, dicimus quod falsum est; quia talis actus locutio non est, sed quedam imitatio soni nostre vocis; vel quod nituntur imitari nos in quantum sonamus, sed non in quantum loquimur. Unde si expresse dicenti "Pica" resonaret etiam "Pica", non esset hoc nisi representatio vel imitatio soni illius qui prius dixisset.

(1) This is our true first language. I do not say "our," of course, because there could be any other kind of language than that of the human being, for indeed speech was given to the human being alone among all existing creatures, because only to him it was necessary.
(7) But should anyone object with what Ovid, in the fifth book of the *Metamorphoses*, says about talking magpies, I reply that he said this figuratively, meaning something else. And should it be said that, today, magpies and other birds actually speak, I say that this is false; for their act is not language, but rather a sort of imitation of our voice's sound; or, at any rate, that they try to imitate us as producing a sound, but not as speaking. So that, if to someone who said *pica* aloud the word *pica* were to be sounded back, this would be nothing but a reproduction or imitation of the sound of the one who spoke first. (*De vulgari eloquentia* I, ii, 1 and 7)

In reading these texts in rapid succession, their close connection becomes evident. They do indeed have much in common with one another. In their shared argumentative structure, for instance, both passages are phrased as responses to a potential objection. They come as a *sed contra* clause in Dante's argument, one that is evoked through the adoption of technical terminology: the phrase "se alcuno volesse dire contra ... rispondo" corresponds to the Latin formula "si vero contra argumenteretur ... dicimus." The two passages also make the same general point. Animals are not endowed with language, affirms Dante, only humans are. Furthermore, in both tracts, language is defined as the vehicle used to manifest the conceptual content of one's mind: as Dante will state elsewhere in the treatises, once again translating himself across the Latin-vernacular divide, language serves to "manifestare conceputa sentenzia," or, in Latin, "enucleare aliis conceptum." Nothing else. Animals, however, have no concepts to encode, decode, and transfer to each other; thus, even when they sound like humans – both works agree – they literally have no idea what they are saying. Animals imitate the exteriority of human behaviour; they do not replicate the semantic process essential for voices to become language. In arguing the same point, both paragraphs also significantly mobilize some shared (and inter-translated) technical terms. Dante's Italian "parlare" is an equivalent of "loqui" and "locutio"; "ripresentare" is the precise technical antecedent of the synonymic rendering "representatio vel imitatio" (in a redoubling typical of translations), and the force of the verb in the nexus "intendono ... ripresentare" is stabilized in the Latin rendering "nituntur ... imitari" – they *strive* to, rather than *mean* to, imitate human sounds, as the vernacular might have paradoxically implied.

Nonetheless, there is also a specific difference in clear contrast to the ways in which these passages almost perfectly match. When Dante "translates" his emphatic vernacular phrase "massimamente della gazza e del pappagallo," he renders it with the Latin expression "pice ... et alie aves." Moving from one statement to the other, readers are presented with a textbook case of under-translation, which relegates the parrot specifically named in *Convivio* to the indistinct group of "some other birds." To my knowledge, this curious phenomenon has not received much commentary, possibly because it has been considered an accidental feature of the text.[5] It is, however, possible to propose a rationale for the parrot's disappearance. Since this discrepancy appears across texts that are intrinsically involved in a common project of cultural translation and in the context of a systematic inter-linguistic argument, it certainly is not accidental. As he drafted these pages, Dante was clearly thinking in (and across) two languages at the same time. Thus, his omission of the parrot is not a neutral act, but may signal some divergence in the lines of thought he develops in either tract. Of course, both works ultimately agree that the vernacular is the "new sun" that will shine instead of the old Latin, as *Convivio* proudly states in its opening gambit; similarly, one passage is clearly an immediate rephrasing of the other, as the careful terminological choices across the two texts suggest. Nonetheless, the ultimate coherence of Dante's arguments should not distract from their radical divergence in one element: the presence of the parrot, in one instance, and its absence, in the other. I would argue that this single difference invites interpretation.

Several elements compel readers to move beyond simply witnessing the deviation. First, the disappearance of the "pappagallo" in the translation from the vernacular to the Latin was not a case of lexical difficulty. Dante knew perfectly well how to say "parrot" in Latin. The association of the parrot and the magpie, specifically as animals who can reproduce human speech ("verba et voces") without producing sense, was a commonplace in Dante's sources. Isidore had treated it in the *Etymologiae*, in the first paragraph of his entry on birds in Book 12, noting that there are some birds able to imitate the human words and voices. While pairing parrots and magpies in his Latin, Isidore stated:

De avibus. Unum nomen avium, sed genus diversum. Nam sicut specie sibi differunt, ita et naturae diversitate. Nam aliae simplices sunt, ut columbae; aliae astutae, ut perdix ... aliae verba et voces hominum imitantur, ut psittacus et pica.

On birds. One term designates all birds; yet, they are of different kinds. They differ, in fact, not only in their species, but also in the different natures they possess. Some are innocent like doves, others are cunning like the partridge ... some imitate human words and voices, as do the parrot and the magpie. (*Etymologiae* 12, 7, 1)[6]

Thus we may confidently assume that it was most likely *not* an issue of lexical competence that kept the parrot out of the Latin treatise, and again enlist Isidore to speculate about the reasons for its disappearance. Something else about the parrot, a detail in its traditional descriptions, could be the trigger for Dante's avoidance. When we compare the two individual entries for the magpies and the parrots which Isidore includes in later paragraphs of the same book, we realize that they are closely related, but do contain a meaningful distinction. On the magpie, Isidore writes:

Picae quasi poeticae, quod verba in discrimine vocis exprimat, ut homo. Per ramos enim arborum pendulae inportuna garrulitate sonantes, et si linguas in sermone nequeunt explicare, sonum tamen humanae vocis imitantur. De qua congrue quidam ait: *Pica loquax certa dominum te voce saluto; / si me non videas, esse negabis avem* (Mart. XIV, 76).

The word for magpie, *pica*, in some way recalls poetry, *poetica*, since this bird can produce words in an articulated voice, like humans. Magpies hang from tree branches and chatter annoyingly. They are unable to adjust their tongues to produce speech; still, they imitate the sound of human voice. Of this, appropriately, some poet wrote: I, the chattering magpie, salute you, my lord, with a distinct voice; / were you not seeing me, you would deny it was a bird (Martial, *Epigrams* 14.76). (*Etymologiae* 12, 7, 24)

The main thrust of the passage is, unsurprisingly, the impossibility of classing the words that magpies produce with their articulated voice as speech. It is the same point Dante makes across his texts. What these birds produce is only an imitation of the *sonum* of human talk. What they have access to is, in other words, the material, non-intellectual, aspect of the verbal sign. As Dante will claim, too, Isidore remarks that all that magpies can do, when they appear to be articulating human speech, is to echo back what they have heard.

Things are quite different for the parrot, however. Here is what Isidore has to say about this other kind of speaking bird:

Psittacus Indiae litoribus gignitur, colore viridi, torque puniceo, grandi lingua et ceteris avibus latiore. Unde et articulata verba exprimit, ita ut si eam non videris, hominem loqui putes.	The parrot comes from the coasts of India. It is green with a purple collar and tongue that is broader than that of other birds. It can speak articulated words, so that if you did not see it, you would think it was a person speaking. (*Etymologiae* 12, 7, 24)

What this second, seemingly articulate, bird has in common with the magpie immediately comes to the fore. Both birds sound "human." Isidore makes the point by transferring a detail that he had provided about the magpie by way of a classical quotation into his own expository prose. Martial's pentameter "si me non videas, esse negabis avem" is now appropriated as a fact of nature, not a poetic exaggeration: "si eam non videris, hominem loqui putes." What specifically differentiates the parrot from the *pica*, however, is just as clearly spelled out in Isidore's prose. While no mention is made of the magpie's original, non-imitative call in the dedicated entry, for the parrot Isidore reports that there is one:

Ex natura autem salutat dicens: "have," vel χαῖρε. Cetera nomina institutione discit. Hinc est illud: *Psittacus a vobis aliorum nomina discam / hoc didici per me dicere: 'Caesar have.'* (*Mart.* XIV, 73).	By nature, it greets people by saying "Ave" or *Chaire*. All other words are learned when instructed. From this came the famous lines by Martial: "I, a parrot, will learn to say the names of others from you, / but I learned on my own to say: 'Hail Caesar.'" (*Ibidem*)

While the parrot learns all names by way of formal instruction, it also, by its own nature ("ex natura"), does have a call. This call is not only articulate, but also meaningful. Under the proper circumstances, we might even say that the parrot's call is not simply animal. The fact that the parrot possesses a call that is "not inarticulate" and "not simply animal" does not mean, of course, that it is endowed with a "human" voice. According to Isidore – and later, to Dante – the parrot does not *mean* to say something when it hails the emperor, as he extrapolates from Martial's epigram.[7] No matter how encomiastically the Latin poet wrote about his imaginary parrot, Isidore's entry is perfectly clear about the non-semantic quality of the call. But the fact remains that the parrot produces *by nature* a sound that does indeed mean something. When drawn into the process of human semiosis by the presence of a human listener, the parrot's call coincides with a meaningful phrase. It is a greeting that the animal extends unwittingly, but it is a greeting nonetheless. And it does not seem to be just any greeting. Two aspects of the parrot's call are worth noting. First, in the way Dante and traditional avian lore treat them, the parrot and the magpie have something in common and something that differentiates them. What the two birds share is the echoing of their own name: in the "pica" entry that Dante devotes to this bird in *De vulgari eloquentia*, the reduplication of the name coincided with the chosen example of the bird's imitative speech. The same echoic quality of the call may be detected in the parrot's case, as Isidore constructs it. The only non-learned word of this other speech-imitating animal is, at the same time, its name (*avis*, abl. *ave*) and an allusion to a transcendence of the echolalic condition of artificially acquired language. In extending a greeting, in sum, the parrot also identifies itself. The point of divergence is, however, also clear. While Roman (and imperial) in origin, in Christian discourse, "Ave" (hail) is a charged word, one that points beyond any echolalic self-identification. As readers of Dante could hardly avoid considering, the term corresponds to the angel Gabriel's greeting to Mary, which opened up the process of human redemptiovn and inaugurated the new dispensation, the age of grace. As we are about to see, the process heralded by that word of greeting possessed a clear and essential linguistic dimension: the coming of Christ, the Word made flesh, also brought with it the potential for the redemption of human language, which had been involved in the post-lapsarian decadence affecting all things human.[8]

2. *Instabilissimum animal:* A Brief History of Human Languages

To measure the potential impact that the traditional association of the parrot with its native call "ave" may have on Dante's avoidance of the bird in *De vulgari*, it is useful to move into a survey of human linguistic history as delineated by Dante in his Latin treatise, paying special attention to its inception phase in Eden.[9] The biblical narrative has a lot to say about the linguistic dimension of the early history of humankind. As the book of Genesis makes clear from the start, Adam was tasked with the performance of a basic linguistic act: naming the animals. The biblical text insists on this point:

[19] formatis igitur Dominus Deus de humo cunctis animantibus terrae et universis volatilibus caeli adduxit ea ad Adam ut videret quid vocaret ea omne enim quod vocavit Adam animae viventis ipsum est nomen eius [20] appellavitque Adam nominibus suis cuncta animantia et universa volatilia caeli et omnes bestias terrae.

The Lord God, having formed from the earth all animals of the earth and birds of the sky, brought them before Adam, so that he might see what to call them. For indeed whatever Adam called it is the name of each living creature. So Adam named all the living creatures with their proper names and all the birds of the sky and all the beasts of the earth. (Gen. 2:19–20)

A diminished version of the divine creation act, in which language was the means for the coming into being of a rationally ordered (and sapientially mediated) cosmos, Adam's language was still endowed with several positive qualities. Since Adam developed it in his (and humankind's) pre-lapsarian state, and since it was the result of a divine mandate, the language he used had every quality necessary to carry out its task, which was the orderly description by an orderly mind of an orderly reality. As Dante notes, today humankind would still use that first language, the unsurpassable language Adam deployed in Eden, were it not for the diffraction and confusion of tongues that took place later in history. As humankind lost Eden, its original place on earth, with original sin, so too it lost its original Edenic language with another act of defiance of God's orders, the attempt to build the Tower of Babel. In his study of the origin and causes of linguistic vernacular differentiation, Dante recalls this essential turning point of human history in the following terms:

(4) Redeuntes igitur ad propositum, dicimus certam formam locutionis a Deo cum anima prima concreatam fuisse; dico autem 'formam', et quantum ad rerum vocabula, et quantum ad vocabulorum constructionem, et quantum ad constructionis prolationem: qua quidem forma omnis lingua loquentium uteretur, nisi culpa presumptionis humane dissipata fuisset, ut inferius ostendetur.
(5) Hac forma locutionis locutus est Adam; hac forma locutionis locuti sunt omnes posteri eius usque ad hedificationem turris Babel, que turris confusionis interpretatur; hanc formam locutionis hereditati sunt filii Heber, qui ab eo dicti sunt Hebrei.

(4) Returning, then, to my subject, I say that a certain form of language was created by God within the first soul; I say "form" for what pertains to the words used for things, and to the construction of words, and to the arrangement of the construction. This form of language would still be used by all speakers, had it not been shattered through the fault of human presumption, as will be shown below.
(5) In this form of language Adam spoke; in this form of language spoke all posterity of his until the building of the Tower of Babel (which is interpreted as "tower of confusion"). This is the form of language inherited by the sons of Heber, who are called Hebrews because of it. (*De vulgari eloquentia* I, vi, 4–5)

As Dante notes, in alignment with his culture, the original, Adamic and Edenic vernacular was all but lost to humankind after Babel. With the sole exception of the Jews, who did not take part in the construction of the tower, all guilty parties received a mutilated and decaying means of communication. Dante explains that the Jews, as the chosen people, retained the privilege of using Adam's language for a specific and transient reason: in order for the Saviour, who would be born from them according to the flesh, to continue speaking an idiom of grace. The text of *De vulgari* is clear on this point: Hebrew is the lost language of Eden, preserved in one people, but only for a specific reason and, it appears, viable only until that reason has become obsolete. Cause and consequences of this special status are neatly articulated in the treatise:

(6) Hiis solis post confusionem remansit, ut Redemptor noster, qui ex illis oriturus erat secundum humanitatem, non lingua confusionis, sed gratie, frueretur.
(7) Fuit ergo hebraicum ydioma illud quod primi loquentis labia fabricarunt.

(6) To them alone it remained after the confusion, so that our Redeemer, who was to be born from them (according to His humanity), should not use the language of confusion, but that of grace.
(7) Thus, the Hebrew language was that which the lips of the first speaker made.
(*De vulgari eloquentia* I, vi, 6–7)

With the end of Adam's monolingualism, continues Dante's argument, the current state of affairs begins. Human language exists as a broken, multifarious plurality of idioms. All languages respond to the need to provide people with a tool to conceptualize reality and share that conceptualization with each other, but each is also destined to clash against every other after the confusion arisen at Babel – a confusion that was a product as much of geographical dissemination as of temporal fluctuation.

One element of Dante's compact reasoning should be highlighted: while it certainly lost the stability and unity with which it was endowed in the beginning, human language did not lose its underlying potential to serve as a means of communication in precise historical settings. Even in its post-Babel state, for human language the loss of universal functionality did not amount to a loss of functionality *tout court*. Both the desire and the potential to communicate remained alive in the state of linguistic fragmentation to which humankind was relegated. What changed was humankind's ability to endow the languages used by each section of the world's population with coherence and stability. Being, at this point, a merely human product, human language necessarily began to reflect humankind's own natural instability. As such, Dante compellingly argues, it became subject to change:

(5) Hee omnes differentie atque sermonum varietates quid accidunt, una eademque ratione patebit.

(5) It will be clear that one single reason motivates all these differences and varieties of speech.

(6) Cum igitur omnis nostra loquela,
preter illam homini primo concreatam
a Deo, sit a nostro beneplacito reparata
post confusionem illam que nil fuit aliud
quam prioris oblivio, et homo sit insta-
bilissimum atque variabilissimum animal,
nec durabilis nec continua esse potest; sed
sicut alia que nostra sunt, puta mores et
habitus, per locorum temporumque dis-
tantias variari oportet.

(6) Since all our language – except that
created by God within the first man – has
been reconstituted after the great confusion
(which was nothing but the oblivion of the
earlier language), by our own device, and
since the human being is a highly unstable
and variable animal, our language can be
neither durable nor uniform. To the contrary, like everything else that belongs to us
(such as customs and habits), it must vary
with the differences of space and time. (*De
vulgari eloquentia* I, ix, 5–6)

To remedy this situation, Dante continues, humankind responded in two ways. A small portion of humanity, the chosen people, needed to do nothing; their language remained unaffected by Babel, immune from dissension and decay. In the hands and on the lips of the chosen people, that language remained free from the accidents of history and geography, so that Christ could inherit it and begin, from that unaffected linguistic sphere, the process of Salvation. There was also, however, a remedial strategy put in place by the international community of intellectuals, those Dante calls the "inventores gramatice facultatis." These intellectuals, he notes, used the building blocks of the individual vernaculars they had come to possess in order to construct the artificial cultural koine that in the West is called Latin, a translational and transcultural prosthetic language, designed to allow the encoding and decoding of information across linguistic communities separated by temporal and spatial gaps. *De vulgari* devotes a dense paragraph to the genesis of this artificial language:

(11) Hinc moti sunt inventores gramatice facultatis; que quidem gramatica
nichil aliud est quam quedam inal-
terabilis locutionis idemptitas diversis
temporibus atque locis. Hec, cum de
comuni consensu multarum gentium
fuerit regulata, nulli singulari arbitrio
videtur obnoxia, et per consequens nec
variabilis esse potest. Adinvenerunt
ergo illam, ne, propter variationem sermonis arbitrio singularium fluitantis,
vel nullo modo, vel saltem imperfecte
antiquorum attingeremus auctoritates
et gesta, sive illorum quos a nobis locorum diversitas facit esse diversos.

(11) This was the point from which the inven-
tors of the art of grammar began; for their
gramatica is nothing less than a certain immutable identity of language in different times
and places. Its rules have been formulated with
the common consent of many peoples; thus, it
can be subject to no individual will. As a result,
it cannot be mutable. Those who devised this
language did so lest, through changes in the
language that fluctuates according to individual
wills, we become either absolutely unable,
or at best only imperfectly able, to access the
wisdom and history of the ancients, or of those
whose difference in location renders them different from us. (*De vulgari eloquentia* I, ix, 11)

Dante's enthusiastic support for this process readily transpires from the way he phrases his account of the invention of Latin and Greek as grammatical languages. Deemed able to bridge time and space differences, grammar guarantees that those who possess it may literally reach the "auctoritates et gesta" (the philosophical elaborations and historical narratives) of either ancient or foreigner cultures – and do so completely, with no residual incomprehension. Dante is not alone in this optimistic outlook on the power of cultural and grammatical languages to supply humankind with a defence against the consequences of the sin at Babel. The search for a perfect language, as Umberto Eco called it, was a widespread philosophical and cultural trend in the Middle Ages, one possibly culminating (at least for Dante) in the theories and investigations of the Modistae (as Maria Corti proposed). Whatever the trigger for his interest in logical-grammatical theories and the intellectual coordinates of his reasoning may be, at this point in his intellectual history Dante appears to share the Modistae's trust in the advantages of adopting such an information-transmission protocol for culture.[10]

Thinking of language in grammatical terms helped to overcome an implicit difficulty in the two-pronged "solution" to Babel, as Dante described it in *De vulgari*. Of the two antidotes to linguistic differentiation that he reviewed, the first was only temporary. Hebrew, the language Dante ascribes to the chosen people of the Old Testament, was destined to lose its historical function in humankind's providential, and hence sacred, history with the coming of Christ, his eventual redemptive sacrifice, and the resulting vendetta visited upon the Jews in the year 70 CE. In reading Dante's text, we are to understand that with the destruction of the Second Temple and the ensuing diaspora, the historical function of Hebrew ceased. With it, the last link to Edenic language was lost, and even the last trace of original linguistic unity disappeared. The invention of the *gramatica* was, instead, a more permanent solution to the problem of inter-temporal and inter-spatial communication. And it was apparently also a good solution, one matching widespread cultural associations and practices. After all, the idea of "culture" in Dante's time was primarily identified with a chronologically and geographically wide-ranging corpus of texts, all drafted in the common idiom of Latin, which appeared to set different times and spaces in seamless dialogue with one another. As a practically bilingual writer, who had begun his education with a canon of Latin *auctores* (*maiores* as well as *minores*) that encompassed, for instance, both Ovid's distant and ancient elegies and the elegiac composition of a quasi-contemporary and fellow Florentine, Arrigo da Settimello, Dante perceived and presented Latin as a viable diaphasic rather than exotically diatopic or archeologically diachronic alternative to the vernacular. The integration of what we now consider the "classical" set of authors and texts into a synchronic, contemporary-oriented canon was not just a trademark of Dante's poetics, but a critical notion he shared with his culture.[11]

No matter how enthusiastically endorsed and unquestionably practised it might have been for Dante and his readers, however, the artificial solution to the multilingualism inaugurated at Babel was not without problems. At least, not according to Dante. If we look at the reciprocal system of oppositions through which he presents grammar and the vernacular in his review of their respective worth at the start of *De vulgari*, we can appreciate some of the problems and begin to explore some of the tensions present in his thought.

Dante draws a complete syncrisis of vernacular and Latin in the opening section of *De vulgari eloquentia*:

(2) ... vulgarem locutionem appellamus eam quam infantes adsuefiunt ab adsistentibus, cum primitus distinguere voces incipiunt; vel quod brevius dici potest, vulgarem locutionem asserimus, quam sine omni regola, nutricem imitantes, accipimus.
(3) Est et inde alia locutio secondaria nobis, quam Romani gramaticam vocaverunt. Hanc quidem secundariam Greci habent et alii, sed non omnes. Ad habitum vero huius pauci perveniunt, quia non nisi per spatium temporis et studii assiduitatem regulamur et doctrinamur in illa.
(4) Harum quoque duarum nobilior est vulgaris: tum quia prima fuit humano generi usitata; tum quia totus orbis ipsa perfruitur, licet in diversas prolationes et vocabula sit divisa; tum quia naturalis est nobis, cum illa potius artificialis existat.

(2) ... I call "vernacular language" that which infants are accustomed to from those around them when they first begin to distinguish voices; or, more briefly said, I define vernacular language the one we acquire without any rule, by imitating our nurses.
(3) There also exists a language that is secondary to us. This the Romans called *gramatica*, grammar. The Greeks and some other peoples (not all) also have this secondary language. Few, however, acquire it fully, since it is only through some length of time and dedicated study that one assimilates its rules and principles.
(4) Of these two languages, the more noble is the vernacular. It is so because it was the language first used by humankind; because the whole world employs it, though with different pronunciations and vocabulary; and because it is natural to us, while the other is, on the contrary, artificial. (*De vulgari eloquentia* I, i, 2–4)

The passage articulates a neat series of strategic oppositions. The vernacular, the language that Dante is interested in discussing and promoting in the treatise (which is, we should remember, *not* drafted in said idiom), is superior to its grammatical counterpart for several reasons. First, it is a primary language, since humankind used it first, and speakers learn it first. Ontogenesis and phylogenesis of the vernacular correspond to each other, and thus coherently project the "other" language as secondary. *Gramatica*, as we have seen, came later in history, and, we are now told, individuals only acquire it later in life, through a controlled process of acculturation. Vernacular is also common to all humankind, Dante continues, though it is implemented according to different pronunciations and lexica in different times and spaces. Grammatical languages, however, exist for some cultures but not for all. Finally, the vernacular is a natural feature of human nature, while the "other" language is – in explicit contrast – an artificial, cultural construct.

The neat system Dante developed in the Latin treatise has a counterpart in the vernacular tract he wrote during the same span of years. There are several essential continuities between the two texts, not least among them the fact that *Convivio* preserves the trace of Dante's inception of *De vulgari*. There are, however, differences as well.

In an argument devoted to justifying his choice of producing a prose commentary in the vernacular to accompany his vernacular *canzoni*, Dante notes that he was compelled by the relative worth ("nobiltà") of each language. He wrote the prose section of his treatise in the vernacular, among other reasons, because Latin is a superior language owing to its stability and incorruptibility:

(7) … Ché, primamente, [il latino] non era subietto ma sovrano, e per nobilità e per vertù e per bellezza. Per nobilità, perché lo latino è perpetuo e non corruttibile, e lo volgare è non stabile e corruttibile.
(8) Onde vedemo nelle scritture antiche delle comedie e tragedie latine, che non si possono transmutare, quello medesimo che oggi avemo; che non aviene del volgare, lo quale a piacimento artificiato si transmuta.
(9) Onde vedemo nelle cittadi d'Italia, se bene volemo aguardare, da cinquanta anni in qua molti vocaboli essere spenti e nati e variati; onde se 'l picciol tempo così transmuta, molto più transmuta lo maggiore. …
(10) Di questo si parlerà altrove più compiutamente in uno libello ch'io intendo di fare, Dio concedente, di Volgare Eloquenza.

(7) … Firstly, [Latin] is not subject but sovereign, when measured by its nobility, virtue, and beauty. By nobility, because Latin is eternal and incorruptible, whereas the vernacular is unstable and corruptible.
(8) This is why we see, in the ancient writings of the Latin comedies and tragedies, which cannot be transmutated, the same Latin as we have today; this is not what happens with the vernacular, which, being fashioned according to preference, does transmutate.
(9) This is why we see, in the cities of Italy, if we look closer, that in the span of fifty years many words died, were born, and varied; if a short period of time transmutates language so much, much more does a greater period transmutate it …
(10) This will be more fully discussed elsewhere, in a book I intend to write, God willing, on Eloquence in the Vernacular. (*Convivio* I, v, 7–10)

Coming to this passage from a reading of *De vulgari*, the divergent evaluation of the respective nobility of each language jumps out. In one work, Dante asserts that the vernacular is nobler than Latin; in the other, he states the opposite. This discrepancy, which has been the object of a general conclamation throughout the history of the two treatises, is both critical and inessential, since the inverted ranking assigned to the two languages was a matter of intratextual argumentative coherence (and rhetorical expediency) more than anything else. As such, it should not detain us long. Secondly, we may note that one element, which is at the core of Dante's thinking in *De vulgari*, is not emphasized. The definitional interrelation of vernacular and grammar, which entailed the projection of the first into the sphere of the natural in opposition to the artificial quality of the latter, is not part of his reasoning here. Some of the elements that will be crucial in the differential definition of the two linguistic options are certainly present in this passage, but not the notion of the vernacular's natural quality. Naturalness is the main acquisition of the second treatise. Instead, what *Convivio* has to say about the distinctive linguistics of the vernacular revolves around the notion of change. Instrumental as it is to a defence of the project of writing a vernacular commentary to vernacular lyric texts, Dante's reasoning in *Convivio* stresses only one side of the equation. Latin, as a grammatical language, is stable. Ancient texts demonstrate this stability by preserving a language that is fully congruent with the one used in modern Latin texts. The vernacular, on the contrary, is subject to individual "piacimento," individual fleeting preference, and is thus unstable across geographical and chronological divides, so much so that it mutates from generation to generation, even in the small space of the very same city.

Beyond these points of intertextual continuity and discontinuity, there are other elements which deserve attention. The reciprocal indifference or irreconcilability of Dante's statements *across* the two works is matched, in fact, by other tensions *within* each of them. These internal conflicts are worth exploring in detail because they may help with appreciating some elements of Dante's later reflection on language, which are present and yet marginalized at this stage in his thinking. In both texts, Dante approaches each option with some measure of ambiguity, and his prose preserves the traces of a silenced minority report. In other words, while the dichotomies he establishes seem neat, his reasoning is not immune to internal contradictions. The general apparent irreconcilability of the two statements about the "nobility" of Latin and the vernacular develops in a wider field of tensions that both *Convivio* and *De vulgari* enter when they consider the primary and secondary *locutiones* in terms of natural instability and artificial stability.

In *Convivio*, Latin is programmatically defined as the grammatical artificial language, one which cannot and does not change. Dante's statements on this point are incontrovertible. The fact that the language of ancient texts has undergone no transmutation and is still the same one used in Dante's present is, for him, sufficient proof of this quintessential stability. The counter-fact that the vernacular has mutated in the short span of fifty years, a piece of information that Dante trusts his readers are able to verify through their own experience, confirms the point *e contrario* and *a fortiori*. However, in the same treatise in which inter-time stability is predicated as the essential trait of Latin, Dante also suggests the puzzling association of the discipline of grammar with the Moon, the most mutable of all celestial bodies. And he does so specifically on the authority of a major Latin theorist, Horace, who in the *Ars poetica* pointed out the internal mobility of Latin's building blocks. The internal contradiction is as crucial as it is seemingly left unaddressed in Dante's work:

(9) Dico che 'l cielo della Luna colla Gramatica si somiglia, perché ad esso si può comparare [per due propietadi] … L'una si è l'ombra che è in essa … l'altra si è la variazione della sua luminositade, ché ora luce da uno lato e ora luce da un altro, secondo che lo sole la vede. (10) E queste due propietadi hae la Gramatica: ché per la sua infinitade li raggi della ragione in essa non si terminano, in parte spezialmente delli vocabuli; e luce or di qua or di là, in tanto [in] quanto certi vocabuli, certe declinazioni, certe construzioni sono in uso che già non furono, e molte già furono che ancor saranno: sì come dice Orazio nel principio della Poetria, quando dice: "Molti vocabuli rinasceranno che già caddero".

(9) I say that the heaven of the Moon resembles Grammar because it may be compared to it [for two properties] … One is the shadow in it … the other is the variation of its luminosity, since it at times shines on one side, at time on the other, depending on how the Sun regards it. (10) Grammar has these two properties; since, because of its infinitude, the rays of reason do not reach their end, particularly insofar as words are concerned; and it shines now here, now there, for certain words, certain declensions, certain constructions are now in use that formerly were not, and many have ceased to be in use that will be in use again. As Horace says at the beginning of his Poetics, when he says: "Many words, which have fallen, will be born again." (*Convivio* II, xiii, 9–10)

Evidently, the lexical and syntactical turnover of which Horace spoke, which implicitly clashes with the stability Dante avers for Latin, suggests that this language too, no matter how grammatical in nature it may be, is not fully stable. Within the systematic reasoning of the vernacular work, in other words, there is an element of tension.

Correspondingly, and contradicting his own earlier axiologically charged insistence on naturalness, in *De vulgari eloquentia* Dante presents the vernacular as liable to be stabilized. While it is, by nature, a mobile and ever-morphing language, Dante sees the vernacular as possessing a limit-like potential for stability. According to the argument he develops in the Latin treatise, this potential for the language in which he writes his poetry is realized in his own and Cino da Pistoia's exemplary reliance on grammar as a model for their poetic idiolect. In his comparative ranking of the languages and literatures of *oc*, *oïl*, and *sì*, Dante notes that his vernacular is superior to the others in the *tripharium idioma* because its practitioners have stayed closer to the common grammar – that is, closer to Latin – than did their colleagues who wrote in other Romance languages. The argument proceeds with remarkable cogency, apparently unaware of the potential drawbacks of the point it advances:

(4) Tertia quoque, que Latinorum est, se duobus privilegiis attestatur preesse: primo quidem, quod dulcius qui subtiliusque poetati vulgariter sunt, hii familiares ac domestici sui sunt: puta Cinus Pistoriensis et amicus eius; secundo, quia magis videntur inniti gramatice, que comunis est, quod rationabiliter inspicientibus videtur gravissimum argumentum.

The third part, which belongs to the Italians, proves superior on account of two privileges: first, because those who have written vernacular poetry more sweetly and subtly, such as Cino da Pistoia and his friend, are familiar and homely to it; and second, because they appear to rely more on the *gramatica* which is shared by all, and this, to those looking into it rationally, appears a most weighty argument. (*De vulgari eloquentia* I, x, 4)

As emerges from this passage, the cogent logic of the treatise also allows for historical counterpoints. In the same breath as he declares that the "naturalness" of the vernacular (which is manifested in its mutability) is an essential and positive feature of the language, Dante also values the opposite ability of the same language to approach itself to, and even depend on, the artificially wide-reaching and stabilized *gramatica*. This linguistic argument receives a second, reinforcing treatment in the stylistic section, devoted to the poetics of the illustrious vernacular, again through the evocation of the model of those writers Dante defines as "regulated." The artificial quality of their language is again not an impediment to their being featured as exemplary to vernacular authors, who are supposed to use a natural language in their works. On the contrary, what makes them suitable for that function is their being *regulati poete*; and *regula* is, as we have seen, a key concept in Dante's account of how grammatical languages function and are acquired. This is suggested by the use of the verb *regulamur* in the context of the development of a *habitus* for Latin in the opening section of the treatise:

(7) … Et fortassis utilissimum foret ad illam habituandam regulatos vidisse poetas, Virgilium videlicet, Ovidium *Metamorfoseos*, Statium atque Lucanum, nec non alios qui usi sunt altissimas prosas, ut Titum Livium, Plinium, Frontinum, Paulum Orosium, et multos alios, quos amica sollicitudo nos visitare invitat.

(7) … And perhaps it would be most useful, in acquiring it [the highest construction], to look at the regulated poets – that is, Virgil, Ovid of the *Metamorphoses*, Statius, and Lucan – as well as others who have produced the highest prose, such as Livy, Pliny, Frontinus, Paulus Orosius, and many others whom an affectionate solicitude invites us to revisit often. (*De vulgari eloquentia* II, vi, 7)

The field of tension in which Dante's reasoning moves borders on a logical impasse. Strictly speaking, if being natural is a positive feature of a language, then its fully natural temporal and geographic instability should be accepted and valued. Endowing it with stability (the same achieved artificially by Latin) would be an inconsistent move, one which is both anti-historical and denaturalizing. If, on the contrary, we wish a language to have a transhistorical function, then its artificiality needs to be accepted as necessary, a logical necessity that contradicts the axiom that makes naturalness an essential badge of honour for the vernacular. Dante's overall argument across the two treatises cannot reconcile these contradictory options, which also arise, as we have seen, from within each work.

Thus, while the two treatises apparently espouse each of the two options, they do so with their own language and arguments seemingly working at cross purposes. The Latin treatise, in which Dante declares that the vernacular is the more noble language while writing in the grammatical one, insists on the naturalness of the vernacular as a positive trait, while also insinuating that the best possible vernacular is actually the one patterned on the artificialness of grammar. The vernacular treatise, in which Dante declares that Latin is the more noble language, as he drafts his vernacular prose commentary to his vernacular lyric and doctrinal poetry, insists that the absolute stability conferred on Latin by its being a grammatical language is a positive trait – while insinuating that in Latin, too, change has been possible and indeed endemic from the start. The general instability of the chosen subject also seems to produce a deep instability in Dante's overall line of argument.[12]

It is time to return to the initial case of local instability I introduced, which now has hopefully begun to appear semiological (cultural) rather than simply philological (textual). The tensions that emerged from taking the coeval and co-implicated, and yet somewhat diverging passages by Dante and setting them against each other may also begin to account for the absence and presence of the parrot from which we started. In Dante's *Convivio*, both magpie and parrot featured as icons of inauthenticity, of linguistic artificiality. Their false languages were dependent on the mindless echolalic training and imitation of human speech. The artificial quality of the language that Dante imagined for the magpie was nonetheless absolute. That is, Dante's text fell perfectly in line with what Ovid wrote about the magpies in the final lines of *Metamorphoses* V: "picae omnia imitantes" (the total mimicry of the magpies). However, the artificiality that his culture ascribed to the parrot was less absolute. As we have seen, this bird was not treated as just echolalic – it was not, that is, bound only to repeat what was being said to it. In medieval thinking, the parrot also possessed a native call, one that drew it into the sphere of the natural. For Dante, who is developing that notion exactly at this juncture in the two treatises, that sphere belongs to the vernaculars and to them alone. For its association with a native ability to articulate sound beyond technical training – an involuntarily semantic utterance, to be sure, and yet an interpretable one – the parrot was seen in Dante's polarized pairing of talking birds as the one closer to the natural quality of the vernaculars, and also to their natural instability.

The parrot's presence in *Convivio* did not contradict, but rather went hand in hand with the perceived instability of all languages, even grammar, intimated in the text. This tacitly endorsed cultural precondition allowed the bird to fit the context. Correspondingly, in the opposite direction, in *De vulgari eloquentia*, a treatise in which the vernacular was made to approach, at least tendentially, the status of a grammaticalized idiom, the magpie was a perfectly suitable emblem but the parrot was not. Its disappearance was far from coincidental: the "psittacus" turned out to be a less appropriate point of contrastive reference for human languages, in a treatise in which the vernacular was certainly valued, but especially valued because it could potentially be drawn into the stabilizing gravitational field of grammar. If grammar is the *locutio secundaria* designed from the start to supplement human natural instability with stability in space and time, then the "natural" call of the parrot is the wrong symbol for it. When he advocates the imitation of the *regulati poete*, and when he vaunts the higher reliance on grammar that his own vernacular poetry displays, Dante is moving in this same direction. For the author of *De vulgari eloquentia*, culture consists in moving what is natural away from its endemic mutability, edging it toward artistic – that is, artificial – stability. On the contrary, in his cultural imagination, the parrot was the bearer of a natural positivity that was accepted and valued as such, but that could not be endorsed by the logic of the treatise. What in language is natural is also unstable, and instability is what the Latin treatise, by excising the parrot from its prose, is apparently willing to exorcise.

At this point it may be useful to remind ourselves of the specific call that Isidore attributes to the parrot: "Ave." I pointed out quite cursorily its uncanny coincidence with the angelic greeting at the Annunciation. Its implications deserve closer consideration: associated with Incarnation, and accordingly with the promise of regaining Eden in a better and more stable form than any artificial regression would grant, the parrot's instability in Dante's text appears as linguistic as it is hermeneutic. As the turning point in salvation history, Incarnation represented for Christian thought a mystery that involved a further specific and highly charged reversal in addition to and in full cohesion with those mentioned above: namely, that of Mary and Eve. As the poles between which the history of fall and redemption unfolded, medieval typological thinking treated these two central feminine figures in human history as co-implicated in several ways, but most notably in the correspondence established in the scene of the Annunciation by the angelical greeting "Ave," considered as a reverse echo of the first woman's name, "Eva." The connection is nothing short of topical in medieval spirituality and culture. One example may suffice here, to show how Dante too was aware of, and capitalized on, the topos.

In the penultimate canto of the *Commedia*, Dante epitomizes this typological relationship by having Saint Bernard begin his review of the heavenly rose with the visual correspondence between Mary and Eve established by their assigned seats in heaven. Surveyed in strict and immediate relation to one another, Mary and Eve are specifically made to appear in the same column of seats in the amphitheatre of the blessed, precisely because of their inverse relation to original sin:

La piaga che Maria richiuse e unse,	The wound that Mary closed and healed was
quella ch'è tanto bella da' suoi piedi	opened and pierced by the woman, so fair,
è colei che l'aperse e che la punse.	now at her feet. (*Paradiso* 32.4–6)[13]

The "reverse symmetry" (as Vicky Kirkham defined it) of the world-historical roles the two women are called to play in Dante's lines produces the typological pairing. As it marks the turning point of redemption history, and thus fulfils the promise of Incarnation and the coming of Christ as the new Adam, the "Eva-Ave" connection triggered by the greeting of the angel is appropriately palindromic.[14] Historical-salvific time and the time of linguistic utterance are both undergoing conversion through Gabriel's voice. The name of the first sinner recapitulates (in a technical sense) the primal scene of sin, in the same breath as the greeting to Mary begins the process of redemption from that sin. Biblical typology binds together not only original sin and redemption, but also their narrative contexts. The expulsion from Eden and the Annunciation, a motif that will become a visual topos in several early Renaissance paintings, are strictly connected.

Together with the incarnational undertones of its call, other elements link the parrot to the context of Eden. In medieval imaginary, the birds of the earthly paradise sing a *canticum novum*. They are associated with renewal, not repetition; they herald Christ and look forward to a nature made whole and holy again. Like the birds of the earthly paradise (and as the bird that perhaps most properly belongs to the imagery of that space), the parrot has a call that is not pure echolalia. Unlike the magpie, its greeting is natural, and its call undoes Eve even as it anticipates Mary. The parrot's greeting associates human language with the new dispensation, projecting as forced echolalia those artificial human enterprises that rely solely on the surrogacy of art.

Suspended between artificiality and potential naturalness, the parrot appears part and parcel of the system of tropes that established the garden of Eden at once as a lost space of human perfection, an unattainable object of post-lapsarian desire, and a symbol of the inbuilt promise of human redemption.

3. *Instabilissimus locus*: Contingency, Irony, Solidarity in the Cantos 26

Let us take stock of what we have determined thus far about the acquisitions of Dante's pre-comedic works in matters of historical linguistics. The theoretical dichotomy between the artificial stability of grammar and the natural instability of the vernacular is at the core of his reflection. Projected on the plane of linguistic history, the dichotomy corresponds to the post-lapsarian status of all languages that began at Babel. Both divine providence and human ingenuity reacted to the Babelic crisis, though they articulated their response along two different axes. The former's response consisted in exempting a portion of humankind from the punishment itself. Dante stipulates that one group and one group only, those who spoke Hebrew, did not take part in the act of pride consummated at Babel. Thus, they could maintain their language – which is to say Adam's language – intact. The neo-testamentary reason for their special status was, Dante insists, the Jewishness of Jesus (born from the chosen people according to his humanity). A language of Grace and not of confusion thus seems to have existed after Babel, God's punishment having been selective and not absolute. At the same time Dante proposes that a second, divergent response to linguistic differentiation was launched by the grammarians, the intellectuals who discovered and devised the art of regulated and artificial languages. In creating a transparently and contractually organized language, they were able to obviate both the negatively charged temporal metamorphosis and the progressive spatial differentiation affecting all natural human idioms. This artificial koine, which Dante attributes to Greek and Latin cultures (and some others, but not all of them), granted his own culture access to the intellectual achievements of distant times and spaces.

Both options – one archeological, the other prosthetic – left something to be desired. For one thing, the archeological option, consisting in a return to Adam's central vernacular, was bound to be impossible to achieve: Dante knew that, by his time, modern vernaculars had grown too distant from the original idiom. For another, this option was also constructed as apostatic in quality; if pursued, it would result in an attempted but unattainable regression, a return to a pre-Christian (more accurately, pre-incarnational) time. Once the mandate of the first chosen people had been fulfilled with the coming of Christ, and once that mission's exhaustion had been signalled by the destruction of the Second Temple in Jerusalem, any effort to recapture the old linguistic dispensation could only result in a reversion to a time before the later positive developments of salvation history. Going back to Adam's language would amount, for Dante's culture, to an attempt to re-enter Eden or, worse yet, to rebuild the Temple. Correspondingly, the prosthetic option, though promising in terms of the spatial breadth and temporal depth of reach that came with grammar, would force language into a state of unnatural stability, a rigour embodied both in the restrictive poetics that Dante's own treatise deems necessary to impose on the vernacular poet (using the illustrious vernacular only for the highest topics, only in poems drafted in the highest register and style) and in the latent drive to grammaticalization that *De vulgari* appears to recommend for the natural language of his day.

In essence, a close examination of Dante's pre-comedic works leaves us with nothing but a blocked alternative. If no singular vernacular may claim the necessary stability to become a language of culture (an enduring and supralocal idiom for intellectual communication) and no grammar may be coopted for that task (because of its unnatural quality), what language was a new poet and intellectual to use? The only open option would be that of a vernacular which not only accepted instability as necessary evil, but also embraced it. While out of reach in the pre-comedic works, at a certain point of his intellectual history that option did become viable for Dante. His ensuing realization that the blocked alternative between grammatical artifice and vernacular instability could be mediated changed the course of his writing, producing the impetus for the *Commedia*. The new course Dante impresses on his poetry with the *Commedia* is not solely the product of internal tensions in his thinking. Rather, it may be shown to resonate with elements of his culture that possessed a different, more complete view of the matter than it may seem when we take his other works as the sole point of entry into the question. The solution existed, in other words, but was not to be found in the theory of either *De vulgari* or *Convivio*, two works that for several reasons – not least among which were their common problematic linguistics – were left in different but congruent states of incompleteness.

As the previous sections have suggested, *Convivio* and *De vulgari* were coherent with each other in addressing linguistic and poetic questions, and in both works Dante seemed to reach a theoretical impasse while searching for a vernacular that could be at once natural and non-historically bound (a language that would undo Babel). The stage he reached in the treatises is not, however, the last act in his theory of language. As has been observed and as I propose in the following pages, the *Commedia* does eventually revisit all these questions. Beyond the blocked alternatives set up by *De vulgari*, the forced choice between the regressive pre-Babel unity of a lost vernacular and the artificial Esperanto-like unification in a grammaticalized language, Dante found a third way and articulated it throughout his *Commedia*, most keenly in the end sections of the three cantos starring Ulysses, Arnaut Daniel, and Adam.

In other words, Dante's reflection on language did not stop with his theory that posited the diffraction at Babel as final and only saw a way past it in the artificial reconstruction of a koine that produced grammatical systems of communication. Though no longer in a formalized way, he continued to think about language, but did so directly in the body of his poem. By writing a poem that was both *not* in Latin and sustained by paradoxical universal aspirations, Dante crossed the theoretical limits of his pre-comedic works in his poetic practice. He did so also in the linguistic theory that came together with it. Several moments in the *Commedia* rehash questions of linguistic history, providing new answers to the theoretical questions opened up there. In all these cases, as we are about to see, the earthly paradise is a recurring image. Dante's idiosyncratic version of Eden is clearly visible in the background of the three vertically connected episodes on which this section focuses: Virgil's dialogue with Ulysses in *Inferno* 26, the speech in Provençal that the poem assigns to Arnaut Daniel in *Purgatorio* 26, and Adam's own account of the earliest phase in human linguistic histories in the heaven of the Fixed Stars in *Paradiso* 26. As we may remember, Eden is the plateau Dante imagines located at the top of the mountain, "una montagna bruna per la distanza" (*Inferno* 26.130–3), that the Greek hero tries to reach on his ill-fated journey an adventure retold to the vernacular poet by his Latin intermediary in the fiction of the *Commedia*. Eden is also the destination of the protagonist's visit after his exchange with Arnaut, the *miglior fabbro* "of the mother tongue," and the last penitent soul with whom Dante interacts in Purgatory, who calls it, in his untranslated Provençal the "som de l'escalina" in his final words recorded in the poem (*Purgatorio* 26.145–7). Finally, Eden is the "eccelso giardin" in which God placed Adam, and he made his primal, mutable (we learn now) language at the beginning of human time (*Paradiso* 26.109–14). The invitation to read these cantos "vertically" – that is, in connection with one another as specific steps in a coordinated reflection on multilingualism and translation – is perhaps subtle and in fact, to my knowledge, has not been picked up in scholarly treatments, but it is strong. Connected by more than their simple numerical correspondence across the three sections of Dante's *Commedia*, the codas of the three Cantos 26 are all involved in reflecting on issues of linguistics. And they appear to do so consistently through the trope of the Edenic garden. In all cases, Eden appears in the poem as a space in which and through which Dante revisits issues of linguistic transmission, variety, and mutability. It is featured, that is, as a space of translation.[15]

Let us begin by looking at the interconnection of *Inferno* 26 and 27, the cantos of the Greek hero Ulysses and his modern counterpart, Guido da Montefeltro. There is little need to expound on the multilingual dimension of Dante's text. The narrative of *Inferno* 26 reports the conversation between Dante, a modern Italian vernacular poet, and Ulysses, a Greek Homeric hero, with a Latin poet, Virgil, being called upon to act as cultural and possibly linguistic mediator. The text focuses, in other words, on an inter-age and inter-cultural exchange based on the twofold crossing of linguistic differences. Virgil's preemptive warning to the protagonist, as he entreats him to be allowed to interact with Ulysses, speaks to this dimension. In vindicating his own role, Virgil insists on correlating the ethnic aversion of the interlocutors with linguistics: the souls wrapped in the split flame whom Dante wants to interrogate may, as Greeks, be "schivi" (a word whose meaning ranges from "shy" to "hostile") around his words:

"Lascia parlare a me, ch'i' ho concetto ciò che tu vuoi; ch'ei sarebbero schivi, perch' e' fuor greci, forse del tuo detto."

"Let me do the speaking, since I have understood what you would like to know: they are Greeks, and they may recoil from engaging with your words." (*Inferno* 26.73–5)

The lexicon of the passage is technical: the terms "parlare," "concetto," "detto" evoke language and issues of linguistic communication, alongside ethnic-national ones. The question is, of course, and as the commentators hasten to note, eminently cultural. Dante is a modern poet and a practitioner of a more "modest" brand of literature than the epic poetic canon to which the ancient souls belong. The mediation of Virgil, who is at once speaker of an ancient language and steeped in a classical poetic ethos, is thus deemed necessary to bridge the cultural gap. The mediation is all the more necessary, since, from a historical and philological point of view, it is through Virgil's texts – and his Latin – that Dante was granted access to the ancient stories. Commentators of all ages have unfailingly added a philological-cultural gloss to that effect, as captured in the distanced dialogue between Benvenuto da Imola's fourteenth- and Charles Singleton's twentieth-century commentaries:

> The traditional pride and haughtiness of the Greek constitute part of the reason for Virgil's words here, no doubt; but the fact that Dante is a modern, of a time and culture remote from those of ancient Greece and such heroes as these, enters into the matter, too. Virgil, poet of ancient Rome, would be much closer to the two Greek heroes. Indeed, as Benvenuto observes in his comment on vs. 84: "Sic est verum quod autor devenerit in cognitionem istorum mediante Virgilio" ["Thus it is true that the author made their acquaintance through Virgil"]. (Charles Singleton, *Commentary*, ad loc.)

Although a wider issue of cultural arbitration may be at stake, I insist, what emerges in the immediate narrative context is linguistic mediation. The narrative starring Dante's Ulysses unfolds within the arguably homogeneous literary genre of epic, one area in which other episodes in the *Commedia* fail to thematize any communication problem: in *Inferno* 4, for instance, Homer speaks to his fellow Latin poets in a language that Dante is expected to (and apparently does) fully understand. Despite this, Ulysses' account of his final journey and eventual demise, which is the core of what Dante wants to learn from him, reverberates across three culturally interconnected languages that require an intermediating process to become mutually non-exclusive. The words Virgil uses to preface his stepping into the narrative evoke translation.

As we have seen while examining Chrétien's version of *translatio*, medieval writers employed this tag to indicate the historical phenomenon that saw the transference across time and space of the cultural centre of the western world from Greece (and Greek) to Rome (and Latin), and from Rome to the French writing culture (in Chrétien de Troyes' formulation) or, in Dante's own reworking of the trope, to the decentralized space of vernacular literacy in the Italian peninsula. The agonistic dynamic intrinsic to the phenomenon of cultural *transference* and linguistic *translation*, of which *translatio* consists, is hardly hidden. The same is true for Dante. Though seldom noticed, when Dante reaches all the way back to Homer's Ulysses via Virgil's interpretation, the context of the narratives that he interrogates and plans to supplement with his addition is war. The subject matter of Greek and Latin epics is essentially martial. What is more, the struggle for an identitary supremacy lies at the core of both Homer's and Virgil's narratives, taken both in themselves and in dialogue with one another. Whether they are devoted to the return home of a victorious raiding party (the Greeks in the *Odyssey*) or the search for a new land by a defeated people (the Trojans in the *Aeneid*), the epic texts pertinent for Dante's episode offer a narrative centred on a clash of civilizations. The *Odyssey* is a poem that relays the homecoming of one of the few veterans of the *Iliad* who made it back, just as the *Aeneid* recounts the fate of another raiding troop which, by reaching the shores of Italy, is destined to become the embodiment of their own past nemesis for the local peoples of the new land. By unleashing a landgrab war in Latium, the Trojans, refugees turned invaders, are to the Latin people what the Greeks were to them. The plot reversal mirrors a cultural shift: among many other things and despite its own subtly exhibited guilt complex, the *Aeneid* is an antagonistic rewriting of the Greek narrative of Greek epic success from the point of view of the defeated party now turned conqueror.

Together with the narrative *translatio*, the literary-historical supersession is carried out, in Dante as much as was the case in Chrétien de Troyes, by linguistic *translation*. Dante constructs the infernal meeting by staging the conditions for such acts: Homer's Greek linguistic identity is taken over by Virgil's Latin (interposed in the conversation), and Latin is ultimately displaced by the vernacular of the text we are reading. This dynamic of translation is, in turn, not peaceful either. The new power and culture rise from the ashes of the old ones and in turn silence their voices: nobody speaks of the Greeks and Romans anymore, as Chrétien bittersweetly noted in the prologue of his *Cligès*; Troy is, for Dante, in *Purgatorio* 10, "in cenere e caverne" (reduced to ashes and ruins). In sum, the historical multilingualism of the western literary canon is intrinsically linked to a dynamic of violent suppressions that takes place across time. Each new language replaces its predecessor as the central language of the West through *translatio*.

While it mimics the agonistic movement of linguistic supersession from Greek to Latin and from Latin to the vernacular, however, *Inferno* 26 also inserts an element of surprise. If we assume that the text is asking us to imagine the interaction between the three characters as a vignette in which Virgil would carry out his linguistic mediation by speaking Greek to the Greek Ulysses and by translating into grammatical Latin for Dante's benefit, we are soon proven wrong. This possible version of the proceedings, one that the text does not rule out but suggests in Virgil's phrasing of his alleged merit toward them, is not what readers are next told has actually taken place. At least, it is not all that happens in the exchange. At the start of the *Inferno* 27, readers learn that the exchange between Virgil and Ulysses extended beyond the Latin poet's invitation to the Greek hero to recount the circumstances of his death. In the episode's coda, they also discover that they might have been wrong in imagining that the linguistics of the exchange were moving retrogressively beneath the surface of the vernacular text, that is, using Latin as intermediary language of culture to gain access into the sphere of ancient Greek poetry. Rather, judging from

Guido da Montefeltro's words, it appears that Virgil was speaking in his own "native" vernacular – a very local brand of Lombard – to Ulysses. He certainly did so when he dismissed him. Here is what the soul of Guido, the modern Ulysses whom Dante meets in the same *bolgia* as his ancient prototype, has to say, reporting apparently verbatim the exchange he has just heard:

"O tu a cu' io drizzo
la voce e che parlavi mo lombardo,
dicendo 'Istra ten va, più non t'adizzo'
..."

"You, to whom I address my voice, and
were speaking a moment ago in Lombard,
saying, 'Go then, I won't stoke you any
longer'..."
(*Inferno* 27.19–21)

Virgil's curt aside to Dante, "It's your turn to speak: this one is Latin" ("Parla tu, questo è latino"), retrospectively confirms that linguistics was indeed a concern of the previous canto, one that interwove geographical as well as chronological differences and implicitly mediated between them, but it does so along unexpected lines. The effect of Guido's abrupt intervention in the text is to reframe, by yoking together the cantos, the sense readers may have had while internally wrestling with the interlinguistic dynamics of the dialogue between the "ancient flame" of the Greek hero and the Latin poet. Virgil's language, which for a moment – the long moment in which they read the canto of Ulysses as an exercise in cultural *translatio studii* – appeared a haughty and mighty idiom, the ennobled vehicle for the transmission of grand cultural material, is reduced to the level of trivial and local domestic chit chat. The prosthetic, grammatical model of inter-age and inter-nation language that we may have attributed to Virgil, in other words, is displaced and collapsed. If there is a cultural confrontation (and there is one in this episode), the *Commedia* suggests, it is not resolved through the adoption of that artificial protocol for information encoding and transmission called grammar. In the linguistics of Dante's poem, the classicizing return to Latin evoked in Virgil's mediating role is evidently not offered up as a solution.

The move has larger than local effects on the implicit linguistic dynamics embedded in Dante's text. If, thanks to Latin's mediation and Greek's ascendance, Dante's vernacular staked a cultural claim to the same centrality as the other two languages of culture in the process of *translatio*, it was only seemingly so. *Inferno* 27 comes to dissociate the subject matter of Ulysses' speech from its expected linguistic and poetic vehicle. The language Virgil uses with Ulysses, his "native" Lombard, is no language for a centralizing power of an imperial court (as Dante imagined his illustrious vernacular might have become, in his *De vulgari eloquentia*), no idiom designed to bridge authoritative past and identitary present (as *Convivio* confidently indicated it would). It is a local variety of the *volgare di sì*, one subject to the vagaries of time and space mutation. If there is in fact a felicitous transmission of weighty cultural material between the ancient world and Dante's present, this process is not mediated by the artificial languages of culture.

What may come as a surprise in the superimposed sections of Cantos 26 and 27 of *Inferno* is confirmed more systematically and openly in the codas of the other two Cantos 26 in the *Commedia*. Interestingly, while the coda of *Inferno* 26 displaces Virgil's Latin as a grammatical and prosthetic option, thus denying that Italian (as in, a classicizing and grammaticalized version of it) may play a role at the centre of a vertical line of textual transmission and cultural tradition, *Purgatorio* 26 revisits the linguistic question by acknowledging the presence of various languages of culture in the poetic canon and frames it as a potentially non-conflictual system. The episode is set up carefully, placed as the final movement in a stretch of cantos devoted to questions of poetics and modern literary history. The long section devoted to a reflection on vernacular poets began in *Purgatorio* 24: when Dante met Forese Donati among the penitent gluttons, a Florentine friend with whom he most likely also exchanged sonnets, in a poetic vernacular and often thematically vulgar *tenzone*. The encounter with this first poet develops into a short but poignant metapoetic exchange with another local vernacular versifier, Bonagiunta da Lucca, who asks whether Dante is the author of the "new rhymes" inaugurated with the canzone *Donne ch'avete intelletto d'amore*. When he hears Dante call himself an inspired poet of Love, the answer forces him to admit that all poetry before that text, including the Sicilians', Guittone d'Arezzo's, and his own, has been outdone and is, thus, utterly outdated at this point in literary history. Finally, coming to the ledge of the penitent lustful, the metapoetic imaginative section culminates with the protagonist's affectionate meeting with two penitent poets of love: first Guido Guinizzelli, whom Dante openly acknowledges as one of his poetic father figures, and credits with a success that will last as long as the "uso moderno" (modern fashion) will endure, and then Arnaut Daniel, whom Guido carefully compares to other poets of the previous generation, in particular to Giraut de Bornelh.

It is at this narrative juncture, which has been prepared by a long portion of text peppered with discussions of what vernacular poetry does or should do, that Dante allows the longest stretch of alloglot poetry to enter the text of the *Commedia*, writing eight lines of original Provençal and placing them in the mouth of his penitent Arnaut:

El cominciò liberamente a dire:
"Tan m'abellis vostre cortes deman,
qu'ieu no me puesc ni voill a vos cobrire.
Ieu sui Arnaut, que plor e vau cantan;
consiros vei la passada folor,
e vei jausen lo joi qu'esper, denan.
Ara vos prec, per aquella valor
que vos guida al som de l'escalina,
sovenha vos a temps de ma dolor!".

He freely began to say: "I appreciate your courteous question so much that I cannot nor do I want to hide myself from you. I am Arnaut, who weeps and goes on singing; I now see with concern my past folly and look ahead with glee at the joy which, I hope, awaits me. Thus, I pray you, by that power that leads you to the top of this stairway, to remember, when the time comes, my pain!" (*Purgatorio* 26.140–7)

As we realize, coming to them not only by way of the horizontal sequence of metapoetic cantos but also reaching up vertically from *Inferno* 26, these lines have an essential metalinguistic dimension to them. Through Arnaut's speaking part in the poem, Dante not only projects the canon as a synchronic rather than diachronic organism; he also presents it as a collaborative poetic space from which attempts at interlinguistic supersession and drives for supremacy are banished, or at least downplayed. The *langue d'oc* – both Arnaut's original and Dante's own, no less valuable version of it – becomes central to its individual conditions of existence. Its truth coincides with both the personal truth of its originator, to whom in its contingency it is perfectly appropriate, and in the apperception of the audience, which is invited to provide an internal interpretation of the text that stands in solidarity with it. Significantly, no translation is given; there is no linguistic supersessionism at play in the episode. Nor does there seem to be any room for the contradictions between vernacular transiency and grammatical artificial stability that marked *Inferno* 26. The internal mechanisms of translation between the coplanar vernaculars of Dante and Arnaut are presented as intrinsically, if ideally, non-supersessional. If Dante is ventriloquizing Arnaut, that is, he does so by taking the linguistic identity of his interlocutor upon himself.

Accordingly, the section starring Arnaut is dotted with courteous declarations, which prefigure the interpretive charity that the text models for the reader through the protagonist's behaviour. These professions of deference range from Guinizzelli's pointing to Arnaut as "miglior fabbro del parlar materno" (l. 117, a better craftsman of the mother tongue), a respectful and nonconfrontational move if there ever was one, to the protagonist's elegantly phrased claim that he has prepared a place of welcome for his interlocutor's name: "al suo nome il mio desire / apparecchiava grazioso loco" (ll. 137–8). Correspondingly, Dante's Arnaut – in the implicit abdication of a *trobar clus* style, a renunciation that critics have long since recognized as characterizing his lines, and in his explicit desire to reveal himself to the protagonist, something that he candidly declares – embodies a new openness of poetic language that is made meaningful through the interpretive encounter with its audience.

We should note that the kind of translation at play toward the end of *Purgatorio* 26 is not the aggressive cultural *translatio*, first foreshadowed and then surprisingly dispelled, in the corresponding canto in *Inferno*. Rather, it is the new cornerstone of the poem's linguistics, one that relies, as Alison Cornish has recently stressed, on openness to translation. However, the foundation of the democratic vernacularity that the exchange embodies is even more clearly spelled out in *Paradiso* 26, the last canto in this vertically connected triad. Here too, questions of linguistic identity and mutability are paramount. They emerge in the last block of verses in the canto, a coyly motivated narrative coda to a context concerned with other doctrinal and theological matters. The episode, in which Adam as first speaker eventually appears, unfolds in the heaven of the

Fixed Stars, where the protagonist is being examined on the three theological virtues by the apostles Peter, James, and John. As he is misguidedly attempting to see John's body, despite the brilliance that constitutes the latter's soul, Dante is momentarily blinded. When he finally recovers his sight, there is a fourth light next to those of the apostles. This new soul, as Beatrice explains, is Adam's. So that he may hear them answered more quickly, the traveller mentally poses four questions to him. Adam rephrases Dante's unspoken queries in his reply: when did God place him in the garden of Eden, how long did he enjoy it for, what was the exact nature of the sin that determined the loss of the garden, and, finally, what was the language that Adam formed and used. Evidently, the linking of all these questions makes them directly pertinent to the trope of the garden, but it is perhaps the last one that most specifically connects the concluding passage of *Paradiso* 26 with its antecedents in *Inferno* and *Purgatorio*, since it concerns the origin and the original status of human language.

Here is the answer Dante receives from Adam about Edenic language:

"La lingua ch'io parlai fu tutta spenta
innanzi che a l'ovra inconsummabile
fosse la gente di Nembròt attenta;
Che nullo effetto mai razïonabile,
per lo piacer uman che rinnovella
seguendo il cielo, sempre fu durabile.
Opera naturale è ch'uom favella;
ma così o così, natura lascia
poi fare a voi secondo che v'abbella.
Pria ch'i' scendessi a l'infernale ambascia
I s'appellava in terra il sommo bene
onde vien la letizia che mi fascia;
e El si chiamò poi; e ciò convene
che l'uso d'i mortali è come fronda
in ramo, che sen va e altra vene."

"The language that I spoke was all but gone before Nimrod's people set themselves to the unfulfillable task: no product of reason is, in fact, ever durable, given the variability of human taste, which renews itself with every season. It is a natural effect that Man should speak, but whether in one way or another, Nature leaves it to you, who act following your pleasure. Before I descended to the agony of hell, *I* was the name on earth of that highest good, from which issues the bliss that envelops me, and *El* the name thereafter. And this must be the case because the usage of mortals is like foliage on a branch, which goes away as another arrives." (*Paradiso* 26.124–38)

Two essential points emerge from Adam's account of the process that brought about the birth of the original vernacular and precipitated its aftermath. The first is expressed positively, and the second is phrased as the dispelling of a potential misconception. The first point Adam makes is that the language he produced and used was fully human in origin, and thus its lexicon underwent natural change, as it is bound to happen for any human artifact. Naturally, and intrinsically, humans have the faculty of speech; but individual arbitrium controls the production of all languages, and they are thus subject to change. Secondly, and consequently, Adam insists that Babel played no part in changing the essence of the first vernacular. God's punishment did not introduce change to an allegedly stable protolanguage: it was there from the start. Instability already was, so to speak, written in its genetic code. Even the name of God mutated, Adam concludes, during his own lifespan, moving from "I" to "El." The implicit authority Adam uses to gloss the phenomenon is by now familiar: the locus classicus of Horace's *Ars poetica*, the same that planted the seed of impermanence in Dante's theoretically compact reasoning on the absolute stability of grammatical languages. The usage of mortals is like seasonal foliage, always renewing language itself.

By calling into question Adam's role as the maker of the first language and indicating that even his idiom held no exceptional position, Dante radically revisits and revises the stances he articulated in *De vulgari eloquentia*. Several notions have practically disappeared. Gone is the idea that Adamic language enjoyed a unique status; as is, accordingly, the possibility to advocate for any archeological rank. When Dante's Adam claims that the language he spoke was completely extinct even before Nimrod attempted to build the tower, he deflects all ontological or genetic claims to superiority of any language over any other. It is in the nature of all languages that they are historically transient and locally different. Multiformity is the primal essence of language. The arbitrary work of all speakers – "secondo che v'abbella" – is the guiding principle and active force behind all change and differentiation. Neither evil nor good, change in time and multiplicity in space are presented as neutral. They are, originally and quintessentially, the only possible state for human language. Any option advocating for an apostatic and impossible regression to a pre-Babel (or pre-lapsarian) unity, a counter-historical regression into an Edenic linguistic dispensation, is dispelled in *Paradiso*.

4. *Instabilissima signa*: Dante's New Linguistic Ecology and the Art of Acrostics

The three episodes surveyed in the previous section allow us to look with Dante in a different, perhaps less traumatic way at Babel and the diffraction of languages associated with it: *Inferno* 26 and its coda in 27 contribute a healthy dose of *irony* to the treatment of linguistic differentiation, by unsettling any dynamic ranking of cultural languages; *Paradiso* 26 dwells on the *contingency* of all speaking acts, beginning with the absolute first one, Adam's *primiloquium*; and *Purgatorio* 26 insists on readerly *solidarity* as the basis for all successful interlinguistic communication, a process based on the internal mechanisms of translation.[16] Taken together, these three intratextually connected episodes articulate the new linguistic poetics of the *Commedia*, introducing readers to the idea that for Dante any attempt to undo multilingualism – by way of either the artificial or the regressive options opened up at Babel – is ultimately ill conceived. The *Commedia* seems, rather, to rely on different principles.[17] Openness to interpretation, interpersonal and interlanguage translation are the key tenets defining a new literature, which not only accepts multilingualism but also capitalizes on it. The witnesses who have been called upon to vouch for this new sense of vernacular and translational optimism are, however, all characters in Dante's poem. It is true that, in both the episodes they recount and the interactions they have with the protagonist, they cover the widest possible range of time and space: from the most distant past and the farthest East, with Adam, through the Mediterranean world of antiquity, with Virgil and Ulysses, to the relatively close present of the vernacular Provence, with Arnaut. They are, however, all "internal" to the workings of the poem, and readers may resist automatically accepting them as straightforward indicators of the author's poetics. The various intra-narrative engagements and exchanges between characters in the poem may help to position Dante, but none may be said to embody a point of view that automatically coincides with his. To phrase the same idea more precisely, not one of the speaking characters encountered so far is given a statement that may be considered an unadulterated version or a transparent expression of what the author of the poem thinks or does. As intermediate narrators, they may be representing Dante's metapoetic positions, but they also may not.

This kind of sceptical approach is both sound and familiar in Dante studies, and my argument takes it into honest consideration. As is the case for issues of theology and ethics, so too, in matters of poetics; Dante's intermediate narrators are to be trusted only up to a certain point. There are, however, other passages in the *Commedia* that help us move beyond this potential objection. I have selected two such passages, both from the last cantica, which may be taken to represent, due to the space they occupy in the phenomenological unfolding of the writing, a semi-final manifestation of authorial intent. The first locus is *Paradiso* 5, where in a daring simile, designed to represent the emergence of a school of souls from the luminous background of the celestial sphere of Mercury, Dante inserts a retrogressive acrostic linking the incipit of five tercets. The second one, which we have already begun to address, again revolves around a simile: Adam's characterization of humans' arbitrary play with the lexical building blocks of language as seasonal foliage. I address them in the opposite order to that in which they appear in Dante's text, starting with a review of the final vertically connected canto, which takes into account both the poetic imagery that innervates it and the dialogue in which it engages with some of its prosaic prodromes. The episode of Adam in *Paradiso* 26 contains, embedded in both the character's and the author's language, a recitation and recantation of explicit statements and, more importantly, implicit figural associations that were critical for Dante's linguistics in *De vulgari*.

As we are about to see, when they are presented together in the arboreal simile of *Paradiso* 26 quoted above, and especially in the line "che l'uso d'i mortali è come fronda," linguistics and botany are not new to Dante readers. The metaphorical field that binds them together is well established, and the terminology essentially stable. The coherence of terminology and metaphors is not, however, an automatic guarantee that perfect syntony is achieved through their message. There is a profound symbolic opposition between the compact pre-comedic account of human language and its later treatment in *Paradiso*: while it is true that Dante apparently returns, at different times and in different writing projects, to the same metaphors and terms to treat the same question, those terms and metaphors acquire systematically opposed connotations in transit. There are two incompossible elements in his metaphorical system. On the one hand, there is the negative connotation that Dante attributes to the linguistic history of the vernaculars, which are marred by progressive chrono-topographic diversification. As we observed, diversification is not only the most palpable marker of their post-Babel quality, but also the element on which Dante's illustrious vernacular, the peculiarly literary brand of speech that his *De vulgari* seeks and at once strives to define, is designed to intervene. On the other hand, there is the conceptualization in terms of "work," specifically agricultural work, which Dante develops in the treatise to indicate what actions he envisions for the poets to whose linguistic training he devotes great attention. Dante imagines this work as the careful control and strict regimentation of the linguistic environment of the various local vernaculars they use in their poetry. Their activity as *non-municipal* poets, as Dante envisions it, coincides with their work on and management of the supralocal variety of their vernacular language. In *De vulgari*, these two components are essentially correlated in Dante's reasoning.

A. Adam's Edenic Speech

When he reaches the threshold of the *Primum mobile*, the last material heaven of his universe, Dante decides to go back, once again and for the last time in his poetic career, to address the origin and function of language, and he selects a privileged interlocutor, Adam. This choice may appear banal: after all, language – in particular, the variety with which Dante is most concerned, the vernacular, the natural idiom intrinsic to human nature – started with Adam. However, Dante's choice is associated with novel and somewhat surprising connotations in *Paradiso* 26, especially when compared to the way language was presented in *Convivio* and *De vulgari eloquentia*, where it was the object of a considerable, sustained theorization. In the Adam episode readers find, in fact, a dense thicket of metaphors that propagate into neighbouring portions of the text and connote Dante's idea of language with a new set of imaginary associations.[18] The semantic field of vegetation and the cultivation metaphors within it that Dante deploys in his discussion of the origin of language offer a significant point of entry into the discussion. They first inform the powerful, generalizing statement that Dante puts in the middle of his report: "the usage of mortals is like foliage" (l. 137). As readers of *Convivio* and *De vulgari* know, *uso* is a loaded term, when deployed in the context of vernacular linguistics. Dante's discussion of the historical differentiation affecting vernaculars and the contrastive immunity to change attributed to grammatical languages focused specifically on this term. In the words of Dante's Adam, too, all human language is subject to *uso*, the fleeting and arbitrary convention of speakers, who modify its forms and thus engender its perennial renewal. Something, however, has changed in the tone of the simile that is associated with this notion that recurs across the treatises and the poem.

To measure the systemic change in connotations that affects Dante's metaphorization of language as vegetation, it is advisable to begin with a statistical observation. In the wider context of *Paradiso* 26, the term "fronda" (which I have rendered above as "foliage" in the sense of "leafy branch") appears several times in the span of about sixty lines. In Dante's text, more than one thing is labelled "fronda." First, "fronda" is the "usage" of the speakers, which is intrinsically unstable and thus causes continuous mutations in the language that it governs (l. 137). There is also the whole cohort of the blessed, who are described as the "branches" with which the luscious metaphorical garden of heaven tended by God, the eternal gardener (ll. 64–6), is "embranched" ("s'infronda"). There is Dante the protagonist himself who is a "branch" bowing forward, bent by the surprise of realizing that the soul who "breathes" words toward him is the first human being (l. 85). The arboreal semantic field explored in the Adam episode is so rich that it crosses into the next canto and into the next heaven beyond that of the Fixed Stars in which this episodic coda takes place. Then it is called upon again in the conceptualization of Time as a plant that shoots its root in the last sphere before the Empyrean and extends "its branches" into the lower material heavens, as stipulated in *Paradiso* 27.118–20. Without leaving the confines of Canto 26, however, the four instances of this metaphor, one of which is redoubled thanks to an etymological figure linking noun and verb, leave a deep mark in the text. While it is structural to the imagination of the whole canto, the metaphorical overgrowth readers encounter there also points to Adam's specific role as language user and maker. Images from the same semantic field of vegetation and cultivation were in fact widely deployed in Dante's reflection on linguistics in *De vulgari eloquentia*.

The structural role of the vegetation simile is evident from the start of the Latin treatise. For instance, Dante already conceives of and describes the linguistic environment in which humankind is immersed in terms of plant life in the first recitation of the foundation myth that sets Eden against Babel. In the first book of *De vulgari*, Dante notes:

Et cum radix humane propaginis principalis in oris orientalibus sit plantata, nec non ab inde ad utrunque latus per diffusos multipliciter palmites nostra sit extensa propago demumque ad fines occidentales protracta, forte primitus tunc vel totius Europe flumina, vel saltim quedam, rationalia guttura potaverunt.

And since the main root, from which humanity propagated, was planted in the orient, and since from there our plant stretched into all directions, extending through many branches up to the western limits, perhaps it was then that rational throats first drank from the rivers of all Europe, or at least from some of them. (*De vulgari eloquentia* I.8.1)

The terminology sustaining his reasoning is cohesive. It is also coherent with the metaphorical field of plant life: "radix," "propago," "plantata," "palmites," "protracta" are all words that technically imagine the propagation of human-kind throughout the world as a vegetative process. In continuity with this idea of humanity, Dante also offers a coherent image of language as vegetative. In defining the second phase in his work as a selective linguist, when he begins his hunt through the various dialects of Italy for the most appropriate and illustrious vernacular, Dante phrases his work as an attentive and rational deforestation of the main, secondary, and sub-secondary vernacular varieties of Italy. The metaphorical substratum of the passage is, again, telling:

> Quam multis varietatibus latio dissonante vulgari, decentiorem atque illustrem Ytalie venemur loquelam; et ut nostre venationi pervium callem habere possimus, perplexos frutices atque sentes prius eiciamus de silva.

> Let us hunt, then, for the most elegant and illustrious speech, and do so within the many and discordant varieties of the Italian vernacular. To have an unobstructed path for our hunt, let us first clear out the tangled shrubs and brambles from this wood. (*De vulgari eloquentia* I.11.1)

In the metaphorical logic of the treatise, local linguistic varieties are the intricate growth that Dante aims to uproot. This linguistic undergrowth, we should remember, exists because of the idiosyncratic variations that individual speakers introduce into any given idiom and which, thanks to local agreements about customs and habits that characterize small communities, take root in narrow and reciprocally isolated territories, as established in *De vulgari eloquentia* I.9.10. In botanical terms, we may say that Dante's programmatic work of deforestation is designed, at least metaphorically speaking, to respond to the natural progressive afforestation of vernacular languages, and potentially undo it.

Notably, the work of the poet who avails himself of the illustrious vernacular is placed under the aegis of a specific work ethic. Consisting in the violent transformation of the linguistic municipal ecosystem, the *eradicatio sive discerptio* of *De vulgari eloquentia* I.11.2 is not only preliminary. When, in chapter 16, Dante moves on to define the essential features of the illustrious vernacular, a process he calls a second (this time rationally "deductive") *venatio*, he adopts virtually the same set of metaphors deployed earlier. In defining the second necessary feature for the vernacular he deems apt for the highest poetry, Dante introduces three only partially coordinated metaphors in rapid succession. First, the vernacular he defines should be "cardinal," because other idiolects revolve around it (this is what it means for the vernacular to be a "hinge," from the Latin root *cardo*); secondly, these minor vernaculars are like a flock tended by an individual; finally, this individual is the true *paterfamilias* of the group. To these three metaphors, which appear to be organized in a syllepsis chain ranging from the realm of the inanimate to the animal, and from the animal to the human, Dante adds a final one: the vegetative. What else does the vernaculars' *paterfamilias* do, he asks rhetorically, if not tend the wooded landscape of Italy? The tone of the passage is heightened, but the metaphors that sustain it are not simply ornamental:

> Nonne cotidie exstirpat sentosos frutices de ytalia silva? Nonne cotidie vel plantas vel plantaria plantat? Quid aliud agricole sui satagunt, nisi ut amoveant et admoveant, ut dictum est?

> Does he not daily eradicate the thorny brambles of the Italian forest? Does he not daily plant new plants and plantings? What else do his farmers do but take out and bring in, as I said above?   (*De vulgari eloquentia* I.18.1)

The deforestation terminology returns to the fore, this time with the autochthonous brambles of the Italian forest being eradicated and replaced by graftings and shoots of new species. The poets who are conquering space for the illustrious vernacular are now called to work as "agricole" on the language they both use and serve. Their activity involves the violent uprooting of the dense underbrush of the vernaculars, which is imagined as the elimination of local varieties of vegetation that are to be replaced with different, standardized species. The metaphors piled on in this emphatic passage are far from neutral. They have a precise biblical antecedent. In the first book of Genesis, in the threefold meting out of individual sentences to the three actors in the drama of original sin, God establishes a specific punishment for Adam:

> [17] ad Adam vero dixit quia audisti vocem uxoris tuae et comedisti de ligno ex quo praeceperam tibi ne comederes maledicta terra in opere tuo in laboribus comedes ex ea cunctis diebus vitae tuae [18] spinas et tribulos germinabit tibi et comedes herbam terrae.

> To Adam he said: Since you heeded the voice of your wife and you ate from the tree, from which I forbade you to eat, let the ground be inimical to your work. You will labour to draw fruit from the ground your whole life. It will produce for you thorns and brambles, and you will eat the grass of the earth. (Gen. 3:17–18)

The recurring of the same images in Dante's text suggests, thus, that the work on language carried out by the poets who are pressed into service of the illustrious vernacular is conceptualized in terms of biblical *labor*, the post-lapsarian toil assigned to Adam in his exile from the Garden. It is violent work, intended to punish both man and environment, which according to Dante is to be exercised on the natural, spontaneously varied linguistic landscape, and which aims at its aggressively rational standardization. The same processes and principles seem to control the post-Edenic condition of human beings and the specific condition of the poet-linguists who work in the field. It is they who remove some (bad, infesting) linguistic forms and promote (better, controlled) others.

As noted above, the metaphorical implication of language in the semantic field of vegetation that marks Dante's discourse in the pre-comedic treatises also extends to *Paradiso*. The underlying, negative characterization of the model he developed in his other works is, however, notably absent. In its place, readers now find Dante matching the same terminology with an opposing set of connotations. Several new elements emerge from his meeting with Adam. The first novelty is the sense that successive alterations in the lexical component of the vernaculars are a natural phenomenon, free from any axiological determination. The second is the axiological assessment of nature, which is perceived, in its technically Edenic phase, as independently fertile and generous. The last new element is the ensuing absence of any punitive connotation from the idea of human work. *Paradiso* 26 is clear in articulating the principles underlying the new understanding of language, surgically targeting the linguistic model that it comes to supplant. The lexical choices Dante makes here, in describing the setting in which the vernaculars are born and the lines along which they develop, are as neat as they are unmistakably different. The space he singles out for his reflection on the origin and development of the vernaculars is now the garden, understood both in terms of Eden (the garden where Adam was the first, provisional *ortolano*), and Paradise, its figural completion (the "eccelso giardino" of l. 110, where God is the *ortolano eterno*). What, in *De vulgari eloquentia* I.18.1, Dante imagined as the soil in which natural vernaculars are rooted was not a garden, but a naturally hostile space, a terrain that necessitates the hard work of the poets who foster the selection and rationalization of the linguistic landscape by embodying it in their poetry. The new space of which Dante speaks in the *Commedia* is different, and a side-by-side reading of the texts that construct these two places produces a jarring effect.

The irreconcilable quality of the two accounts of Dante's imaginary botanic-linguistic nexus is the sign of two main acquisitions that mark his developing reflection on the task of the poet. The first, already present in *De vulgari*, is the conviction that change is the natural condition of human language. In the Latin treatise, Dante fleetingly but forcefully accused any negationist profession to the contrary of intellectual obtuseness (he calls it "quasi-bestiality" in I.9.9): change is endemic to language. The same principle is at the core of his thinking in *Paradiso*, but now Dante extends it to Adamic language, the idiom he artificially exempted from the process before, by identifying it with Hebrew, as the language of grace. With this essential continuity, however, Dante also associates an axiological dimension that mutates, from negative to positive, in the fifteen or so years separating the pre-comedic works from the final cantos of *Paradiso*. Over this time, mutability has ceased to be treated as a problem that the poet diagnoses and desires to remedy by devising a linguistic therapy. Dante's change of direction, away from any normalizing poetics and toward acceptance of change and multiformity, of linguistic instability, is radical. The impact it has on the metaphorical system he uses to articulate his thought is also clear. Dante still stipulates that individual vernaculars have grown different from one another because time has passed, and the arbitrium of speakers in individual communities has altered them differently in different places. However, this situation does not trigger any repressive or regressive reaction in the poet. In the new linguistic ecology established by the *Commedia*, Dante does not conceptualize the task of the poet as an onerous disciplining of language or a curbing of its natural processes. In *Paradiso* 26, in sum, there is no trace of the regression by way of logical induction from multiplicity to oneness, which is what chapters 16–19 of the first book of *De vulgari* explicitly attempt to do while defining the illustrious vernacular. Similarly, there is now no attempt to oppose the flow of time by way of genealogy, traversing the various stages of genetic differentiation from the first post-Babel *trifarium idioma* to the secondary threefold language common to the Franco-Italo-Provençal zone, which is what, implicitly, chapters 8–10 in the same book established, as they outlined the linguistic geography and history of humankind.

Adam's speech is free from all hints of the regressive movement underpinning the tendential disappearance from the vernaculars of all municipal forms, a process that for the author of *De vulgari* was supposed to culminate in the lexical uniformity of the illustrious vernacular, the idiom marked by the *simplicissima signa* of linguistic and social identity on which his text insisted. That process of delocalization corresponded to a regression toward archetypal and progressively less differentiated linguistic stages that is now set aside. For the poet of *Paradiso* 26, in other words, time no longer produces an inevitable degeneration in language, a constant mutation that the poet is called upon to counteract by normatively adopting a technical, artificial language. On the contrary, language, like time, is associated with a natural Edenic fertility, with its branches extending through the heavens of creation and its seeds that, scattered from the centre of the earthly paradise, take root everywhere.

B. The Acrostic of Paradiso *5: An Anti-Babel Fish*

While the lexicon of vegetation is shared between the author and the character in the Adam episode concluding *Paradiso* 26, the next passage to be examined contains a perhaps puzzling but crucial assertion by the poet. In it, through a statement in authorial first person, Dante articulates his steady commitment and profound allegiance to the principles this chapter has attempted to tease out of his texts. With its theological as well as poetological associations, the retrogressive acrostic *Pesce* contained in *Paradiso* 5 moves us from Edenic linguistics to considerations of translation theory and poetic praxis. The felicitous encoding of a Christological symbol, transferred from one language to another, suggests that Dante now claims full ownership of two related notions: first, that no linguistic artifact is technically untranslatable, not even the most difficult and resisting poetic feature in a text; second, that this is the case because of the new dispensation that Christ opened in human history and for human language with Incarnation.

Before looking closely at the *Paradiso* 5 segment, however, we should dwell on one of Dante's most explicit pronouncements on the issue of translation, one that appears to signify the opposite. With the stark declaration he advanced in *Convivio* I that no poetic text may or should be translated, a point supported by a careful literary-historical sampling of classical and biblical examples of translation attempts gone awry, Dante took a clear position. Engaging in an apparent paradox, I am about to reason against the grain of what Dante says explicitly in a metapoetic statement, to clarify what he may have meant indirectly in the block of poetic texts just surveyed. As I hope to show, Dante is hedging his bets in *Convivio* and, just as importantly, he explicitly revises his position when he allusively redeploys the same charged technical language to make the opposite points in *Paradiso*. In the reading I propose, in other words, the passage from the first book of *Convivio* that indicts translation as a costly activity is to be taken as both partial and provisional. In it, Dante says less than he is often credited for, and his pronouncements are not his ultimate stance on the issue, since they are eventually provided with a direct corrective counterpoint in *Paradiso*.

The text and context from which to start are clear. In the first book of *Convivio*, while discussing the reasons why he did not write his commentary in Latin (or translate his poems into that language), Dante frames his decision within a larger discourse on the drawbacks of translation. Moving a poetic text from one original language to another produces radically negative effects, he states. Based on the idea that translation deprives texts of their sweetness and musicality, Dante makes what appears to be a strong case for untranslatability.[19] Here is the passage in question:

… E però sappia ciascuno che nulla cosa per legame musaico armonizzata si può della sua loquela in altra transmutare sanza rompere tutta sua dolcezza ed armonia.

… E questa è la cagione per che Omero non si mutò di greco in latino, come l'altre scritture che avemo da loro. E questa è la cagione per che i versi del Salterio sono sanza dolcezza di musica e d'armonia: ché essi furono transmutati d'ebreo in greco e di greco in latino, e nella prima transmutazione tutta quella dolcezza venne meno.

… Thus, let it be known to anyone that no composition arranged through the harmony of musaic ties may be transposed from its language into another, without utterly disrupting its sweetness and harmony.

… And this is the reason why Homer was not transposed from Greek to Latin, as other writings we have from them. And this is the reason why the verses of the Psalter are without sweetness of music and harmony: they were transposed from Hebrew to Greek and from Greek to Latin, and in the first transposition all their sweetness disappeared. (*Convivio* I.7.15)

Dante openly declares that no translated poem may retain its original sweetness and harmony. This loss is evident, he continues, in both Homer (who was spared such unpoetic translation and hence is not available to his readers in Latin, unlike Greek prose works) and the poetry of the Bible, the Psalms, which were indeed translated from Hebrew to Greek and from Greek to Latin (and lost all of their poetic quality in the first leg of that journey). The statement sounds "modern" to ears used to perceiving the negative effects of translation as endemic. The loss connected to the movement from the original text to its subsequent and secondary instantiations in other languages is now so widespread that the attendant idiom "lost in translation" is as common as it is uncontested. Today's readers should, however, be wary of that effect: in truth, what Dante appears to say is not just "modern," but all too modern. This may be so, at least when taken at face value and as an absolute statement.

In fact, what Dante declares in this passage may not necessarily contradict the qualified, but certainly marked, optimism that he attains in the *Commedia* about the necessity (as well as the positive effects) of translation. There are at least two reasons. The first is that the point he makes is functional to a specific, specious argument. When Dante isolates the features that are at stake in, and eventually compromised by, the action of translating, he mentions only sweetness (of diction) and musicality (of harmony). These are aspects of poetic texts that he not only appears to treat as purely contingent in the argument, but that he will also quite significantly discount in what is now the final book of the work. On the one hand, that is, Dante proceeds to quote quite liberally from the Psalms in Italian throughout the body of *Convivio*, thus suggesting that loss of sweetness and musicality does not reduce the availability of the biblical text for purposes of intellectual argumentation. Similarly, in the final book of that same work, he declares that in his own current poetry he has moved from singing of love to treating rectitude, and thus he has abandoned "le dolci rime," the sweet rhymes of previous poems, to embrace a poetics of subtlety – a "rima aspra e sottile." Neither the meaning of the translated texts nor the "un-sweet" style he is pursuing now as a poet is affected by the process of translation that he ostensibly indicts at the start of the work.[20]

Secondly, and perhaps more importantly, this pronouncement may well be the most explicit one on the process of translation, what Dante calls "transmutare," but it certainly is not the final statement he makes on the issue. As we have seen from our vertical reading of the Cantos 26, he adopts a quite divergent attitude in the *Commedia*. Notably, in these cantos Dante revisits the issue of translation, returning both to the Homeric question first broached in *Convivio* and to the issue of biblical poetry, by enlisting the key figure of Adam himself to discuss matters of linguistic history. In the *Commedia*, that is, he pointedly resorts to Homer as a monitory example of the dangers intrinsic to a specific kind of "centralizing" *translatio*, rather than as proof of the untranslatability of poetic texts. Similarly, he returns to Adam to point out the essential vernacularity (which is to say, instability and multifariousness) of all human languages, not the sacrality of the original biblical idiom.

Finally, a rather technical supplement of revision may be detected in Dante's eventual take on the matter of translation. In the vocabulary Dante mobilizes to discuss the alleged inadvisability of translation for poetic texts, there is an idiosyncratic term: rather than "translare" (or "translatare"), the common forms used in metaliterary statements about vernacularizations in his day, Dante calls the activity a "trasmutare." This lexical choice has several consequences. This term, which quite often appears in the *Commedia* to indicate transformation, reappears, with the same meaning as it had in *Convivio*, in a pointed passage in *Paradiso*. There, given the context of heightened self-awareness in which it is used, it may be read as the signpost for a subtle and technical palinode.

Just about a decade ago, Antonio Soro published a brilliant essay on *Paradiso* 5, proving for all intents and purposes the presence of a retrograde acrostic in a stretch of five tercets in the middle of the canto.[21] The text in question is the following, and the context is Dante and Beatrice's access into the second material heaven, Mercury:

E se la stella si cambiò e rise,
qual mi fec' io che pur da mia natura
trasmutabile son per tutte guise!
Come 'n peschiera ch'è tranquilla e pura
traggonsi i pesci a ciò che vien di fori
per modo che lo stimin lor pastura,
Sì vid' io ben più di mille splendori
trarsi ver' noi, e in ciascun s'udia:
"Ecco chi crescerà li nostri amori".
E sì come ciascuno a noi venìa,
vedeasi l'ombra piena di letizia
nel folgór chiaro che di lei uscia.
Pensa, lettor, se quel che qui s'inizia
non procedesse, come tu avresti
di più savere angosciosa carizia.

Now, if the star changed and smiled, what became of me who, by my own nature, am ready to transform in any fashion! Just as in a fishpond, calm and clean, fish emerge to meet what comes from the outside, provided they consider it food, so I saw more than a thousand lights draw toward us, and in each one heard: "Here is someone who will increase our love!" As each came closer to us, one could tell the shade was filled with joy thanks to the light that emanated from it. Think, reader, if that which begins here did not proceed, how you would anxiously desire to know more. (*Paradiso* 5.97–111)

Soro's discovery is as convincing as his argument is cogent. The text talks about fish, in a daring simile that describes the nearing movement of the new group of souls – a movement of ascent from the depths of the heaven toward the protagonist that is perfectly reflected in the need for the reader's gaze to move *up* the page to spell out the five letters of the words *Pesce*. Perhaps even more intriguingly, the text also coyly but unequivocally signals the starting point of the acrostic with the word "Pensa" (consider) and emphasizes something that begins but may not progress. Hence, by exclusion, it insists on something that should regress. Lino Pertile has recently returned to the same text and acrostic and explored the Christological aspect of the symbol of the fish, an image that was traditionally associated in Christian culture with an acrostic reading of the five Greek words Ἰησοῦς Χρειστὸς Θεοῦ υἱὸς σωτήρ, that is, Jesus Christ, the Son of God and Saviour, the initials of which spell out the word ΙΧΘΥΣ (Fish).[22] As Pertile notes, the Christological underpinnings of the *Paradiso* 5 passage are crucial, as is the critical dialogue in which Dante engages with Augustinian material that hinges on the same elements. In *De civitate Dei* 18.23, Augustine recounts that he saw a Greek codex containing the *carmina* of the Eritrean Sybil, in a passage where the line headings were arranged so as to spell out the name and attributes of Christ. The initials of these five words, as noted above, spelled out the word for "fish," in which, as Augustine says, "mystice intellegitur Christus" (Christ is mystically understood). With the acrostic marking his entry into the heaven of Mercury, Pertile concludes, in the vernacular of his poem Dante recovers and allusively reproduces a drama of cultural transmission and interpretation that was based on the presence of the same acrostics in a pre-Christian but prophetic text. The Augustinian passage, at least the prose framing the new Latin "version" of the Sybil's prophecy, deserves a more extended quotation here, since several elements in it may be relevant for the subtle intertextual dialogue Dante's Mercurial canto establishes with it. Augustine writes:

23. 1. Eodem tempore nonnulli Sibyllam Erythraeam vaticinatam ferunt. Sibyllas autem Varro prodit plures fuisse, non unam. Haec sane Erythraea Sibylla quaedam de Christo manifesta conscripsit; quod etiam nos prius in latina lingua versibus male latinis et non stantibus legimus per nescio cuius interpretis imperitiam, sicut post cognovimus. Nam vir clarissimus Flaccianus, qui etiam proconsul fuit, homo facillimae facundiae multaeque doctrinae, cum de Christo colloqueremur, graecum nobis codicem protulit, carmina esse dicens Sibyllae Erythraeae, ubi ostendit quodam loco in capitibus versuum ordinem litterarum ita se habentem, ut haec in eo verba legerentur: Ἰησοῦς Χρειστὸς Θεοῦ υἱὸς σωτήρ, quod est latine: Iesus Christus Dei Filius Salvator. Hi autem versus, quorum primae litterae istum sensum, quem diximus, reddunt, sicut eos quidam latinis et stantibus versibus est interpretatus, hoc continent ...

1. Some report that in that time the Sybil from Eritrea prophesied. Varro stipulates that there existed many Sybils, not just one. And this Eritrean Sybil did indeed write several clear assertions about Christ, which I at first read in Latin in verses that were barely Latin and shabby on account of the ineptitude of the translator (whoever that was), as I realized later. This was when the most esteemed Flaccianus, who was also proconsul, a person of the most spontaneous eloquence and deep knowledge, during a conversation about Christ we were having, showed me a Greek codex, saying it was by the Eritrean Sybil, in which he pointed to a specific place where the start of every line was arranged in such an order that the letters spelled out the words: Ἰησοῦς Χρειστὸς Θεοῦ υἱὸς σωτήρ, which means Jesus Christ, Son of God, the Savior.

These lines, whose initial letters as I said produce that meaning, in another translator's linguistically and stylistically adequate rendering, have the following content …

What follows in the text is a twenty-seven-line hexametric poem, rehashing the main elements of Christ's Second Coming, including the presence in the flesh of the judged faithful and heathens, the conflagration of the Earth and celestial bodies, and the final unveiling of all metaphysical truths. Beyond the apocalyptic message contained in the acrostic poem, what is interesting here is Augustine's attention to the translative quality of the exercise. At stake is not only the interlinguistic dimension of the phenomenon but also, more precisely, the attention Augustine pays to the technical difficulties that the new version of the text he offers to his readers has apparently overcome, beginning with a literal one:

In his latinis versibus de graeco utcumque translatis ibi non potuit ille sensus occurrere, qui fit, cum litterae, quae sunt in eorum capitibus, connectuntur, ubi Y littera in graeco posita est, quia non potuerunt latina verba inveniri, quae ab eadem littera inciperent et sententiae convenirent. Hi autem sunt versus tres, quintus et octavus decimus et nonus decimus. Denique si litteras quae sunt in capitibus omnium versuum connectentes horum trium quae scriptae sunt non legamus, sed pro eis Y litteram, tamquam in eisdem locis ipsa sit posita, recordemur, exprimitur in quinque verbis: Iesus Christus Dei Filius Salvator; sed cum graece hoc dicitur, non latine. Et sunt versus viginti et septem, qui numerus quadratum ternarium solidum reddit. Tria enim ter ducta fiunt novem; et ipsa novem si ter ducantur, ut ex lato in altum figura consurgat, ad viginti septem perveniunt. Horum autem graecorum quinque verborum, quae sunt Ἰησοῦς Χρειστὸς Θεοῦ υἱὸς σωτήρ, quod est latine: Iesus Christus Dei Filius Salvator, si primas litteras iungas, erit ἰχθύς, id est piscis, in quo nomine mystice intellegitur Christus, eo quod in huius mortalitatis abysso velut in aquarum profunditate vivus, hoc est sine peccato, esse potuerit.

In these Latin lines, which have been translated in some way from Greek, it was not possible to obtain the meaning that the incipit letters produce when connected, in the cases in which the Greek letter Y was used, since it was impossible to find Latin words beginning with that letter that could fit the meaning. The lines in question are three: the fifth, eighteenth, and nineteenth. In conclusion, if, when reading the incipit letters of the poem, we do not read the letters which now appear in the aforementioned lines, but substitute the letter Y, as if it were used there, we obtain five words that mean something: *Jesus Christ, Son of God, the Savior*, but in Greek not in Latin. The text comprises twenty-seven lines, which gives us a three-dimensional triangle. Three by three yields nine, and when we multiply nine by three (which is the equivalent of raising each side into the third dimension), we reach twenty-seven. The five Greek words we obtain are Ἰησοῦς Χρειστὸς Θεοῦ υἱὸς σωτήρ, which in Latin is *Jesus Christ, Son of God, the Savior*. If you connect the initials of each, you obtain ἰχθύς, which is to say, "fish." That term may be mystically interpreted as Christ, insofar as he could remain alive (that is, without sin) in the abyss of mortality as if in the depths of water.

In addition to being concerned with matters of prophecy, and thus with the dynamics of obscure foreshadowing and clear fulfilment typical of the Christian understanding of history, the passage is interested in matters of poetics as well as of translation. For the specific quality of the vehicle that the Sybil adopts to convey her messianic message – that is, poetry – Augustine's analysis is appropriately grammatical, moving between linguistic and stylistic considerations. Furthermore, because of the specific interlinguistic nature of the textual negotiations involved in the successive revelation of the layered meaning (a literal acrostic that contains a symbolic sub-acrostic), Augustine's attention is focused on questions of version and interpretation. He begins by keenly noticing the impossibility for the Greek original text to signify anything (that is, not only to produce meaning but also to convey it) because of its botched translation. That the difficulty was a product of the quality of the version, not of the nature of the exercise itself, is demonstrated by the immediately following "new" and "better" version that the text produces. The first version was linguistically quasi-illegible and poetically incoherent because its translation amounted to the transfer of an overwrought and overcharged meaning from one language into the next. While the first version of the Sybil's poetic prophecy fails, the second one, which apparently handled all technical difficulties better, is able to carry over the meaning of the original. To be sure, while an alphabetic adjustment is needed in the process (and is promptly acknowledged), the embedding of the symbolic message into the exact poetic measure of the new version (precisely twenty-seven lines, a signpost for divine numerology) guarantees that the new version succeeds in responding not simply to the linguistic challenge of the original but also to its intrinsically poetic nature. This optimistic attitude on the part of Augustine did not, I believe, go unnoticed by Dante.

Building upon Soro's and Pertile's arguments, and mobilizing the significance of Augustine's passage in full, I propose a rereading of Dante's allusive acrostics centred on the tercet appearing at the beginning of our excerpt. This tercet has a double nature. It is at once the first we encounter while reading the text for the first time *and* the one we reach last when we read up the page to the final letter of the acrostic. Two elements are worth noting: what Dante states about the effects that his arrival in the heaven of Mercury triggered in the planet, and how he says it. His use of the verb "trasmutare" points to the term's technical meaning, the same one it had in the metapoetic *Convivio* section quoted above:

E se la stella si cambiò e rise,
qual mi fec' io che pur da mia natura
trasmutabile son per tutte guise!

The recurrence of this specific verb intimates the translative quality of the refined literary game that Dante is playing with his own past textual self and his readers. As he toys with poetry's graphic ability to form acrostics and evokes the original Greek acrostic that spelled out the same word that his own acrostic now spells out, translated into Italian, Dante reverses his position both on translatability and on the peculiar translative fragility he had envisioned for poetry. According to the author of the *Commedia*, even the most allusive and elusive of texts may be made to undergo transmutation across languages, as proven by his successful attempt to move the Christological Greek acrostic – lifting it from the exemplar of the Sibylline poetic books – into his own vernacular poem.

At this point, two final corollaries may be advanced. First, Dante relies here (as elsewhere) on the reader's collaboration for his poetry to achieve its intended meaning and, beyond that, its full semiotic potential. For the word *Pesce* to emerge literally from the text, readers need to become active producers of meaning, going against the flow of the narrative and reading against the grain of the text. They need, that is, to become active interpreters, so that the poetry may produce meaning. Not coincidentally, the acrostic appears in an episode that takes place in the heaven of Mercury. The acrostic starts with the change, a felicitous one, that affects the star when the smiling Beatrice enters it. But Mercury is not only, as we know from what Dante writes about it in *Convivio* and partly restates here, the smallest and most easily influenced planet. Mercury is also profoundly associated with hermeneutics. A further Augustinian passage may help to succinctly gauge the value of this association, which is widespread in Dante's culture:

> Nam ideo Mercurius quasi medius currens dicitur appellatus, quod sermo currat inter homines medius; ideo Graece Hermes, quod sermo vel interpretatio, quae ad sermonem utique pertinet, ἑρμηνεία dicitur.

> For indeed Mercury is called *Mercurius*, insofar as it is said to run between, as speech runs and mediates between people. Thus, in Greek it is called Hermes, since *hermeneia* is speech or, better, interpretation – a part of speech. (*De civitate Dei* 7.14)

It is certainly true, as Pertile argues while discussing the relevance of the intertext for *Paradiso* 5, that the heaven of Mercury is the theatre for Dante's invention of hidden and subtle things in his poetry ("l'espressione ermetica," as he puts it).[23] The connection between Mercury and language, however, also relies on the corresponding mechanism involved in communication: hermeneutics, which is the active involvement of the addressee in decoding meaning. Inversely linked to the act of expression, interpretation is an equally Mercurial art. Once again, just as crucially, what Dante proposes for his readers in the Christological acrostic is a process that takes place at the intersection of several languages in which translation and interpretation go hand in hand: the Sibylline original Greek, Augustine's

Latin, and Dante's own vernacular. In this multilingual sphere, however, all individual idioms are conceived not as impermeable systems, containing secret and inscrutable messages that a translation would elide. Rather, they are, in their iridescent surfaces, and in the poetic prowess of their composer-translators, an ever-changing vehicle of truth.

The second corollary is just as important. Dante here states something about himself (character and poet) that has a metapoetic consequence. When he declares that he is "trasmutabile ... per tutte guise," the protean openness to endless change is of course predicated, first and foremost, on the character. As such, in an *a fortiori* rhetorical move, the tercet speaks to the effects of the ascent into the changeable heaven of Mercury in terms of a sympathetic moment of mutability. But the mobility intrinsic to the character also extends to the author. In using the present tense in the passage, the author of the text takes upon himself the burden of articulating his full availability to, and considerate trust in the positive effects of, the mutability that he now confidently associates with hermeneutical translation. After all, and as we have just observed, without that faith in the potentially infinite and always recurring play of language, his call to the reader to discover the sign of Incarnation at the precise crossroads of two languages – the ancient Greek and his modern vernacular – would only be a refined but utterly sterile rhetorical game written out in the dead letter of his text. The "star" of Mercury, the protagonist of the action, and the author of the poem are all, by their very nature, changeable; and their mutability is no sign of imperfection or decay.

Conclusion

Beginning as a philological inquiry into Dante's diverging discussion of the seemingly speaking birds that appear in two closely related contexts in *Convivio* and *De vulgari eloquentia*, this chapter has now come to a diffuse nexus of sources and analogues. This shift from intertextual to interdiscursive considerations is more the result of the necessary linear progression of the argument developed here than a feature of the material. None of the philological observations I have made should be read without considering the cultural context in which these texts were intended to circulate and with which they resonate. Correspondingly, none of the general points I have advanced about cultural paradigms should be removed from the specific space they occupy in Dante's texts. If the inverse matrix of presence and absence of the parrot from two strictly related argumentative contexts in Dante has any meaning, it is so because of cultural reasons. Dante's mention of the parrot as a nonviable example of a speaking animal – an animal, that is, only seemingly capable of producing linguistic utterances – in one text, and his omission of the same from the other are not the product of contingent factors, but a meaningful choice because of the larger cultural associations explored along with it. Dante's self-translating avoidance behaviour has become "interpretable" because it is coherent with a set of cultural assumptions about the nature and significance of that bird developed outside Dante's text, with no apparent textual interconnection. The disappearance of the parrot, as Dante moves the same reasoning from a vernacular to a Latin text and from *Convivio* to *De vulgari*, is coherent with some of the elements that constitute the trope of the Edenic garden as a locus for imagining, practising, and reflecting upon translation. These assumptions often seem to escape modern readers. Yet, I argue, they were present in the mind of his contemporaries. The specific set of cultural associations that makes the mentioning of the parrot in the specific context of Dante's *De vulgari* somewhat unseemly has something to do, in sum, with the trope of Eden.

Conversely, the material surveyed in this chapter has also revealed the pertinence of Dante's diffracted moments of reflection on language and translation to the general argument of the book. A vertical survey of the closing sections in the Cantos 26 revealed their shared concern with geographical multilingualism and the historical mutability of language. This observation would be of limited relevance for this book were it not for the relationship that each of Dante's soundings into the potentialities of translation establishes with the trope of Eden. Eden is a multiform presence in these connected cantos: it is featured as the always-receding horizon of Ulysses' last voyage in *Inferno* 26, as the space awaiting the protagonist just beyond the threshold of the last ledge of *Purgatorio*, where he dialogues with the Provençal-speaking Arnaut Daniel, and as the backdrop of both the first sin and the first act of vernacular communication in the early vicissitudes of human history, as recalled by Adam at the end of the corresponding canto of *Paradiso*. These episodes, distant as they are across the wide span of the *Commedia*, never take readers far from the Garden of Eden.

Connecting these episodes vertically makes the field of cultural tensions through which Dante moved also become more visible as the framework for his reflection on vertical (inter-age) and horizontal (inter-vernacular, but also inter-generational) translation. In working across diverging texts and insisting on philological and hermeneutic details, this chapter suggests that the trope of translation included for Dante, as did for his predecessors, incarnational associations. Once today's readers realize that, in his most subtle and most hidden acrostic in the poem, the technical language related to the act of translation controlled the protagonist's experience in the heaven of Mercury, Dante's change of mind from the pre-comedic works to the poem becomes both apparent and understandable. Also emerging along with Dante's radical change of perspective are its cultural underpinnings; in particular, the recovered and reactivated nexus between acts of interpretive translation and the incarnational promise contained in the garden. These are all elements in a complex and evolving system of thought that Dante is both receiving from his culture and in turn helping to shape. They are the root of the same tensions that we have detected at the core of earlier vernacular fictional representations of Eden and that we will encounter again, in the ambivalent treatment of the same trope in Boccaccio's *Decameron*.

Chapter Three

Making Paradise on Earth: The Second Garden of Boccaccio's *Decameron*

> Et sachiez que je cuidai estre
> Por voir em paradis terrestre:
> Tant estoit li leus delitables,
> Qu'i sembloit estre esperitables:
> Car, si com lors m'ert avis,
> Il ne fet en nul paradis
> Si bon estre com il fessoit
> el vergier, qui tant me plesoit.
>
> *Roman de la Rose*, ll. 633–40

In this chapter, my argument will move from an analysis of a specific element in the *cornice* of the *Decameron* to the two stories that bookend it. The frame element under scrutiny is the specific space into which the *brigata* moves at the start of Day 3 and that it continues to use as a backdrop for the storytelling until the foray into the Valley of Women in Day 7. Attesting both to the generous bounty inherent in the natural world and the achievements of human work, this indulgently described place is explicitly treated as a hypothetical counterpart to the earthly paradise. As the narrators themselves note, the second garden of the *cornice* is a surrogate of (or a limit case, tending to) the garden of delights of the biblical narrative. In this sense, the pertinence of the text to the general thrust of the book needs little elaboration. There is, however, a further dimension of this connection that I propose exploring here. The literary garden that the text of the *Decameron* constructs is not only biblical, but also possesses a marked translative quality. The natural and artistic space visited by the *brigata* owes its general architecture (shape, waterworks, planting patterns, and fauna) to a specific ancient model along with a vernacular one: the clearly evoked garden of the *Roman de la Rose* and the more recondite classical garden of Pliny's epistolary fiction. Both texts, independently and through one another, are quite literally translated into Boccaccio's new Italian vernacular literary garden.

The second section of this chapter explores a related element in the body of Boccaccio's collection of *novelle*: the correlation of the *cornice* with the two liminal stories that mark the boundaries of this block of narrative. This connection may appear more elusive, but it runs similarly deep and is similarly meaningful. The tales Boccaccio uses to frame the four days of Edenic storytelling in the second garden are deeply involved in negotiating the value and uses of human language, each exploring an opposite pole in the range of possible linguistic perversions: strategic mutism and quick-witted oratorial proliferation. Located precisely at the opposite end of this narrative stretch, Frate Cipolla, the protagonist of 6.10, and Masetto, the main character of 3.10, emblematize two coordinated perversions of the linguistic mandate that Christianity associated with the original Edenic setting of humankind's *primiloquium*. While doing so, they also each establish a typological relationship with the prototype of the garden that is topographically evoked in the stories and frames their telling. Both these relationships point to the ethical dangers entailed in approaching Eden as a reachable goal while forgetting that such an act is damningly regressive because it is anti-incarnational by nature.

It is no coincidence, I argue, that the tales of Masetto and Cipolla are the first and last to be told in the second garden and contain clear references to both the Edenic setting and the two birds, the magpie and the parrot, that we have already seen associated with it. Placed on the margins of this carefully localized narrative sequence, they reactivate and retrospectively confirm the connection between the space of the garden and the practices of translation at the core of this book. In other words, they rehash the correlation of the garden-visit topos with the topic of inter-language and inter-age translation. In connecting so deeply with the linguistic aspects of the Eden trope, they also act as interactive glosses, illuminating the *brigata*'s first careful assessment of the new setting for the activity of storytelling as an allusive Edenic space. They also give the reader a heightened awareness of the dangerously regressive quality that making Eden on earth may entail. As we are about to see, in the case of Masetto, the ethical danger signalled in the texts consists in what Boccaccio's culture would have constructed as a typological regression into a carnal understanding of Eden. Although, in the novella's plot, Masetto is a young man replacing an old one, and hence would have a wide set of positive typological associations on his side, his chosen means of gaining access to the enclosed garden of the nuns with whom he will eventually have unsanctioned sex are marked negatively in the same typological imagination. His assumed mutism, which amounts to a renunciation of language, and the sexual exertion he chooses to take upon himself, presented in the text on par with physical labour, converge in coding him as an unredeemed and parodic replica of Adam, one who has paradoxically renounced the task of making and using language and who adheres, in his reading of the biblical pre-lapsarian mandate to "tend the garden," to the most carnal and literal interpretation possible. In the case of Frate Cipolla, the ethical danger evoked in Boccaccio's story consists in a similar regressive attitude projected on the protagonist, paired, this time, not with strategic silence but with a profluvium of words. In his improvised speech, the friar invents a fanciful journey in search of blessed relics, one that allegedly takes him first to the Orient, the traditional location of earthly paradise in biblical and medieval cartographic imagination, and then to Jerusalem, a city that his sermon figurally associates not so much with the inception of a new religion, Christianity, as with the frustrated attempt, favoured by the apostatic Roman emperor Julian, to rebuild the Temple of the city, the central place of cult of a religion that the text projects as old. Typological resonances control and enrich several elements in the stories. Just as, in Masetto's overabundant carnal labour in the convent's garden, the text sees the "cuckolding of Christ" via the intercourse with his mystical brides, so too, in Frate Cipolla's divagations, Christ's incarnation, the Word becoming flesh, is evoked only to be parodically reformulated and vernacularized. Similarly, just as in Masetto's becoming a new Adam readers could see his becoming a perverse version of the resurrected Christ, in Frate Cipolla's promised miracle of the fire-protecting crosses they could see the uncanny evocation of the crosses which, according to widely circulating medieval exempla, marked the garments of the Jews who had taken part in attempting to restore the Temple in Jerusalem.[1]

Seen in this light, both the stories told at the beginning of Day 3 and at the end of Day 6, as well as the narrative frame in which their telling is imaginatively staged, respond to the Eden trope and contribute to articulating it one more time in the tradition. For Boccaccio, as for his predecessors, Eden is not simply a paradigmatic model for the interaction of the original benignity of nature and the value of human work, but also a setting for a specifically linguistic drama and the symbolic place to stage a discourse on language. The linguistic dimension of the earthly paradise also reverberates, in sum, with its biblical and patristic connotations, in the secular *Decameron*.

1. The Intertextual Garden of the *Decameron*

Let us begin with the garden, a literary garden if there ever was one. In the carefully orchestrated topography of the *Decameron*, Boccaccio gives an expectedly rhetorical treatment to several locations in the narrative. Having begun with a happenstance meeting in a church in Florence and moved, first, to a nearby villa on the same day, the small and well-organized troupe of storytellers – whose verbal and gestural interactions make up the frame tale – reach a second villa on their third day of communal living. The garden pertaining to this new dwelling place will be the backdrop of all upcoming activities, save the intermezzo of the Valley of Women, where the *brigata* will tell their stories in Day 7, and the rather anodyne oak wood to which they pay a quick visit on Day 9, only to return to the villa for the last two days of activities.[2] Boccaccio matches the narrative predominance of the second natural and cultivated space with rhetorical emphasis, producing one of the most celebrated and topical description of gardens in medieval vernacular prose. A detailed consideration of his account will detain us for a little while, since its building blocks belong to a long intertextual and interlinguistic tradition that also makes Boccaccio's garden a translative cultural space.

Boccaccio's description of the garden in the second *Decameron* villa proceeds through several stages in an orderly fashion. As I anticipated in the first chapter of this book, I will present it in tandem with the description of the garden in Guillaume's section of the *Roman de la Rose*. I start from the first fundamental feature that connects them: the garden is a specific enclosure, which is at the same time round and square. The peculiar but by now familiar shape of Boccaccio's garden is constructed by the interference of two independent architectural and topographic notations: roundness and linearity. The first general impression is of the former:

Appresso la qual cosa, **fattosi aprire un giardino** che di costa era al palagio, in quello, **che tutto era da torno murato**, se n'entrarono. (*Decameron* 3.Intro.5)

Quant j'oi un poi avant alé,
Si vi un vergier grant et lé,
Tout clos de haut mur bataillié,
Portret dehors et entaillié
A maintes riches escritures…
Rose 129–33

After that, they ordered that a garden, which was alongside the palace and was walled all around, be opened, and they entered it.[3]

After I had proceeded a while, I saw a garden, beautiful and spacious, walled all around and crenellated, which had images outside and several beautiful, sculpted inscriptions.[4]

The circularity suggested in the term "tutto … da torno" (all around, as seen from the outside), a note which is immediately struck again in the phrase "dintorno da sé" (all around, seen from the inside), is also balanced by a topographical squaring, with the straight lines of the paths traversing the demarcated space. Once again, the *Rose* provides readers with a paradigmatic antecedent.

Esso avea **dintorno da sé** e **per lo mezzo in assai parti vie ampissime, tutte diritte come strale** e coperte di pergolati di viti, le quali facevano gran vista di dovere quello anno assai uve fare, e tutte allora fiorite sì grande odore per lo giardin rendevano. (6)

Li vergier par compasseüre
Fu toz de droite quarreüre,
S'ot autant de lonc con de large.
Rose 1321–3

The garden had several wide paths, stretching all around and throughout it. They were straight as arrows and covered with pergolas of vines, which looked as if they were going to yield a large vintage that year. They bore many flowers which spread their intense fragrance through the garden.

The green space all around was in a perfect square, being exactly as long as it was wide.

In chapter 1, I discussed the peculiar geometry of the matching space in the *Roman de la Rose*, and there should be no need to rehash the point here. Suffice it to say that, discreetly as ever, Boccaccio's text maps this new garden onto the expected coordinates of the internally squared circle, the same one we have observed as a recurring Edenic marker. Boccaccio's topical insistence on the all-encompassing collection of spices and seeds present in this space is also coherent with the image of the garden as a micro-orb that acts a concentrated specimen of vegetative variety within the larger *sectus orbis*:

[Odore] che, **mescolato insieme con quello di molte altre cose che per lo giardino olivano, pareva loro essere tra tutta la spezieria che mai nacque in Oriente**. Le latora delle quali vie tutte di rosa' bianchi e vermigli e di gelsomini erano quasi chiuse: **per le quali cose, non che la mattina, ma qualora il sole era più alto, sotto odorifera e dilettevole ombra, senza esser tocco da quello, vi si poteva per tutto andare. Quante e quali e come ordinate poste fossero le piante che erano in quel luogo, lungo sarebbe a raccontare; ma niuna n'è laudevole la quale il nostro aere patisca, di che quivi non sia abondevolemente.** (6–7)

Il ot ou vergier mainte bone espice,
…
Et mainte espice delitable,
Que bon mangier fet aprés table. (*Rose* 1337–44)
Mes li rain furent lonc et haut,
Et por le leu garder de chaut,
Furent si espés par deseure,
Que li solaus a nes une eure
Ne puet a la terre descendre,
Ne fere mal a l'erbe tendre. (1367–72)
Qu'iroie je ci acontant?
De divers arbres i ot tant,
Que mout en seroie encombrez,
Ainz que jes eüsse nombrez; (1359–62)
Nul arbre n'i a, qui fruit charge,
Se n'est aucuns arbres hideus,
Dont il n'i ait **ou trois ou deus**
Ou vergier, **ou plus**, se devient. (1324–7)

A fragrance which, mixed with that of many other sweet-smelling things in the garden, made them think they were in the presence of all spices that ever grew in the East. The sides of those paths were almost enclosed by white and red rose bushes as well as by jasmines. One could thus walk everywhere in a fragrant and pleasant shade without being touched by the sun – not just in the morning, but also when it was at its height. It would take long to tell how many, and which ones, and how arranged were the plants in that place. Suffice it to say that all the praiseworthy species which grow in our climate were present, and in abundance.

In the garden, there were many good spices. … And many pleasant spices, which are good to have at the end of a meal. The branches were long and high, and woven densely so as to guard the place from heat: the sun could never reach the ground – at any time of day – and harm the tender grass. What should I add to this? There are so many trees that one would be at pains to try and count them. There are no fruit-bearing trees (except for a few ugly ones) of which there are not three or two or eventually more in the garden.

A similarly tame and beneficial fauna corresponds to the luscious and valuable flora collected in the garden, contributing to the peaceful and harmonious atmosphere of the place. The text moves into this new area via a narrative ploy, accounting for the delayed introduction of the new feature through the progressive focalization of the *brigata*:

Andando adunque contentissimi dintorno per quello, faccendosi di varii rami d'albori ghirlande bellissime, tuttavia udendo **forse venti maniere** di canti d'uccelli quasi a pruova l'un dell'altro cantare, s'accorsero d'una dilettevol bellezza, della quale, dall'altre soprappresi, non s'erano ancora accorti: ché essi videro **il giardin pieno forse di cento varietà di belli animali, e l'uno all'altro mostrandolo, d'una parte uscir conigli, d'altra parte correr lepri, e dove giacer cavriuoli e in alcuna cerbiatti giovani andar pascendo e, oltre a questi, altre piú maniere di non nocivi animali, ciascuno a suo diletto, quasi dimestichi, andarsi a sollazzo**: le quali cose, oltre agli altri piaceri, un vie maggior piacere aggiunsero.

El vergier ot dains et chevriaus,
Si ot grant planté d'escuriaus,
Qui par ces arbres gravissoient;
Conins i avoit qui issoient
Toute jor hors de lor tanieres,
Em plus de quarante menieres
Aloient entr'aus tornoiant
Sor l'erbe fresche verdoiant.
Rose 1373–80

They thus joyfully wandered around the garden, making beautiful garlands with branches of different trees, while all along hearing perhaps twenty different kinds of bird call, the birds singing as if engaged in mutual contest. At one point they became aware of a further pleasant quality that, while enthralled by the others, they had not yet noticed: they saw the garden teeming with perhaps a hundred kinds of beautiful animals. They began pointing them out to each other: here appeared some rabbits, there dashed forth some hares; in another place rested some roe deer and in yet another grazed young fawns. In addition to these, there were many other kinds of pleasant animals, all roaming around in sport, as if they ware tame. These features, together with the other delights, engendered in them an even greater pleasure.

In the garden there were fallow and roe deer, and a great number of squirrels climbing the trees; there were rabbits coming out of their warrens, and they engaged in more than forty kinds of sport on the fresh green grass.

In addition to their intertextually comparable flora and fauna, Boccaccio's and Guillaume's gardens also have quite similar hydraulic features, a detail that is worth mentioning at least in passing. Both spaces have a fountain at their centre that supports an elaborate irrigation system, charged with ensuring the growth of the garden's vegetation. If the review of these common structural imaginary and practical literary features has one merit, it is that it points to the translative quality of Boccaccio's operation. To be sure, many of the features I have highlighted as corresponding across the Italian and Old French texts are "traditional"; that is, they were available to Boccaccio's readers as points of reference in literary works that were both culturally closer and textually more local than the *Rose*. One may find examples of this garden variety in the Italian vernacular, which may be flagged as contextual antecedents for Boccaccio. Ranging from Folgore da San Gimignano's sonnet on the month of June to the garden setting for the "Questioni d'amore" in Boccaccio's own *Filocolo* 4.7 or Pomena's garden in his *Comedia de le Ninfe* 26, the topos of the perfect garden does not necessarily entail the crossing of linguistic boundaries. Nonetheless, the density of lexical connections, the clusters of thematic and verbal resonances, the presence of differential elements such as the choice of spices, the perhaps merely accidentally divergent numberings in the catalogue of peaceful animals (forty kinds of "sport" in the *Rose*, twenty kinds of "bird call" in the *Decameron*), and the rhetorical insistence on a summative *praeteritio* in enumeration, all have a cumulative effect in singling out the Old French garden as the target of a specific allusion for the *Decameron*.

If one accepts the connection of Boccaccio's and Guillaume's gardens as the predominant (if not the only) one, the redeployment of the *Roman de la Rose* in the *Decameron* may be configured as an act of translation. Of course, since it involves the transfer of recognizable narrative material across two "modern" languages, we might call it a horizontal translation, though Boccaccio's culture might have had a keen perception of the chronological distance between the *Rose* and the new text. After all, as an attentive reader and editor of Dante's texts, Boccaccio was aware of the gap between the inception-time of vernacular literatures that Dante had registered in the *Vita nuova* and in *De vulgari eloquentia*.[5] At the same time, Dante's historical perspective, as articulated in several sections of the Latin treatise, was balanced by a radical synchronic assessment of the literary canon for each vernacular, as is the case in the syncrisis he outlined in *De vulgari eloquentia* I.10.2, where each literature claims control (the *oïl* specifically in the present) of a definite literary genre – and the French are confined to the use of prose: "quicquid ... ad vulgare prosaicum, suum est."

It is challenging to establish the value of Boccaccio's "translative" operation from the *langue d'oïl* to the Italian vernacular. On the one hand, his "translation" of the *Roman de la Rose* may be framed as a confirmative response to Dante's non-deferential attitude toward the French narrative-poetic tradition. Dante systematically marginalized the French element, not only in his theoretical account of the reasons for excellence that each of the three vernacular tongues, the three "mothers" of Latin, may invoke, but also in the *Commedia*, a poem that never mentions the *Rose* outright, even in places where its presence is clearly recognizable. On the other hand, Boccaccio's dependance on the *Rose* as an identifiable cultural paradigm aligns well with the development of a writer who took his first steps in the French and Italian environment of the Anjou court in Naples, and certainly had access to its library. Perhaps a choice between the two options is not necessary, especially because Boccaccio's text not only translates one vernacular antecedent, thus engaging in what we may consider a horizontal or short-range vertical translation, but also probably a classical, Latin one.

The description of the second garden in the *Decameron* is, in fact, reminiscent of another celebrated and doubly foreign antecedent: the account of one of his villa properties that Pliny the Younger, at the turn of the first century CE, drafted for his friend Domitius Apollinaris and included in his epistolary collection.[6] In this letter, Pliny added several moments of garden description that may have specific parallels in the *Decameron*. A word of cultural caveat, together with one of philological reassurance, is in order here. Pliny's *Epistles* are not an obvious antecedent for Boccaccio. In general, Italian Trecento authors seem to have been more familiar with the corpus of writings belonging to Pliny the Elder, in essence his *Naturalis Historia*, than with his nephew's epistolary collection. They even laboured under the prosopographical illusion that there was only one Pliny. It is only thanks to the intervention of a particularly informed witness, a librarian at the Verona library (a centre of study specifically well suited to preserve exact biographical details for some among her "famous sons"), that the question *de duobus Pliniis* was first addressed and resolved. All this being said, however, some manuscripts preserving a partial and limitedly rearranged collection of the younger Pliny's letters were available in the time and place of the *Decameron*'s composition and first circulation, and some within reasonable philological reach of Boccaccio and his immediate educated Florentine audience. A specific codex, the Laurenziano San Marco 284, preserves Pliny's text in a perhaps significant codicological arrangement, namely as the last item in a collection containing one hundred letters. Below I cite relevant portions of that text, as they appear in that manuscript, flagging the points of potential intertextual connection with Boccaccio's own prose.

When one pays attention to the younger Pliny's writing, several potential points of contact with Boccaccio's text readily emerge. One may start from a general geographical consideration: Pliny's villa is in Tuscany, as of course are all the narrative spaces of Boccaccio's frame narrative. Just as importantly, Pliny's exercise in epistolary ekphrasis shares structural and lexical elements with the *Decameron*. As per consuetudinary rhetorical norms, both in Pliny's epistle and in the Introduction to Day 3, the text devotes its opening to a general *descriptio locis*, which Pliny elegantly situates within the expected frame of a *Gebrauchsbrief*, offering the addressee's affectionate concern for his health as an excuse for his long description of the villa:

Caius Plinius [Domitio] Apollinari Suo Salutem. 1 Amavi curam et sollicitudinem tuam, quod cum audisses <maiestate> [me aestate] tuscos meos petiturum, ne facerem suasisti, dum putas insalubres. 2 Est sane gravis et pestilens ora tuscorum, que

per litus extenditur; sed hi procul a maris recesserunt, quin etiam appennino saluber-
rimo montium subiacent ... 7 Regionis forma pulcherrima. **Imaginare amphithe-
atrum aliquod immensum, et quale sola rerum natura possit effingere. Lata et
diffusa planities montibus cingitur**, montes summa sui parte <progenera> [procera]
nemora et antiqua habent ... 8. Inde c<a>eduae silvae cum ipso monte descendunt.
Has inter pingues terrenique colles ... 9. Sub his per latus omne vinee porriguntur
unaque facie **longe lateque** contextunt ... 11 **Prata florida et gemmea trifolium
aliasque herbas teneras semper et molles et quasi novas alunt**. Cuncta enim per-
hennibus rivis nutriuntur; [sed] ibi aque plurimum, palus nulla, quia devexa terra,
quidquid liquoris accepit nec absorbuit, effundit in tyberim. (Laurenziano, San
Marco 284, ff. 75v–77r)

Dear Apollinaris, I really appreciated the anxiety and concern you showed when, having heard I was going to visit my Tuscan estate in the summer, you endeavoured to
dissuade me, since you consider that region unhealthy. The air is certainly pestilential,
in that part of Tuscany which stretches along the coast. But my property is set back
from the shore, located at the feet of the Apennines, most wholesome mountains ...
The general form of the region is astounding. Imagine an immense amphitheatre, one
that only nature could create. A wide and spacious plain is surrounded by mountains,
whose peaks are occupied by tall and ancient forests ... Following the downward
slopes one finds lower, coppiced woods, and in between them hills of fertile land ...
Beneath them stretch vineyards on every side, which impress on the landscape a sense
of uniformity far and wide ... Luscious and fertile meadows produce trifolium and
other kinds of forage, always tender, moist, and as if ever fresh. They are all nourished
by steady streams, but even though waters are abundant here, there is no swamp: the
sloping ground pours into the Tiber all moisture that it receives but cannot absorb.

As readers of the *Decameron* will be able to appreciate, while not directly pertinent
for the Introduction to Day 3, Pliny's rhetorically copious account of the larger
topographical coordinates of his villa anticipates those of the Valle delle Donne on
which Day 6 concludes. Boccaccio's description of this temporary narration space
hinges, like Pliny's, on the conceit-like topos of Nature imitating Art imitating
Nature. Most importantly, Boccaccio and Pliny share the peculiar metaphor of the
amphitheatre and the insistence on the anxious correlation of their spaces with the
technical/natural divide:

Secondo che alcuna di loro poi mi ridisse, il piano, che nella valle era, cosí era ritondo
come se a sesta fosse stato fatto, quantunque artificio della natura e non manual
paresse ... Le piagge delle quali montagnette cosí digradando giuso verso il pian dis-
cendevano, come ne' teatri veggiamo dalla lor sommità i gradi infino all'infimo venire
successivamente ordinati, sempre ristrignendo il cerchio loro ... Il piano appresso,
senza aver piú entrate che quella donde le donne venute v'erano, era pieno d'abeti, di

cipressi, d'allori e d'alcun pini sí ben composti e sí bene ordinati, come se qualunque è di ciò il migliore artefice gli avesse piantati: e fra essi poco sole o niente, allora che egli era alto, entrava infino al suolo, il quale era tutto un prato d'erba minutissima e piena di fiori porporini e d'altri. (*Dec.* 6.concl.20–4)

As one of them told me afterwards, the valley's plain was as perfectly round as if it had been made with a compass, although it seemed the artificial product of nature and not of manual work ... The plots of these hills gradually descended toward the plain in always narrower circles, in the same way we see in the progressive order of steps in the theatres ... The plain, which had no access beyond that through which the women had entered, was rich in fir, cypress, laurel, and pine trees, shaped and organized so well, as if they had been planted by the best possible practitioner of the art. Very little or no sun could penetrate between these trees, even at the highest point of its course, and reach the ground, which was a meadow of the thinnest grass, all filled with flowers, red and of other hues.

Boccaccio's and Pliny's spaces have more in common than the general lay of the land, however. Architectural and landscaping details also correspond across the texts. Pliny's description of the garden and grounds at his villa runs as follows:

14 Villa in colle imo sita prospicit quasi ex summo: ita leviter et sensim clivo fallente consurgit, ut cum ascendere te non putes, sentias ascendisse. [**Dec. 3.intro.3**] ... 17 Ambit hunc ambulatio pressis varieque tunsis viridibus inclusa; ab his gestatio in modum circi, quae buxum multiformem humilesque et retentas manu arbusculas circumit. [**Dec. 3.intro.6**] Omnia macheria muniuntur [**Dec. 3.intro.5**]: hanc gradata buxus operit et subtrahit. 18 Pratum inde non minus natura quam superiore illa arte visendum [**Dec. 3.intro.8–9**]; campi deinde porro multaque alia prata et arbusta.

The villa is placed at the bottom of the hill but has a view as if it were on the top. The slope rises so gently and smoothly that you would not realize you are climbing until you had climbed it ... All around stretches a path, closed by dense and variously shaped greenery. From there a trail stretches, shaped like a round chariot track, which encircles a varied array of topiary and low, artificially curved trees. The whole space is surrounded by a wall, which is hidden by carefully scaled hedges of boxwood. Then there is a lawn, as naturally remarkable as the previous spaces are for their art. Beyond are the fields and meadows and shrubs.

32 Hanc dispositionem amoenitatemque tectorum longe longeque precedit hippodromus. Medius patescit statimque intrantium oculis totus offertur, platanis circumitur; ille edera vestiuntur utque summae suis ita ime alienis frondibus virent. Edera trunculum et ramos pererrat vicinasque platanos transitu suo copulat. Has buxus interiacet; exteriores buxos circumvenit laurus, umbraeque platanorum suam confert. 33

Rectus hic hippodromi limes in extrema parte hemicyclio frangitur mutatque faciem: cupressis ambitur et tegitur, densiore umbra opacior nigriorque. [***Dec. 3.intro.6***]

The hippodrome is far more beautiful than the pleasant arrangement of the buildings. It is wide open in its middle section, and thus visible in its entirety to those who enter it. It is surrounded by plane trees, which are covered by ivies so that they bear luscious foliage, both their own, on the top, and, in the lower parts, a borrowed one. The vines move along the trunks and branches, thus interconnecting the neighbouring plane trees. Boxwood plants are placed between the trees, and on the outside laurels surround the boxwood, contributing their shade to that of the plane trees. The long rectilinear stretch of the hippodrome then bends into a semicircle, changing its form: darker and gloomier, it is surrounded and protected by cypress trees, which cast a thicker shade.

Nature and art collaborate in constructing a pleasant space, enriched by various waterworks. As I did earlier, I have grouped Pliny's descriptions of different elements in his villa according to their architectural class, thus going back to the building part of his villa and from there moving again into the hippodrome:

20 Contra mediam fere porticum dieta paulum recidit, cingit areolam, quae quatuor platanis inumbratur. Inter has marmoreo labro aqua exundat [***Dec . 3.intro.10***] circumiectasque platanos et subiecta platanis leni aspergine fovet … 23 Fonticulus in hoc, [in] fonte crater; circa sipunculi plures miscent iocundissimum murmur. In cornu porticus amplissimum cubiculum triclinio occurrit; aliis fenestris xystum, aliis despicit pratum, sed ante piscinam, quae fenestris servit ac subiacet, strepitu visuque iucunda; 24 nam ex edito desiliens aqua suscepta marmore albescit. [***Dec. 3.intro.9–10***]

Opposite the midsection of the porch there is a slightly recessed apartment which encloses a small garden patch and is shaded by four plane trees. In their midst water pours out of a marble basin, which nourishes with a light mist both the plane trees surrounding it and the plants beneath them … In this room, there is a small fountain, and in the fountain a basin; all around several waterspouts produce the most pleasant sound. On the wing of the porch, a most spacious chamber matches the dining room. From some windows it overlooks the terrace, from others the lawn. Before the lawn, however, there is a pool, which is pressed into service of these windows. One can see it and hear it, lying pleasantly right beneath them, with its albescent water cascading from on high into its marble.

36 … In capite stibadium candido marmore vite protegitur; vitem quattuor columellae Carystie subeunt. Ex [s]tibadio aqua velut expressa cubantium pondere siponculis

effluit, cavato lapide suscipitur, atque ita occulte temperatur, ut impleat nec redundet. 37 … Contra fons egerit aquam et recipit; nam expulsa in altum in se cadit iunctisque hiatibus et absorbetur et tollitur.

40 Hic quoque fons nascitur simulque subducitur … Per totum hippodromum inductis fistulis strepunt rivi, et qua manus duxit sequuntur: his nunc illa viridia, nunc [haec,] interdum simul omnia iuvantur. [*Dec*. 3.intro.9–11]

At the end [of the hippodrome] there is a white marble seating area, protected by vines. The vegetation is supported by four little columns of Greek marble. From the seats, as if pressed out by the weight of those who sit there, water flows out, is collected by the carved stone, which is subtly arranged so as to be always filled but never overflowing … On the opposite side a spring pours out and recovers the water, which is jetted up into the air, falls back into its own column, and is thus absorbed and pushed out again by connected mouths.

Here, too, a spring is at once flowing out and controlled … Throughout the hippodrome, flowing from artificial spouts, some streams murmur and follow the design imposed by human hands: they are used to water at times some green spaces, at times [others], and sometimes even all of them.

When one reads Pliny's text with Boccaccio's in mind, pointed and general resemblances emerge. Both gardens are fully enclosed ("che tutto era da torno murato" : "omnia maceria muniuntur"); both contain tender trees ("albuscelli" : "arbusculas") and meadows ("pratelli : prata"); both have a central, prominent space ("un cortile nel mezzo" : "diaeta cingit areolam"); both have a fountain pouring forth abundant water ("una fonte di marmo da cui usciva l'acqua che soprabondava al pieno" : "marmoreo labro aqua exundat"); both include channels irrigating the meadows ("canaletti" : "spicunculi plures … inducti rivi") with murmuring waters ("dilettevole suono" : "iucundissimum murmur"), all deriving from a central water display ("l'acqua alta verso il cielo, che … nella fonte chiarissima ricadea" : "ex edito desiliens aqua"). Of course, readers of this chapter, and presumably readers of the *Decameron*, have already seen most of what Pliny's villa has to offer: they have found its beauties detailed in the *Roman de la Rose*. The majority of the highlighted elements are, in other words, part of a "common discourse" on villa gardens. The commonplace quality perceivable in the descriptions of these spaces should not, however, be held against their proposed intertextual pertinence. Some elements in Pliny's description remain unmatched in other accounts, a circumstance that makes a peculiarly pointed operation of Boccaccio's redeployment. The moments of topic coincidence are, however, as important as the points of direct and targeting allusion. In fact, one common element emerges from Boccaccio's practising of both contextual and textual dialogue: the unchanging way in which he proceeds. What is striking in Boccaccio's rehashing of Pliny's text – if this is indeed what he is doing, in layering his garden description with discernible, if subtle, allusions to the *Epistles*, along with references to widespread commonplace elements – is the confidently optimistic approach he brings to the literary operation of "contaminating" ancient and modern versions of the trope he deploys. In defiance of the philologist's scruples that I just evoked in my terminology, as a "translator" from Pliny's epistle as well as from Guillaume's *Rose*, Boccaccio makes it difficult to distinguish between his reuse of a vernacular text (albeit one that is culturally and chronologically noncontiguous) and that of a Latin one (albeit one that contains traditionally widespread motifs). Any reader, I surmise, would be hard pressed to tell a loan from the *Rose* and one from the *Epistles* apart – unless, that is, they had access to the rare Pliny tradition.[7]

One more element is worth noting: the canon of literary models that Boccaccio mobilizes for his garden description certainly covers a large span of time; yet once the material is transferred into his page, any chronological difference in the original context is seemingly elided. Staged in a garden and affecting a garden description, Boccaccio's translation of Guillaume and Pliny's antecedents domesticizes both, downplaying chronological difference in imitation. Boccaccio's intertextual game is, in other words, not a product of his classicism. Rather, his work is of one cloth with the confidence in the enriching potential available in acts of translation: the same "optimism" that this book has been tracing throughout.

But what is the connection of Boccaccio's peculiarly intertextual space with Eden? In my survey of the interconnected Latin and vernacular antecedents of the *Decameron*'s second garden, I deliberately skipped the *brigata*'s initial reaction to entering the garden. In its simplicity, their first observation notably established, as a hypothetical, the same typological connection that runs through the material presented in this book: the garden in which and about which the translation takes place is deeply reminiscent of the traditional tropes of Eden. What the narrator reports about the characters' reaction upon entering that familiar narrative (and tropological) space is, however, new. While it is certainly celebratory in tone, the complimentary appreciation of Boccaccio's characters is also clearly articulated as a caveat:

> Il veder questo giardino, il suo bello ordine, le piante e la fontana co' ruscelletti procedenti da quella tanto piacque a ciascuna donna e a' tre giovani, che tutti cominciarono a affermare che, se Paradiso si potesse in terra fare, non sapevano conoscere che altra forma che quella di quel giardino gli si potesse dare, né pensare, oltre a questo, qual bellezza gli si potesse agiugnere.

> Seeing this garden, its orderly beauty, the trees and fountain, the streams issuing from it, delighted each woman and the three young men so much that all began affirming that, could one make Paradise on earth, they did not know what other form one could give it beyond that of this garden, nor were they able to think, in addition, what other element of beauty could be added to it.

In the epigraph to this chapter, I have provided readers with the corresponding statement in the *Rose*. Upon entering the walled garden of pleasures in which he finds the enamouring rose, the protagonist-narrator in the French visionary narrative believes he is in the earthly paradise as well. His confidence in the correctness of his perception will remain unshaken throughout, and the *Romance* will come to reassess and redress it only from a distance, in the corrective and retrospective juxtaposition of the Park of the Lamb and the Garden of Deduit. Boccaccio's *brigata* takes its interpretive steps much more carefully than the lover in the *Rose*, phrasing their appreciation of the space within a radical hypothetical. As we are about to see, their narrative activities within this special garden reflect such a prudent awareness.

What about Pliny's text? Is it too, in any way, connected to the Edenic trope? As one may easily expect, no allusion to the Edenic quality of the space created in his Tuscan villa is present. Pliny's epistle is unaffected by the Eden topos, and for good cultural reasons. Though one of Pliny's claims to fame is having composed and sent to the emperor Trajan a letter about what he considered the appropriate treatment of Christians (advocating persecution of the reticent among them), his writings do not exhibit any familiarity with Jewish or Christian topoi or themes. There is something in his epistle, however, that might have struck a reader like Boccaccio not so much as prescience of but, rather, as convergence toward Christian themes. Pliny's remark that he has lost none of his servants in his estate points to his Tuscan villa, and the grounds around and within it, as a special space. Though the air is pestilential all around it, as Pliny admits, the villa is notably free of death. In a perfect ring-composition. the opening and farewell paragraphs of his text match one another, circling back to the theme of death. In so doing, they provide readers of the *Decameron* with a further element of intertextual pertinence:

> 45 Placida omnia et quiescentia, quod ipsum salubritati regionis ut purius caelum, ut aer liquidior accedit. Ibi animo, ibi corpore maxime valeo … 46 Mei quoque nusquam salubrius degunt; usque adhuc certe neminem ex iis, quos eduxeram mecum, (venia sit dicto) ibi amisi.

> Everything is peaceful and tranquil there, which adds to the healthful quality of that area, as do the clear sky and breezy air. There I am in my best mental and physical health … My servants too are nowhere healthier than there; certainly (may it remain so) thus far I have not lost any one of the men I brought there with me.

In the context of the *Decameron*'s frame tale, which insists on confronting death from a carefully constructed distance, there is no need to stress the relevance of this incidental feature in Pliny's estate. Not describing an Eden in itself, Pliny's text may thus have appeared to a reader of the *Decameron* as containing an intimation, a "dream" of it. The double inverted commas I use to mark the word dream are not scare quotes, used to alert readers that my prose indulges in an acritical use of colourful language. Rather, they signal a quotation from Boccaccio's perhaps favourite vernacular author, Dante, who, in accounting for the classically resonant quality of his own description of Eden in *Purgatorio* 28, has the Proserpina-like character of Matelda state that those who, in antiquity, wrote poetry about the Golden Age perhaps had a dream intuition of the actual Eden that the poet-protagonist is about to enter: "Quelli che anticamente poetaro / l'età de l'oro e suo stato felice, / forse in Parnaso esto loco sognaro" (ll. 139–41). As the smiling Virgil and Statius who are escorting Dante also agree, the place is the same, though the paths designed to access it – dream vision versus actual journey – have historically been altered by the intervening discontinuity of Incarnation.[8]

2. Two Stories for One Place

The first story told in the pseudo-Edenic garden of the *Decameron* forces readers to move within a similar field of tensions. As remarked by Filostrato in his prologue, the story is designed to highlight the protagonist's *ingegno*, the resourcefulness that is the very element chosen by the Day's queen as the running theme for all the stories. The partly different set of parameters which are mobilized in Masetto da Lamporecchio's tale, however, do not distract from the specific setting of the main character's adventures: the garden of a nunnery where he offers himself up as *ortolano*. The rubric of *Decameron* 3.1 clarifies all the elements in the plot, presenting Masetto's choice to "make himself a mute" and "become gardener" of the convent as, at first, simply circumstantial and instrumental to his becoming the object of the nuns' sexual attentions:

> Masetto da Lamporecchio si fa mutolo e diviene ortolano d'un monistero di donne, le quali tutte concorrono a giacersi con lui.

> Masetto from Lamporecchio makes himself mute and becomes the gardener of a women's convent, who all manage to lie with him. (*Decameron* 3.1.Rubric)

While not every garden of medieval narratives may or should be seen in typological connection with Eden, readers of the *Decameron* who reach Masetto's story in the frame of the Edenic setting of the second garden of the work are likely invited to do so. Readers of this book may also be struck by the similarly topical connection the story establishes between language – in Masetto's case, the renunciation of language – and the garden space in which he moves. In line with other narratives, Filostrato's story plays with the traditional elements of the garden-visit trope, constructing a compact system of cultural allusions which is not difficult to map.[9]

When we look at the novella with an awareness of its typological filigree, for instance, we may note that the narrative seems to set up the character positively:

Masetto is from the start introduced as a young man who replaces an old one in the service of the convent garden. As Filostrato establishes, the old gardener Nuto (perhaps the bearer of a parodical speaking name himself: he is, etymologically, a *nutus* – a mute sign) verbally recounts all the reasons why he is not happy with his work in the convent to a young man, who sees the job vacancy thus created as an opportunity to work in the same garden. While Nuto is literally old and literally a gardener, Masetto, biographically young and viably a gardener as well, interprets the situation metaphorically, allusively constructing the garden work that awaits him as sexual rather than simply agricultural: "Se voi mi mettete costà entro, io vi lavorerò sí l'orto che mai non vi fu cosí lavorato" (If you put me in there, I will so work the garden for you as it has never been worked before, *Dec.* 3.1.18).

The system of biological oppositions (old and new), as well as the juxtaposition of literal and metaphorical (if certainly not spiritual) interpretation of the gardening work at hand, is both traditional and tense. Simple typological associations would make Masetto a viable counterpart of the type of Christ as the Gardener – *Christus hortolanus* of John 20:15. In this light, he would represent an instantiation of the new and now resurrected Adam, evoking and at once transcending the task given to the first man to tend the Garden in Eden. Yet – and here lies one prominent element of tension – the way in which the protagonist of the tale gains access to that carnally paradisal space of the convent, by choosing mutism, and the way he lustily interprets the mandate of tending it, by working in the nuns' service with almost relentless sexual energy, cast an eerie light on his attempts to make paradise on earth for himself.

We should not forget that the linguistic dimension of his adventure is crucial to the plot and ultimate message of the tale. While Masetto certainly sets out to figurally become a new Adam, he also bypasses Christ, the Verbum, by giving up, at least temporarily, his own speech. The rubric notably presents his choice as not simply a feigning (*si *finge*, as do other trickster characters in the *Decameron*) but as an intrinsic transmutation ("si fa mutolo," he literally becomes dumb), thus carnally essentializing his play through a renunciation of speech. As a result, Masetto is offered to the readers as paradigm of a paradoxical non-new new Adam. He is at once an Adam who renounces his role as first speaker and flattens his horizon on the earthly and material sphere of life, as well as a non-Christ, that is, a non-Verbum who renounces the option of giving new life and new substance to human language. To be sure, the protagonist is literally young; just as clearly, however, he is presented as spiritually old – as in old testamentary – in his attachment to the flesh. His paradise on earth, the space from whose pleasant fertility he will reap his reward, is a garden of carnal delights. Similarly, his way of responding to the mandate issued in Genesis to tend that garden unfolds just as carnally in an erotic vein, and the beautiful convent grounds he works become the staging space of his sexual exertions.

Correspondingly, his final blasphemy – that of having succeeded in cuckolding Christ – is integral to, and the crowning of, his carnal reading of reality:

Cosí adunque Masetto vecchio, padre e ricco, senza aver fatica di nutricare i figliuoli o spesa di quegli, per lo suo avvedimento avendo saputo la sua giovanezza bene
adoperare, donde con una scure in collo partito s'era se ne tornò, affermando che cosí
trattava Cristo chi gli poneva le corna sopra 'l cappello. (43)

Thus, to conclude, Masetto – now old, a father, and rich, having dispensed with the
toil and expenditures of raising children – thanks to his ability to use his youth well,
returned to the very place he left bearing only a hatchet, affirming that thus Christ
rewarded those who put horns on his hat.

Masetto's statement as retired "patriarch," the wealthy father of many children he
did not have to support, confirms the regressive quality of his progress through
life. When his biographical age has apparently caught up with his symbolic age,
he is persistent in his regressive understanding of what the course of human life
should be. In his final declaration, he proves himself immune to Christ's launch-
ing of a new age of grace and recalcitrant to the radical renovation of time that
Incarnation and Passion have brought about. Masetto's own words denounce his
physical and spiritual "oldness," inviting readers to bring critical distance to the
narrative pleasure of hearing his adventure told.

Now, in advocating for critical distance in reading Boccaccio's novella, I am not
inviting a univocally and blindly unsympathetic reading of the tale, based solely
on the potentially negative (or simply disquieting) association of the protagonist's
behaviour and the Christological paradigm which may be applied to it. On the
contrary, if I have pointed to the negative, ominous side of Masetto's actions,
the dense field of dichotomies and ambiguities that emerges when we project his
adventures against traditional images of Eden, this is because Boccaccio's work
exploits, without ever resolving them into either of their extremes, the interpretive
polarities associated with that space. The narrator's preface is charged with voic-
ing such counterclaims, when it insists on associating a story about a young man's
resourcefulness with the "natural" desires of his counterparts, the nuns whose status as consecrated virgins does not absolve them from their natural desires. Here
are Filostrato's words:

Assai sono di quegli uomini e di quelle donne che sì sono stolti, che credono troppo
bene che, come ad una giovane è sopra il capo posta la benda bianca e in dosso messale la nera cocolla, che ella più non sia femina né piu senta de' feminili appetiti se
non come se di pietra l'avesse fatta divenire il farla monaca. (2)

Many men and women are so foolish that they too easily believe that young women
cease to be females, as soon as one puts a white veil on their head and a black cowl on
their body, or that they cease to feel the female appetites, as if their becoming nuns
had turned them to stone.

In Filostrato's framing of the tale, there would appear to be nothing wrong with tending the garden the way Masetto does. There is nothing, that is, theoretically wrong with contesting – as the story does incidentally – the practical loss of earthly fertility, not to speak of heavenly fruitfulness, triggered by a woman's convent seclusion in the absence of spiritual vocation, which is one of the themes Filostrato emphasizes in the tale. The actions that Masetto performs are, after all, his answer to a biblical mandate: as noted, tending the garden is the primeval task the first parents were assigned in Eden. The problem with Masetto's behaviour is, however, that it unfolds in a space (and according to an idea of time) that is made to regress to the negative side of an endemic interpretive ambivalence. Boccaccio's readers would hardly have failed to notice that move.

In making his own paradise on earth, Masetto seems to be oblivious to the fact that, for a Christian living in the Christian dispensation, Christ's process of redemption has opened up a new and better paradise – one that is not on earth. By only conforming to one side of the biblical mandate, Masetto proves to be regressive. He is a literal-minded reader who voluntarily indulges in a purely carnal understanding of Eden as a place on Earth's surface, patently oblivious to both its actual historical supersession and its possible ethical transcendence. Through the interaction of Filostrato's preamble with the dense fabric of Edenic and Christological allusions interspersed in the novella, readers may be called upon to see an additional significant element, one that allusively connects the Eden trope activated in the story with issues of language. A specific detail in Filostrato's tongue-in-cheek prologue points in that direction. As the plot of the tale will highlight, the protagonist's mutism is matched by repeated instantiations of the verbosity that characterizes the nuns with whom he will have sex. Allusions to their "vaniloquium" (idle chatter) constellate the novella, starting from the first encounter with the young man they wrongly assume cannot hear them: "le monache incominciarono a dargli noia e a metterlo in novelle … e dicevangli le piú scellerate parole del mondo, non credendo da lui essere intese" (the nuns started to harass and tease him … and they were saying to him the most unholy words in the world, thinking he would not understand them, 3.1.20). As the story progresses, other verbal exchanges between the nuns are also shared, with constant attention paid to their vacuity. The mini dispute about broken vows, which the first two nuns hold before having sex with Masetto, insists on the frailty of such verbal binding acts: "Oh … quante cose gli si promettono tutto il dí, che non se ne gli attiene niuna" (How many things we promise [God] every day, and never stick to any of them! 26). Similarly, the mutability of the other nuns' minds, who prove ready to turn their initial conviction to denounce the sexual liaisons of some among their number into participation in their pleasures, is entrusted to a verbal exchange: "prima tennero ragionamento insieme di doverle accusare alla badessa; poi, mutato consiglio e con loro accordatesi, partefici divennero del poder di Masetto" (at first they discussed the matter and decided they should denounce them to the abbess; then, having changed their minds and made an agreement with them, they acquired a share in Masetto's farmstead, 33). The juxtaposition of male silence to female loquacity is not solely functional to the plot and, as has been noted, culturally structural.[10] In the context of the novella, it is also allusively charged, pointing to a visual association already contained in the prologue of the story, but thus far unobserved.

When Filostrato insists that there are too many men and women who would like to believe that a woman loses her sexual appetite when she is made to become a nun, he phrases the idea in both technical and traditional terms, insisting on the colours of their habit: "come ad una giovane è sopra il capo posta la benda bianca e indosso messale la nera cocolla" (2). Certainly, as Filostrato notes and the "moral" of the story may also be insinuating, the habit does not make the monk or, in this case, the nun: the white veil and black cowl do not rid these nuns of their carnal desires. However, it is also clear that by associating them with the black-and-white plumage of magpies, the specific habit of these nuns allusively anticipates their notable contrastive loquacity. This detail is, in other words, both historical and suggestive of a figurative connection, which will become relevant in the analysis of the next tale in this chapter.

In sum, placed at the intersection of rhetorical and imaginative tensions, Boccaccio's man-made Eden is a profoundly ambivalent object. Correspondingly, the evaluation of the specific character's behaviour, who is exploiting its dual quality, is open to an ambivalent evaluation. On the one hand, Eden is the earthly place of Adam's fall, a lost carnal space embodying the memory of sin, a space essentially forbidden to humanity in the post-lapsarian dispensation. On the other hand, it is also the "sign" of the eventual overcoming of sin, itself destined to be replaced by a heavenly state of redemption, a spiritual space opened to human beings once again by Christ's sacrifice. Depending on whether a text, as a cultural object, emphasizes one or the other of these facets of Eden, the value of the place veers toward either interpretive option. Masetto's actions, along with the narrative determinants associated with them, locate him squarely on the negative, provisional side. What he sees in the adventure in the convent, and works for throughout his life, is paradise on earth, a space he constantly sees as an earthly, carnal reality. For the audience of the *Decameron*, however, Eden is culturally coded as potentially something more and something else, being at once the lost, irrecoverable place of innocence *and* the promise of a better one. As such, as the locus for a negotiation of the same cultural oppositions dividing old (carnal and literal) from new (spiritual and symbolic) approaches to reality, Eden is a reading test for Masetto as well as for his readers.

The same set of oppositions around the visit-to-Eden trope also controls another tale, the last one in the compact three-day stretch of narration taking place in the second garden: *Decameron* 6.10, the story of Frate Cipolla's crafty comeback from a trick played on him. In this tale, too, Eden is evoked through a series of pointed allusions that again revolve around the typological co-implication of old and new dispensation, original sin and incarnation. While Masetto's story thematized the tensions between the figure of Adam as both archetype of the fallen man and type of Christ, Cipolla's tale explores a different typological correspondence between two different actors in the drama of fall and salvation: Eve and Mary. By promising to display an exceptional and deeply incarnational relic, a feather from the wings of the Angel Gabriel, lost at the time of the Annunciation, Frate Cipolla allusively activates the latent and corrective promise of the earthly paradise, the same space perversely carnalized by Masetto with his indefatigable toiling in the wrong kind of Eden.[11]

As anticipated in my discussion of Dante's reaction to the traditional call attributed to the parrot ("Ave"), echoing the annunciation scene, and its palindromic relation to the name of Eve as proto-sinner ("Eva"), medieval theology treated the conceit connecting Eve's original sin (a sin of pride and an act of disobedience) with Mary's defining acceptance of her role as mother of the Redeemer (based on the virtue of humility and consisting in an act of obedience) as a commonplace in its typological understanding of salvation history. Antitypical to the original sin Eve consummated in Eden, the Virgin's reaction to the angelic greeting brought together the scene in the Marian *hortus conclusus*, the mystical enclosed garden, and Adam and Eve's exclusion from the *hortus deliciarium*, the garden of Eden.

Incarnation, as noted above and as we shall see more in detail below, is the appropriately fulfilling complement to Adam's fall and banishment from the garden. In the allusive theology of the *Decameron*, Masetto's Adamic role, both achieved in his taking upon himself the task of tending the garden and perversely obtained by re-entering the garden as a mute and a carnal interpreter of divine mandates (hence, essentially an old man), is balanced by the coming of Christ, who, as the Word made flesh and the paradigm of the new man, opens the way to a better space, heaven as non-earthly paradise. Cipolla's pointed allusions to the primal scene of incarnation, mobilized by his invention of a particularly sensitive relic, serve this narrative purpose. Within these parameters, it is not difficult to see how Dioneo's novella moves within a system of typological correspondences that extend from theological tenets to narrative structural ploys. In impressing a sharp turn to the plot of the story, however, the narrator proves he has more than a simple distant confirmation of Filostrato's allusive strategy. In his telling of Frate Cipolla's rhetorical exploits, Dioneo explores a different aspect of the connection of linguistics and Edenic space: its external geography. The remainder of my analysis will accordingly address questions of space.

Let us begin with the central object of the novella: the parrot's feather. In discussing the nature and role of this fictional relic in the plot, I shall resist the temptation to treat it as the reappearance of the same parrot, elided in the transition and translation from the vernacular of Dante's *Convivio* to the Latin of *De vulgari eloquentia*, which I noted in the previous chapter. However, there are several details referring to that one individual feather that make the Dantean context pertinent for Boccaccio's tale as well. When we come to the reading of *Decameron* 6.10 from a reflection on Dante's linguistics, we cannot fail to appreciate the irony of a story that proposes a new case of missing parrots. There is no need to insist on the importance of this item for the plot. The *rubrica* does a perfect job in isolating the object at the centre of the *beffa*, the prank of which Cipolla is the chosen but amazingly resilient victim:

> Frate Cipolla promette a certi contadini di mostrar loro la penna dell'agnolo Gabriello; in luogo della quale trovando carboni, quegli dice esser di quegli che arrostirono san Lorenzo.

> Fra Cipolla promises to some people from the countryside a feather of the Angel Gabriel; but, when he finds coals in its place, he says that they are part of those on which Saint Lawrence was roasted. (*Dec.* 6.10.Rubric)

Just as it was the case, albeit only allusively, in Dante, so too also in Boccaccio's story the parrot is linked to the Annunciation scene. This time, however, the connection is fully, if of course parodically, explicit. Cipolla's short advertising segment to the assembled congregation, which prepares his audience for his relic-based preaching the next day, pointedly establishes that the feather is angelic in quality:

> Di spezial grazia vi mostrerò una santissima e bella reliquia, la quale io medesimo già recai dalle sante terre d'oltremare; e questa è una delle penne dell'agnol Gabriello, la quale nella camera della Vergine Maria rimase quando egli la venne ad annunziare in Nazarette.

> By special grace I will show you a most holy and beautiful relic, which I brought with me from the holy lands beyond the sea. This is none other than a feather of the Angel Gabriel, which was left in the Virgin Mary's room when he came to make her the annunciation in Nazareth. (11)

Readers know – and not just from reading the story – that what Cipolla plans to exhibit as a marvellous relic he retrieved in the Holy Land is not a feather of the Angel Gabriel but one taken from the tail section of an exotic bird – exotic, that is, for the naïve people of Certaldo. While their innocence is suspended between naïveté and candour in the allusive prose of the novella, which mobilizes an evidently Dantean and subtly damning subtext (*Par.* 15.108), their passive acceptance of the feather as one that had belonged to a clumsily shedding or "naturally" moulting archangel is presented as an implicitly culpable credulity:

> E certo egli il poteva a quei tempi leggiermente far credere, per ciò che ancora non erano le morbidezze d'Egitto, se non in piccola quantità, trapassate in Toscana …

Anzi, durandovi ancora la rozza onestà degli antichi, non che veduti avessero pappagalli ma di gran lunga la maggior parte mai uditi non gli avean ricordare.

And for sure he could have easily made them believe this because, in those days, the luxuries of Egypt had not come, save for a minimal part, to Tuscany … To be sure, since the rough honesty of the ancients still reigned there, the greatest part among them had not only never seen parrots, but also never heard any mention of them. (27–8)

In the dynamics of the tale, the missing relic produces an overflow of deceiving words and impossible relics at once. Both abundances are significant. Cipolla's verbal *copia* does not come as a surprise, the character having been labelled a Tullius or Quintilian himself in the opening – and the story is, Dioneo's privilege notwithstanding, about a *motto*, a verbal comeback that delivers the speaker out of a social predicament. In the amazing verbal profluence of which the friar shows himself capable, he does not simply match, *e contrario*, Masetto's strategic mutism. We know from the rubric that, forced by the tricksters who leave coal in place of the feather, Cipolla will call upon Saint Lawrence's trial by fire to extricate himself from the preaching impasse. What the rubric does not tell us is that, in order to get to the coals from the feather, he takes his listeners for a dazzling verbal journey through an imaginary geography of distant lands and an equally absurd typology of holy objects.[12]

In what follows, I concentrate more on the geographical than the material dimension of these objects. If I insist on the former, it is because it has received less critical attention, not because I do not acknowledge that the same verbal brilliance is displayed in lists of both places and objects. While readerly pleasure in the novella may be equally distributed between the two lists, Cipolla's rhetorically constructed relics appear today more physically than geographically untenable. But this imbalance might not have been true for Boccaccio's first audience. To a medieval reader, their provenance is an equally sensitive element that the story activates and questions. To them, the vagaries in the journey that the friar completed to obtain them are not simply quixotic, but specifically eerie. Cipolla's relics are obtained at the end of a long and fanciful journey that matches clear directional notations with fantastic and deceitful toponymy. To be sure, the immediate falsity of Cipolla's imaginary relics is factual. That he is a fraud is evident. That his talismans are intended to be appreciated as similarly false by the refined intra- and extra-diegetical audience of the story is also clearly established in the tale. His purportedly "holy" relics are false in themselves, since they are nothing more than verbal constructs that cannot be indicated by any actual referent. They are part of a deception, however, also because of their fanciful geographic origin, having been brought back from a fictional, rhetorically constructed Holy Land. In addition to being a humorous parody of what relics should be, that is, the verbal objects created by Cipolla's on-the-spot oratory harbour a just as deadly danger. Once readers are able to put together their quality and their provenance, the friar's marvels show themselves as regressive and specifically "apostatic" relics.

When it comes to their nature, it is clear how, in his fanciful account of his journeys, the friar systematically turns spiritual notions into material objects, thus adhering to the paradigm of frenetic literalism and fanatical materialism topically associated with pre-incarnational times. The story offers readers two sets of relics. The first are the ones Cipolla is shown on his journey:

Egli primieramente mi mostrò il dito dello Spirito Santo cosí intero e saldo come fu mai, e il ciuffetto del serafino che apparve a san Francesco, e una dell'unghie de' Gherubini, e una delle coste del Verbum caro fatti alle finestre, e de' vestimenti della Santa Fé catolica, e alquanti de' raggi della stella che apparve a' tre Magi in oriente, e un ampolla del sudore di san Michele quando combatté col diavole, e la mascella della Morte di san Lazzaro e altre. (45)

First he showed me the finger of the Holy Spirit, as safe and sound as it ever was, and a tuft of the Seraph who appeared to Saint Francis, and one of the Cherubs' nails, and one of the ribs of the dear Word-made-fresh-at-the-window, and some garments belonging to the Holy Catholic Faith, and some rays of the star which appeared to the three wise Kings in the East, and a vial with Saint Michael's sweat, which issued when he fought the devil, and the jawbone of Saint Lazarus' death, and others yet.

Secondly, we are given a list of the relics that the Holy Patriarch of Jerusalem, Nonmiblasmete Sevoipiace, gave Cipolla to take home:

Donommi uno de' denti della santa Croce, e in una ampolletta alquanto del suono delle campane del tempio di Salomone e la penna dell'agnol Gabriello, della quale già detto v'ho … (47)

He gifted me one of the teeth of the Holy Cross, and in a small flask quite a bit of the sound of the bells in Solomon's temple, and the very feather of the Angel Gabriel about which I have already told you.

Post-enlightenment readers are all too ready to see in Boccaccio's lighthearted treatment of the false-relic business, in which Cipolla customarily engages, a critical dénouement of the rhetoric of material holiness of such relics. Readers from the time of the *Decameron* might have been aware of a different yet related set of issues at work in Cipolla's sermonizing as well. The relics he advertises are, patently and admittedly, of the "wrong" kind to readers of today as much as they were to medieval spirituality, but not simply because they belong to a commonly discredited class of objects. Cipolla's relics are unacceptable for a set of deeper, less contingent reasons than their being technically fraudulent. They systematically consist either in hyper-materialized tokens of immaterial beings and realities, be they archangels (like Gabriel and Michael), or a Seraph, or one of the Cherubim, or the Holy Catholic Faith (a grammatically personified virtue). Alternatively, they may be set in a curious relationship with the whole, and considered a representative part of it. This same kind of untenable relationship appears in the case of the beams of a star or the sound of bells (impermanent material traces of material objects). Similarly, a "tooth" of the Cross (analogically related to its metaphorical "arms") or the jawbone of Lazarus' Death (an iconographic shift from an immaterial entity, death, to its material signifier, a skull) are presented as blatantly unacceptable to any and all audiences. As Jonathan Usher keenly noted, the nature of the relics themselves is involved in linguistic questions as well. The relics are not simply "fatte di parole" (made of, and "made up" with words), they are also involved in how "si fanno le parole" (how words are made and come into being). Thus, the falsity of Cipolla's relics is not simply logical. It is perhaps, just as dangerously, of a precise historical-linguistic kind.[13]

But there is more: the geographic provenance of the relics and the itinerary the friar has allegedly completed to reach their place of origin contribute to the negative light in which the text presents them. Cipolla's story pairs the insistent and comically detailed catalogue of false relics with a just as florid account of the friar's movements on an imaginary world map. Cipolla's journey toward the east (toward the earthly location of Eden) and then south (toward what will eventually result in a carnal Jerusalem) is contained in a celebrated and delightful passage that is especially amusing for a Florentine audience familiar with urban topography and street onomastics. To be appreciated, the passage needs to be quoted in full.

> Signori e donne, voi dovete sapere che, essendo io ancora molto giovane, io fui mandato dal mio superiore in quelle parti dove apparisce il sole ... Per la qual cosa messom'io cammino, di Vinegia partendomi e andandomene per lo Borgo de' Greci e di quindi per lo reame del Garbo cavalcando e per Baldacca, pervenni in Parione, donde, non senza sete, dopo alquanto pervenni in Sardigna. Ma perché vi vo io tutti i paesi cerchi da me divisando? Io capitai, passato il braccio di San Giorgio, in Truffia e in Buffia, paesi molto abitati e con gran popoli; e di quindi pervenni in terra di Menzogna ... E in brieve tanto andai adentro, che io pervenni mei infino in India Pastinaca ... Ma non potendo quello che io andava cercando trovare, perciò che da indi in là si va per acqua, indietro tornandomene, arrivai in quelle sante terre dove l'anno di state vi vale il pan freddo quattro denari, e il caldo v'è per niente. E quivi trovai il venerabile padre messer Nonmiblasmete Sevoipiace, degnissimo patriarca di Ierusalem. (37–44)

Ladies and gentlemen, you should know that, when I was still young, I was sent by my superior in those lands where the sun shines ... Thus, having set forth, I left from

Venice and passing through the borough of the Greeks and thence riding through the kingdoms of Garb and Baldric, I came to Parione. From there, not without thirst, after a while I reached Sardinia. But why should I list in detail all the countries I sought? I ended up, having crossed Saint George's channel, in the land of Menzogna … And, in a short time, I went so deep into it, that I reached the Indies of Pàstina … However, since I could not find there what I was looking for, and since one cannot proceed thence if not by water, coming back, I reached those holy lands where cold bread is sold at four thalers, and the heat is for free. Here I found the venerable father Blamemenot Ibegyou, most worthy patriarch of Jerusalem.

As Branca's gloss points out, while presenting itself as a grandiose voyage through foreign lands, Cipolla's journey only amounts, in practice, to the allusive description of his crossing of the city of Florence from east to west. The editor's note is at once illuminating and disorienting:

> Le determinazioni geografiche … si riferiscono in gran parte a Firenze attraversata da est a ovest. Porcellana era via e spedale presso San Paolino, Vinegia e Borgo dei Greci sono contrade fra Piazza della Signoria e Santa Croce, Garbo era l'attuale via Condotta, Baldacca una strada presso Orsanmichele … Parione la via da Santa Trinita alla Carraia, Sardigna una piaggia deserta fuori San Frediano, San Giorgio contrada presso la Dogana e anche località Oltrarno. Ironico *iter hierosolomitanum*.

> Most of the geographical indications … relate to the east-west crossing of Florence. Porcellana was a street and hospital near San Paolino, Vinegia and Borgo dei Greci are neighbourhoods between Piazza della Signoria e Santa Croce, Garbo was what today is via Condotta, Baldacca a street near Orsanmichele … Parione the street from Santa Trinita to the Carraia, Sardigna a stretch of uncultivated land outside San Frediano, San Giorgio a neighbourhood in the vicinity of the Dogana, and also a locality across the river Arno. An ironic *Journey to Jerusalem*. (Branca, commentary *ad loc.*)

In mapping the geography of the imaginary journey back onto the more modest city-scale to which it alludes, Branca's explanation has the merit of correctly noting and generously explaining the subtext of Cipolla's double-speak to non-Florentines. Nonetheless, the gloss misleads readers when it labels the trip as a journey to Jerusalem. The misdirection is partial but significant because it elides the first distinctive leg of the friar's trip. The movement Cipolla reports is, in fact, at first not toward Jerusalem, but due east, through lands of wonder. This first half of the journey is modelled on Alexander the Great's itinerary of conquest. As Branca duly and acutely notes in a later commentary on the same passage, Boccaccio's text contains a pointed cultural allusion:

> *India Pastinaca … da indi in là si va per acqua.* Questa frase e la seguente possono forse, con allusività caricaturale, avvicinare Fra Cipolla e il suo favoloso viaggio a

Alessandro Magno e alla sua vittoriosa marcia arrestatasi proprio in India di fronte all'acqua.

India Pastinaca ... thence one only travels by water. This sentence, together with the following one, may allude by way of caricature to a correspondence between Fra Cipolla's fabulous journey and Alexander the Great's victorious march, which came to a halt in India, right in front of a body of water. *(Ibidem)*

Significantly, this directional thrust is not only toward a generic East, but also, more specifically, toward the traditional location of the earthly paradise, a place that, several sources insist, the Macedonian king was destined neither to find nor have access to. Boccaccio's allusion to the pseudo-historical material concerning Alexander's journey of exploration and conquest evokes the trope of the visit to Eden in the novella. The traditional association was deeply familiar to Boccaccio's audiences. As, for instance, the widely circulating *Epistola Alexandri de situ et mirabilibus Indie* reported, Alexander lamented that, having reached the farthest parts of the continent, he could not progress by land. This realization, which was triggered by informed advice, forced him to divert his steps:

Ultra deinde progressi ut memorabile aliquid cerneremus, nihil propter desertos campos silvasque et montes vidimus in quibus elephanti et serpentes esse dicebantur. *Pergebamque ad mare occeanum,* volens si posset *orbem terrarum circiter* navigare, quem quidem tenebrosum et periculosum mihi incole affirmabant, dicentes quod mihi Herculis et magnorum deorum metas transire non liceret. *Unde, his pretermissis, sinistram partem yndie perscrutavi.* (Biblioteca Medicea Laurenziana, Pluteo 29.8 sup. c. 43v)

Having moved forward from there, in search of something else worthy of note, we saw nothing but barren fields, forests, and mountains, in which it was rumoured lived elephants and snakes. I moved toward the ocean, intending, if possible, to circumnavigate the world, though some people who lived there asserted that it was indeed dark and dangerous. They said that I was not allowed to go past the limits set by Hercules and the great gods. Thus, having foregone these matters, I set out to inspect the left side of India.[14]

Once he had run out of lands to explore and subjugate, the ancient hero turned away, forced to abide by the human limitations imposed on him by providential history. Similarly, Frate Cipolla notes that, "since one cannot proceed thence if not by water," he too is forced to reroute on his quest. He has reached India (or the town of Pàstina, depending on who is listening to his words), and he too gives up on finding what he was journeying toward.

Through this short but pointed allusion, Boccaccio's tale suggests that the far East, the traditional location of Eden, is lost to both Alexander and Cipolla alike.

Unlike Alexander's, however, Cipolla's journey does not end with any realization or a return home. The second section in his travels takes him due south-west, back toward Jerusalem, the Jewish city which appears in the text as the site of his successful discovery of relics. As Branca also notes, generalizing the coverage of his label, this sharp turn changes the nature of the friar's trip, which now morphs into a truly parodic pilgrimage to Jerusalem. Mapped onto the imaginary and fraudulent journeys of the friar, the localities of Eden and Jerusalem emerge in quite an ambivalent light: they are both sacred spaces, but neither is immune from the potential charge of being the destination of a regressive journey.

As we have seen, a crucial tenet of Christian theology regarding Eden is that the garden is *not* to be regained by way of travels and conquests (whether military or intellectual). The idea was shared by readers of the story of Alexander the Great's frustrated travels, as much as those familiar with the post-mortem realization of Dante's Ulysses, who in *Inferno* 26 acknowledges the folly of his "flight" toward the "world without people" (l. 117). In a similar way, Jerusalem is certainly a Holy City, but one that, just as certainly, has for Boccaccio's culture exhausted its function as place of redemption with the supersession of Judaism by Christianity, a world-historical event that was sealed and signalled by the destruction of the Second Temple. Now, it is a specifically Jewish Jerusalem that Cipolla finds at the end of the second leg of his journey, the locus in which literal, physical, and carnal relics are produced and found. The humorous rhetoric and insistent wordplay on the clerical onomastics in the passage are bound to cause discomfort in the theologically and culturally informed reader. When Jerusalem is seen not so much as a holy city but as the centre of a superseded religion, it cannot fail to appear an inappropriate endpoint for a Christian pilgrimage. It is, perhaps more precisely, an inappropriate destination *tout court*. Just as the relics that originate there are purely verbal and literally carnal, so too the place from which they emerge is unredeemed. To corroborate my last point, let me move on to the final discussion of the novella's motifs, centred on the "extinguished coals" of Saint Lawrence, the replacement relic that Cipolla produces at the end of his performance in Certaldo and uses to make his final rhetorical escape.

3. Taking the Cross

In the previous section, I proposed seeing Cipolla's loss of the parrot's feather as the trigger for an oratorical perversion that is also a regression to the literal and the carnal, a movement that I would call technically apostatic. I choose this term neither lightly nor in a generic sense. The final act of Cipolla's sermon, his marking of the Certaldesi's Sunday bests with black coal crosses, is a no less comical than disturbing scene for more than one reason, the first being the allusion it contains to Jerusalem as a retrogressive location. Let us look at the final act in Cipolla's speech, which is just as dazzling as what preceded in his sermon:

"E per ciò, volendo Idio che io, col mostrarvi i carboni co' quali esso fu arrostito, raccenda nelle vostre anime la divozione che in lui aver dovete, non la penna che io voleva, ma i benedetti carboni spenti dall'omor di quel santissimo corpo mi fé pigliare. E per ciò, figliuoli benedetti, trarretevi i cappucci e qua divotamente v'appresserete a vedergli. Ma prima voglio che voi sappiate che chiunque da questi carboni in segno di croce è tocco, tutto quello anno può viver sicuro che fuoco nol cocerà che non si senta."

E poi che cosí detto ebbe, cantando una laude di san Lorenzo, aperse la cassetta e mostrò i carboni; li quali poi che alquanto la stolta moltitudine ebbe con ammirazione reverentemente guardati, con grandissima calca tutti s'appressarono a frate Cipolla e, migliori offerte dando che usati non erano, che con essi gli dovesse toccare il pregava ciascuno. Per la qual cosa frate Cipolla, recatisi questi carboni in mano, sopra li lor camisciotti bianchi e sopra i farsetti e sopra li veli delle donne cominciò a fare le maggior croci che vi capevano, affermando che tanto quanto essi scemavano a far quelle croci, poi ricrescevano nella cassetta, sí come egli molte volte aveva provato. (*Decameron* 6.10.51–4)

"Thus, since the Lord intended me to kindle in your souls the devotion you should have for him, by showing you the coals on which his [Saint Lawrence's] body was roasted, he made me reach not for the feather I intended to, but the blessed coals extinguished by the humours of that holiest of bodies. Therefore, blessed children, remove your hoods and devoutly draw closer to see them. But before that, let it be known that whoever is marked with a sign of the cross drawn with these coals shall for a whole year be sure that no fire will burn them unawares." Having said this, singing a laud for Saint Lawrence, he opened the box and showed the coals. After the members of this stolid crowd had looked at the coals reverently and with admiration, they all came pressing closer to Friar Cipolla, each asking him to please be touched with them and giving better alms than they were used to. Therefore, having picked up these coals, Friar Cipolla began drawing the biggest possible crosses on their white shirts and doublets as well as on the women's veils, swearing that the more they were consumed in drawing these crosses, the more the coals would grow back in the box, as he had had proof many times.

The first disquieting realization the text invites in its alert readers is that the gullible citizens of the town, both men and women, go home with their garments dirty but happily convinced that the crosses the friar has drawn on them will protect them from the dire effects of fire. At least, as the preacher's aside "fuoco … che non si senta" stipulates, they will be safe from a "fire … that is not felt." While they would be protected from feeling the carnal flames enveloping them, at any rate, nothing is said about the eternal ones that will eventually be visited upon them – at least according to Dante's pertinent perspective on the episode. Should we judge Cipolla's performance in light of the antecedent of *Paradiso* 29, an episode in which Cipolla's order is put under vitriolic attack by several matching points of theology, his words truly are "moneta sanza conio" (worthless coins), and those who receive them share in the blame.

The second potentially disturbing detail in the passage is the specific form of the ritual which the preacher performs as envoy for his audience. To my knowledge, no specific antecedent has been offered to gloss this last stretch of narrative, in which all the Certaldesi are made into ash-marked crusaders – or, at least, literally into *crucesignati*. Examining a possible "source" of the episode (more precisely, a wide range of literary and hagiographic antecedents) may help us to see why Cipolla's Jerusalem is not a holy city after all. Two elements are worth noting. First, the regeneration process peculiar to the coals that Frate Cipolla claims are Saint Lawrence's is not unprecedented. Similarly, there exist notable precedents for the ability to shelter from fire that Cipolla claims cross-marked garments possess. Both elements appear in widely circulating historical examples contained in ecclesiastical and homiletic sources, to which it may be useful to turn.

Let us begin with the coals themselves. Jonathan Usher suggestively connects the peculiar self-regenerating ability Cipolla claims to have witnessed on many an occasion in his miraculous coals with the golden-bough replay scene on the shores of Dante's purgatory, when Virgil girds the protagonist with a miraculously regenerating rush (*Purgatorio* 1.134–6). A closer and perhaps more pertinent antecedent, however, may be found in the legends circulating about Saint Lawrence. A canonical account of Saint Lawrence's life and death is found in its fullest form in a text from his *Martyrologium* penned by Ado of Vienne, in the ninth century, for the Day *V idus Augusti*. The culminating episode in the saint's life takes place in the other holy city of Christianity: Rome. Pressed by the Roman authority to produce the wealth he had been administrating on behalf of the Christian community of the Urbs, Lawrence is credited with using a strategy of delay and frustration on the authorities. Here is the passage in full:

"Da mihi inducias biduo aut triduo, et proferam tibi thesauros." Ab eadem die coepit colligere caecos, et claudos, debiles et pauperes, et abscondit eos in domo Hippolyti. Valerianus autem nuntiaverat Decio, quia promisisset, datis sibi induciis, Laurentius thesauros. Completis igitur tribus diebus, praesentavit se in palatio Salustiano. Et dixit ei Decius: "Ubi sunt thesauri, quos pollicitus es praesentare?" Beatus Laurentius collectam multitudinem pauperum introduxit in palatium, et voce magna dixit: "Ecce isti sunt thesauri aeterni, qui nunquam diminuuntur, nec decrescunt; qui in singulis aspergitur, et in omnibus invenitur."

"Grant me a delay of two or three days, and I will bring out the treasures." From that very day he began gathering the blind and lame and weak and poor and hid them in the house of Hippolytus. Valerian, however, had announced to Decius that Lawrence had promised to give up the treasures after the granted delay. At the end of the three days, Lawrence showed up at the palace of Salust. Decius said to him: "Where are the treasures that you pledged to deliver?" The blessed Lawrence brought in the multitude of paupers he had assembled into the palace and with loud voice he said:

"Here, these are the eternal treasures which never wane nor diminish! This is what, while divided among them singularly, still is found in all." (*Acta S. Laurenti* 4 Aug II., pp. 518–19)[15]

Cipolla's dislocation and distortion of Saint Lawrence's legend is significant for more than one reason. First, in claiming that this relic comes from the east, Cipolla activates a radically impertinent location for the Lawrence legend. As any reader familiar with basic martyrology knew, Lawrence's history is fully and exclusively Rome-based. Both the details in the topography of his legend and the personnel involved in his prosecution and eventual martyrdom, in which star the two notorious emperors Decius and Valerian, remove any ambiguity.

That Cipolla goes to Jerusalem to find a relic of a Roman saint is, however, not simply a geographical and historical absurdity. It is, more dangerously, a regressive act. Substituting Jerusalem for Rome, in fact, amounts to going back in history, an act that asserts that one is unwilling or unable to acknowledge that Jerusalem's centrality, both in the old dispensation and in the early phases of the new one, has been outmatched and truly superseded by a new centre for the spiritual life of the world, Rome. It would be impossible for Boccaccio, his fictional *brigata* of storytellers, and even his minimally culturally aware real readership to think otherwise. That, though grounded in Jerusalem, salvation history proceeds through Rome is such a central tenet in Christian thought that the argument is not simply a staple in the pro-papal Guelph propaganda but also is accepted by a Guelph as eccentric as Dante in his *Monarchia* and confirmed by the joint argumentative force of *Paradiso* 6 and 7. No matter how deep the political divergences opposing theocratic and imperial approaches to history may have been, in sum, for a medieval reader the postulate that the apostolic Rome was both the historical fulfilment and the actual supersession of Jerusalem could hardly be questioned.

Secondly, the inverted connection between material and spiritual values that Cipolla's financial exploitation of his flock establishes could similarly not go unnoticed. The figural fleecing of his flock that Cipolla performs on the square of Certaldo is a pointed and, of course, negative type of a salient moment in Lawrence's legend: his parading of Rome's poor in front of the persecuting and venal imperial officer. In systematically pursuing material gain, Cipolla's final preaching act replaces the true (because spiritual) treasure of the Church with a false (because material) one. His never-ending coals, which are divided among the parishioners singly and will be found in all, are a blasphemous parody of the never-waning, never-diminishing treasure in Saint Lawrence's speech. Again, Cipolla's move is technically regressive, since it goes from spiritual to material, from a (holy and charitable) use of the earthly goods by the Church, intended to benefit the brethren in Christ, to the (sinful and predatory) exploitation of one's flock, which Cipolla's order perpetrates daily. Again, Dante's merciless diagnosis in *Paradiso* 29, entrusted to the sententious statement "così s'ingrassa il porco Sant'Antonio," resonates in the background of Cipolla's trickery together with, and against the background of, the story of Saint Lawrence.

Thirdly, even Cipolla's crafty control of the calendar, his pointing to a *modicum tempus* separating the day of his sermon from the actual feast of Saint Lawrence, is useful for more than simply anecdotal reasons. Thanks to its appearance in the traditional legends about Saint Lawrence, we are able not only to establish the imaginary date of the incident in Certaldo, but also to perceive a relevant element of contrast with the matter (and the goal) of the friar's sermon:

> "Il quale io non reputo che stato sia errore, anzi mi pare esser certo che volontà sia stata di Dio e che Egli stesso la cassetta de' carboni ponesse nelle mie mani, ricordandom'io pur testé che la festa di san Lorenzo sia di qui a due dí." (*Decameron* 6.10.50)

> "A delay that I do not think is a mistake; rather, it seems to be certain it was God's will and that he himself put the box of coals into my hands, since I just remembered that the feast of Saint Lawrence is in two days' time."

When readers come to *Decameron* 6.10 from the reading of Saint Lawrence's *martyrologium*, they quite easily realize that a further chronological parody is entailed in the preacher's phrasing. His transparently mocking reflection that the feast of Saint Lawrence is only a few days away, which serves to remotivate the accidental shift in relics, becomes the effect of an extemporaneous divine inspiration.

Finally, and perhaps most importantly, the notion that a cross on one's garment is a talisman against fire is well attested in saints' legends and thus hardly surprising in the context in which it is introduced. While it is, to my knowledge, unrelated to the Laurentian corpus of narratives, the motif is widespread. One can find an especially economical version in Magister Matthias' *Copia exemplorum*, a collection dating to the same years (though from a distant locality) as the *Decameron*:

> 46. Crux. Domus cuiusdam cruce signati succensa est et omnibus, que in ea erant, in fauillam redactis pars uestis, in qua crux erat, inuenta esta illesa inter fauillas.

> The home of a man who had taken the cross went up in flames. Everything in it turned to ashes. The part of his garment, in which was the cross was, however, found perfectly intact by the fire. (*Copia exemplorum*, p. 26)[16]

In Magister Matthias' narrative repertory for preachers, the exemplum of the miraculous powers of the cross is connected by way of internal reference to another exemplum from the *Alphabetum narrationum*: "232. Cruce signatam vestem inter flammas illesam Deus custodit" (A garment signed with a cross was kept safe by the Lord within the flames). In this much more detailed narrative, we read that a certain Cesarius of Susa enjoyed the protective effects of the cross, effects which were then witnessed and appreciated by his fellow citizens collectively. His story, in turn, connects to a different anecdote in which the sign of the cross is again central: the miraculous appearance of black (ashen?) crosses on the garments of all the Jews involved in the failed (allegedly supernaturally thwarted) attempt to rebuild the temple at Jerusalem. This exemplum, which is collected under the rubric of "Providence" in Magister Matthias' work, had less local or anecdotal origins and enjoyed an even larger circulation. Looking at its development in some detail may help us to appreciate a layer of Boccaccio's narrative that has thus far remained unexplored. Magister Matthias recounts the episode from late antique history as follows:

150.2 Prouidentia. Iulianus apostota in odium cristianorum iussit reparari templum iudeorum sumptus largissime administrans, et dum cementi magna congesta fuisset, uentus uehemens ueniens totum dispersit, deinde terre motus factus est magnus et postmodum ignis uehentissimus, qui plurimos concremauit. Alia uero die signum crucis in celo apparuit et iudeorum uestes nigro colore crucis signaculo sunt replete.

Concerning Providence. Julian the Apostate, on account of his hatred for Christians, ordered that the Temple of the Jews be repaired and thus dispensed considerable amounts of money. While a great amount of material was being assembled, a strong wind came to scatter all. An earthquake then came. And, after that, a raging fire that burned many people. The day after, the sign of the cross appeared in the sky, and the garments of Jews were filled with the marking of the cross. (*Copia exemplorum*, p. 99)

The ambitious enterprise of rebuilding Solomon's Temple was, all sources report, promoted and financed by the Emperor Julian the Apostate, the last of the Pagans, in the first half of the fourth century CE. The premise of the miraculous story is in truth historical (there was an earthquake in the year 363 in Galilea), and it is referred in Ammianus Marcellinus' account of the basic facts in his *Res Gestae* XXIII.1–3:

2. [Caesar]… ambitiosum quondam apud Hierosolymam templum, quod post multa et interneciva certamina obsidente Vespasiano posteaque Tito aegre est expugnatum, instaurare sumptibus cogitabat inmodicis, negotiumque maturandum Alypio dederat Antiochensi, qui olim Brittannias curaverat pro praefectis.

   3. Cum itaque rei idem fortiter instaret Alypius iuvaretque provinciae rector, metuendi globi flammarum prope fundamenta crebris adsultibus erumpentes fecere locum exustis aliquotiens operantibus inaccessum, hocque modo elemento destinatius repellente cessavit inceptum.

The emperor was planning to spend an inordinate amount of money to rebuild the once lofty temple in Jerusalem, the one that had been destroyed after many bloody battles by the sieging army of Vespasian and then at high price by Titus. He gave the task to bring to fruition this project to Alypius of Antioch, who had been in charge of the administration of Britannia in lieu of the prefects. Thus, as Alypius, who had been charged with the care of the province, was dealing with the issue with determination, a terrible barrage of globes of fire, erupting from near the foundations, attacked the place and made it inaccessible – not before having burned some of the workers. In this way, with the harshest opposition of one of the elements, the project was abandoned. (*Res Gestae*, vol. II, 310–13)[17]

Missing from Ammianus' account is, of course, the miraculous marking of the garments with the crosses, but this detail does not deter Christian writers from appropriating the idea of a (quasi-) supernatural opposition to the project and spinning it to include a secondary miracle. In the *Alphabetum narrationum* by Arnald of Liège, all the elements are recovered and redeployed in compact form. The anecdote appears under the entry *Signum*, bearing a significant subtitle and commentary: "Signis evidentibus aliquando impedit Deus malos ut non compleant quod ceperunt" (By way of clear signs God sometimes hinders evil men from bringing to fruition what they started). The exemplary story is related as follows:

> Ex cronicis. Iulianus Apostata in odium Christianorum templum Iudeorum iussit reparari, ipsis Iudeis sumptus largissime subministrans. Sed dum maximam cementi copiam ministrassent, subito uentus uehemens totam dispersit. Denique terremotus magnus est factus et postmodum ignis a fundamento ingrediens, plurimos concremauit. Alia uero die signum crucis in celo apparuit, et Iudeorum uestes nigro colore crucis signaculo sunt replete.

> Drawn from the chronicles. Julian the Apostate, on account of his hatred for Christians, ordered the Temple of the Jews to be rebuilt, providing the Jews with considerable capital. As they had prepared a great amount of building material, however, a sudden windstorm scattered everything. Later there was a strong earthquake and, after this, flames issuing from the foundations burned many people. Another day, furthermore, the sign of the cross appeared in the sky and the clothing of the Jews was filled with black signs of the cross.[18]

The anecdote is drawn verbatim from the *Legenda Aurea* (Chapter 121: *De decollatione Sancti Iohannis Baptiste*) and originates in the scathing section devoted to the highly sacrilegious life of Julian the Apostate, who was guilty, among other things, of having ordered that the Baptist's bones be burned and scattered. As such, the story could be found in a far from recondite corner of the hagiographic tradition, but as an appendix to the martyrology of the patron saint of Florence. After being plagued by several appearances of the cross, which ranged from miraculously shaped dewdrops on his garments to signs embedded in the entrails of a sacrificial victim he examined, Julian the Apostate was also punished, the *Legenda Aurea* says, by the burning of the Temple's worksite he sponsored and the textually concomitant, miraculous appearance of the ashen crosses. The branding of the garments of the regressively enterprising Jews with miraculous signs of crosses should resonate in our reading of Boccaccio's novella, adding a new harmonic dimension to it. What Frate Cipolla leaves in his wake in Certaldo is no different from what Julian the Apostate produced: a flock of superstitious believers with their garments marked by crosses. The dynamics of Boccaccio's story has, however, an added twist. As the *Legenda Aurea* states, the miracle of the burnt crosses in Jerusalem led many Jews to confess Christ as the Lord. On the contrary, the parodic marking of Frate Cipolla only confirms a group of Christians in their literal-minded and carnal beliefs and practices, turning them into a parodic post-figuration of the apostatic inhabitants of Jerusalem. The problem his sermon leaves in its wake is not only that, after such a long and twisted hagiographical peregrination, his flock (like the *Decameron* readers and perhaps readers of this book) find themselves back in Florence, a place they truly never left. The potentially negative effects of their inability to read through his rhetoric extend to their ethical standing as well.

Having reviewed the main typological elements mobilized in Frate Cipolla's story, it is time to return to a passing reference the preacher makes to incarnation in his sermon. In reacting to the subtraction of his marvellous angelic or ornithological relic with a no less marvellous *multiloquium*, Cipolla engages in an activity that has the potential to be highly problematic. We have seen how several elements he mobilizes in his review of relics are part of the dynamics of world-historical change through which salvation history progresses. More pointedly, they allusively (as well as systematically) connect original sin with redemption – and, significantly, from a topographical point of view, Eden with Jerusalem. Within this framework Cipolla's incidental trivialization of the formula of the Incarnation, the words "verbum caro factum est," which he renders as "Verbum caro fatti alle finestre," is all the more significant. In his successfully dazzling attempt to lead his hearers from the feather to the coals, Cipolla's rhetoric produces two related effects. In claiming he has received "una delle coste del Verbum caro fatti alle finestre" (one of the ribs of the "dear Word-made-fresh-at-the-window"), he points to the theological locus of Christ's humanity: his *costato*, from which blood mixed with water will pour forth. In the same breath, Cipolla also typologically evokes the moment of Eve's creation (from Adam's *costa*). His rhetorical move technically regresses human history from the moment of redemption with Christ's death on the cross to its Edenic inception with the creation of the first sinner. Just as Mary is a new Eve, her fulfilment *in bono*, Christ is a new Adam, similarly (if incommensurably) a better one. The short circuit of redemptive history evoked in Cipolla's words passes through a misrepresentation of Incarnation.

A final word on the linguistic dimension of the tale is in order here. By first being forced by the *beffa* (his incarnational feather having gone missing), and then deciding, to explicitly remove incarnation from his world view (the miracle and mystery of the Word being made flesh degenerating into a street cry), Cipolla obtains the ability to produce theologically uncontrolled and socially unchecked discourse. The spiritual, religious, and pastoral consequences of his decision are readily manifest. In exchange for detracting what Christianity held as the ultimate basis for language to speak the truth – the transcendental guarantee that language is not an endless and meaningless production of signifiers – Cipolla achieves immediate success, garnering the sympathy of both his *beffatori* and today's reading public. However, by engaging in the virtuoso production of an endlessly proliferating speech, Cipolla also dispenses with a historical, though not merely earthly, option for his words: the possibility, opened up by Incarnation, to speak a language of recovered grace. Without any hope of finding external reference or truth, the friar's discourse squarely situates itself on the dark side of the typological ambiguity figured in Eden, which in his perspective remains an inaccessible and barren place. Without Christ, even his Jerusalem remains an all-too-earthly city. Its allure, complicated by the regressive evocation of the Temple's rebuilding in the marking of the flock with charcoal crosses, also reveals itself as a perversely apostatic impulse.

Conclusion

The natural and artistic space that the *brigata* members experience at the start of Day 3, and that they will temporarily leave only at the end of Day 6, is explicitly treated as a hypothetical counterpart to the earthly paradise, the garden of delights of the biblical narrative. The second garden in the *Decameron* is not only a limit case, a paradigmatic model for the interaction of the original benignity of nature and the value of human work, but also a setting for a specifically linguistic exploration of the values and limits of human discourse. The two stories that frame it are deeply involved in negotiating the uses humans may make of language, each exploring the opposite pole in the range of possible linguistic perversions. The first kind of perversion, that of Masetto, is regressive in nature. The story sets him up positively: he is, after all, a young man who replaces an old man. But the way in which he gains access to that carnally paradisal space and the way he interprets the mandate of tending it eventually produce ethical disaster: he is an Adamic figure who gives up Christ, the Verbum, by going temporarily silent; and he eventually cuckolds Christ with a gardenful of nuns.

The other perversion, located precisely at the opposite narrative end of the stretch of stories told in the second garden, is, instead, apostatic. In his fanciful account of the relics collected in his journeys east (toward the earthly location of Eden) and then south-west (toward a carnal Jerusalem), Frate Cipolla systematically turns spiritual notions into material objects, thus adhering to the paradigm of frenetic literalism and fanatical materialism that Boccaccio's culture projected on the figure of the Jew, the bearer of the old dispensation. In reacting to the loss of his parrot feather, which he was going to display as a feather of the Angel Gabriel, and in trivializing in his speech the formula of the Incarnation, Cipolla removes the central event in Christianity from his world view. Masetto cuckolded Christ with a flock of chattering magpies, while Cipolla aborts him by reducing the archangel to a deplumed parrot. Not unlike his predecessor, who became a patriarch at the end of his life, Frate Cipolla also succeeds in his endeavour. But his rhetorical triumph in the square of Certaldo comes at a high price. It is a price that today's readers, but not, I would say, Boccaccio's contemporaries, have seemingly forgotten was there to be paid.

Chapter Four

The Old and the New:
Chaucer's Garden of Delight

And now is Mirthe therin, to here
The briddes, how they singen clere,
The mavis and the nightingale,
And other Ioly briddes smale.
And thus he walketh to solace
Him and his folk; for swetter place
To pleyen in he may not finde,
Although he soughte oon in-til Inde.

Encores est léens, sans doute,
Déduit orendroit qui escoute
A chanter gais rossignolés,
Mauvis et autres oiselés.
Il s'esbat iluec et solace
O ses gens, car plus bele place
Ne plus biau leu por soi joer
Ne porroit-il mie trover.
The Romaunt of the Rose, ll. 618–24

Chaucer's *Canterbury Tales* occupy a special space in the argument of this book. Because of their literary multiformity and internal multivocality, they represent an instance of the heightened impact that the medieval translational practices surveyed here have on the production of new vernacular texts. They are also a historical point of arrival for the garden trope in the literary imagination. The unfinished journey of his pilgrims, with its ultimately – and endlessly – delayed point of arrival, allusively conveys Chaucer's attitude about the literary tradition he inherits and powerfully transforms. All elements are in place for a new literary paradigm, the one programmatically sketched by Petrarch in the letters this chapter will survey, but Chaucer's text strategically delays them, opting for a summative reconsideration of the cultural capital it possesses in lieu of a radical redefinition of it. Chaucer is – pardon the cliché – if not the last of the medieval writers, the last one in the nonlinear and diffracted lineage this book attempts to trace. Culturally and historically speaking, he was perfect for this role. His library was multilingual, comprising Latin as well as French and Italian works, which we will see carefully redeployed in his tales. He worked within the context of a newly emerging language of culture, the idiolect of his native London, which during his lifetime was also the seat of the court and the capital city of a rapidly and dramatically changing kingdom. He not only was a diplomat, repeatedly and intensively travelling to

France and Italy on behalf of the English crown, but at the same time also a tireless translator and cultural mediator, with a strong awareness of the nature of his work that resonated with contemporary questions of biblical translation and interpretation in the Wycliffe movement. The lighthearted tone of most of his texts – and certainly of the tales on which this chapter focuses – should not distract from the clear and refined literary games Chaucer plays with the authoritative Latin and vernacular traditions he translates into his present.

In this chapter, I move between two texts, mutually imbricated, Petrarch's *Griselda* (*Seniles* 17.3 and 4), his translation of Boccaccio's concluding story in the *Decameron* (*Decameron* 10.10) that Chaucer also translated in the Clerk's Tale, and the Merchant's Tale, another story with elements that also stem from Boccaccio's *Decameron*. Considered in their interplay, these texts help define the chronologically latest case and the methodologically limit stage in which the trope of the garden visit is articulated in the tradition examined in this book. My study will be an exercise in contrast, first registering a difference at the level of garden imagery. Although Petrarch's translational texts make gestures toward an antecedent for which allusions to Edenic gardens were crucial, gardens are absent from their immediate narrative horizon. On the contrary, the trope dominates both the plot and the imagery of Chaucer's Merchant's Tale. Secondly, but just as importantly, I will contrast the diverging values that Petrarch's and Chaucer's texts associate with the act of translation. Petrarch's sequence of epistles to Boccaccio, which he placed in a summative position at the end of his collection of *Letters of Old Age*, was intended to be both a theoretical reassertion and a practical demonstration of the value of a "reverse" translation – a translation that moved from what Petrarch defined as the potentially exclusive vernacular of the original to the inclusive linguistic garb of Latin. In line with recent readings of Petrarch's *Griselda*, I see Petrarch's theory and practice of translation in that letter sequence as modelling a specific way of reading: one that could stabilize the ethical meaning of Boccaccio's concluding novella in the *Decameron*, endowing it with a clear ethical and spiritual message for a select readership. The choice of Latin, a language that Petrarch marked explicitly as "my words" in his preface, converged with his interpretation of the original text, framed within a value system in which oldness (both as exemplary antiquity and psychological maturity) and masculinity (associated with both spiritual constancy and ethical self-coherence) were contrastively coded as positive. As I will note, Petrarch's deliberate intervention in the value system of Boccaccio's story registers already at the level of the characterization of the tale's protagonists. In translating Boccaccio's account of the repeated trials that Gualtieri, the ruler of the city of Saluzzo, imposes on his wife, Griselda, pretending first to have their children killed and then to repudiate her, Petrarch stresses their exceptional maturity. A "senile" spirit – thus writes Petrarch – manifests in the husband's keen insight into the great worth hidden by his wife's humble station in life as well as in the wife's virile steadfastness confronting the reversals of fortune that befall her.

These narrative details are matched by metapoetic statements that Petrarch entrusts to the preface and conclusion of his epistles to Boccaccio. In their insistence on the value of the past, *Seniles* 17.3 and 4 are not only a manifesto of the classicist attitude of Petrarch-the-humanist. Consisting in an act of translation, they are also meant to oppose and ultimately discount, from related points of view, the specific hermeneutic productivity associated with translation in vernacular works of fiction. As we shall see, asserting the original author's authority, which remains crucial for establishing the singular meaning of a text, as well as signalling the irreconcilable differences between the original message conveyed in a work and its potential ethical redeployment in different spatial and temporal coordinates, Petrarch's theoretical setup in these epistles seems to work at cross purposes with the translation tradition studied in this book. For Petrarch, the possibility or even the advisability for a text to "mean" different things to different readers by being translated into new interpretive coordinates appears to be more a problem than an opportunity.

Favouring a new "philological" approach to textuality, as he does in the postface to his translation of the *Griselda* in *Seniles* 17.4, Petrarch raises doubts about the possibility that texts may open themselves fruitfully to translation. In staging two contrastive reading scenes to account for the immediate and polarized reception of his version of Boccaccio's story, Petrarch contrasts a compassionate reading, deeply indebted to the scene of conversion by reading in Book 8 of Augustine's *Confessions*, with a stern and dry-eyed interpretation based on a systematic scepticism about the historical possibility of a character as virtuous as the story's heroine. To respond to the apparent "failure" of the story he has just translated to communicate its message, Petrarch insists that the veracity of the plot is guaranteed by a wide range of classical examples and models. While it is intended to defend a new text, in pointing to this closed canon of past exemplary figures Petrarch's vindication of his rendering of Boccaccio's *Griselda* ends up advocating for a literary practice based on the unmatched linguistic, stylistic, and ethical exemplar of classical culture. This very principle is designed to signal differences, rather than continuities, in the redeployment of literary material; and it ultimately unsettles the possibility of fostering a purely empathetic reading of the text based on its significance for the subject's immediate present circumstances.

In this brief account of the stance that Petrarch takes on issues of translation and interpretation in his last letters to Boccaccio, I have deliberately glossed over the significant internal tensions that mark not only the specific texts I discuss, which will be addressed below, but also a historical fact: Petrarch's own career as bilingual writer. Notwithstanding the historical-philological and authorial-originalist classicism he professes in his late Latin epistles, Petrarch was the author of two ambitious and immensely influential vernacular works, the *Canzoniere* and *I Trionfi*, which were militantly engaged in reviving and revisiting classical models and poetic traditions in a new poetic idiom. I am aware that, while it may result in a simplification (or, at least, be the by-product of taking the author's own autobiographical fiction at face value), the outline of Petrarch's position on these matters I have sketched here may also prove useful. Useful, at least, as an agent of contrast for Chaucer's texts, which may be seen as a pointed response to the very reading and writing paradigm delineated in Petrarch's letters to Boccaccio. As I will show in the conclusion of this section, both the Clerk's Tale, indirectly, and the Prologue and Envoy that frame it, more directly, critically review Petrarch's statements. They provide readers with a forceful and imaginative response in which the new trumps the old, the vernacular reasserts its productivity over Latin, and philogyny replaces Petrarch's prescriptive homosocial horizon of reception.

In the second section of this chapter, I accordingly concentrate on the interplay of the Clerk's Tale and the Merchant's Tale, a story that, immediately following the retranslation of Petrarch's translative *Griselda*, is, like its antecedent, concerned with translation. This story too, through its plot and the attending set of values with which it endows its protagonists, advances an alternative model to Petrarch's: one in which the choice between the old and the new is systematically reversed. In both tales, in fact, discursive modernity and subversive femininity are paired together to create the element of value in their connotative systems. Weaving classical and biblical material into a typical triangular, fabliau-inspired plot, the Merchant's Tale recounts the deception (and self-deception) of Januarie, featured as the stock character of the *senex amans* now turned husband, at the hands of Mayus, his young wife, and Damyan, a crafty squire. Staged within the space of a garden, the conclusion of the tale revolves around the magical intervention of another arguably mismatched and yet mythologically pacified couple, Pluto and Proserpina, who will resolve the plot, moving its action forward to a comic resolution. When the rulers of the underworld and their cortège of fairies gather around the laurel-shaded well at the centre of the locked garden and catch the young woman and her hidden lover about to cuckold the old husband, their polarized gifts – clear sight to Januarie, and unstoppable speech to Mayus – not only begin the trial against the woman, who is caught in *flagrante adulterio*, but also provide her with the means to avoid its aftermath. In her ability to produce a counter-discourse and a rebuttal in every dispute with a man into which she is dragged, Januarie's young wife becomes not only a valiant counterpart to the extra-diegetical character of the Wyf of Bath, to whom the Clerk had addressed words of amused appreciation in the conclusion of his tale, but also an emblem of copiousness as a rhetorical and poetic device.

It is significant, and perhaps not particularly surprising, that, in a vernacular text which narrates incidents taking place in a garden, a young woman is given the power to provide an endless, always regerminating retort to any authoritative rebuke she may receive. In light of the trope that this book reconstructs, it could hardly be otherwise. In the same context in which it imaginatively and ironically discovers for modern readers the first act in the sexualized history of copiousness,

Chaucer's Merchant's Tale also foregrounds the connection that this rhetorical feature has with the nexus of vernacularity and ever-renewing discourse. By practising a reticent art of translation from the *Roman de la Rose* as well as Claudian's *De raptu Proserpinae*, and by carefully deploying charged symbolic elements throughout the plot, the story advances this point forcefully. The garden itself, along with familiar ornithological stock presences – the magpie and the parrot – that appear allusively (and metapoetically) in the tale, connects the setting and the activities that unfold there to the trope of the Edenic garden, and aligns the tale's own work to the activity of translation.

Indeed, the story conspicuously features an Eden-like garden, amid allusions to other literary gardens that the text strategically mobilizes but *does not* reproduce. As we will see, when Chaucer refers allusively to the *locus amoenus* at the centre of Claudian's *De raptu Proserpinae* (which is a point of reference for the disoriented Dante entering Eden in the last leg of his journey through Purgatory), and when he openly refers readers back to the garden of the *Roman de la Rose* (a text he has translated elsewhere, in a different work), he does so not only to evoke antecedents he may assume are in his audience's library, but also to point out the translative quality of these texts. The trope of the visit to Eden is, once again, the lens through which specific meaningful aspects of the text may be brought into focus. It is also an important object in the text in its own right, an imaginary space built with topical elements of the literary and hermeneutical tradition.

1. Reversion: Translating in Petrarch's *Griselda* and the Clerk's Tale

Let us begin with Petrarch. As the direct antecedent of Chaucer's Clerk's Tale, it is good to start with a consideration of his *Griselda*, perhaps his most famous involvement in matters of translation.[1] His Latinization of the last *Decameron* tale is embedded in the compact sequence of epistolary exchanges with Boccaccio that forms the concluding book of the *Seniles* (Book 17). The liminal positioning is significant, pointing to the summative quality of these texts, which are followed only by the single *Epistle to Posterity*, Petrarch's intellectual and cultural testament. There are several elements in the text of *Seniles* 17.3 and its immediate context that make it relevant to the argument of this book. The first is, evidently, that it is a translation exercise (although one that goes in the opposite direction to the cases studied thus far), moving from Boccaccio's vernacular narrative antecedent to Petrarch's Latin prose. The epistle is also ostensibly intended to pay a compliment to Boccaccio's literary achievement in the vernacular, since the source story, Dioneo's novella of Gualtieri and Griselda, is labelled as the most weighty and valuable of the tales in the collection. The compliment is partly backhanded, and Petrarch's epistle is at pains to qualify any praise with disclaimers pointing to the youthful quality of Boccaccio's early enterprise and his related, objectionable choice of reading public. Contemporary women, those whom the author of the *Decameron* believes capable of finding both reading "pleasure" and "useful counsel" in his work (*Decameron* Proemio, 13), become for Petrarch, and quite trenchantly so, merely unlearned vernacular readers. Juvenility and lightness are two features that Petrarch points out in Boccaccio's original. As we are about to see, these are two somewhat problematic elements of the *Griselda* rhetoric, which, among other things, his Latin version is designed to address and remedy.

The second element of interest is that Petrarch's version of Boccaccio's story is given a precise theoretical framework *qua* translation. The interpreter immediately explains his motivation for undertaking the work. He fears that the original vernacular will prevent an international segment of its potential readership from having access to the valuable content of the story. He also brings an ancient authoritative maxim on the art of translation to bear on his decision to take a freestyle approach, quoting Horace's permissive statement that one should not, as a "faithful interpreter," strive "to render word by word" the original version of a text (*Ars Poetica* 133–4). Petrarch will take this principle as a licence not only to take lexical or syntactical liberties while "translating" Boccaccio's original, but also to introduce significant variations into his version of the tale – including grafting a new overarching moral for the story. Explicitly labelling the provider of a new version as a *fidus* (overly faithful) *interpres* (controlling agent for the original), Horace's line anticipates the tension between the translator's active intervention in the original text and his respectful reliability in preserving the author's authority, a double commitment to which Petrarch strives to adhere in his epistle. The activation of a "new" meaning, which is intrinsic in the act of interpretation and actualized in Petrarch's translation, is a principle that potentially contradicts the requirement that a translator abstain from crossing into the precincts of the "original" author, as Petrarch notes he did not do, while refraining from becoming "too faithful," as Horace put it. This contrast is a crucial concern in Petrarch's epistle, both for its theoretical framing and translational practice.

The third element of relevance for this discussion is that Petrarch consistently deploys technical translative language to define his literary intervention, but does so in a particularly tense setting. Downplaying the differences between the original text and its new instantiation, Petrarch locates the main disjunction between his and Boccaccio's versions of the story solely on the level of style. While he frames his translation as an act of interpretation, he also limits the weight of his intervention by carefully juxtaposing the authority of the author and that of the interpreter and ultimately abdicating responsibility for the "real" meaning of the tale, which allegedly remains Boccaccio's and not Petrarch's own. Petrarch accordingly deploys charged sartorial metaphors to define his work, focusing on translation as a mere change of linguistic "garb," literally a re-dressing of a body that stays essentially the same. The metapoetic framing of Petrarch's theory of translation uncannily mirrors the text's insistence on the repeated spoliation and reclothing experienced by its female protagonist, postulating the same constancy in her ethics as in the hermeneutics of the translated text.

Finally, in addition to describing the circumstances triggering his translation exercise, Petrarch recounts an episode he deems significant in the immediate reception of his work. With this last step, his reflection becomes all-encompassing: it stretches from the inception and framing of the work, passes through the practical aspects of its implementation, and ends with an evaluation of the dissemination and impact of the translated text. While discussing the truth-status of the story he has translated, in the opening paragraphs of *Seniles* 17.4, he describes the polarized reactions of two of his and Boccaccio's friends, a gentleman from Padua and a learned man from Verona. As he reports, the first was so moved by the story that he could not finish reading it and passed the text to another man in his company, while the other was able to keep his composure throughout the reading. This person's stern reaction was not due to a particular moral disposition, Petrarch notes, but to the deep conviction that the virtues attributed to the protagonist were utterly implausible, and that, accordingly, the story could only be a fictional plot. However, Petrarch now argues that his stance was untenable, since there are historical records of equally imposingly exemplary figures, whom the author lists in a concluding display of both literary erudition and polemical punctiliousness.

All these elements will be addressed again in detail in my close reading of Petrarch's epistle. Thus far, suffice it to note that in approaching that text readers of this book may find themselves on largely, but perhaps not fully, familiar terrain. The phenomenon under scrutiny is presented as an instance of translation across the Latin-vernacular divide, like most of the cases studied here. Theoretical reflections accompany the translational practice, containing pointed references to classical antecedents. The process of linguistic transformation is associated with an active hermeneutic intervention on the part of the interpreter, who delineates for his contemporary readers the boundaries for their reception and use of the translated text. What seems to be missing from the imaginary context of Petrarch's translation is the garden. I maintain, however, that this absence is both apparent and deeply significant, as it is balanced by a subtle allusion to a famous scene of reading that unfolds in a tropological Edenic garden. The twofold reading scene described in the postface to Petrarch's translation (*Seniles* 17.4) evokes the trope of the garden visit in two ways. It does so indirectly, as the reaction of the first reader – who weeps profusely, proves unable to read further, and must give the text to a companion to complete the reading – gestures toward the garden setting of Augustine's famous reading-cum-conversion. It also does so pointedly, by emphasizing the second reader's contrasting style of reading – he reads the whole text without interruption, remains unflinching throughout, and criticizes the fictional quality of the text – and indicating that Augustine's scene is ultimately a nonviable model for the reading acts that it presents. In sum, for a readership alert to the trope of the garden, Petrarch evokes said trope with utmost clarity.

Now we shall move on to a closer analysis of the text, beginning with the epistle that frames Petrarch's Latinization of Boccaccio's tale. The first fifteen paragraphs in this letter to Boccaccio are particularly dense and worth dwelling upon at length. In them, Petrarch provides a carefully arranged account of the circumstances that led him to translate his friend's text and, in so doing, provides an initial framing for his own text. The context is, apparently, his chance encounter with the *Decameron*, a work Petrarch immediately casts in an ambivalent light:

> Librum tuum, quem nostro materno eloquio, ut opinor, olim iuvenis edidisti, nescio quidem unde vel qualiter ad me delatum, vidi. (2) Nam si dicam: "legi", mentiar, siquidem ipse magnus valde, ut ad vulgus et soluta scriptus oratione, et occupatio mea maior et tempus angustum erat, idque ipsum, ut nosti, bellicis undique motibus inquietum … (3) Quid ergo? Excucurri eum et festini viatoris in morem hinc atque hinc circumspiciens nec subistens animadverti alicubi librum ipsum canum dentibus lacessitum, tuo tamen baculo egregie tuaque voce defensum … (5) Delectatus sum ipso in transitu et, siquid lascivie liberioris occurreret, excusabat etas tunc tua, dum id scriberes, stilus, ydioma, ipsa quoque rerum levitas et eorum qui lecturi talia videbantur; refert enim largiter quibus scribas morumque varietate stili varietas excusatur. (6) Inter multa sane iocosa et levia quedam pia et gravia deprehendi, de quibus tamen diffinitive quid iudicem non habeo, ut qui nusquam totus inheserim. (7) At, quod fere accidit eo more currentibus, curiosius aliquanto quam cetera libri principium finemque perspexi; quorum in altero patrie nostre statum, illius scilicet pestilentissimi temporis, quod pre omnibus nostra etas lugubre ac miserum mundo vidit, meo quidem iudicio et narrasti proprie et magnifice deplorasti; in altero autem historiam ultimam et multis precedentium longe dissimilem posuisti.[2] (*Seniles* 17.3)

I have seen your book – the one I believe you produced in our maternal tongue some time ago, as a young man. I am not sure from where or how it was brought to me. Now, I won't say "I read it" because that would be a lie, since it is rather big – addressed, as it is, to the common folk and written in prose – and even bigger was the amount of work before me, and the little time I had was also, as you know, troubled by the commotion of ubiquitous war … What, then? I ran through it and, looking here and there, like a hurried traveller, without ever stopping, I noticed that that book of yours had been attacked by the teeth of dogs but also excellently defended by your cane and your voice … I found pleasure even in just going over it: if I was met by something lewd, a little too frankly put, you were excused by the age at which you wrote it, the style, the language, as well as the lightness of the subject matter and of those who were supposedly going to read such things. In fact, it is of paramount importance to whom you write, and one's variety in style is justified by the audience's variety in moral standards. Among many playful and lighthearted matters, I also noticed some pious and serious ones, about which, however, I won't pass a definitive judgment, since I never stopped to devote full attention to them. Yet, as almost always happens to those who run in this way, I did scrutinize the beginning and ending of the book somewhat more deeply than the rest. In the former, I feel you aptly recounted and magnificently lamented the sorry state of our homeland at the time of the great plague – a time that our age saw as the saddest and most tragic ever for the world. In the latter, however, you placed the last story, so different from the many that precede it.

The ambivalence of Petrarch's stance in the passage is quite palpable and multiform. While it certainly contains noteworthy elements, on which Petrarch lavishes praise, Boccaccio's bulky volume ("magnus valde") is presented as an uneven work. It contains morally questionable narrative elements ("… quid lascivie liberioris") in its mix. It is the product of a "past" (as in younger) authorial persona, implicitly contrasted with what readers are supposed to consider the more serious, present cultural stance and literary activities of the aged correspondent. It is addressed to a specific audience (the *vulgus*) and, accordingly, has been penned in a particular "language and style": that is, vernacular prose ("materno eloquio … soluta oratione"). It encompasses a mix of subject matter, ranging from the most "lighthearted" ("levia") to the most "serious" ("gravia") topics, a variety ultimately justifiable on the basis of all of the above. The exculpatory logic Petrarch adopts in the passage indicts Boccaccio's project more than it acquits it. The classical principle of *convenientia*, which dictates *a parte subiecti* that different literary projects are suited to different stages in an author's life and *a parte objecti* that subject matter and style should be chosen according to the audience being addressed, may well account for Boccaccio's decision to write in the vernacular, in prose, and to an audience for whom levity is appropriate terrain. Nonetheless, these same principles do not hide Petrarch's implied preference for a different set of linguistic, stylistic, and aesthetic as well as ethical parameters, which his epistle both assumes of, and helps establish in, his readers.

Moreover, readers can find expressions in Petrarch's balancing act that are perhaps even more damning, starting with the characterization of his encounter with Boccaccio's text as not exactly a canonical "reading." Petrarch employs the simile of the hurried traveller to report his own reading and qualify his appreciation of Boccaccio. Just as a hasty traveller might explore a new land, Petrarch the uncommitted reader looks around as he traverses the book; he finds a measure of delight in crossing its varied terrain and tolerates accidental encounters with various matters along the way, but his attention is always elsewhere. The chance event with which the epistle opens, with the book reaching Petrarch through an unknown intermediary in unknowable circumstances, in turn inaugurates a series of sensible professions of disengagement from fulfilling the requirements of what would in contrast be a "proper" act of reading. The writer states that "he saw" ("vidi") his friend's book, immediately drawing a distinction between this way of experiencing the work and the discounted alternative "I read" ("legi"), an activity that involves lingering and undivided attention, specifically what Petrarch could not give to the book at hand ("ut qui nusquam totus inheserim").

Imaginatively phrased as cursory ("excucurri"), with the reader stopping only at key points to make note of something, Petrarch's experience of the *Decameron* was just as uneven as the work itself. For one, he realized ("animadverti") that the book had come under attack, but that the author valiantly defended it. This is most likely a reference to Boccaccio's introduction to Day 4, a setting from which Petrarch could appreciate having been deliberately left out, excluded from the authoritative examples of Dante, Cavalcanti, and Cino da Pistoia, a canon of love poets who Boccaccio claimed stayed true to their vocation even in old age. Petrarch also caught sight ("deprehendi") of the fact that, interspersed within its larger body of blithe tales, the *Decameron* contained "a few" serious and pious ones; his telling use of the plural "quedam" invites speculation about which, in addition to the last story in the book, these "pia et gravia" stories may be. Significantly, Petrarch also only paid closer attention ("curiosius … perspexi") to the beginning and ending of the volume: the first section he praises as a convincing rhetorical tour de force ("narrasti proprie et magnifice deplorasti") that condemns the deadly effects of the plague in Florence, and the latter as distinctly unlike the rest, on account of the singularly powerful tale it contains (a "historiam … longe dissimilem").

Upon reaching this last story, the epistle sharply changes its tone and rhetoric, with the praise it dispenses becoming less qualified. The pleasure he derived from reading the concluding tale in the *Decameron* ("ita michi placuit"), Petrarch continues, is such that his readerly haste yielded to calculated lingering ("ut … meque detinuit"), his fleeting impressions were replaced by mindful determination ("memorie mandare voluerim"), and his initial distraction turned into active engagement with the transmission ("ut et ipse … repeterem … renarrarem") of the text:

(8) Que ita michi placuit meque detinuit ut inter tot curas, que pene mei ipsius immemorem me fecere, illam memorie mandare voluerim, ut et ipse eam animo quotiens vellem non sine voluptate repeterem et amicis, ut fit, confabulantibus renarrarem, si quando tale aliquid incidisset.

This tale I liked so much, and was so seized by, that despite the many worries that were almost making me forgetful of myself, I wanted to learn it by heart. In this way I could repeat it to myself every time I desired (and not without pleasure) as well as retell it to friends with whom I fell into conversation, when something of the sort happened to be on point.

As is often the case in Petrarch, the epistle is just as concerned with recording the subject's reaction to an experience as it is with presenting the object of the experience itself. What the text relates in this second section, thus, is presented as mostly taking place in Petrarch's mind (and as an intimation of his working method), rather than in (and around) Boccaccio's text. Yet, something about that text – or to be more specific, about the relationship between Boccaccio's and Petrarch's texts – is quite precisely and compellingly said. Moving the attention from anecdotal circumstances to metaliterary considerations, the epistle addresses the translative quality of the text it accompanies, and it does so in technical terms. In addition to entrusting the story to memory, Petrarch notes that the exceptional quality of the subject matter, to which he had pleasantly been exposed years before, and which Boccaccio had evidently found fascinating enough to give the place of honour in his vernacular work, deserves additional attention: it needs to be translated. This is how the epistle handles the point:

(9) Quod cum brevi postmodum fecissem gratamque audientibus cognovissem, subito talis inter loquendum cogitatio supervenit, fieri posse ut nostri etiam sermonis ignaros tam dulcis historia delectaret, cum et michi semper ante multos annos audita placuisset et tibi usqueadeo placuisse perpenderem, ut vulgari eam stilo tuo censueris non indignam et fine operis, ubi rhetorum disciplina validiora quelibet collocari iubet.

Once I had done that a short time later, and had realized that the listeners liked the tale, I suddenly realized something while I was still speaking. Namely, I thought it possible that such a sweet story would please people who don't know our language, just as I had always liked it since the first time I heard it many years before, and I realized that you also must have liked it – to the point of considering it not unworthy of your vernacular pen and placing it at the conclusion of your work, the place where the art of rhetoric orders the strongest elements should be placed.

The first element that establishes Petrarch's upcoming exercise as a translation is the inter-linguistic preoccupation that motivates him while writing. There is a chance, he thinks, that such a sweet story may also turn out to be pleasant for "people who do not know our language." The "why" of the operation is, thus, simple: to allow the tale to cross historically determined linguistic boundaries. The "how" is, rather, a more belaboured aspect of the work, starting from the immediate personal and spiritual circumstances that precipitated the translation, an activity that Petrarch also labels as noticeably exceptional:

(10) Itaque die quodam inter varios cogitatus animum more solito discerpentes et illis et michi, ut sic dixerim, iratus, "vale" omnibus ad tempus dicto, historiam ipsam tuam scribere sum aggressus, te hauddubie gavisurum sperans ultro rerum interpretem me tuarum fore; quod non facile alteri cuicunque prestiterim. (11) Egit me tui amor et historie, ita tamen ne horatianum illud *Poetice artis* obliviscerer: *Nec verbum verbo curabis reddere fidus / interpres.* (12) Historiam tuam meis verbis explicui, uno

alicubi aut paucis in ipsa narratione mutatis verbis aut additis, quod te non ferente modo sed favente fieri credidi. (13) Que licet a multis et laudata et expetita fuerit, ego rem tuam tibi non alteri dedicandam censui. (14) Quam quidem an mutata veste deformaverim an fortassis ornaverim, tu iudica; illic enim orta, illuc redit; notus iudex, nota domus, notum iter, ut unum et tu noris et quisquis hec leget, tibi non michi tuarum rationem rerum esse reddendam. (15) Quisquis ex me queret an hec vera sint, hoc est an historiam scripserim an fabulam, respondebo illud Crispi: "Fides penes auctorem", meum scilicet Iohannem, "sit". Hec prefatus incipio.

And so, on a day in which I was, as usual, troubled by different thoughts that tore at me and angry, so to speak, both at them and at myself, I said "good-bye" to all for some time, I began writing that story of yours. I was hoping that you would certainly be happy that I was spontaneously turning to be your translator, something that I have hardly done for anyone else. My love for you and your story compelled me, but not so deeply that I forgot Horace's point in the *Ars poetica*: "One should not translate word by word, / as a zealously faithful interpreter." I have told your story with words that are mine, changing or adding in some places one word or a few more in the narrative itself – something I trusted you would endorse not simply endure. Although it had been both praised and requested by many, still I deemed it should be dedicated to you, since it belongs to you. Whether I have deformed or adorned it by changing its dress, you be the judge: it is going back to where it originated; it knows the judge, the home, and the path it should take. I have only added that you and whoever reads these things should know that it is up to you, not me, to account for your things. Whoever would ask me whether these things are true or false – i.e., if I have written a history or a fable – I will answer with the words of Crispus: "It's up to the author" (i.e. my friend Giovanni) "to do so." Having said this, I begin.

From a personal point of view, Petrarch's writing of Boccaccio's tale is designed to be a welcome, if temporary, distraction from the usual dissension of thoughts that agitates his mind. From the point of view of his friendship with Boccaccio, it is an attempt to produce something about which his addressee will rejoice. The twofold aim of Petrarch's work is not the only redoubled element in his account. There are two further sets of dichotomies, one related to the kind of writing that is at stake in Petrarch's translation of *Decameron* 10.10, and the other affecting the authority of all involved parties. From a metapoetic perspective, both are crucial distinctions.

On the first matter, there is a measure of tension in Petrarch's juxtaposition of the verb "scribere," which he uses at first to label his version of the story, and the more specific qualification of the writer as "interpretem" for the same act, which immediately follows in the paragraph. Used to mark the difference between committing a text to memory and writing it in another language, the root verb "interpretare" establishes that Petrarch's operation entails a higher degree of activity than "scribere." We have only to take stock of the wide application he makes of Horace's dictum to appreciate the divergence. For Horace, an interpreter should not strive to proceed word-by-word in his renditions, and thus risk becoming pedantically faithful in his work; for Petrarch, the desire to interpret may be motivated by love for his friend and his story ("tui amor et historie"), but such love is not idolatrous of the text's letter – or, we might add, the author's intention. Consequently, while Petrarch downplays his intrusions into Boccaccio's text and strives to present them all under the umbrella of "authorially welcomed alterations" ("te non ferente modo sed favente"), his changes to narrative details are often radical and meaningful. What is more, his translation is framed as a hermeneutical intervention. In the concluding paragraph of the epistle, a passage to which I will return momentarily, Petrarch provides readers with the precise coordinates of his own "interpretation," what the story is intended to "mean," thus clarifying for them the nature and measure of this difference.

Readers find a similarly tense situation when it comes to the second point, the question of ownership of the text. No matter how different from Boccaccio's original the text has become thanks to its interpreter's interventions, Petrarch's version of the story still belongs to its first author. No matter how "interpretive" Petrarch's "writing" has been, the translated text is cogently said to be Boccaccio's. In Petrarch's preface, authorial sameness is established through insistent notations of property. When the new author respectfully invokes the authority of his exemplar to delimit his own, he insists that he has worked on "historiam ipsam tuam," one of "rerum tuarum" (10). Shortly thereafter, similar characterizations recur verbatim, leaving little doubt about how Petrarch constructs the interrelation of the two texts. What Petrarch is sending Boccaccio is still "historiam tuam" (12) and "rem tuam" (13), his uncontested property. This idea can be seen as somewhat surprising, especially given the Horatian authority Petrarch brings to bear on his activity as translator: the expression *fidus interpres* was, in fact, used in a context where Horace instructed new authors on how to "make what is public property their own" ("publica materies privati iuris erit," *Ars poetica* 131), and mobilized legal language that is echoed in Petrarch's text ("vetet … operis lex," l. 135). In short, although the tale has been made the object of an "interpretation," Petrarch claims that the final responsibility for its meaning rests with the original author. Programmatically, what Petrarch the interpreter has written belongs to Boccaccio the author, in both an original and ultimate sense.[3]

The final disclaimer Petrarch adds to his operation, that single element ("unum") he deems essential for Boccaccio as well as for future readers to keep in mind when approaching the text, is far from standard. Coyly phrased as a question of vouching for the veracity of the tale, a feature in the text to which Petrarch will return in the postface to his translation, the application of the classical principle that the author is responsible for his texts ("fides penes acutorem erit") is not limited to the veracity of the narrative. Even in the new garb that has been provided for it, Petrarch notes, the story remains one of Boccaccio's assets. His ownership affects it at a deeper and more essential level. Apparently exonerating Petrarch from being liable for its truth-value, the fact that the only author of the translated text is "meus … Iohannis" also exonerates Petrarch from accounting for the tale's meaning. As he trenchantly states, "it is you, not I, who is called to account for your things" ("tibi non michi tuarum rationem rerum esse reddendam"). After all, as the epistle puts it, in anticipating the story's own insistence on dressing and undressing scenes, the translation has merely been a change of clothing ("mutata veste") for the text; by being sent to its first author for evaluation, the translated story (or its protagonist) is simply retracing well-known steps. Just like Griselda the character, so too Griselda the tale returns from whence it came, and by treading the same road. If the epistle can say that the circumstances of the journey are familiar and "the judge, the home, and the road" are known, this is because the story is still essentially the same – just as, for better or for worse, a person is after having undergone a change of clothing.[4]

But is Petrarch's protestation of utter and essential sameness acceptable? A consideration of the concluding paragraph in the epistle may help assess the limited validity and instrumental quality of his claim. In this companion piece to the metapoetic preface, Petrarch returns to discussing the reasons for his work. This time he does so by addressing its purpose, the *causa finalis*. Unsurprisingly, as is common for medieval writings, his goal is ethical:

(143) Hanc historiam stilo nunc alio retexere visum fuit, non tanto ideo ut matronas nostri temporis ad imitandam huius uxoris patientiam, que michi vix imitabilis videtur, quam ut legentes ad imitandam saltem femine constantiam excitarem, ut quod hec viro suo prestitit, hoc prestare Deo nostro audeant … (144) Abunde ego constantibus viris ascripserim, quisquis is fuerit, qui pro Deo suo sine murmure patiatur quod pro suo mortali coniuge rusticana hec muliercula passa est.

It seemed right to redo this story in another style, not so much to invite the womenfolk of our time to imitate the patience of that wife – something that to me seems hardly imitable – as to invite all readers to imitate that woman's constancy, so that they dare keep for our God what she kept for her man … I would certainly count among men of constancy whosoever would suffer without complaint for his God what this little peasant woman suffered for her mortal spouse.

The purpose of Petrarch's reworking of Boccaccio's text in a different style (a story that is now significantly "hanc historiam" and no longer "tuam historiam") is to provide an example to be imitated. Notably, while the novella is ostensibly about a woman, and the title of Petrarch's epistle cites "fides uxoria" as its core concern, the example it is supposed to provide is not one addressed to women and has nothing to do with patience in marital matters. Rather, as Petrarch states, it is addressed to men, and has everything to do with constancy in the spiritual realm. Faced with the interpretive openness of his exemplar, which leaves the ultimate import of Dioneo's tale unadjudicated, simply registering that the story was robustly debated by the storytellers (*Dec.* 10.concl.1), Petrarch opts for providing a single interpretive point of entry into it. Refraining from even dignifying the original storyteller's subversive reading of the tale – as an example not of any virtue Griselda might have had, but rather of Gualtieri's "mad bestiality" (*Dec.* 10.10.3) – with an answer, Petrarch's original but this time non-originalist interpretation takes a sharp ethical-allegorical turn. His Valterus is a figure of God, and his Griseldis one of the human spirit. Given the theological impasse of attributing to God the same intentions as Boccacio's Gualtieri, a notion which flew in the face of the Epistle of James he prudently quotes, Petrarch is keen to remark that the tests to which the husband subjects his wife are, from the spiritual perspective he recommends, not tests at all but rather ethical reminders of human fragility. Such tests, if one wants to be counted among the virtuous, require steadfast and unmurmuring acceptance.

Not content with such a conclusive indication of the story's meaning – or, at least, of his own intention in writing it – Petrarch returns to explore the possible effects of his text in his next epistle, this time choosing to outsource the reading. Using the first sentence to suture the two epistles together with a recapitulation, Petrarch notes:

(1) Ursit amor tui ut scriberem senex quod iuvenis vix scripsissem, nescio an res veras an fictas, que iam non historie sed fabelle sunt, ob hoc unum, quod res tue et a te scripte erant, quamvis hoc previdens "fidem rerum penes auctorem", hoc est penes te, fore sim prefatus. (2) Et dicam tibi quid de hac – historiam ego quam fabulam dixisse malim – michi contigerit. Legit eam primum comunis amicus patavinus, vir altissimi ingenii multiplicisque notitie, et, cum epistole medium vix transisset, subito fletu preventus substitit; post modicum vero, cum in manus eam resumpsisset firmato animo perlecturus, ecce iterum quasi ad condictum rediens lecturam gemitus interrupit. (3) Fassus itaque se non posse procedere eam uni suorum comitum, docto satis viro, legendam tradidit. (*Seniles* 17.4.1–3)

My love for you urged me to write, as an old man, what I would hardly have written as a young one – things that I am not sure are actual or fictional (since these are not histories but fables) – for the sole reason that they belonged to you, and you wrote them first. I did, however, foresee this and thus I prefaced my work with the saying "vouching for the truth of this matter is up to the author": that is, it's up to you. Now I will tell you what happened with this tale, which I would prefer to call a story rather than a fable. It was first read by our mutual friend from Padua, a man of high intelligence and wide culture; he had hardly passed the midpoint of the letter when he stopped, hindered by sudden weeping. After a little while, having taken it up again to read through to the end with a steeled spirit, it happened once more – as if he had reached an appointed place – that his reading was interrupted by a sob. Confessing, then, that he could not go further, he passed it on to one in his retinue, a sufficiently learned man, to read.

To his profession of friendship with Boccaccio ("amor tui") Petrarch adds a reiteration of the alienating clause with which he prefaced his translation of the dubiously true story ("res tue et a te scripte erant"), and Bocaccio is again featured in the role of *auctor*. However, the translator also adds an additional retrospective detail that we should keep in mind because it is pertinent for this analysis. He has completed this work – a project that he would hardly have undertaken even as a young person ("iuvenis") – at a specific age: he is now old, a "senex." Thus framed, the first reading scene of the new text then ensues. The person reading is a mutual friend from Padua, a randomly chosen reader ("quid … contigerit" expresses this facet of the situation). Petrarch notes the inchoate quality of his reaction. Having barely crossed the midpoint of the letter, this intelligent and learned man is overwhelmed by the tale and halted by a crying spell. Having regained his composure, he tries to continue, but is once again interrupted by his own sighs. Fortunately, there is another person in his retinue, to whom he passes the text to read. Just as we are supposed to understand that his reading this time reached the story's ending, we are not told the reaction of this secondary reader. The shift in reader is, however, significant. It is not difficult to see an allusion to another paradigmatic reading scene here: the *lectio interrupta* that Augustine narrates as the turning point of his life in Book 8 of his *Confessions*. In that prominent episode of his intellectual and moral biography, Augustine recounts that, caught in the pangs of a spiritual crisis that manifested itself in copious weeping, he heeded a mysterious call to "pick up and read" ("tolle, lege") a book he had with him; in it, he found words that touched him so deeply that he needed to read no further, having received the final spur to achieve his long-sought conversion to Christianity (8.8.28–9). In the original passage, Augustine's narrative is peppered with references to crying: first, the storm in his soul brings a heavy rain of tears ("imbrem lacrimarum"); he then retreats to a more solitary spot to undertake the work of weeping ("negotium flendi"); he is pregnant with crying ("fletu gravidus"); his eyes are rivers of tears ("flumina oculorum meorum"). The mysterious voice that compels him to "pick up and read" reaches him while he is speaking and weeping at the same time: "Dicebam haec et flebam." The effect of the mysterious message he receives and immediately interprets as an invitation to read the book he has brought with him is drastic. He changes his expression ("statim … mutato vultu"), stops the impetus of his tears ("represso … impetu lacrimarum"), and opens the book. Rather than depicting crying as a reaction to reading, Augustine's text thus presents reading as a response and an antidote to weeping.

Still, the analogies between the old and new reading scenes narrated in the *Confessions* and in Petrarch's epistle, respectively, extend to the climactic moment in Augustine's account. Upon opening the book, Augustine reads words that he finds perfectly fitting to his situation and that he immediately applies to himself. This act is explicitly presented as the repetition of another exemplary interpretive act, the one that precipitated Saint Anthony's conversion, who also converted to Christianity when he heard words being read that he took as being addressed to him ("tamquam sibi diceretur quod legebatur"). Augustine's conversion by reading also marks his pause in reading:

> itaque concitus redii in eum locum ubi sedebat Alypius: ibi enim posueram codicem apostoli cum inde surrexeram. arripui, aperui, et legi in silentio capitulum quo primum coniecti sunt oculi mei: "non in comessationibus et ebrietatibus, non in cubilibus et impudicitiis, non in contentione et aemulatione, sed induite dominum Iesum Christum et carnis providentiam ne feceritis in concupiscentiis." nec ultra volui legere nec opus erat. statim quippe cum fine huiusce sententiae quasi luce securitatis infusa cordi meo omnes dubitationis tenebrae diffugerunt. (*Confessiones* 8.8.28)

Thus, I started off and went back to the place where Alypius was seated, for that was where I had put down the book of the Apostle when I had stood up. I fetched it, opened it, and silently read the first chapter on which my eyes came to rest: "Clothe yourself not in banquets and drunkenness, not in lust and shamelessness, not in discord and rivalries, but in the Lord Jesus Christ, and make no provision for the flesh's desires." I did not desire to read any further, nor was there any need to. All at once, with the end of that sentence, the shades of my doubt were all scattered, as if by a light of assurance pouring into my heart.

His calm restored, Augustine passes the book to his friend Alypius, who is with him and about to partake in the same experience. Continuing the reading from where Augustine had left off, he too finds a message that leads him to a spiritual conversion:

> Tum interiecto aut digito aut nescio quo alio signo codicem clausi et tranquillo iam vultu indicavi Alypio. at ille quid in se ageretur (quod ego nesciebam) sic indicavit. petit videre quid legissem. ostendi, et attendit etiam ultra quam ego legeram. et ignorabam quid sequeretur. sequebatur vero: "infirmum autem in fide recipite." quod ille ad se rettulit mihique aperuit. (29)

Then, using a finger or some other sign to mark the place, I closed the book and, with a now peaceful expression, showed it to Alypius. In response, he showed me what was happening in him (something I did not know). He asked to see what I had read. I presented it to him. He looked beyond what I had read. I did not know what would follow in the text. But this is what followed: "Do, however, receive the one who is weak in faith." He interpreted this as concerning himself and disclosed it to me.

The resonances of the Augustinian context with Petrarch's are essential. In both cases a subject's empathetic reading of a text, marked by copious tears, is interrupted, and in both cases a companion carries the reading forward to its natural (and salvific) conclusion. Again, what seems to be missing in the dialogue between the new text and its antecedent is any remark about the setting. It is important to note that, while we have no indication of where Petrarch's Paduan friend encounters the epistle, the conversion scene in Augustine's *Confessions* was staged in a specific setting: the garden adjacent to his home in Milan. Although adding few details, the *Confessions* make this point with poignant clarity:

> hortulus quidam erat hospitii nostri, quo nos utebamur sicut tota domo: nam hospes ibi non habitabat, dominus domus. illuc me abstulerat tumultus pectoris, ubi nemo impediret ardentem litem quam mecum aggressus eram, donec exiret – qua tu sciebas, ego autem non: sed tantum insaniebam salubriter et moriebar vitaliter, gnarus quid mali essem et ignarus quid boni post paululum futurus essem. abscessi ergo in hortum, et Alypius pedem post pedem. neque enim secretum meum non erat, ubi ille aderat. (19)

> There was a small garden next to our lodgings, which we used on par with the rest of the house, since the host, the master of the house, did not live there. The turmoil in my chest had brought me there, where no one would hinder the harsh lawsuit I mounted against myself until its conclusion – what that would be only you knew, since I did not. I was only raging toward sanity and dying to be alive, conscious of what was wrong with me and unconscious of what was so very soon to be right. I went, thus, into the garden, as Alypius followed step by step: after all, I was no less alone with myself when he was with me.

Presented with a tearful and interrupted reading scene that also includes a second reader who just so happens to be standing by, readers of Petrarch's epistle can hardly avoid recalling the Augustinian antecedent – and also, I would suggest, its setting. The absence of the garden-visit trope from the context of Petrarch's account of the act of reading is thus neither complete nor coincidental. On the contrary, it is evocative.

Dominated by repetition and a vivid sense of *déjà lu*, Petrarch's vignette is clearly patterned after the decisive moment of the *Confessions*, in both the dynamics it reports *and* the locale in which it unfolds. The close patterning – with the protagonist responding to an impulse to open the book, having a witness by his side who would become part of the reading experience, and encountering a text that he feels has been written for him – is designed to evoke a sense of repetition grounded in sameness. The context of Augustine's conversion narrative suggests how this sameness is rooted in a specific place: "Ego sub quadam fici arbore stravi me nescio quomodo, et dimisi habenas lacrimis" (And I stretched myself under a tree of figs, I don't know how, and gave free rein to my tears, *Confessiones* 8.12.28). As has been noted, the words he uses here – "a tree of figs": neither just "a tree" nor just "a fig tree" – are a literal echo intended to evoke at least two different trees (from Genesis [2.3.7] and the Gospel of John [1.47–8]). Augustine's words apply just as perfectly to these already typologically related trees – their respective singularity notwithstanding – as they now apply to the tree in Milan. In other words, the *Confessions* accept the notion that these words were spoken about a different object and to a different audience before, and that their present appropriation and repetition subtract nothing from either referential act. Rather, it is in their repetition that they find fuller (moral) meaning. The strategy of de-emphasizing difference in time, locale, and characters involved in the scene is not only crucial for the operation of an ethical reading, but also it is linked to the precise space in which that reading unfolds.[5]

Instead of a garden-scene, while remaining in the realm of the effects of reading and interpreting a text, what Petrarch's letter gives us is a second-degree interpretation. Petrarch transcribes his "reading" of the effects that the reading of his epistle has produced in the first reader in great detail:

(3) Quod accidens quorsum alii traherent, incertum habeo; ego in optimam parte traxi mitissimumque viri animum intellexi; vere enim homo humanior, quem ego quidem noverim, nullus est. (4) Redit illo flente ac legente ad memoria satyricum illud: *mollissima corda / humano generi dare se natura fatetur, / que lacrimas dedit; hec nostri pars optima sensus.*

I am not sure how others may interpret what happened. As for me, I interpreted it in the best possible way; namely, as indicating the spirit of a most gentle person. And, in fact, I knew no man more humane than him. His reading and weeping brought back to my mind a passage in the *Satires*: "By giving tears to humankind, / Nature reveals that she has given them the softest of hearts: / that is the most noble part of our emotions."

Petrarch actively chooses to see an intimation of the man's meekness in his weeping. His reading is, technically, *in bono*. No one, he notes, is "more human than this man" (3). Aligning himself with Boccaccio's opening sentence in the *Decameron*, namely, that "umana cosa è aver compassione degli afflitti" (it is properly human to feel compassion for those who suffer, Proemio.1), and citing Juvenal 15, Petrarch characterizes this first reaction as positive, a proof that weeping indicates the best possible disposition in a human being (their *pars optima*), and a validation of the good kind of fidelity that his translation kept to its original.

But this is not all, and the epistle is keen to offer a counterexample, one that involves a reading that goes very differently. The epistle takes the compassionate, involved reading of the Paduan friend and juxtaposes it with the stern behaviour of another mutual friend from Verona. Having heard what happened to the first reader, this man is willing to put himself to the test and asks to gain access to the text:

(5) Post tempus amicus alter noster veronensis, – sunt enim nobis, ut relique, sic amici etiam comunes– audito quid alteri inter legendum accidisset, eandem legere optavit. (6) Gessi morem ingenioso et amico viro. Legit eam totam nec alicubi substitit nec frons obductior nec vox fractior nec lacrime nec singultus intervenere et in finem "Ego etiam" inquit "flessem – nam et pie res et verba rebus accomodata fletum suadebant nec ego duri cordis sum –, nisi quod ficta omnia credidi et credo. (7) Nam, si vera essent, que usquam mulier, vel romana vel cuiuslibet gentis, hanc Griseldim equatura sit? Ubi, queso, tantus amor coniugalis, ubi par fides, ubi tam insignis patientia atque constantia?"

A little bit later, another friend of ours from Verona (of course, we share friends as we share everything else), having heard what had happened to the other one while he was reading, desired to read it as well. I complied with the request of this intelligent and dear friend. He read it all. He did not stop at any point, nor did he show perturbation in his brow or hesitation in his voice: no tears and no sighs came from him. In the end, he said: "I too would have cried – for indeed the subject matter is pious, and the words, well-suited to the matter, did invite weeping, and I am not hard-hearted – but I was sure, and still am, that the whole thing is fiction. For, if it were true, what woman, whether Roman or of any other people, could ever equal this Griselda? Where, I ask, might one find such a great conjugal love? Where a similar faith? Where such a notable patience and constancy?"

The outcome of this second reading test could hardly be more different from the first. The friend from Verona reads the letter in its entirety, his eyes are never lowered, his voice never trembles, and he has no tears to shed or sighs to emit. Petrarch notes that in the end his behaviour was not a result of any shortcoming of the text or in his character. What kept him from feeling any kind of emotion was his certainty that the whole story was pure fiction. He reached this conclusion through a reasoning per absurdum. The exceptional quality of Petrarch's Griseldis was such that no ancient, Roman or foreign, example of conjugal love, faithfulness, patience, and constancy could ever match her. This notion – that a heroine from the present might outdo her counterparts from the past – was, however, an utter impossibility. Hence, it followed that the tale must be fictional. At this point, Petrarch insinuates that although he did not want to enter into a polemical exchange with his friend, he had a reply ready – one he now shares with Boccaccio and his readers. Petrarch's response takes the form of a catalogue of classical examples of moral determination that includes Roman heroes such as Mutius Scaevola and the Decii, along with distant figures such as the Athenian Codrus and the Philenii of Carthage, and heroines including Cato's Portia (wife of Brutus), Hipsicrathea (one of Mithridate's wives), and the mythical Alcestis:

> (10) Quis est enim exempli gratia qui non Curtium ex nostris et Mutium et Decios, ex externis autem Codrum et Philenos fratres vel, quoniam de feminis sermo erat, quis vel Porciam vel Hipsicratheam vel Alcestim et harum similes non fabulas fictas putet? Atqui historie vere sunt. Et sane qui pro alio vitam spernit quid non spernere, quid non pati possit non intelligo.

> Who wouldn't consider, for instance, Curtius and Mutius and the Decii, to speak of our own people, or, to mention foreigners, Codrus and the Phileni – or, since the topic was women, Portia or Hipsicrathea or Alcestis and others like them – to be sheer inventions? And yet, theirs are true historical narratives. And I really cannot understand how there could be something that anyone who has renounced life for the sake of others would not be able to renounce or endure.

To respond to his friend's indictment of the story as implausible, Petrarch insists on the presence of all these characters on historical record. They existed, and their heroic actions are documented: any attempt to discount the virtues of the Latin Griseldis (or the original vernacular Griselda) as impossible should therefore be refuted. Petrarch's defence is not compelling solely because of its high-register rhetoric, but also its underlying principle. Whereas Boccaccio hedges his bets in the proem of the *Decameron*, inclusively classifying his *novelle* as "o favole o parabole o istorie, che dire le vogliamo" (fables or parables or histories, however we wish to call them, Proemio.13), Petrarch insists on the historical veracity of the tale he has translated. At last clarifying why "he prefers to call this a *historia* rather than a *fabula*," the question that was actually the starting point of this second epistle dedicated to Boccaccio's tale, he also vigorously advances the principle that worthy literature should be rooted in history – and ancient history at that. For him, ancient examples vouch for modern ones. In other words, the Veronese friend's conclusion is false because the second premise of his syllogism is also false. It is simply not true that Griselda's virtues must be fictional because they exceed all classical examples. They do not, and Petrarch knows of several cases that disprove this claim. In short, were his friend better read then he too would be able to appreciate the story as a valid and compelling moral tale.

So, how are we to interpret this second reading scene? I propose doing so in the same way as we did the first one. In that example, Petrarch accepts the core element in the empathic reading – namely, the possibility that the text may speak directly to a reader's immediate spiritual circumstances, moving him to tears (in an Augustinian setting). Similarly, in the case of the alienating scepticism of the new reading, which is based on the sense of difference between textual past and interpretive present, Petrarch responds by accepting the interlocutor's hermeneutic premises and actual reading practices. He sees the two reading scenarios as only outwardly divergent, but necessarily co-implicated. When taken together, they allow the text to perform its ethical work. Petrarch appears to argue that each reading should entail both an acceptance of sameness and an appreciation of difference.

In his epistles to Boccaccio, in sum, Petrarch deliberately coordinates the historiographical and autobiographical mode of reading his text, but the tension between the two modalities remains. His insistence on the necessary pastness of the past and, at the same time, on its relevance for the present is coherent with the axiological system that he imports into Boccaccio's novella through his translation. As a conclusion for this section, I would like to draw attention to two moments in Petrarch's text, in which this very point is given a relevant narrative articulation. Incidentally, this rapid examination will allow us to highlight one of the elements that marks Chaucer's later translation of Petrarch's translation as a purposely divergent work. There is a pivotal moment in the plot, when Valterus, who has been asked by his subjects to enter into matrimony and thus provide for his dynastic future and their tranquillity, chooses his bride. Both characters are described, in an uncharacteristic (and certainly non-Boccaccian) way, as biographically young but ethically old. The description of Petrarch's Griseldis begins with her station in life, but soon turns to establishing her moral character:

(40) Fuit haud procul a palatio villula paucorum atque inopum incolarum, quorum uni omnium pauperrimo Iannicole nomen erat. (41) Sed ut pauperum quoque tuguria nonnunquam gratia celestis invisit, unica illi nata contigerat Griseldis nomine, forma corporis satis egregia, sed pulcritudine morum atque animi adeo speciosa ut nichil supra. (42) Hec, parco victu in summa semper inopia educata, omnis inscia volupatits nil molle nil tenerum cogitare didicerat, sed virilis senilisque animus virgineo latebat in pectore.

Not far from the palace there was a small village with few, impoverished inhabitants, the poorest of whom was called Iannicole. But, since sometimes heavenly grace visits even the humblest dwellings, he happened to have an only daughter, named Griselda, of remarkable physical attractiveness, but unsurpassed in the beauty of her habits and spirit. Having grown up with few means and in constant poverty, completely unaware of pleasure, she had never learned to contemplate anything refined or soft. On the contrary, she had, hidden in her virginal breast, a manly and mature spirit.

The notion that a female protagonist be distinguished by her physical form but unsurpassed in the remarkable beauty of her spirit and manners is certainly traditional, expected in rhetorical portraits of women. Her upbringing, too, is unsurprisingly coherent with her fortunes: if Griseldis has not learnt to contemplate anything soft and tender, readers are told, it is because of her meagre diet and the utmost poverty in which she lives. The notion that a virile and mature spirit is hidden in her *pectus*, however, is independent of any rhetorical and narrative circumstances. These features fully and solely belong to her, not to a literary tradition or the narrative premises of the tale. Correspondingly, Valterus also is biographically young but morally old:

(44) In hanc virgunculam Valterus sepe illac transiens quandoque oculos non iuvenili lascivia sed senili gravitate defixerat et virtutem eximiam supra sexum supraque etatem, quam vulgi oculis conditionis obscuritas abscondebat, acri penetrarat intuitu, unde effectum ut et uxorem habere, quod nunquam ante voluerat, et simul hanc unam nullamque aliam habere disponeret.

Valterus, who often passed by that spot, had already at times laid eyes on this little maid. He did so not with youthful lust, but with mature poise. And thanks to his penetrating gaze he noticed her remarkable virtue, one exceeding her sex and her age, which the obscurity of her status concealed to the eyes of the common folk. On those premises he disposed himself both to take a wife, something he had never wanted before, and, at the same time, to take this one and no other.

Again, the fact that – unlike the common folk – the noble Valterus has a sight keen enough to discern what is hidden by the obscurity of Griseldis' condition is not unprecedented, and this idea can also be found in Boccaccio's text. It is, however, remarkably Petrarchan that the gaze Valterus directs at his future wife is, from the start, said to be driven not by youthful lust but mature gravity.

It is true that in my translation I have somewhat edulcorated Petrarch's text. In his Latin, the lexical vehicle used to describe the protagonists that I have rendered as "mature" is the word *senilis*. This term has deep and wide resonance outside the plot. A lexical triangulation connects Petrarch, the author of "senile" epistles that vindicate his literary energy, who is also a "senile" writer of a tale he wouldn't have endeavoured to compose as a young man, and the two morally "senile" protagonists of the story, who are given this matching ethical trait to offset their (narratively necessary) young age. The intervention in the system of the original tale that Petrarch makes through this tendentious lexical choice is significant, even more so since we can demonstrate that Chaucer registered and carefully responded to it. The moral "senility" of the protagonists is an element that Chaucer's Clerk systematically undoes in his tale.[6]

Chaucer's retelling of Petrarch's story pays attention to the dynamics of old and new, but it is never Walter or Grisildis who is presented as old. Although old age is, moralistically, evoked on his existential horizon, Chaucer's Walter is explicitly characterized as young by his subjects. As their spokesperson puts it:

"And thogh youre grene youthe floure as yit, / In crepeth age alwey, as stille as stoon" (The Clerk's Tale, 120–1).[7] Similarly, Chaucer's Grisildis is soberly virtuous like Petrarch's Griseldis, but there is nothing senile about her spirit: "But though this mayde tendre were of age, / Yet in the brest of hire virginitee / Ther was enclosed rype and sad corage" (218–20). Comparably young, but pointedly "mature" ("rype") rather than "old," she is a perfect future match for Walter. Even in the close rendering of the pre-nuptial interest the *markys* took in her, which he too marks as serious and reflective, Chaucer explicitly eschews the marker of senility in the moral setup of both interested parties:

> And whan it fil that he myghte hire espye,
> he nogth with wantown looking of folye
> his eye caste on hire, but in sad wyse
> upon hir chiere he wolde hum ofte avyse,
> commendynge in his herte hir wommanhede,
> and eek hir vertu, passynge any wight
> of so young age, as wel in chiere as dede   (ll. 235–41)

> [So, when he chanced to see her, he did not cast his gaze on her with wanton and foolish look, but he would often ponder in a serious way upon her expression, praising in his heart her womanly qualities and also her virtue, by which she surpassed anyone of her young age, both in her expressions and acts.]

On the other hand, two connected elements of the tale are consistently signalled as old: Janicula, Grisildis' father, and all that is associated with him, especially the markers of his daughter's initial nubile status, her "old" condition (the note appears first in line 222 and then again in 904). In what the text presents as of considerable figurative importance, her dress, and not she, is explicitly labelled as old. It appears as "olde geere" (l. 372), at the very moment of Grisildis' forced undressing and redressing before the wedding, when she is clothed from head to foot "al newe" (378). The same garment again comes under narrative scrutiny when she returns home after Walter has ostensibly repudiated her. On that occasion it is Janicula – who, in his prudent scepticism about the lasting quality of his daughter's marriage, has kept her old clothing at the ready – who unsuccessfully attempts to cover her body. Remarks on the aging of her dress take up significant narrative space. They appear even more meaningful since they constitute Chaucer's expansion of a single word in Petrarch's text, "seminuda," and have no antecedent in Boccaccio:

> And with hire olde coote, as it myghte be
> he covered hire, ful sorwerfully wepynge.
> But on hire body myghte he it nat brynge,

for rude was the clooth, and moore of age
by days fele than at hire mariage   (ll. 913–17)

[And he covered her with her old coat, as well as it could, weeping sorrowfully. But
he could not bring it over her entire body for the cloth was coarse and it was older by
many days since her marriage.]

Measured by Janicula's inability to cover his daughter's body, the time that has
elapsed in her marriage seems to affect everything but Grisildis herself. It is important to note that according to the syntax of the passage (if not to its logic), it is not
the body but the garment that has aged. Even in the last trial Walter sets up for
his wife, when the text insists on the youthful appearance of the "fresshe" damsel
whom he is pretending to be about to marry (and who, in reality, is his and Grisildis' daughter), no comparison between her and her mother is ever established.
Chaucer's heroine may well be endowed with all the things that maturity brings to
a person's character – "pacient benygnytee, / discreet and pridelees, ay honurable, /
and to hire housbonde evere meke and stable" (ll. 929–31) – but, unlike Petrarch's
Griseldis, what she never is is "old."

The mismatching of clothing to body registered at this point in the narrative
also has metaliterary significance. As Petrarch maintains when he defines his work
as providing "alia veste" to Boccaccio's story, and as Chaucer accepts, noting that
Grisildis' first change of clothing meant that "she translated was in swich richesse"
(l. 385), the process of translation is tantamount to a change of linguistic garb. If
this is true, however, for Chaucer there seems to be something intrinsically awry
in the attempt to reclothe a body with an old garment. In particular, the specific
blend of authorial originalism (the story he has translated belongs to its original
author) and classicizing authentication (its truth status and ultimate significance
may be measured against ancient examples) that Petrarch creates in his version of
Boccaccio's Griselda seems to clash with translation – at least as Chaucer intends it.

Another, doubly articulated, point of advised contention between the two renditions of the story has to do with the choice of examples used to confirm its moral
message. While Petrarch, as I have noted, insists on detailing a list of classical
characters, mostly drawn from Latin historiography (Valerius Maximus has been
acknowledged as his source in this passage), Chaucer chooses a different reference
point for his Grisildis' actions: the biblical character of Job. The tale's narrator
does so in a self-reflexive moment, calling into question rhetorical and interpretive
habits traditionally associated with the Clerk's profession:

Men speke of Job, and moost for his humblesse,
as clerkes, whan hem list, konne wel endite,
namely of men, but as in soothfastnesse,
though clerkes preise wommen but a lite,

there kan no man in humblesse hym acquite
as womman kan, ne kan been half so trewe
as wommen been, but it be falle of newe.   (ll. 932–8)

[Men speak of Job, mostly on account of his humility, since clerks, when they want,
know how to write, principally of men. Yet, in truth, though clerks praise women just
a little, there is no man who can perform so well in humility as a woman can, nor can
be half as true as women are – unless it happened recently.]

Three elements in this dense passage are particularly worthy of commentary.
First, instead of classical characters being offered as comparable points of reference (and implicitly as limits) for Grisildis' exemplarity, the text offers readers a
biblical one. Chaucer asks his readers to access a very different mental library (or
specific section of it) from the one Petrarch indicated for the interpretation of his
own Griseldis to evaluate the new material before their eyes. Second, Chaucer's
Clerk proves perfectly aware of the scholarly bias against women that motivates
his peers' choice to praise Job as an unparalleled example of humility, since they
systematically refrain from praising women. What is more, he calls them out for
the voluntary quality of their bias: after all, they know how to write well, that is,
in bono, "when they want." Third, Grisildis is an example not of an individual,
but of a whole gendered category: it is not just one woman who can outdo a
man in practising humility, the Clerk maintains, but all women who may do so,
prevailing over any man. Unless, of course, something has happened, and men
have produced an unparalleled example of humility: "but it be falle of newe."
Ever so ready to accept the idea that the present may outdo the past, Chaucer's
Clerk is revealed to be the exact opposite of Petrarch's learned friend from Verona,
who cannot accept the idea that a story about the present could portray a new
character so powerfully exemplary as to have no equal among the champions
from the Greco-Roman world. While he aligns himself with Petrarch's rebuttal in
offering a refutation of this critique, Chaucer takes a different route to do so. In
the unspoken part of their dialogue, Petrarch responds to his friend's biased position by providing classical examples of virtuous constancy from antiquity that
outdid his Griseldis. In contrast, rather than looking back to the classical past to
authorize the present, Chaucer chooses to look to the present to measure the past.
In doing so, he also keeps an eye on a possible future. The "new" is for him so
axiologically superior to the "old" that it always contains a salutary excess. Unlike
the closed ethical canon that both Petrarch and his interlocutor saw recorded in
history, the Clerk maintains his optimism about the time to come, even though
it may eventually prove him wrong.

To conclude and provide a rapid summary of what has emerged thus far, let us note the following. My interpretation of *Seniles* 17.3 and 4 suggests that Petrarch's translation of Boccaccio's story involved four steps. First, Petrarch took a text that he deemed appropriate to represent the best that vernacular literature could offer, in terms of ethical messages and rhetorical prowess, and pulled it out of context. Second, he provided this exceptional tale with a new linguistic and stylistic garb, adopting Latin because of its status as the internationally recognized medium for highbrow communication, thus bypassing the text's limitations of time and place. Third, he made sure to validate the veracity of his subject matter against a treasure trove of authentically historical paradigmatic examples drawn from the classical (Greco-Roman) world. Fourth, he addressed the new text to a specific audience of learned men of letters, who were keen (and able) to move within such cultural coordinates. Chaucer's narrative, rhetorical, and stylistic strategies in the Clerk's Tale deviate so greatly from Petrarch's that they can also be outlined in four contrasting steps. First, Chaucer took Petrarch's Latin manifesto and problematized its ethical and cultural message by reframing it within a polycentric and polyphonic narrative system. Second, he measured Petrarch's female protagonist against biblical rather than classical antecedents, insisting on her exemplarity not as an individual but as a representative of her gender. Third, he strategically re-translated the text, couching it in modern vernacular, in a programmatically "low" style. Fourth, he addressed its parodically divergent message to a specific vernacular, female, and contemporary audience. All these countermoves are, I argue, not simply coherent but also interdependent. As is the case with Petrarch's procedures, they cannot be separated from one another.

Chaucer's choices, as we are about to see, are also coherent with the wider corpus of imaginatively translated texts studied in this book. That he understands his reaction to Petrarch's literary moves specifically within the field of translation is suggested not only by his strategic redressing of Petrarch's text in the Clerk's Tale, but also by the metapoetic and allusive coda he uses to imbricate it with his next tale. A close reading of this text as a proem to the Merchant's Tale will bring us closer to and then eventually fully back into the frame of Eden-like garden spaces, where we will linger for a significant amount of time.

2. Elision and Recantation: The Garden of the Merchant's Tale and Januarie's Songs

It is not a gratuitous act to approach the Merchant's Tale through a reflection on translation, since this story not only directly follows the Clerk's Tale but also is narratively and structurally interconnected with it.[8] Appended to the Clerk's Tale and at times attributed to the character's voice, squarely at the centre of the marriage triptych making up Fragment IV (Group E), readers find *Lenvoy de Chaucer*. With sombre and solemn wording, the author commemorates and laments the death of Grisildis, the exemplary heroine of the story that the group of pilgrims has just heard. Undoing, in just one line, the tale's potential for exemplarity, which was the feature on which the narrator had insisted, Chaucer declares: "Grisilde is deed, and eek hire patience / And bothe atone buried in Ytaille" (Griselda is dead, and her patience too: both are buried together in Italy, ll. 1173–4).[9] The geographic dimension of the first statement is noteworthy. In "burying" both the character and her meaning in a specific place, the epilogue preempts any potential reappearance (and redeployment) of both the figure and her ethical exemplarity anywhere else. In contrast to the highly mobile text of her story, which has been moved from Italian to Latin, and from Latin (and French) to English, the protagonist of the tale and any potential value she may be made to acquire in the ethical sphere are consigned to a dead end. While the language is topographical, the point is literary. Unlike the body of a saint that may become the object of a translation, in the Envoy Grisildis' body and virtue are given programmatic stability.

From this assertively articulated postulate, the author moves on to make a related, if lighthearted point:

> O noble wyves, ful of heigh prudence,
> Lat not humylitee yore tonge naille,
> Ne lat no clerk have cause or diligence
> To write of yow a storie of swich mervaille
> As of Grisildis, pacient and kynde.   (ll. 1183–7)

[O noble women, filled by high prudence, do not let humility nail your tongue nor any clerk have reason to write of you a story of such exceptionality as that of Griselda, the patient and kind.]

The considerations developed here are partly aligned with Petrarch's own interpretive reframing of Boccaccio's story, but they are also surprisingly diverging. As it was the case for Petrarch, who recommended a reading of his story as an invitation to exercise constancy rather than attempting to imitate the heroine's patience, Grisildis' model is also no longer a viable one. Accordingly, Chaucer provides a new interpretive take. The new message of the story is that for contemporary women patience and kindness are out of the question, and hence they should learn another art: that of endless retort. They should never allow their tongues to be tied; rather, so the Clerk's Envoy states, they should do better "to follow Echo," and always provide a valiant response to any possible accusation of which they are made the target. Certainly tongue-in-cheek, the meaning of the Envoy is also clear: "Folweth Ekko, that holdeth no silence, / But evere answereth at the countretaille" (Follow Echo, the one who holds not silence, but ever answers in counterpoint, ll. 1189–90).

It is not silence, writes Chaucer, that becomes women, but piercing and rhetorically sustained speech, "crabbed eloquence": this is what ensures their triumph over men (l. 1203). With such premises in place, it is not surprising that the upcoming story both is concerned with a series of rhetorical debates on the advisability for any man to enter into a contract of marriage (all as rhetorically elaborate as they are inconclusive) and also, in its final section, hinges around the decisive oratorial gift that Proserpina bestows upon the young female protagonist of the tale – and, through her, to all women. The magical untying of Mayus' tongue in the Merchant's Tale connects back to the satirical advice of the author, a recommendation that is inspired, *e contrario*, by the dead Grisildis. The thematic imbrication of the two tales could not be clearer – and, in a way, more troubling.

Moving beyond its framing, two elements have been traditionally isolated as main components in the tale, both connected with the garden theme. First, the classic debates about the nature and value of the institute of marriage that ricochet across the text, and in which the dialogue via opposing authorities with other narrators in the *Canterbury Tales* progresses. Second, the counter-exemplary plot onto which these inconclusive debates are grafted: the Merchant's Tale offers a specific, utterly fictional case of a mismatched December-May marriage, with a fully expected conclusion – in the tradition of a *fabliau* – of cuckoldry in the bawdy, sexually explicit scene of the coupling in the pear tree, the same structural twist that readers of the *Decameron* found in the tale of Lydia and Pyrrhus (7.9). While both these elements are deftly intertwined in the plot, only the latter will be analysed here, with only a few pointed remarks devoted to the former.

The discussions about the advantages and drawbacks of marriage that make up a substantial portion of the tale are, in fact, not completely unrelated to the main argument of this chapter. On the contrary, they make some crucial forays into the field of Edenic imagination as well. This is not surprising. Anyone arguing the relative merits of marriage could hardly dispense with the natural biblical setting of the Adam and Eve story, which was, after all, the scriptural root for the establishment of marriage as an institution. Quite naturally, the Merchant's Tale articulates the idea in its opening gambit, when it defines marriage as "That hooly bound / with which that first God man and womman bond" (The holy bond with which God bound together the first man and woman, ll. 1261–2). There is, in sum, a topographic connection between the clerkly debates that the story stages and the Edenic setting, mobilized in the exemplary narrative starring Januarie and Mayus. While Chaucer's Grisildis is buried in Italy and Januarie and Mayus live in Italy as well, the spatial coordinates of their story take us to a different archetypal place.[10]

Similar considerations also apply to the discussion of marriage as "a ful greet sacrement" (l. 1319), in which, again, the biblical story of Adam and Eve, set in Eden, is taken as the justification for the institution and the institute of marriage. Between lines 1325 and 1332, where the text assures the reader that the wife is her husband's "paradys terrestre," the theme is this time explicitly mirrored in the poem's lexicon. The association is so close that it triggers an interesting shift of attention from the "historical" circumstances of the institution of the sacrament to its "metaphorical" value. The text does not only state that marriage happened to take place for the first time in Eden and that this circumstance is evidently sufficient to determine its nature even today. It says more, connecting the locale where marriage originated with its definition: what marriage "is" (metaphorically, of course) and what it "consists in" (in what it results, that is, in present ethical terms). Biblical, historical, and semiotic dimensions of the discourse on marriage are collapsed onto one another, with the effect that they treat the earthly institution and earthly paradise as the same thing.

As we are about to see in the use that Januarie makes of this nexus and its associated notions, this conflation produces the leading metaphorical and spatial setting of the narrative: an unstable and morally problematic paradise on earth. As Boccaccio's narrators and the readers of his two stories detailing regressive and apostatic approaches to Eden had already established in a quite orthodox way, constructing this artificial space of delight is a rather bad idea for Chaucer's protagonist as well. One should not seek to recreate Eden on earth, either by attempting to retrogress into it (to regain paradise independently of Incarnation) or by attempting to create a technical – which is to say artificial – reproduction of its features in the here and now (to make surrogate Edenic spaces and invest them with value). Theologically speaking, as the two stories examined in the previous chapter and the two gardens in the *Roman de la Rose* remind us, regaining paradise is something that humans are not supposed to do – at least, not by way of travel or of technical artifice. As we have seen, in Christian discourse and across the texts of a wide vernacular fictional canon, going back to Eden is both an impossible feat and a misguided endeavour. No one is granted access to it; but, more importantly, that garden is the wrong garden to pursue. A different and better garden exists, one that awaits not the resourceful but the faithful. And *this other* mystical but no less real garden is a place of eternal bliss, the access to which has been obtained by Christ's incarnation and sacrifice. In the case of Januarie, the Canterbury pilgrims are given an opportunity to witness for themselves how bad the idea of remaking paradise on earth will prove and see the misguidedness of any attempt to do so by appealing to the Edenic sacrament of marriage.

While these notions are, of course, part of the picture that this chapter attempts to draw, and while they certainly are part of the overall message of Chaucer's tale, my argument will not focus on the debating contexts in which they appear. As is the case in any literary rehashing of medieval intellectual controversies or rhetorical demonstrations, the *auctoritates* framing the argument and the exempla providing it with evidentiary force are hardly separable.[11] Focusing on a single strain of the story, however, will shed a sharper light on several details that intrinsically connect the Merchant's Tale with the translational Edenic trope *per se*. In the text,

Eden is not simply a cultural point of reference to be evoked and a narrative space to be explored. It is the stand-in for the metaliterary question that Chaucer's tale will answer in its conclusion: how the textually old and new may be fruitfully paired together.

One of the possible points of access to the material is the language that old Januarie repeatedly uses to talk about the marriage he wants to contract. The first words we hear from him contain the first mention of Eden, associated with the idea of marriage:

> "Noon oother lyf," seyde he, "is worth a bene;
> For wedlok is so esy and so clene,
> That in this world it is paradys."
> Thus seyde this olde knyght, that was so wys.   (ll. 1263–6)

> "No other life," said he, "is worth a bean. Wedlock is so tranquil and so clean, that it is paradise on earth." So said this old knight, who was so wise.

It is worth dwelling on the text's insistence on advanced age. Not only is Januarie inappropriately seeking a status more befitting a younger person, his statement that matrimonial life is tantamount to heaven on earth is attributed to an authority explicitly labelled as "old." To be sure, the notation is biographical and functional to the plot. The text has just established that Januarie is "a worthy knyght" from the Italian city of Pavia, he is sixty years old and prosperous, he has spent his life unmarried but not celibate, and has finally decided, after sixty years of life (the text repeats this piece of information twice), to take a wife. The quality of "oldness" is, however, in a larger sense, a cultural one. Januarie's decrepitude – the darker side of Petrarch's mature senility – accompanies his viewpoints, reasonings, and actions throughout the story. While he marries a young woman, one should note, the matrimonial bond he has contracted does nothing to improve his condition. This central determinant for the character is more than a merely biographic element in the symbolic system of the tale. When Januarie collapses the idea of heavenly life onto the category of "paradis," he points those who can detect the etymological value of the word toward a garden (that is, as we shall see, toward an earthly, man-made pleasure garden). But he also admits to a form of materialism and literalism that allusively associates him, in the eyes of a trained Christian humanistic audience, with the old worldly dispensation: the age of the Father and the carnal understanding of the Law. In partaking of an old conception of reality – most specifically, of a vetero-testamentary way of looking at the world – Januarie is presented as carnally and spiritually old.

Notably, this element in the symbolic layer of the text spawns two extended treatments, one jokingly resolved, the other left ambiguous and thus interpretively challenging, of the potential shortcomings (ethical and metaphysical) entailed in

Januarie's approach to life on earth. The first is the scruple, which readers are naturally expected to receive as ridiculous, that Januarie shares with his friends once he has decided not only that he will marry but also who his bride is going to be. We are again given Januarie's unmediated words to ponder:

> "I have," quod he, "herd seyd, ful yoore ago,
> Ther may no man han parfite blisses two, –
> This is to seye, in erthe and eek in hevene."
> (ll. 1637–9)

"I have heard," he said, "said a long time ago, that no one may have two perfect states of bliss. That is to say, on earth and also in heaven."

Based on this principle, and with a clear, if illusory, picture of the blissful state that awaits him, Januarie fears that by way of marriage he may lose the eternal bliss to which he feels entitled in the afterlife:

> "Yet is ther so parfit felicitee
> And so greet ese and lust in mariage,
> That evere I am agast now in myn age
> That I shal lede now so myrie a lyf,
> So delicat, withouten wo and stryf,
> That I shal have myn hevene in erthe heere.
> For sith that verray hevene is boght so deere
> With tribulacion and greet penaunce,
> How sholde I thanne, that lyve in swich plesaunce
> As alle wedded men doon with hire wyvys,
> Come to the blisse ther Crist eterne on lyve ys?"
> (ll. 1642–52)

"Yet, there is such a perfect happiness and great contentment and delight that, if I start to lead now, at my age, such a merry life, so delicious without woe and strife, I will have my heaven here on earth! If true heaven is bought at such high price of tribulation and great discipline, how can I, who live in the same sweet pleasure as all wedded men do with their wives, reach the bliss in which Christ eternally lives?"

Unlike his assessment of married life, Januarie's theology is, though damning for someone like him who is after heavenly bliss in earthly terms, actually sound. This is, of course, not because his scruples have any real ethical merit, but because they speak to the point of the double significance that Eden assumes in both its typological and moral dimensions. Januarie's doubts will soon be dispelled, not only by the plot of the story, in which he will be shown to be ready to quickly overcome any hesitation, but also by the joking insinuation that his minor premise (i.e., that marriage is filled with "swich plesaunce") may after all be false, and hence his syllogism vain. The way in which this character's doubts are articulated here, with typical Chaucerian double-edged humour and earnestness, reveals the weightiness of the issue at hand. There is something seriously wrong in enjoying heaven on earth, since such allegiance does prevent a person from desiring to access the only stable and complete state of bliss: heavenly paradise. Stated in cultural rather than solely theological terms, Januarie's dilemma points to the notion that any attempt to make and enjoy one's own paradise on earth – a regressive act that the plot embodies in the garden he constructs for his sexual delights – is potentially apostatic in quality.

The problem Chaucer's protagonist faces is as ethical as it is hermeneutical. In eliding the dichotomy between earthly and heavenly delights, Januarie's perspective also betrays his essentially carnal and literal reading of what the Eden of biblical narrative was (and is) supposed to signify. A more correct, non-exclusionary reading exists, one that considers earthly paradise as a token, an incomplete and subordinate prefiguration, of the heavenly one. This reading – which rests on the ability to see the earthly garden as a sign of the heavenly one, to perceive in Adam the promise of Christ, and to consider the carnal dimension of pleasure as a sign of a higher spiritual condition – is available to anyone professing faith in the incarnational fulfilment of history. But this is not, the tale contends, Januarie's case. His perspective is missing the ability to see beyond the artificial (and remedially surrogate-like) materiality both of his marriage and of the garden he will build and in which he will play Adam and Eve with his wife. For him, in other words, the polarized assessment of the earthly garden that Patristic thought provided is moot: whereas, according to Ambrose, the earthly garden is both a *shadow* (and thus a foil) and a *token* (and thus a promise) for the heavenly one, for Januarie his earthly garden of delights, in its carnal self-sufficiency, is all there is. With these framing considerations in mind, it is now time to move on to this little literary heaven on earth, and to the strange birds inhabiting it, since the cluster of symbolic elements present there seems to control one aspect of the interpretation of the tale.

Even before being admitted to it by way of topical description and narrative development, readers are given clear indications about the quality and identity of the garden Januarie has attached to his house in Pavia. Even before they are asked to evaluate his artificial Eden, that is, the text provides readers with the necessary cultural coordinates to do so. The introductory language is in fact both technical and ethically charged:

> Somme clerkes holden that felicitee
> Stant in delit, and therfore certeyn he,

This noble Januarie, with al his myght,
In honest wyse, as longeth to a knyght,
Shoop hym to lyve ful deliciously.   (ll. 2021–5)

According to some learned men, happiness consists in pleasure. Thus he, this noble Januarie, most certainly with all his might, with the dignity proper to a knight, tried to live in full delight.

Just one of the many accessories of his pleasure-bent and essentially Epicurean life, Januarie's garden is, by implication but also explicitly, a garden of delight: a *hortus deliciarum*.[12] It is also, we should note, an explicitly literary garden. In an apparent case of missed descriptive opportunities, the tale provides only scant details about the locale (l. 2143 ff.). We are told that it has a well at its centre, where the fantastic "feérie" of Pluto and Proserpina will come for sport in the last leg of the tale; that this well is shadowed by an evergreen laurel; that among the fruit trees there is a pear tree, where the final coupling of Damyan and Mayus will take place; and that it is "enclosed al aboute." While there are few details about its features, the text clearly places Januarie's architectural creation within a specific metaliterary framework:

He made a gardyn, walled al with stoon;
So fair a gardyn woot I nowher noon.
For, out of doute, I verraily suppose
That he that wroot the Romance of the Rose
Ne koude of it the beautee wel devyse.   (ll. 2029–33)

He made a garden, walled all with stone. So charming a garden was never seen before. For, indeed, I truly think that not even the author of the *Romance of the Rose* could have adequately described its beauty.

The evocation of the antecedent of the *Roman de la Rose* serves a double purpose. On the one hand, by insisting on the exceptional and thus beyond-description quality of the object at hand, it reinforces an attitude that the poem had already exhibited in the case of the wedding feast a few hundred lines earlier. There, the topical establishment of the absolute bliss involved in the proceedings is conveyed by a just as topical silencing of the most pertinent classical antecedent:

Hoold thou thy pees, thou poete Marcian,
That writest us that ilke weddyng murie
Of hire Philologie and hym Mercurie,
And of the songes that the Muses songe!

> To smal is bothe thy penen, and eek thy tonge,
> For to descryven of this mariage.   (ll. 1732–5)

> Hold your peace, Martian the poet, who wrote about the happy marriage of Philology and Mercury, and of the songs that the Muses sang. Too small is your pen, too small your tongue to treat this wedding.

Accusing Martianus Capella, a notoriously copious writer, of literary feebleness is of course part of the humorous deployment of the literary cliché according to which poets aggressively impose silence on the models who, of all their predecessors, most directly influence them. The topos establishes that any increase in the subject matter also triggers the poetic insufficiency of even the most prolific writers of the past. It is thus that room is made for the new text, as the only truly adequate space for the task of giving the new subject its due. This rhetorical move, one should note, is usually combined with a virtuoso exhibition on the part of the new poet: the new rhetorical performance is designed to show that the new author is able to both outdo the technical difficulty of the poetic task at hand and outmatch any literary antecedent. In Chaucer's allusion to both the *De nuptiis Philologiae et Mercurii* and the *Roman de la Rose*, however, the play with literary models heads in a different direction. Instead of pointing to the surpassing of the old model *in* and *by* a new work as preliminary and a preamble to a copious production of a new text, Chaucer's Merchant uses the commonplace to stifle his own narration, in a concluding and perhaps conclusive move. In the case of Januarie's garden, there is no luscious and rhetorically competitive translation upon the evocation of the *other* garden. Rather than using the mobilization of models in order to outclass them in an allegedly respectful fashion, Chaucer invites readers to take a textual detour, if not a shortcut. Here, literary filiation does not result in poetic imitation but in literary bypassing of the sources.

The pointed evocation of the *Romance of the Rose*, which with its bare-bones, reference-like style takes the place of any detailed description of the tale's garden, adds a further layer of metaliterary irony to the topos, since it comes in a text penned by the same author who was responsible for the first translation of that same text into the English language. The garden in the Merchant's Tale is, thus, both allusively literary and, more specifically, translative. True to the literal paradox his lines construct, the garden in this text will not be described in full by any author: neither the one who wrote the *Roman de la Rose*, be it Guillaume or Jean, nor the new one, Geoffrey. Reduced to a strategically nondescript place, the garden of the vernacular tradition only creates a space for the consummation of the story with carnal love and cuckoldry – nothing more. Its precise descriptive coordinates are apparently *not* the point of the work.

Chaucer's choice to forego any description of the place in the Merchant's Tale is a telling index of the value that his culture associated to the literary act of representing Eden. The decision to frame the garden of earthly delights belonging to Januarie exclusively from the protagonist's point of view is functional to his portrayal as unwilling and unable to enter into the semiotic Christian dispensation. His carnal intentionalism coincides with a hermeneutically literal approach. While the protagonist can translate other texts (as he does, though poorly, in the case of the Song of Songs), he cannot provide the garden with a new linguistic instantiation. The lexical and translative richness of the Eden trope remains systematically beyond his reach: translating means renewing the old, and this is precisely what Januarie is constructed as constitutionally incapable of doing.

Nonetheless, the preterition affecting the unimaginably rich and practically unimagined garden, built by Januarie as his heaven on earth, does not only create a void. The allusive silence in the text triggers one internal and one external effect. First, internally, the same invitation that the Merchant extends to all readers, to go and read the relevant antecedents of the tale for themselves, is matched by another moment of pointed but elusive allusion to a classical school text, Claudian's *De raptu Proserpinae*, an obvious reference text for a plot that also eventually features the God of Hades and his queen. Here is the scene in full:

> And so bifel, that brighte morwe-tyde,
> That in that gardyn, in the ferther syde,
> Pluto, that is kyng of Fayerye,
> And many a lady in his compaignye,
> Folwynge his wyf, the queene Proserpyna,
> Which that he ravysshed out of [Ethna]
> Whil that she gadered floures in the mede –
> In Claudyan ye may the stories rede,
> How in his grisely carte he hire fette –
> This kyng of Fairye thanne adoun hym sette
> Upon a bench of turves, fressh and grene.   (ll. 2225–35)

And it so came to pass that, on that bright morning, in the remotest area of the garden, Pluto, who is the king of fairies, escorted by many dames who were in the retinue of his wife, Queen Proserpina, whom he had ravished, snatching her from Etna while she was gathering flowers in a meadow (you may read the story in Claudian, how he took her on his fearful chariot), this king of the fairies sat on an earthen bench covered with fresh and green grass.

The allusion to the Latin work is once again pointed and silent. Proserpina is simply described as Pluto's wife, whom he carried away from the Etna region.

However, readers of Claudian could not fail to note that Pluto actually abducted Proserpina from a more specific place than the slopes of the volcano in Sicily. In the account of the flower-gathering party that immediately precedes Proserpina's abduction, Claudian's text indulged in a long description of the *locus amoenus*, a garden-like space placed under the tutelage of a character named Henna. In a rhetorically copious entreaty she addressed to Zephyrus, the wind most closely connected to spring, asking him to bring blossoms to the natural space under her control, Claudian's Henna produced a detailed account of all the species of trees and odorous spices that she would produce. This is not the place for a detailed examination of the long passage from the *De raptu Proserpinae* (II.71–136) that is the elided target of Chaucer's allusion. However, even just one extract may provide readers with a sense of its pertinence to the garden trope. Henna's words to the god of the winds insist on the variety of vegetation that will spring from his presence, immediately associating her meadows and fields with gardens:

> "Nunc adsis faveasque, precor; nunc omnia fetu
> pubescant virgulta velis, ut fertilis Hybla
> invideat vincique suos non abnuat hortos.
> quidquid turiferis spirat Panchaia silvis,
> quidquid odoratus longe blanditur Hydaspes,
> quidquid ab extremis ales longaeva colonis
> colligit optato repetens exordia leto,
> in venas disperge meas et flamine largo
> rura fove ..."

"I pray you, now, be present and propitious. Let all the young trees bring fruit now, so that fertile Hybla may be jealous and admit that her gardens ["hortos"] are surpassed. Spread through my veins all that Panchaia breathes forth from her incense woods, all that fragrant Hydaspes sweetly sends out from afar, all that the long-living bird collects from the most distant fields when it seeks new beginnings from a welcome death. Be propitious now, with your generous breath, to my fields. (*De raptu* II.78–86)

In the description of the place that follows, Claudian lists flowers and plants, putting the classical catalogue form to good use. He mentions roses, hyacinths, and violets, brilliant in the sun's light; as well as the shadowy groves of pines, oaks, cypresses, and holms; and along with laurels, boxwoods, ivies, and vines creeping on helm trees. In the elided copiousness of the passage, Claudian's text appears a fitting point of reference for Chaucer's garden, one that brings another literary place to intersect with the garden of the *Roman de la Rose*.

The silencing of the garden description is not limited to internal resonances in the tale. One external connection may be pointed out as well. When Chaucer's Merchant intimates that other texts contain other iterations of the topos mobilized in his tale, all the while providing no narrative space for them, readers may realize that other narrative voids exist in the tradition. As we have seen, readers of Italian may observe how the elusive behaviour of Chaucer's tale coincides with that of the *Fiore*, which was essentially a faithful and yet partial "translation" of the *Roman de la Rose*. In an eerily similar fashion, that text too had skipped the description of the garden while "translating" its French antecedent. To suppose a textual connection between Dante (or pseudo-Dante) and Chaucer would stretch philological speculation too far, but it is certainly intriguing to consider that the onomastics of Chaucer's story, as transparent and proverbial as it may be, quite perfectly matches a detail in the *Fiore*.

In its rather unorthodox seasonal setting, as its first memorable incipit establishes, the action of the Italian poem begins in winter: "Nel mese di gennaio e non di maggio" (in the month of Januarie and not of Mayus). In the uncanonical setting of its narrative time, the *Fiore* is found in eerie consonance with the onomastics of Chaucer's tale. More than philological contact, of course, the similarities in onomastics and setting of two poems that clearly *do not* engage in garden description speak of a semiological participation in a shared discursive field. Both the *Fiore* and Chaucer's Merchant's Tale participate in the same translative garden trope and do so by both consistently bypassing the *Roman de la Rose* antecedent in garden-description. If the Merchant's Tale can dispense with detailed recitation of one of the sources that it still admits to being necessary for its narrative to function, it is on account of its own translative quality. In evoking the *Rose*, that is, Chaucer points to the already established intertextual and interlingual quality of vernacular literary gardens – be they French in origin or, we might add, Italian in manifestation.

To summarize what has been established thus far, one may say that from the point of view of garden poetics, Chaucer's text is certainly interested in canon formation, but does not seem to indulge in translation from the secular and allegorical texts to which it points. While it evokes a tradition, that is, the Merchant's Tale dispenses with any detailed recitation of its corpus. Readers are, instead, supposed to gather a complete picture of its central elements by looking outside of the text that they have before their eyes. On the other hand, the tale does engage other texts in practices of re-singing and vernacular reworking: the biblical ones.

Just as there are two rhetorical and metaliterary preteritions in the tale, so too there are two moments in which the old protagonist bursts into uncontrollably happy, carnally delighted singing. In full coherence with his character, which is ever pleasure-bent, both of Januarie's songs issue from either satisfied or rousing lust. After his first night of sexual exertion as a married man, the Merchant notes, Januarie is in the best of moods:

> Thus laboureth he til that the day gan dawe;
> And thanne he taketh a sop in fyn clarree,
> And upright in his bed thanne sitteth he,
> And after that he sang ful loude and cleere,
> And kiste his wyf, and made wantown cheere
> He was al coltissh, ful of ragerye,
> And ful of jargon as a flekked pye.   (ll. 1842–8)

> Thus, he laboured until the break of dawn. Then he took a sip of fine claret, sat up in his bed and sang full loud and clear. He kissed his wife and started to fool around: he was frisky like a colt, filled with lust, and chatty as a spotted magpie.

Full of chatter as a magpie, Januarie finally begins to sing. Though taking place at dawn, his song is no song for the new day. As the text insinuates, with the flapping skin around his neck and his nightcap, Januarie appears to Mayus somewhat like a rooster with comb and wattle, but no matter how traditionally common the association of this bird with new beginnings may be, his image is parodic. Unlike a chanticleer, Januarie is not announcing a new day. Rather, his song infects the day with connotations of oldness: "The slakke skyn about his nekke shaketh / While that he sang, so chaunteth he and craketh" (His slackening skin shook around his neck while he sang: in this way he chanted and croaked, ll. 1849–50).

As the text glosses, only God knows what Mayus thought in her heart, seeing her husband sitting up in the bed, in his nightcap and lean neck. While, once again, the text is reticent on that point, readers are able to appreciate both the essential vanity of the unspecified song Januarie sings (as in its emptiness) and the ethical vanity of the singer (as in his narcissism). The song, a reaction to sexual gratification, is loud and clear, to be sure, but rather than the rejuvenation that its tone may anticipate, it only produces juvenile behaviour. Throughout the tale, but here perhaps most plainly, Januarie is described as an old man: old in his body as well as in his attitudes. The proximity to his young wife does not produce any renewal in him; only a starker contrast emerges. Similarly, the Christological symbolism that may accidentally be associated with him – the resurrected Christ, the chanticleer announcing the end of worldly darkness – is destined to remain mute. Readers can see the cluster of Christological gestures and elements around Januarie – the dawn, the rising, the song – but the effect is contrastive.

Similar considerations extend to the second song. By the time readers reach this new, again unspecified, moment of singing, elements in the plot have matured. The young bride has received entreaties from the young squire Damyan for her love and readily accepted them; the two have decided to find a way to consummate their love and plotted to do so in the garden Januarie has built and jealously keeps. For his part, Januarie has gone blind and, accordingly, his love for Mayus has turned to constant fear of being betrayed and raging jealousy. On the day he is cuckolded, Januarie enters the garden, holding Mayus by her hand and unaware of the fact that Damyan is already there, waiting to receive instructions from his soon-to-be lover on how to approach her undetected:

> This Januarie, as blynd as is a stoon,
> With Mayus in his hand, and no wight mo,
> Into his fresshe gardyn is ago,
> And clapte to the wyket sodeynly.   (ll. 2156–9)

> Our Januarie, blind as a rock, holding his Mayus's hand and no one else around, went into his fresh garden and immediately locked the gate.

While Januarie is strolling blindly in the garden, we are told, Pluto and his wife happen to be there as well, and they notice the trick that is going to be played on him. A debate ensues between them on the treacherous nature of women (Pluto's thesis), opposed by protestations of their innocence and worth (Proserpina's counterpoint). Pluto vows that he will give Januarie back his sight at the very moment in which he will be betrayed, so that he may be able to catch Mayus in the act (ll. 2258–61). Proserpina counters with a corresponding gift for Mayus: the ability to always have an answer ready, to rebut any charge her husband may level against her (ll. 2264–70). As she succinctly states about all women who will inherit Mayus' gift: "For lak of answere noon of hem shal dyen" (No one among them shall perish for lack of a retort, l. 2271). Now that the debate has reached a conciliatory conclusion, the narrator goes back to Januarie to add a detail to the scene:

> Now lat us turne agayn to Januarie,
> That in the gardyn with his faire May
> Syngeth ful murier than the papejay,
> "Yow love I best, and shal, and oother noon."   (ll. 2320–3)

> Now let us go back to Januarie, who is in the garden with his fair Mayus and sings more happily than the parrot: "You I love among all others, you I shall, alone."

The ornithological characterization of Januarie's song is notable. After singing as a magpie, he now does so as a parrot. The same pair of birds that haunted Dante's earlier reflection on language thus reappears. They do so, to be sure, in a joking context, but with demonstrably constant connotations. Both in Dante and in

Chaucer, the birds appear bearing negative markers of inauthenticity and impropriety. Narratively speaking, both Januarie's singing in the bedchamber and his indulging in song here in the garden of delights are hardly in keeping with what an old man is expected to do. Furthermore, and again in a remarkable symbolic alignment with the connotations each bird possessed in Dante's texts, the magpie and parrot are given distinct spheres in which to appear; notably, the parrot is given the garden. What is at stake in this return of the two birds is not an issue of philological imbrication, but one of semiological coherence. The striking parallel in topographical distribution depends on the participation of both texts in a common cultural climate.

There is a final stretch of text that, albeit only spoken rather than explicitly sung by Januarie, is still connected to the category of song: the starkly elegant and quite literal translation Chaucer provides of a portion from Solomon's *Canticum canticorum*, contained in a compact block of eleven lines. Staged at a narrative point in which the cuckolding is only potential, Januarie's singing is again related to the garden. On a sunny day in June, so the tale reports, Januarie is caught by an impelling desire to be alone with his wife. Thus, he summons her with the following words:

> "Rys up, my wyf, my love, my lady free!
> The turtles voys is herd, my dowve sweete;
> The wynter is goon with alle his reynes weete.
> Com forth now, with thyne eyen columbyn!
> How fairer been thy brestes than is wyn!
> The gardyn is enclosed al aboute;
> Com forth, my white spouse! Out of doute
> Thou hast me wounded in myn herte, o wyf!
> No spot of thee ne knew I al my lyf.
> Com forth, and lat us taken oure disport;
> I chees thee for my wyf and my confort."
> Swiche olde lewed wordes used he.   (ll. 2132–49)

"Rise up, my wife, my love, my dear lady! I hear the voice of the turtles, sweet dove, because the winter is gone with all his heavy rains. Come forth now, with your dove-like eyes! Your breasts are sweeter than wine! The garden is enclosed all around: come forth, my spouse. Certainly, you have wounded me in my heart, o wife! I have found no blame in you all my life. Come forth and let us take our pleasure now: I have chosen you as my wife and my comfort." These old and crude words he used.

In this unsung, but rhetorically heightened entreaty to his wife, there are several elements worthy of note. First, the use that Januarie intends to make of these lines, in which we find a combination of verses translated from the biblical text

(Canticum 2:10–14). His translation-cum-appropriation appears in line with the general hermeneutic attitude he reserves for biblical objects. As he has done with the garden of delights, by depriving the biblical text of any potential non-literal meaning, Januarie technically reduces it to a seduction song. The parody in the situation (a serious parody, to be sure) is that the seduction at stake is just as mutual as the exchange of lines between the bride and the groom in the original text. In a paradox of translative literality, Januarie folds back the new text onto the old one. The song he sings is an old song, aimed at no less carnal satisfaction than the garden he has built for his matrimonial dalliances. Incited by his wife, who is plotting to cuckold him by meeting up with Damyan, Januarie sings a song that invites reflection on the space it describes. The tale's narrator does not wait long to provide reasons to do so.

The internal commentary to Januarie's serenade is trenchant and precise: his words are both "old" and "lewed" – old and ignorant. Januarie's own character spills over into his translation of the biblical text. Instead of a *canticum novum*, the old man can only produce an old and literal song. Notably, these are the words not only of an old and ignorant man but also of a blind one. In the tale's plot, Januarie is someone who, quite literally, will not be able to see the "signe" that his wife is going to exchange in a moment's time with her lover. More damningly, he is someone who cannot see the signs that his recitation of the Song of Songs *might* (and, in an active Christian reader and interpreter of biblical texts, *should*) have triggered. His blindness is both physical and hermeneutical.[13] In Christian discourse, biblical texts, in particular Old Testament ones, and among them, in particular, the outwardly scandalous song traditionally attributed to Solomon, "needed" to be read as signs. Reading them literally was felt to be a form of not only culpable carnality but technical idolatry as well. It is no surprise, thus, that it is precisely on these two problems that, in the span of about a hundred lines, Proserpina takes to task the author of the very text that Januarie re-performs. Attacking the authorities that her husband has brought to bolster his argument *de malicia foeminarum*, the Queen of Hades proceeds to rebut his points, opening with a textbook character assassination targeting Solomon:

> What rekket me of youre auctoritees?
> I woot wel that this Jew, this Salomon,
> Foond of us women fooles many oon.   (ll. 2276–8)

> What should I care about your authorities? I know well how that Jew, that Solomon,
> found many foolish women among us.

As she is about to argue, Solomon is an "old" authority. As such, he is steeped in a negative stereotyping of Jewishness, and his negative examples of women's foolishness are readily and easily undone by the counterexamples from the new dispensation. As a matter of fact and of modern historical record, "women ful trewe, ful goode, and vertuous" (l. 2281) do exist, argues Proserpina. They are those "that dwelle in Christe's hous" (l. 2282). In her tirade there is, however, more: Solomon's authority is not simply partial because, as she claims, it is *vetus*. It is also shaky because it comes from someone who has a less than perfect record in matters of morals and faith, even according to Old Testament standards. As Proserpina notes, basing her indictment on good biblical authority: "Pardee, as faire as ye his name emplaster, / He was a lecchour and an ydolastre" (For sure, no matter how hard you try to clean up his reputation, he was a lecher and an idolater, ll. 2297–8). Solomon's old age and carnality quite easily transfer back onto Januarie. In revisiting Solomon's *canticum*, no matter how deftly he renders it in a new idiom, Januarie fails at actually translating it into the present. In his carnal rendering, he technically proves unable to produce a new song: his words are old, stopping on the threshold of the new dispensation brought about by Incarnation. He certainly goes into the garden he has built for himself on earth, but he only perceives its function as connected with carnal pleasures. Just as, in his adopting Solomon's words as a seduction song, he cannot see that texts should be used as signs pointing beyond themselves (their letter), so too he cannot see that the garden itself might be taken as a sign, pointing beyond its earthly contingency to a truth that transcends it. We should note that Januarie is not simply old and blind. His age and blindness are co-implicated as two sides of the same coin. As Januarie himself first remarks, followed by Pluto, the connection is immediate and automatic. The Merchant returns three times to establish the perfect concomitance of blindness and old age: "and though that I be oold and may nat see" (although I am old and cannot see, l. 2168), "by cause, allas, that he is blynd and old" (since he is, alas, both blind and old, l. 2255), "unto this olde, blynde, worthy knyght" (to this old, blind, and noble knight, l. 2259). From a symbolic point of view, however, when it comes to Januarie's blindness and age, simple concomitance points to allusive co-implication. Like the Old Testament author whose text he adopts in his seduction song, Januarie is old *and therefore* he cannot see.

Chaucer's readers can hardly be unaware that there exists a both non-carnal and non-literal hermeneutic move, which would be the appropriate response a Christian should be prepared to give to gardens (as earthly spaces) and biblical texts (as provisional forms of intermediation) alike. Instead, Januarie's use of his garden is presented as literally self-sufficient: a place of delight, it is not designed to point to anything beyond itself. In its unenlightened autonomy, Januarie's identity as garden-owner and garden-singer is fully vetero-testamentary. Blindly insisting on its delights, Januarie regresses into the garden's literality. If he recaptures Eden, that is, he does so as the locus of Adam (and original sin), a place deprived of the promise of renewal that comes from Christ (in Incarnation). For all purposes, old Januarie is the Old Man. He sings the wrong song, the one of the lecherous and idolatrous Solomon. He sings as *pica* and *papagaj*, because he is artificial in his pleasures and vetero-testamentary in his joys. Worshipping in an old and carnal space, he is, put simply, a negative anti-type of Christ. He is old as Solomon's Temple and blind as the iconography of the Synagogue. And he is also sterile, as is alluded to in the tale's final stretch.[14]

Conclusion

Coming full circle, it is time to revisit the point of imbrication of the Clerk's and Merchant's tales from which this section began. I began my analysis with the author's epilogue to the first story; it is now time to dwell on the Merchant's prologue. In transitioning from the story of Griselda to that of Mayus, Chaucer moves from a fully translated tale, with no garden, to an un-translating story that instead revolves around a garden and is full of elements connecting its plot and language to the imagery of Eden. While the Clerk's Tale, which consisted in a retranslation of Petrarch's Latin into a new vernacular, had no Edenic associations, the coyly elusive tale the Merchant tells hovers over matters pertinent to the earthly paradise trope. The sequence of the two tales is not simply meant to be contrastive. One element in the Merchant's lament as *malmaritato* may in fact help coordinate the two contexts, since it contains charged language that reactivates the Edenic trope. In particular, it goes back to the quadriform directionality with which the New Testament, as a translative text, was endowed by Augustine. In summarizing the evils that have befallen him since he got married, the Merchant asserts that his wife's malice is almost beyond accounting:

> What sholde I yow reherce in special
> Hir hye malice? She is a shrewe at al.
> Ther is a long and large difference
> Bitwix Grisildis grete patience
> And of my wyf the passing crueltee.   (ll. 1221–5)

> Why should I rehearse in detail her malice? She is a shrew through and through. There is a wide and deep difference between Griselda's great patience and the extreme cruelty of my wife.

The *difference* between the patience of the dead Grisildis and the malice of the new speaker's wife is "long and large." Both the insistence on distance and the coordinates that articulate the oppositional pairing of the two women are remarkable. In bridging narrative characterization and metanarrative considerations, the text establishes the inapplicable quality of Grisildis as an example. Her tale is an account of something long gone. The clerkly (Latin) tradition of exemplarity is, for the present of the narrative, a dead letter. The past may not extend into the present. Petrarch's original moral, as we noted, is enunciated in clear terms at the end of the tale as a general and atemporal judgment passed on the quality of times: "This world is nat so strong, it is no nay, / As it hath been in olde tymes yore ..." (Our world is not so strong – no, it is not – as it was in olden days, ll. 1139–40).

In his envoy, Chaucer seemingly accepts and endorses both the paradigmatic value of the past and the twist toward a metaphysical meaning that Petrarch imposed on Boccaccio's tale in his reconfiguration of the narrative. In Petrarch's retelling, Griselda's example was given both a place on the historical record on par with classical heroines and a hermeneutic stability that matched her *constantia*, the character's most marked trait, according to the Latin version he gave of her. The Merchant, however, recapitulates the question not only ironically but also with a different aim, choosing actual spatial diffusion over potential otherworldly significance. While Petrarch's dead Griseldis and her patience lie buried in Italy, the existential conditions of the narrator gesture toward an applicability of the story that is geographically inclusive. The "far and wide difference" separating his own situation from the example of the patient Griseldis literally contains the quadriform direction that patristic literature figurally associated with neo-testamentary acts of translation. Chaucer is more than plausibly aware of the metaliterary shade of meaning inherent in the expression. As a translator himself, and while specifically working on the rendering of the *Roman de la Rose*, he gratuitously added exactly the same notation to his English version of Guillaume's garden.[15] In the opening sequence of the dream, when the lover first lays eyes on the Garden of Deduit into which he will eventually be allowed, Chaucer's text takes a slight but significant translation liberty:

And whan I had a whyle goon,
I saugh a Gardin right anoon,
Ful long and brood, and everydel
Enclos it was, and walled wel,
With hye walles enbatailled,
(*The Romaunt of the Rose*, ll. 134–9)[16]

Quant j'oi ung poi avant alé,
Si vi ung vergier grant et lé,
Tot clos d'ung haut mur bataillié.
(*Roman de la Rose*, ll. 129–31)

The pointed translation of "grant et lé" (magnificent and ample) with "long and broad" is telling. Anticipating other clear quadriform allusions that the translation will import from the French antecedent ("the gardin … was as long as it was large," ll. 1349–51), it introduces a directional sense that goes beyond the original meaning of a "spacious" enclosure. The text of Guillaume limited itself to assessing the size of the new place. It is only Chaucer's version that maps it in longitudinal and latitudinal terms. The expression Chaucer adopts is certainly proverbial, but is not unrelated to the context of the two neighbouring and explicitly contrastive stories that the Merchant's prologue connects. The former insists on a fixed place and a specific time, a precise point on a spatial-temporal map; the latter proposes a difference that is ever-increasing along the latitudinal and longitudinal axes of a worldly geography. The differential status of the two juxtaposed stories does not solely concern the incompatibility of one woman's "pacience" and another's "crueltee," or of a monumental tomb and a fertile womb, but also the interconnectedness of translation, interpretation, and figural setting. With this preliminary move, through which Chaucer's text gives Petrarch's stabilizing and retrogressively latinizing and morally epitomizing operation its due, the Merchant's Tale positions itself squarely on the side of positive translative productivity.

Chapter Five

Looking Back and Looking Forward:
Reading Levi Reading Dante

Had their enterprise succeeded, the universal tongue would have been a particular language imposed by violence, by force, by hegemony over the rest of the world. It would not have been a universal language … a transparent language to which everyone would have had access. Rather, the master with the most force would have imposed this language on the world, and, by virtue of this fact, it would have become the universal language. This, then, is their project: to make a name for themselves by imposing their lip on the world.

(Jacques Derrida *Roundtable on Translation*, p. 101)[1]

Poi che la fiamma fu venuta quivi
Dove parve al mio duca *tempo e loco*,
In questa forma a lui parlare audivi.

(*Inferno* 26.76–8)

This final section of the book tackles a text that originates in different cultural circumstances from the rest of the tradition it surveys. Working through a single chapter in Primo Levi's memoir *If This Is a Man*, it interprets its summative and conclusive role somewhat idiosyncratically, engaging in a series of prospective and retrospective interpretive moves. Although it looks back on medieval material from a significant distance and through a specifically twentieth-century lens, the interplay between medieval fictional narrative garden scenes and literary practices of tradition construction and intercultural translation remains at the centre of the argument. What has characterized the block of texts stretching from Marie de France's prologue to her *Lais* to Chaucer's reuse of Boccaccio, passing through the chivalric narratives of Chrétien de Troyes, the *Roman de la Rose*, Brunetto Latini's *Tesoretto*, and Dante's *De vulgari eloquentia*, *Convivio*, and *Commedia*, is still perceivable in Levi's text. While it is not part of the tradition, my reading suggests that "The Canto of Ulysses" attests to the vitality of its basic tenets, long past their official temporal demise. Although there is no visit to a garden, Levi's revisitation of Dante's Ulysses points toward the reactivation of the trope of translation in Dante's text. For Levi, too, the same openness to translation that medieval fictions associated with Eden is the antidote to the dissension of languages originated at Babel. The garden settings and garden scenes that characterize the medieval vernacular fictional narratives this book has examined are still crucial for Levi's framing of the episode, in conceptual and linguistic terms. The cultural connection they established between their reflection on the practices of translation and the trope of the garden visit is what helps to make the central dialogue between languages mediated by translation in Levi's text not only possible, but ultimately successful. In sum, if Dante's poetry resonates in his work so powerfully, it is not solely due to the ethical use Levi makes of the Ulysses episode, but also because a wider discourse on language and translation frames his return to Dante and the reflections it triggers. Even though Levi's text does not directly activate the materials that connected Ulysses to issues of inter-age translation in Dante, it still returns to the questions that Dante broached through them.[2]

In addition to retrospectively examining a redeployment of the medieval trope of translation, my reading of Levi's text also looks forward to the specific cultural present of this book. In doing so, it points to a potential dark side of the tradition on which my analyses have focused: namely, the nationalist option. Predicating the goodness of what is new and unquestioningly commending the powerful takeover that translation carries out on traditional material entail a potentially dangerous corollary. Always considering the present linguistic and cultural circumstances of a text to be positive may lead different communities of writers and readers, especially once they have become an organic part of a nation, to advance a subtextual claim to cultural centrality. The very notion of centrality, be it that of a nation or of a national language, may lead to a specific set of misconstructions. In the history of Europe, such misconstructions have ranged from somewhat benign claims of cultural exceptionalism to more malignant brands of identitarian politics. While qualitatively different, both attitudes are based on the predicated historical centrality of the language and culture that belong to and, in turn, identify a specific community. When a presumed cultural centrality becomes the by-product of exploiting the process of translation, and a text insists on its finality, the triumphant assertion we read in Chrétien's *Cligès*, which codes the force of the temporal dynamics fuelling the *translatio studii et imperii* as irresistible, ceases to be balanced by the self-aware knowledge that no step in the process is ever the final resting place of civilization. When a community ignores the idea that a further turn of historical events may always come and displace the current dominance of its own linguistic and political coordinates, it also loses sight of the possibility that time may precipitate an always impending cultural demise. The awareness of each culture's provisional quality, which was still perceptible in Chrétien's triumphal paradigm of literary supersession from which this book started, could then yield to a static dream of finality. In these cases, the theory and practice of vernacular translation as a contingent effect of historical unfolding get caught in a counter-paradigm: that of the end of history.

My analysis of Levi's *Canto di Ulisse* is founded on two sets of questions. First, is it possible for a text, which is necessarily drafted in a specific language and at a specific point of history that is always already the latest in time, to understand itself simply as a contingent stage, and not the necessary culmination, of a historical translinguistic process? If so, is it possible to imagine a mechanism of cultural transmission through time that does not necessarily coincide with the agonistic vertical succession of national-historical traditions, but rather opens itself up to a horizontal dialectic of translation? Correspondingly, and moving from temporal to spatial terms, is it possible to conceive a de-territorialized vernacular language? Is there a space for interlinguistic and intercultural exchange in which languages do not vie for primacy or rely on cultural prevarication to achieve it? I believe that the tradition of medieval vernacular writers of fiction did indeed answer all these questions in the affirmative, and that in reactivating Dante's model, Levi's text gives a similarly positive response. I would even argue that both the philosophical underpinnings of the medieval narrative tropes encountered in this book and contemporary conceptions of what translation is and does resonate in Levi's answer. In fact, all subsequent languages of culture, even as they are caught in the dynamics of historical supersession, may avoid immediately and univocally associating their circumstantial condition as the "latest" in a cultural lineage with an assertion of being the "last." And this is an idea that medieval texts may be shown to share with contemporary theories of translation.

Let me start with Levi's text, and the linguistic paradigms that it activates. From a narrative point of view, the content of the "The Canto of Ulysses" is simple. The chapter transcribes one isolated and cherished hour of existence as human beings, which Primo and Jean carve out of their time in the Lager during an *Essenholen corvée* they perform for the Chemical Kommando to which they are assigned. In particular, the chapter recounts the salient moments in a lesson that Primo is asked to give to Jean, the *Pikolo* of the Kommando, who wants to learn Italian from him. The lesson takes the form of Primo's mutilated recitation of Dante's text to Jean, accompanied by a translational commentary of some striking parts in it. Levi's retrospective and reflective account is framed by a double set of exceptional circumstances. The first is the tonality that marks this episode in Primo's survival in the Lager, which is recalled as the momentary emergence of one form of shared resistance against the dehumanization machinery of the concentration camp. The second noteworthy element in Primo's experience, as he teaches his native language through one of its culturally central texts, is the exquisitely translative quality of the communicative proceedings it details. There are several elements in Levi's chapter that point in this direction. Passages addressing questions of communication, language acquisition, interlanguage connection, and intercultural translation are not only scattered throughout the text; they also are all marked by a specific affective tonality, being remembered and represented as felicitous.

The signals of felicity interspersed in Levi's text are even more significant, given the contrasting insistence on linguistic dissension and isolation that characterizes his account of the Lager. In Levi's reflection on his momentary escape from the oppression of the Lager, the elements of translational optimism one may detect do not entail oblivion of the violence embedded in the language structure of the camps.[3] If anything, Levi presents the Lager as both the epitome and the final product of Babel. The biblical paradigm of Babel features prominently in his writings. In both *If This Is a Man* and in *The Drowned and the Saved*, it is used to characterize the absurd chaos and linguistic cacophony that marked *Häftling* existence in the Lager as unfolding within a universe of linguistic dissension and violence. Perhaps the most explicit use of the biblical myth in Levi's text is the chapter *A Good Day*, in a passage dedicated to the smokestack of the Buna factory. About the chimney of this industrial complex Levi writes:

> The Carbide Tower, which stands in the centre of the Buna and the summit of which is rarely visible in the fog, it is us who built it. Its bricks have been called *Ziegel*, *briques*, *tegula*, *cegi*, *kamenny*, *bricks*, *téglak*, and hatred has joined them together. Hatred and dissension, like the Tower of Babel. And this is the name we give it: Babelturm, Bobelturm. And in it we hate the demented dream of grandeur of our masters, their contempt of God and human beings – of us as human beings. (*If This Is a Man*, p. 68)[4]

In alignment with the traditional biblical value system, the passage continues by highlighting the curse, "a curse that is not transcendent and divine, but immanent and historical," which hangs over the hubristic and blasphemous building, at the foundations of which lies "the confusion of languages." What Levi will call "the sound and the fury" of the Lager's linguistic hellscape is incorporated in the multilingual chain his text constructs here, a figure of conflictual accumulation that will be repeated for other objects in the book. Because of the multifarious way in which they appear on the page, the daily rations of bread distributed in the camp, as well as the ingredients of the soup that Primo and Jean will fetch in the episode recounted in "The Canto of Ulysses," echo the Babel trope by signalling the utter dissension and violence intrinsic to the Lager.[5]

Babel's "ancient fable," as Levi defines the biblical story, may bring into relief the transgressive elements that "The Canto of Ulysses" introduces when it stages the dialogue between Primo and Jean. First, Jean is an exceptional, and exceptionally positive, character in the universe of the book. Among his distinctions is the fact that "he is fluent in French and German." To be precise, he speaks and thinks in two languages: he is native in both. As the text establishes, on the occasion of a chance encounter with an SS, bilingual utterances are for him the norm:

An SS rides by on his bicycle. It's Rudi, the Blockführer. Stop, at attention, take one's hat off. *"Sale brute, celui-là. Ein ganz gemeiner Hund."* Is it indifferent for him to speak French or German? It is. He can think in both languages. He has spent a month in Liguria. He likes Italy. He would like to learn Italian. I would be happy to teach him Italian. Can we do it? We can. Even now. One thing is as good as any other. What matters is not to lose time, not to waste this hour. (pp. 107–8)

Thus, both for him and in him, languages appear immediately as non-mutually exclusive – even those that, like French and German, have been constructed in nationalist discourses as historically incompatible. In the threatening multilingual landscape of the Lager, Jean's identity as a speaker of two languages, who also wants to learn a third, is an exception – not so much in itself, as Jean is not the sole interpreter in the camps, but rather due to its connotations. The role he plays in the structure of the concentration camp, facilitated by the distinction of his bilingualism, is not what is at stake in the episode per se. While Jean has acquired a privileged position thanks to his fluency in German (he has acquired a linguistic capital of sorts), the narrative insists on what, of that privilege, he decides to share. His multilingualism is not associated with exclusionary practices, but with the work of intermediation it brings about and the community of intents it facilitates.

The second transgressive element of the narrative is that language acquisition starts even before Primo's official teaching through translation and interpretation actually begins. The first words of Italian that Jean is able to pick up and adopt emerge from the living context of a dialogue, by the "natural" and immediate imitation of two native speakers, Primo and another prisoner from Rome, Limentani. The syllabification of the initial vocabulary Jean apprehends, *"zup-pa, cam-po, ac-qua,"* is again not a marker of alienness but of comparticipation. The shared circumstances of life in the Lager remove any opacity from the exchange. Most importantly, the learning process is accompanied by a smile: "Pikolo pays attention, catches some words in our dialogue, and repeats them with a smile." What is more, the lesson Primo soon begins to impart to Jean is deeply interlinguistic, since it shuttles between recitation of Dante's text in the Italian original and its hurried and utilitarian French prose version. The exchange between Jean and Primo is also defined as mutual, at the very basic level of collaboration in language. Jean is not a passive learner, but takes part in the process of communication, which unfolds in a living dialogue and requires that dialogue to exist. A case in point is a suggestion that Jean offers to perfect the exchange of meaning with Primo mediated by Dante. Levi writes:

Lo maggior corno della fiamma antica ... Jean appreciates the bizarre simile of the tongue and suggests the appropriate term to render *antica*. (p. 108)

Even the very word that embodies tradition and archaeological distance, *antica*, is recovered, reshaped, and reactivated in their cross-linguistic work. In the two-way negotiation of meaning across origin and target languages, Dante's text acquires a significance that the new text evokes in a positive light. The importance of this now-elided act of translation – Jean provides Primo with a fitting rendering of an Italian word, while Levi's text does not provide readers with the corresponding French term – may be measured against the opposite insistence on an elided interpretive act, which is instead made available to readers – an observation that Levi's text preserves, but that Primo does not share with Jean. When Primo discovers the echo of one expression in a later phrasing in Dante's poetry, his text registers a philological acquisition. In the context of the exchange between Primo and Jean, however, that acquisition is deemed inessential:

> *Si metta*: I had to come in the Lager to realize that it is the same expression as before: *ma misi me*. But I do not let Jean know about it. I am not sure it is a meaningful observation. (p. 109)

In other words, while the observation may be revealing in a philological vein, addressing a potential original intention in the text, the interaction between Primo and Jean is aimed at producing different results. The remark, which now tells readers something about the meaning of Dante's text, is left out of the dialogue. There is another kind of sense, one that originates from the negotiations of language that Primo is able to conduct successfully, that needs to be more urgently conveyed. This meaning has more to do with shared experience than with any original mechanism of composition or any authorial intent in Dante's poem:

> *Ma misi me per l'alto mare aperto…* Of this I am sure. Indeed, I am sure that I can explain it to Pikolo, to impress why "misi me" is not "je me mis." It is something much more radical and daring: the breaking of a bond, the hurling of oneself beyond a barrier. We know this impulse very well. (p. 109)

All meaning that philology may extract from Dante's text, such as the possible appropriate rendering of the word *antica*, is subsumed by the need to communicate in and through translation. This is the point of the interaction between Jean and Primo. We should remember that the lesson one man asked for and the other agreed to teach is not *about* Dante's canto, but *about the language* that is being taught by way of that text. The meaning is not to be found in what Dante's text may say about itself, but in what it may be used to say about something else. In "The Canto of Ulysses," this further essential meaning is what Primo desperately tries to convey to Jean: the contrastive definition of what it means to be human as a refusal to live like brutes (which is at the core of the words Dante's

Ulysses addresses to his shipmates), and the acknowledgment of the unmerciful and obscure presence of an unknown God (captured in the word *altrui* that Dante's Ulysses uses to seal the account of his death). It is, after all, these coordinated acquisitions, conclusively glimpsed and yet immediately reabsorbed in the mechanical brutality of the Lager, that form the message of Levi's text.[6]

Finally, the exchange between Jean and Primo is not simply based on, and concerned with, translation. It also is utterly charitable, in a further, technical sense. It is based on a systematic practising of interpretive benevolence. It is dominated, that is, by the desire to move beyond linguistic differences and find the common ground that underlies the entire dialogue. When Primo stumbles or forgets, Jean encourages him to go on. For example, at one point Jean meets Primo's admission that he has forgotten what follows the lines of Dante he has just recited, a moment of resignation that Primo expresses in German ("*Keine Ahnung*, as one says here"), with his own heartening exhortation, articulated in French ("*Ça ne fait rien, vas-y tout de même*," 110). The desire to have communication cross any threshold existing between languages is so deeply ingrained in Levi's text that it allows Primo to successfully negotiate the prose-poetry divide. While the lesson hinges on a poetic text, the teacher is also ready to do away with poetry and walk into prose. In Primo's recitation and explanation, where memory of Dante's original fails him, something is admittedly lost, but Levi's text does not dwell on the loss. On the contrary, it vindicates the eventual success of the work:

> And the journey, too. The daring journey beyond the pillars of Hercules: sadly, I am forced to tell it in prose. A sacrilege. I have saved only one line, but it is worth stopping on it: … *Acciò che l'uom più oltre non si metta.* (p. 109)

In his explanation, that is, the narrator accedes to prose reluctantly, but with determination. Any mourning over the "sacrilege" of turning poetry into prose is only momentary. The overall experience, even when the text registers a sense of translational "loss," is connoted as only qualifiedly negative. The translation is, rather, seen as promising from the start:

> Here I stop and try to translate. A disaster. Poor Dante and poor French language! However, the experience seems to bode well … (p. 108)

Readers eventually receive confirmation that the operation is successful. As Levi notes, after having registered Primo's passionate appeal to Pikolo to open his ears and mind to Ulysses' summoning his companions to preserve their humanity, thus refusing to live like brutes: "No matter how dim was the translation, and how rudimentary and hurried my commentary, Jean has received the message." Interlinguistic felicity, which is treated as the vehicle of interhuman connection, culminates in the articulation of Dante's message – a message that Levi establishes as not bound to a specific intention or text:

> Jean has received the message; he has felt that it concerns him, that it concerns all suffering humans, and us in particular. And that it concerns the two of us, who dare to reason about these things with the soup's poles on our shoulders. (p. 110)

That message is crucial for Levi because he sees its truth in two apparently incompatible directions, as universal and panchronic as well as individual and contingent. What Levi's text calls "perhaps the 'why' of our destiny, of our being here today" is not simply contained in Dante's text. Rather, it exceeds it. While it is triggered by the "so human and necessary, and yet surprising anachronism" conveyed in Dante's expression "as pleased another," that message does not coincide with the pastness of Dante's culture. It is not, that is, just "the Middle Ages" that Primo feels compelled to explain to Jean. It is also "something else," a gigantic truth that Primo says he has seen, in the intuition of an instant, while mediating Dante's text to Jean. This central intuition is phrased significantly. With his insistence on the "why" ("il perché del nostro destino") Levi engages in more than a simple abstract denial of one of the most lapidary linguistic inscriptions he associated with the Lager, the answer he received from a guard: "*Hier ist kein warum*" (Here there is no "why"). Dante's message, as conveyed by Primo's translation and Levi's text, actually undoes the force of that sentence through the very grammar of the language that they use.

Seen in this light, the question Primo asks himself when he begins teaching Italian to Jean, "The Canto of Ulysses. Who knows how and why it has come to my mind," may receive both an internal and a cultural answer. Internally, this is a central question for *If This Is a Man* as a book. Asking how the mechanisms of personal and cultural memory work amounts to addressing the very nature of Levi's text as the record of a witness to the horror it recounts. Just as the whole book is based on a challenging, selective, and ultimately revealing process of recollection of an unspeakable past, so too Primo's recollection of Dante's Ulysses challenges, selects, and ultimately reveals individual words, fragmentary lines, and central ideas in Dante's text. The *why* and *how* of this specific act of recollection are in osmotic continuity with the recollections at the core of his testimonial work. What is more, the germinative seed of the book, as Levi himself reports, may be located precisely in this episode. "The Canto of Ulysses" is one of the chapters Levi reports having written first, right after his return from Auschwitz. It is also intimately linked to the eventual title of the book. The precise Dantean coordinates of the Ulysses episode are a privileged subtext of the larger project of *If This Is a Man*. The Italian title *Se questo è un uomo* is the shortened form of the line "considerate se questo è un uomo," a phrase recurring through the *Shemà* poem

Levi uses as epigraph and introduction to his memoir. These words revisit, by way of the omitted verb *considerate*, the incipit of a crucial tercet from Dante's *Inferno* 26. The lines "Considerate la vostra semenza / fatti non foste a viver come bruti / ma per seguir virtute e conoscenza" are, in sum, both at the narrative centre of this single episode and at the root of the message articulated in the book. These wide and deep connections, essential as they are to a possible intratextual answer to Primo's question, are not the only element of interest. Analysing the mechanics of Levi's memory and the mechanisms of his documentary memorialization or evaluating his *dantista* potential on a grand scale are goals that fall outside the scope of this book. The specific and markedly linguistic context of what both Dante's and Levi's texts recount, together with their coherent interest in staging a successful act of translation, may instead serve as point of departure for a cultural answer to Primo's initial question.

The approach to translation, which is so central in Levi's narrative, is both perfectly modern and resonant with the medieval tropes that this book has studied. Reaching all the way back to the introductory chapter, we find the same kind of translative optimism in Augustine's incidental reflection on the positive effects that Babel ultimately had on biblical dissemination and diffusion. At the same time, a twentieth-century text that reflects the same attitude may be used to gloss Levi's positive framing of the episode. I refer to Walter Benjamin's insistence on translation as the cultural practice that best captures the intrinsic drive of all languages to communicate through their apparent mutual exclusiveness. Both Augustine's and Benjamin's approaches converge on the same essential set of points: the openness to horizontal shifts in translation, the availability to displacement from any alleged cultural centre, and the actual polycentric vision of the linguistic-literary map. As the beginning of this book suggested, Augustine treated the multiplicity of languages through which biblical translators worked not so much as the sign of a punishment meted out to humanity, but as a new and equally effective means for the transmission of God's message in a new dispensation. Similarly, as Benjamin posited in his essay, translation does not so much mark the essential isolation and mutual exclusivity of each language as signal their common semantic potential, their shared desire to produce meaning:

> All suprahistorical kinship between languages consists in this: in every one of them as a whole, one and the same thing is meant. Yet, this one thing is achievable not by any single language but only by the totality of their intentions supplementing one another: the pure language. Whereas all individual elements of foreign languages – words, sentences, associations – are mutually exclusive, these languages supplement one another in their intentions. ("The Task of the Translator," p. 257)

In embodying the most essential drive of all languages, the language of translation is for Benjamin ultimately the language of truth – the horizon against which one may perceive the true language of communication. The experience of shared humanity, which Primo and Jean achieve within the Babel of the Lager (and notwithstanding its violence), relies on the same underlying philosophy of language. In presenting Jean's own multilingualism and his desire to open himself up to one more language, as well as in pointing to Primo's endeavour to accede to that request by way of translation, Levi's text intimates how Babel, as a curse on human language, may come undone.

Recent criticism has convincingly suggested that the role of translation can be seen as a response to the violence of history and the Lager at the core of both Benjamin's 1923 essay and Levi's text.[7] Interlingual communication is crucial for Levi to regain momentary existence as a human being, and that aspect of translational felicity is in tune with Benjamin's reflection. There is, however, a further and perhaps more precise antecedent that may be brought to bear on our reading of Levi's episode, one that may contrastively help recover a sense of what translation intrinsically and systematically opposed, both in Levi's text and in the tradition that this book has mapped out. As an antidote to the Babel of the concentration camp, that is, the exchange between Primo and Jean in "The Canto of Ulysses" sheds light on the complementary quality of the language of the Lager. It is an aspect of his experience that Levi acknowledges he was able to conceptualize and formulate only retrospectively and thanks to a notion he borrowed from a different theorist. When he looks back on Auschwitz, Levi points to another work that he feels may illuminate the fundamental linguistic aberration of the concentration camps: Victor Klemperer's 1947 book *Lingua Tertii Imperii: A Philologist's Notebook*. Klemperer's merciless diagnosis of the language of Nazi Germany as the product and the producer of a dehumanizing regime appeals to Levi for one primary reason: the linguist's observation that the language of the self-defined Third Reich was a specific variety of the national language of Germany, bound to a specific time and place. For Levi the obsessive fixation of linguistic forms, on which the language of Nazi propaganda relied, becomes the crucial aspect in the language of the Lager. Intrinsic to the totalitarian and nightmarish reality created in the Lager is the fact that the language it speaks belongs to it alone:

> I did not realize then – I realized it only much later – that the German of the Lager was a self-standing language, it was *orts- und zeitgebunden*, tied to that place and that time. It was a specific, barbaric variety. (*The Drowned and the Saved*, p. 1066)

Klemperer's diagnosis of Nazi German as a language bound to a specific time and place may be used as an agent of contrast to perceive the importance that the nexus of translation, interpretation, and dialogue assumes in "The Canto of Ulysses." When he returns to thinking of the language that his persecutors imposed through the dehumanizing reality of the Lager, Levi sees the boundedness to time and space as its most peculiar and damning aspect.[8] Unbinding not just one text (Dante's) or one language (either Italian or French or even German), but potentially all languages from the constraints of time and space violently imposed on them, is exactly what Primo and Jean accomplish as they carry out their collaborative and translational reuse of Dante. Freeing a text from time and space entails liberating the language in which the text was written from any pretense of stability, which in turn involves freeing all languages from any claim to exceptional historical finality. The possibility of moving out of a *tempo e luogo* a text, a historical language, and ultimately all languages is at the core both of Levi's and Klemperer's understanding of the pathology of Nazi German and the defiant act of resistance that they both envision and practise in their works.

I shall close by adding just one more retrospective detail to what Levi noted about the time- and place-determined quality of the language in the Lager. In the context of the tropes studied in this book, it appears to be far from coincidental that the title of Klemperer's book from which Levi draws this definition is not *The Language of the Third Reich*, but *Lingua Tertii Imperii*. It is an implicit corollary for the language of a self-professed thousand-year empire that it may only portray itself as immune to translation, an immunity that in Klemperer's title is at once coded in, and mocked by way of, a symbol of linguistic entrenchment. The Latin from which medieval writers of fiction systematically departed in their translational vernacular works is, in Klemperer's formula *Lingua Tertii Imperii* and in the body of work carried out in this book, the embodiment of the other side of Babel, seen this time not as an opportunity to have languages collaborate, but as the regressive marker of an insanely pursued end of history. What Levi called, speaking of the Carbide Tower, "una bestemmia di pietra."

Notes

Preface. Beyond Babel: The Tower and the Garden

1 On Eden in western literary culture, see A. Bartlett Giamatti, *The Earthly Paradise and Renaissance Epic*; and, for an even broader perspective, Jean Delumeau, *The History of Paradise*; on its visual-cultural connections, Alessandro Scafi, *Mapping Paradise*; on its visual representations, Marie-Thérèse Gousset, *Eden*; on its anthropological underpinnings, Robert Pogue Harrison, *Gardens*; on theological and political valences, Giorgio Agamben, *The Kingdom and the Garden*; on the philosophical-cultural framing of medieval garden literature, Alastair Minnis, *From Eden to Eternity*; on gardens as actual spaces, E.B. MacDougall, ed., *Medieval Gardens*; Franco Cardini and Massimo Miglio, eds., *Nostalgia del paradiso*; and Sylvia Landsberg, *The Medieval Garden*.

2 On medieval theories and practices of translation, see the contributions collected in the series "The Medieval Translator," published by Brepols, now comprising eighteen volumes; see also the wide contextualization offered by Ralph Hanna et al., "Latin Commentary Tradition and Vernacular Literature"; E. Campbell and R. Mills, eds., *Rethinking Medieval Translation*; and most recently J. Beer, ed., *A Companion to Medieval Translation*.

3 On the value of interrogating different notions of translation in long-period cultural systems, see the seminal study by Maurizio Bettini, *Vertere: Un'Antropologia della traduzione nella cultura antica*. Although it does not cross into the disciplinary field of anthropology as Bettini's does, I understand my work in an ideal methodological continuity with his.

4 The currency of the biased view about the negative effects endemic to translation is, of course, widest among "civilians," as reflected in common-parlance idioms or motion pictures' titles. Naturally, it has not been left unchallenged in contemporary post-modern theorizations. See, for instance, the vindications advanced in contributions as different as Gayatri Chakravorty Spivak, "Translation as Culture";

Edith Grossman, *Why Translation Matters*; Mireille Gansel, *Translation as Transhumance*; and Jhumpa Lahiri, *Translating Myself and Others*.

5　The passage from Ambrose comes from *De paradiso liber unus*, cited according to the CSEL edition (vol. 32.1).

Introduction

1　I cite the text of Augustine's treatise *On Christian Doctrine* from the Lorenzo Valla series: Sant'Agostino, *L'istruzione cristiana*. Unless otherwise indicated, all translations are mine.

2　Biblical texts are cited according to the *Biblia Sacra Iuxta Vulgatam Versionem*, ed. R. Weber, fourth edition.

3　Augustine's *De civitate Dei* is cited according to the Loeb edition: Augustine, *The City of God against the Pagans*, trans. G.E. McCracken.

4　Jerome's *Prologue* is cited according to the text offered in volume 26 of the *Patrologia Latina* edition: Sancti Eusebii Hieronymi *Commentaria in Evangelium Sancti Matthaei*, in *Opera Omnia*, vol. 4: coll. 15–22.

5　For Hrabanus Maurus, I have used the edition *In honorem sanctae crucis*, ed. M. Perrin.

6　On the long-standing debate surrounding Marie's hermeneutic attitude in her *Prologue* to the *Lais*, see the biblical-exegetical framing proposed in Leo Spitzer, "The Prologue to the *Lais* of Marie de France and Medieval Poetics"; for an emphasis on the scholastic methodology, D.W. Robertson, "Marie de France, *Lais*, Prologue, 13–16"; for the term *iuniores* in Priscian (as *moderniores*) in an Augustinian context, extending biblical exegetic tools to secular literature, see Tony Hunt, "Glossing Marie de France."

7　The excerpts from Marie de France's work follow the editions *The "Lais" of Marie de France*, ed. and trans. C.M. Waters; and *The Fables of Marie de France: An English Translation*, trans. M.L. Martin. See also, for Marie's overall intellectual project as embodied in her General Prologue, Logan E. Whalen, "The *Prologues* and *Epilogues* of Marie de France," and, for her use of Latin antecedents, Emanuel J. Mickel, "Marie de France and the Learned Tradition"; and S. Kinoshita and P. McCracken, "Communication, Transmission, and Interpretation." For a novel framing, see also Campbell, *Reinventing Babel*, 122–35 and 170–80.

8　On the interconnection of glossing and translation in the theory of the prologue and the practice of *Guigemar*, see Kristine Brightenback, "Remarks on the *Prologue* to Marie de France's *Lais*"; on the topos of *translatio studii* deployed in the prologue, Alfred Foulet and Karl D. Uitti, "The Prologue to the *Lais* of Marie de France"; on Marie's reader-response approach to literature, Monica Brzezinski Potkay, "The Parable of the Sower and Obscurity in the Prologue to Marie de France's *Lais*."

9　On Marie's reference to other works by Priscian, together with or beyond his *Institutiones*, see Marie-Louise Zanoni, "Ceo Testimoine Precïens."

10　The *Life of Saint Alexis* is cited from *Vie de Saint Alexis*, ed. J.M. Meunier.

11 For the text of Chrétien de Troyes' romances, see *Cligès*, ed. and trans. I. Kasten; and *Erec and Enide*, ed. and trans. C.W. Carroll.

12 On Chrétien's classicism, see Joseph S. Wittig, "The Aeneas-Dido Allusion in Chrétien's *Erec et Enide*," which explores the modelling of the chivalric hero on medieval readings of the Virgilian antecedent; Helen C.R. Laurie, "From *Erec* to *Cligès*," focusing on the Ovidian vein in which Chrétien and his sources redeployed Virgilian material; Douglas Kelly, "*Translatio Studii*," with a long-view and modulated perspective of *translatio* in the Old French tradition, encompassing transmission, adaptation, and allegorization; and Michelle A. Freeman, "The Prologue," again with attention to the Ovidian ascendance of the authorial mask. See also the first half of the essay by Karl D. Uitti, "*Érec et Énide* and *Cligès*," pointing to Martianus Capella's influence on the narrative of the first romance.

13 Virgil's spurious incipit lines are quoted according to the text established in P. Vergili Maronis, *Opera*, ed. R.A.B. Mynors, xii.

14 The text of Ovid's *Tristia* comes from P. Ovidius Naso, *Tristium Libri V – Ibis – Ex Ponto Libri IV*, vol. 3.1. ed. R. Ehwald and F.W. Levy.

15 On the Ovid question in Marie's *Guigemar*, see the anti-Ovidian stance attributed to her by Robert Hanning, "Courtly Contexts for Urban Cultus"; for a structural and structuralist reading of the paintings, see Logan E. Whalen, "A Medieval Book-Burning"; for a perspective sensitive to the socio-historical and hermeneutic gender-inflected violence that the text counteracts, see Suzanne Klerks, "The Pain of Reading Female Bodies in Marie de France's *Guigemar*"; on potential interconnections between Marie's and Chrétien's gardens, see Lindsay Diggelmann, "Gardens as 'Emotional Communities.'"

16 For a problematizing discussion of which "Ovid" (the erotic or the sapiential author) is the object of Venus' book burning, see Tracy Adams, "*Arte Regendus Amor*."

17 For a Pauline reading of the convergency of Marie's and Chrétien's modern-favouring attitude, see Tom Artin, "Sowers of the Word."

1 Encompassing Imperfection: The Garden of the *Rose*

1 On the immediate fortune of and reaction to the *Roman de la Rose*, see Sylvia Huot, *The "Romance of the Rose" and Its Medieval Readers*. On the debate about the interpretation, see Christine McWebb, ed., *Debating the Roman de la Rose*; see also the edition of Christine de Pizan's interventions into the *querelle* in Christine de Pizan et al., *Debate of the "Romance of the Rose*," ed. and trans. D.F. Hult.

2 The text of the *Rose* is cited from Guillaume de Lorris and Jean de Meun, *Le Roman de la Rose*, ed. F. Lecoy.

3 On oneirocritic and metapoetic considerations in the body of the romance, see A.C. Spearing, *Medieval Dream-Poetry*, 16–18 and 24–30; David Hult, *Self-Fulfilling Prophecies*, 10–104; see also, with emphasis on optics, Suzanne Conklin Akbari,

Seeing through the Veil, 45–55. On classical-vernacular imbrications for the lexica of dream and fiction, see Renate Blumenfeld, "Remarques sur *songe/mensonge*."

4 On Jean's translational classicism, see John V. Fleming, "Jean de Meun and the Ancient Poets"; for the satirical, self-deconstructing practices of Ovidian transposition in the *Rose*, see Alastair Minnis, "Lifting the Veil"; and Sylvia Huot, "The Desire for Knowledge and the Knowledge of Desire." For further involvement of Jean de Meun in matters of translation, see John Marenbon, "Jean de Meun, Boethius, and Thirteenth-Century Philosophy."

5 The text of Ovid's *Amores* comes from the Loeb edition of *Heroides. Amores*, trans. G. Showerman, ed. G.P. Goold.

6 On the complexities involved in the experience of narrative time by the protagonist, the authors, and the readers of the romance, see Emmanuèle Baumgartner, "The Play of Temporalities"; Kevin Brownlee, "Pygmalion, Mimesis, and Multiple Endings of the *Roman de la Rose*"; Jacqueline Victor, "Time and the Reader of the *Roman de la Rose*"; as well as Luciano Rossi, "Metalepsis and Allegory."

7 Sources and analogues for the *Rose* garden description, as well as potential allegorical associations entailed in its essential elements, have been amply investigated in a host of traditional contributions. See the seminal study of the light-and-shadow dynamics in D.W. Robertson, "The Doctrine of Charity in Mediaeval Literary Gardens," and his reappraisal in *A Preface to Chaucer*, 91–112; for a wide survey of sources, see Giamatti, *The Earthly Paradise and Renaissance Epic*, 67–86; see also the intertextual commentary in John V. Fleming, *The Roman de la Rose*, 54–103; and, more recently, the discussion of optics and ethics in his "The Garden of the *Roman de la Rose*." For a related line of inquiry into further, destabilizing classical antecedents, see Jamie C. Fumo, "Romancing the Rose."

8 The text of Augustine's *De genesi contra manichaeos* is quoted from volume 34 of the *Patrologia Latina*: Sancti Aurelii Augustini Hipponensis Episcopi *Opera Omnia*, vol. 3.1: 173–220.

9 The text of Isidore's *Eytmologiae* is the one established in Isidori Hispalensis Episcopi *Etymologiarum sive Originum Libri XX*, ed. W.M. Lindsay.

10 On the corrective relation of Genius's Park to Guillaume's Garden, see Nathaniel B. Smith, "In Search of the Ideal Landscape"; Renate Blumenfeld-Kosinski, *Reading Myth*, 78–89.

11 On Brunetto as translator, see Michelle Bolduc, "Bringing Ciceronian Rhetoric to the Florentine Comune," chapter 3 in *Translation and the Rediscovery of Rhetoric*, 115–91.

12 For Brunetto's treatment of Nature, see Anne-Hélène Miller, "Nature and Authorship in Brunetto Latini and Guillaume de Machaut."

13 The edition from which I quote the text is Brunetto Latini, *Tesoretto*, ed. M. Ciccuto.

14 For the cultural and codicological as well as literary context of Brunetto Latini's evocation of Ovid in the *Tesoretto*, see Robert Black, "Ovid in Medieval Italy"; Elisa

Guadagnini, "Les *Métamorphose* d'Ovide dans le Moyen Age Italien"; and most recently Julie van Peteghem, *Italian Readers of Ovid from the Origins to Petrarch*, 3–9. See also, with limitations, Marta Powell Harely, "Narcissus, Hermaphroditus, and Attis."

15 On matters of interpretive competence and hermeneutic frameworks, see the questionably sceptical approach by Douglas Kelly, *Internal Difference and Meanings in the Roman de la Rose*, 12–29; on the text's ultimate openness to acts of interpretation, see Daniel Heller-Roazen, *Fortune's Faces*, 100–31.

16 On the metapoetic status of Faux-Semblant, see Kevin Brownlee, "The Problem of Faux Semblant"; on the historical context of the *Evangile pardurable*, see Marjorie Reeves, "The Scandal of the Eternal Evangel."

17 The present passage from *De Concordia utriusque Testamenti* and the quotations from William of Saint Amour's *De periculis* (see infra) are extracted from "Internal History of the Franciscan Order," in John C.L. Gieseler, *A Compendium of Ecclesiastical History*, vol. 3: 251–63.

18 On the interconnection of (Dante's) *Fiore* and the *Roman de la Rose*, see Earl Jeffrey Richards, "The Translatio Topos and Dante" and Richards, "The Fiore and the Roman de la Rose"; Peter Armour, "The Roman de la Rose and the Fiore"; the wide-ranging collection of essays contained in Z. Barański and P. Boyde, eds., *The "Fiore" in Context*; Kevin Brownlee, "The Practice of Cultural Authority"; and most recently the entry by Antonio Montefusco, "Roman de la Rose," in *The Oxford Handbook of Dante*, 127–41. The *Fiore* contains a further element of interest for the argument of this book: the wintertime setting of the action, which eerily resonates with the names of the protagonists in Chaucer's Merchant's Tale. For a brief discussion of this feature, see chapter 4, pp. 184–5.

19 The *Fiore* is cited from G. Contini's edition, available through the Princeton Dante Project at https://dante.princeton.edu/pdp/fiore.html.

2 Animal Instability: Dante's Theories of Language before and in the *Commedia*

1 On the vital nexus of translation and poetics in Dante, see the seminal work by Teodolinda Barolini, *Dante's Poets*, and by Alison Cornish, *Vernacular Translation in Dante's Italy*.

2 The text of Dante's *Vita nuova* used here is the one established by the Domenico De Robertis for the Società Dantesca Italiana, available in the Princeton Dante Project: https://dante.princeton.edu/pdp/vitanuova.html. The translation is based on Mark Musa's version published on the same site. On Dante's qualified classicism, see John A. Scott, "Dante and Classical Antiquity"; more recently, Robert Black, "Classical Antiquity"; Simone Marchesi, "Classical Culture"; and Zygmunt G. Barański, "Latin Literature." For the potential allusion to a bypassing of the geometry problem of squaring the circle contained in the expression "secondo alcuna proporzione," see Ronald B. Herzman and Gary W. Towsley, "Squaring the Circle."

3 Most recent commentaries for Dante's pre-comedic treatises may be found in
Mirko Tavoni, commentary on *De vulgari eloquentia*, and Gianfanco Fioravanti,
commentary on *Convivio*. Rich cultural framing for these works is provided in Z.G.
Barański and T.J. Cachey, eds., *Dante's "Other Works."*

4 Dante's pre-comedic treatises, *Convivio* and *De vulgari eloquentia*, are cited from
the editions published under the auspices of the Società Dantesca Italiana, available
via the Princeton Dante Project: https://dante.princeton.edu/pdp/convivio.html
and https://dante.princeton.edu/pdp/vulgari.html , respectively. My translations are
based on the versions provided on that same site: *Dante's "Il Convivio,"* trans. R.H.
Lansing, and Dante, *De vulgari Eloquentia*, trans. S. Botterill.

5 On the disappearance of the parrot from the prose of *De vulgari eloquentia*, see the
early proposal by Francesco Mazzoni, "Per il *topos* della gazza e del pappagallo."
On the juxtaposition of creative and imitative bird calls, as conceptualized in the
Occitan lyrical tradition, see the monumental study by Sarah Kay, *Parrots and
Nightingales*, which also contains a relevant chapter on "Dante's Ex-Appropriation of
the Troubadours in *De vulgari eloquentia* and the *Divina commedia*."

6 The text of Isidore's *Etymologies* is taken from Isidori Hispaliensis Episcopi
Etymologiarum sive Originum Libri XX, ed. W.M. Lindsay.

7 Isidore's account of the parrot's natural loquacity, echoing Aristotle, Pliny, and
Solinus, is in turn echoed across multiple traditions. One finds its main element
in several bestiaries (e.g., the Aberdeen Bestiary or Hugo de Folieto's *De avibus*), as
well as, with a significant twist, in Brunetto Latini's *Tresor*, which insists on the local
nature of its greeting: "Papegaus est uns oisaus vers. Si piet et bès sont rouges et a
plus grant language et plus lez que nus oisiaus, per coi il dist paroles articuleres en
sainblance d'ome … E dient li yndienes kil ne naist aillours ke en Inde, et que de lor
nature sevait il s[a]luer selonc l'usage de cele terre" (The parrot is a green bird, but
its feet and beak are red; it has the biggest and largest tongue of all birds, and so it
articulates words resembling man … And people from India claim that this bird is
only born there and that it is able by nature to greet people, in the fashion of that
land, I.v.CLXX). I transcribe the text of Brunetto from Brunetto Latini, *Li Livres
dou Trésor* as attested in the manuscript Morgan Library and Museum, M.814 (fol.
68r). Furthermore, the same distinction between "natural" call and imitative attitude
preserved by Isidore is articulated in another textual strain from antiquity, which
was within Dante's philological reach, at least during the composition of *Purgatorio*
and *Paradiso*. The *Prologus* in Persius' *Saturae* poignantly as much as ironically asks:
"Quis expedivit psittacus suum *chaere,* / Picamque docuit verba nostra conari?"
(Who provided the parrot with *his* greeting "hallo" and taught the magpie to try
and articulate *our* words?, vv. 8–9, emphasis mine). The text of Persius is cited from
Juvenal and Persius, ed. Susanna Morton Braund.

8 For a general orientation, see Kathleen Walker-Meikle, "Pets in Literature"; Bruce
Thomas Boehrer, *Parrot Culture*, 23–49 (on medieval culture); and the introductory
chapter in Elizabeth Leach, *Sung Birds*, which develop, on the side of "birdsong,"

the same rationality-based argument Dante adopts in discussing "birdspeak" as only seemingly human.

9 For Dante's linguistic reflection in *De vulgari*, see Pier Vincenzo Mengaldo, "Preistoria e componenti di una tesi dantesca"; Angelo Mazzocco, *Linguistic Theories in Dante and the Humanists*; Mirko Tavoni, "Che cosa erano il volgare e il latino per Dante" and, more recently, Tavoni, "Language and Style"; Irène Rosier-Catach, "Man as a Speaking and Political Animal"; and Heather Webb, "Language."

10 On the fraught cultural framework for Dante's reflection on linguistics, see Maria Corti, *Dante a un nuovo crocevia*; as well as Umberto Eco, "The Perfect Language for Dante," and Eco, "Dante between Modistae and Kabbalah," responding to criticism levelled at Corti. See also Stephen Nichols, "Global Language or Universal Language?," to which one may add chapters 1 (Costantino Marmo) and 2 (Federica Anichini) in M.L. Ardizzone, ed., *Dante and Heterodoxy*, 1–17 and 18–34, respectively.

11 On a reappraisal of Dante's formative years, with a focus on Latin authors, see Filippo Gianferrari, *Training the Reader*.

12 Further elements of tension between the arguments developed in the treatises abound. As has been noted in the past and signalled again by Gary Cestaro, for instance, in the *Convivio* Dante still insists on the primacy of the vernacular over grammar, as the vehicle language for instruction in it (see *Cv.* I.13.5), and connects the vernacular with desire, linking it to his own generation (I.13.4). Correspondingly, in the *De vulgari*, the normalizing force of the grammaticalized illustrious vernacular is apparently limited to the highest register of literary production and designed as the idiom for the widest intellectual community of the "latini" (see the combined effect of II.1.9 and I.19.1–2, respectively), while the treatise adumbrates a (never written) discussion of the lower forms of poetic writing along with the study of the idiom of a single family, the narrowest possible human community (I.19.3).

13 I cite the text of the *Divine Comedy* from Dante, *Commedia*, ed. G. Petrocchi. Commentaries to the poem follow the digital versions present in the Dartmouth Dante Project https://dante.dartmouth.edu/.

14 For a definition of the typological connection between Eve and Mary, see Victoria Kirkham, *Fabulous Vernacular*, 24; for further information and systematization, see Giuseppe C. Di Scipio, "The Hebrew Women in Dante's Symbolic Rose," 113–14.

15 Locus classicus for a vertical reading of Cantos 26 is Elena Lombardi, "The Poetics of Trespassing." Among the many readings of the individual cantos, the following prove particularly useful for matters of linguistics, rhetoric, and poetics: for *Inferno* 26, see Giuseppe Mazzotta, "Rhetoric and History"; for *Purgatorio* 26, Prue Shaw, "A Reading of *Purgatory* XXVI"; for *Paradiso* 26, this time with a linguistic focus, Elena Lombardi, *The Syntax of Desire*, 129–49.

16 For my threefold characterization of the work the three Cantos 26 perform for Dante's linguistics, I am obviously indebted to the arguments advanced and the formulation adopted by Richard Rorty, *Contingency, Irony, and Solidarity*.

17 For the evolution of core tenets in Dante's linguistic between the treatise and the
    Commedia, see Kevin Brownlee, "Why the Angels Speak Italian"; Zygmunt G.
    Barański, "Dante's Biblical Linguistics"; Brenda Deen Schildgen, "Dante's Utopian
    Landscape"; Gary Cestaro, "Reconstructing Subjectivity in *Purgatorio* and *Paradiso*";
    Albert Russell Ascoli, "Language"; Elena Lombardi, "Plurilingualism *sub specie
    aeternitatis*"; and most recently Teodolinda Barolini, "Difference as Punishment and
    Difference as Pleasure."

18 On metaphorical thinking in *De vulgari*, see Stefano Selenu, "Nella caccia della
    lingua." On the jurisprudential approach informing Dante's thinking in the treatise
    and providing a complementary set of resonances to his discussion of formalized
    norms and arbitrary usage, see Justin Steinberg, "Arbitrium and Poetic License in *De
    vulgari eloquentia*."

19 On Dante's translation theories and practices, see the overview and theorization in
    Massimiliano Chiamenti, *Dante Traduttore*, especially the section "Uno-a-Uno" on
    translation of authorities (pp. 25–55); for a pointed analysis of Dante's individual
    statements, see also Domenico Pietropaolo, "Dante on Translation"; and Antonella
    Braida, "Dante and Translation." For an examination of Dante's case from a wider
    perspective, see the seminal essay by Gianfranco Folena, *Volgarizzare e tradurre*.

20 For this line of argument, see my *Dante and Augustine*, 95–9.

21 For the first notice of the *Paradiso* acrostic, see Antonio Soro, "*PESCE* in *Par.* V,
    97–109."

22 See Lino Pertile, "Dante, Agostino e i pesci di Mercurio (*Par.,* V 85–114)"; on the
    Augustinian connection activated in that context, see also Robert Hollander, "The
    Sibyl in *Paradiso* 33.66 and in *De civitate Dei* 18.23."

23 Pertile, "Dante, Agostino e i pesci di Mercurio," 147.

3 Making Paradise on Earth: The Second Garden of Boccaccio's *Decameron*

1 For a thoughtful re-examination and eventual discounting of the possibility that the
   Decameron may ever yield stable ethical readings of the kind this chapter proposes,
   see Marilyn Migiel, *The Ethical Dimension of the "Decameron,"* 139–60.

2 On the subtle theology deployed in Boccaccio's garden descriptions, see the classic
   contribution by Edith G. Kern, "The Gardens in the *Decameron* Cornice"; for a
   more nuanced assessment, refining the perhaps overly neat progression outlined
   in Kern, see the intertextual reading by Thomas C. Stillinger, "The Language of
   Gardens"; for the interaction between further literary and topographical places
   in Boccaccio's text, see Jonathan Usher, "Frame and Novella Gardens in the
   Decameron." Pointed observations are also available in Tobias Foster Gittes, "*Nel
   Cospetto degli Uomini*." On the theme of the garden as backdrop for storytelling, see
   Lucia Battaglia Ricci, *Ragionare nel giardino*, 125–32 and 166–80; as well as Ilaria
   Tufano, "Nel giardino di Boccaccio."

3 Boccaccio's text is cited from the edition Giovanni Boccaccio, *Decameron*, ed.
   Vittore Branca, which also contains Branca's commentary, with which I dialogue
   throughout. My translation is based on G.H. McWilliam's, available in Giovanni
   Boccaccio, *The Decameron*.

4 As in the previous chapter, the *Rose* is here cited from Guillaume de Lorris and Jean
   de Meun, *Le Roman de la Rose*, ed. F. Lecoy; the translation is mine.

5 For Dante's sense of the time gap between the artistic use of his "new" vernacular
   and its Provençal antecedent, see *Vn.* 25.4 (setting the earliest vernacular writings
   at 150 years earlier), *Dve* I.10.3 (insisting on the chronological primacy of the
   "lingua *oc*"), and, most importantly, the metapoetic discussions of Provençal-Italian
   canonical poets on the ledges of the gluttons and lustful in *Purgatorio* 24–6.

6 On the editorial status of Pliny's epistolary corpus, see Pliny the Younger, *C. Plini
   Caecili Secundi Epistularum Libri Decem*, ed. R.A.B. Mynors, v–xxiii. On the
   Laurenziano, San Marco 284 manuscript, which possibly originated in Arezzo and
   was later moved to Coluccio Salutati's library, see pp. vii–viii; see also L.D. Reynolds
   and N.G. Wilson eds., *Texts and Transmission*, 316–22. For a brief history of the
   disambiguation of the uncle and nephew homonymy, see the *Brevis adnotatio de
   duobus Pliniis* by Giovanni de Matociis (d. 1337); see also Roberto Weiss, "The
   Forerunners of Petrarch," 22–4.

7 An argument may be made that here, too, Boccaccio's text produces an intentionally
   layered allusion, addressing the evocation of a (more recondite) text to a (smaller)
   section of his audience, while allowing for another (larger) component of his public
   to move over a (more familiar) intertextual ground. For a general framing argument,
   advanced through a set of multi-layered readings, see Simone Marchesi, *Stratigrafie
   decameroniane*.

8 On the Dantean filigree of textual and structural allusions present in Boccaccio's
   Decameron, see, at least, Franco Fido, "Dante personaggio mancato nel *Decameron*";
   Albert Russell Ascoli, "Boccaccio's Auerbach"; Robert Hollander, *Boccaccio's Dante
   and the Shaping Force of Satire*; and, most recently, Martin Eisner, "Dante and the
   Author of the *Decameron*."

9 Pointed readings of *Decameron* 3.1 and Masetto's silence are available in
   Millicent Marcus, "Seduction by Silence"; Giuseppe Mazzotta, "Allegory and the
   Pornographic Imagination," 105–16; and Massimo Ciavolella, "The Tale of Masetto
   da Lamporecchio." On the evocation of an ethical, if not theologized, space in the
   novella, see Guido Almansi, *The Writer as Liar*, 76–81; on the mimetic and allusive
   dimension of language evoked, see Marga Cottino-Jones, "Desire and the Fantastic
   in the *Decameron*."

10 After all, the loss of Eden for humankind is routinely blamed on Eve's loquacity, and
   Dante is no exception to this tradition. See Barolini, "Difference as Punishment"
   (153–4), a magisterial contribution on the interrelation of *presumptuosissima Eva*
   and *Beatrix loquax* in Dante's evolving (and gendered) thought, which revisits issues
   first addressed in Barolini, *The Undivine Comedy*.

11 On the rhetorical prowess of and theological dangers embedded in Frate Cipolla's preaching in *Decameron* 6.10, see the seminal essay by Millicent Joy Marcus, "Boccaccio's Singular Cicero"; on the friar's strategy of double entendre, see Joy Hambuchen Potter, *Five Frames for the "Decameron,"* 60–7; and Jonathan Usher, "Frate Cipolla's *Ars Praedicandi*." For the angelic ornithology motif, see Cabrini, "Piume d'angelo."

12 On Frate Cipolla's imaginary journey, see Luca Marcozzi, "Raccontare il Viaggio."

13 Valuable commentary on the purely verbal quality of the allegedly holy relics may be found in Jonathan Usher, "Pieces of Dante among Cipolla's Relics"; and most recently in Cormac ó Cuilleanáin, "The Tale of Frate Cipolla."

14 The extract from the *Epistle of Alexander the Great to Aristotle* is transcribed from Boccaccio's autograph manuscript, the so-called Zibaldone Laurenziano, BML Pluteo 29.8, available at http://mss.bmlonline.it.

15 I quote the "Acta Santi Laurenti" from Ado Viennensis, *Martyrologium*.

16 Passages from the collection of exempla by Magister Matthias quoted here are taken from the edition *Copia Exemplorum*, ed. Lars Wåhlin.

17 For the text of the *Res Gestae* I have used the Loeb edition, Ammianus Marcellinus, *Rerum Gestarum Libri*, trans. J.C. Rolfe.

18 The account of the marking-cross miracle on which Magister Matthias relies is cited from Arnoldus Leodiensis, *Alphabetum narrationum*, ed. B. Brilli. Brilli duly signals Arnald's source in the *Golden Legend*, which I summarize below, and for which see the critical edition, Iacopo da Varazze, *Legenda Aurea*, ed. G.P. Maggioni, 978.

4 The Old and the New: Chaucer's Garden of Delight

1 On the fraught relationship between Boccaccio's (according to Petrarch, "unoriginal") original of this story and Petrarch's (markedly "unique") translation of it, see Luca Carlo Rossi, "La Novella di Griselda tra Boccaccio e Petrarca," in his edition of the texts, *Griselda*, 8–25; on the dialectics between senility and youth (as well as stylistic loftiness and lowliness) in Petrarch's re-styling translation, see Gabriella Albanese, "La novella di Griselda"; William Rossiter, "Translation of Allegory or Allegory of Translation?"; Kenneth P. Clarke, "Reading/Writing Griselda." On the validatory more than restitutive quality of Petrarch's "translation" of Boccaccio's tale, viewed in the framework of Petrarch's (always-provisional and internally fraught) reflection on the interconnection of vernacular and Latin literature, see Jane Tylus, "Petrarch's Griselda and the Sense of an Ending," containing pointed observations on the presence of the *tornata* model in the unfulfilled exchange between the two writers and friends (438–42).

2 Excerpts from Petrarch's epistle are cited according to Francesco Petrarca, *Res Seniles Libri XIII–XVII*, ed. Silvia Rizzo and Monica Berté, on whose Italian translation I have based my own English rendering. *Seniles* 17.3 is on pp. 442–75.

3 Petrarch's insistence on returning the text to its original and legitimate owner – what Jane Tylus has insightfully described as his conceptualization of "translation

as a *tornata* directed ... not at himself but at Boccaccio" ("Petrarch's Griselda,"
442) – qualifies the translator's stance as philological rather than hermeneutical, the
same stance, incidentally, as the one Dante held and practised in the ending of his
Convivio, a model text to which Tylus crucially refers.

4   For the gendering of the tale as "feminine" in the dynamics of "despoliation" and
     reclothing, see Emma Campbell, "Sexual Poetics and the Politics of Translation in
     the Tale of Griselda." In the same gendered vein, but with a particular attention
     to the context of *Seniles* 17, see Kenneth P. Clarke, "On Copying or Not Copying
     Griselda," who reads the very text of the Griselda tale as mediating a homosocial
     exchange between Petrarch and Boccaccio. Further contextual readings of the
     interplay between Petrarch and Boccaccio may be found in Gur Zak, "Petrarch's
     Griselda and the End of Humanism," insisting on the self-destabilizing effect
     triggered by the "ironic reversals" which issue from Petrarch's placement of his
     translation within the last book of his *Seniles*; and, more recently, in Simona
     Lorenzini, "Petrarch and Boccaccio"; Massimo Verdicchio, "Griselda between
     Boccaccio and Petrarch"; and Lorenzo Geri, "*Una nuova veste*."

5   Petrarch evokes this scene in an earlier epistolary text, *Familiares* 4.1, about his
     ascent of Mont Ventoux. Marked by similar metapoetic and hermeneutic tensions
     as *Seniles* 17.4, that text also juxtaposes two different modes of reading and two
     reading scenes, one detailing Petrarch's stumbling upon a passage in Livy's *Ad Urbe
     condita* reporting how King Philip climbed Mount Hemus, the literary trigger
     of his decision to climb the Ventoux, and the other recounting Petrarch's shock
     upon opening his portable copy of Augustine's *Confessions*, only to stumble upon
     a passage that indicts, with ethical self-negligence, those who climb the highest
     mountains and disregard introspection. In that letter, too, the juxtaposition of
     typological and philological readings produces an interpretive impasse. While a
     detailed analysis of this intertextual precedent goes beyond the scope of this book,
     the following contributions may help readers orient themselves by addressing that
     supplementary text. For the philological (dating) issues raised by the letter, see
     Giovanni Billanovich, "Petrarca e il Ventoso"; for the construction of Augustinian
     resonance in the letter, see Pierre Courcelle, "Pétrarque entre Saint Augustine et
     le Augustiniennes," and Évelyne Luciani, *Les Confessions de Saint Augustine dans
     les lettres de Pétrarque*, 65–81; for the infraction of the Augustinian paradigm, see
     John Freccero, "The Fig Tree and the Laurel," and Robert Durling, "Il Petrarca, il
     Ventoso e la possibilità dell'allegoria." For the hermeneutic conundrum embodied
     by the letter, see Jill Robbins, "Petrarch Reading Augustine." For the text's unsettling
     of historical periodization (and historical paradigms in general), see Albert Russell
     Ascoli, "Petrarch's Middle Age."

6   For Chaucer's oblique redeployment of Petrarch's version (through the French
     intermediary of the *Livre Griseldis*) in the Clerk's Tale, see Robin Kirkpatrick, "The
     Griselda Story in Boccaccio, Petrarch and Chaucer"; see also N.S. Thompson, "The
     Three Griseldas," in *Chaucer, Boccaccio, and the Debate of Love*, 279–312, who

insists on the interpretive challenge posed in Chaucer's (and Boccaccio's) versions, designed "to further inveigle the reader in the skeins of interpretation" (p. 300). On Chaucer "dismantling Petrarch" (as per Koff, "Imagining Absence," 282) and the interconnectedness of Clerk's and Merchant's tales, see David Wallace, "Whan She Translated Was." On the inescapable authority of Dante as successful writer of moral tales, to be perceived in the background of all three versions of the story, see Leonard Michael Koff, "Imagining Absence." On lexical "smoking guns" indicating that Chaucer used, along with Petrarch's (Latin) and other (French) vernacular translations, Boccaccio's original, see Jessica Harkins, "Chaucer's Clerk's Tale," with a discussion of previous literature.

7 Chaucer's texts are cited from the Harvard Geoffrey Chaucer Website; I have based my modern English paraphrases on the line-by-line rendition offered there.

8 For the *Decameron* ascendance of the Merchant's Tale plot, see Janet L. Smarr, "*Mercury* in the Garden"; Larry D. Benson, "The Merchant's Tale and Its Analogues"; Peter G. Beidler, "Chaucer's *Merchant's Tale* and the *Decameron*"; N.S. Thompson, *Chaucer, Boccaccio, and the Debate of Love*, 241–50; Carol Falvo Heffernan, "Two 'English Fabliaux'"; Andrzej Wicher, "Geoffrey Chaucer's *The Merchant's Tale*, Giovanni Boccaccio's *The Tale of the Enchanted Pear-Tree*, and *Sir Orfeo*."

9 Petrarch too, as the "worthy clerk" who is the tale's author, is also said to be "deed and nayled in his cheste" (The Clerk's Tale, 29).

10 On the Eden theme bridging the *Roman de la Rose* and the *Merchant's Tale*, see Kenneth A. Bleeth, "The Image of Paradise in the *Merchant's Tale*"; Derek Pearsall, "Gardens as Symbol and Setting in Medieval Poetry"; Lorrain Kochanske Stock, "Making It in the *Merchant's Tale*"; Laura Howes, *Chaucer's Garden and the Language of Convention*, 15–30 and 96–102; and John Zedolik, "*The gardyn is enclosed al aboute*." On further typological associations for the garden, see Jamie C. Fumo, "An Interpretive Crux in Januarie's Garden."

11 On the pro- or anti-gamic debates and Chaucer's interest in rhetoric, dialectics, and the instability of points of view associated to internal narrators, see Joseph Turner, "Rhetoric and Performing Anger."

12 On the ethical and philosophical characterization of Januarie's Epicureanism, see Alcuin Blamires, *Chaucer, Ethics and Gender*, 87–97.

13 On Januarie's translational singing, see James I. Wimsatt, "Chaucer and the Canticle of Canticles"; on the spiritual implications of physical blindness, see Suzanne Conklin Akbari, *Seeing through the Veil*, 223–33.

14 On the allegorical figuration of the Synagogue as blind, see Margaret Schauch, "The Allegory of Church and Synagogue"; Henry Kraus, "Eve and Mary: Conflicting Images of Medieval Woman" and "Anti-Semitism in Medieval Art"; and, more recently, with attention to both antique antecedents and contemporary socio-cultural issues affecting the iconographic type, Nina Rowe, "Rethinking Ecclesia and Synagoga in the Thirteenth Century." On the specific resonance of derogatory

representations of Jewishness in Chaucer, see Christine M. Rose, "The Jewish Mother-in-Law"; and Catherine S. Cox, "The Jewish Pardoner and Chaucer's *Canterbury Tales*."

15 On Chaucer as translator of the *Rose*, see the literary- and socio-cultural framing available, respectively, in Rita Copeland, "Rhetoric and Vernacular Translation in the Middle Ages," and Ardis Butterfield, "The English Subject." See also Caroline D. Eckhardt, "The Art of Translation in *The Romaunt of the Rose*"; Tim William Machan, "Chaucer as Translator"; and more recently, following a compelling recapitulation of Dante's linguistic evolution throughout the *Comedy*, John M. Fyler, "Dante's *Logos*, Chaucer's Words."

16 For the text of the *Romaunt*, I have used the Project Gutenberg EBook of *Chaucer's Works*, ed. W.W. Skeat, volume 1 (of 7): *Romaunt of the Rose; Minor Poems*, available at https://www.gutenberg.org/files/43089/43089-h/43089-h.htm.

5 Looking Back and Looking Forward: Reading Levi Reading Dante

1 For the context of this quotation, referring to the biblical story of Babel, see Jacques Derrida, "Roundtable on Translation."

2 For the presence of Dante in the literature and testimony of the Holocaust, in general, see the analytical stance of Sharon Portnoff, "Levi's Auschwitz and Dante's Hell," arguing for a measured divergence perceptible in Levi's reuse; and the contextual analyses in Lawrence Lange, "The Survivor as Author." See also the preliminary sociolinguistic surveys in Sara Calderini and Marina Riccucci, "L'ineffabilità della nefandezza." Most recently, see Lino Pertile, "Dante and the Shoah."

3 On issues of linguistics and translation in Primo Levi, see Cesare Segre, "Primo Levi nella Torre di Babele"; see more recently Zaia Alexander, "Primo Levi and Translation"; Lina N. Insana, *Arduous Tasks* and, pointedly, Insana, "Translation Matters."

4 My translation of Levi's prose is based on the texts established by Marco Belpoliti, in Primo Levi, *Opere*; the pagination reflects the Italian original.

5 On the multi-language chains in *If This Is a Man*, see now Fabrizio Franceschini, "La Babele del Lager e le serie multilingui."

6 On the dialogue with Dante's antecedent in "The Canto of Ulysses," see Dominique Jullien, "Multilingual Maelstrom: Re-reading Primo Levi's *Canto of Ulysses*," and the rich analysis in Tristan Kay, "Primo Levi, Dante, and the Language in Auschwitz."

7 See Peter Arnds, "Translating Survival"; Pietro Frassica, "At Loggerheads with *Lager* Jargon"; and Mirna Cicioni, "*Labour of Civilization and Peace*."

8 For *The Language of the Third Reich*, see Victor Klemperer, *Lingua Tertii Imperii*.

Works Cited

Primary Sources

Ado Viennensis. "Acta Santi Laurenti." In *Martyrologium*, vol. 123:322–5. Paris: J.-P. Migne, 1844.

Ambrose, Saint. *De paradiso liber unus*, in *S. Ambrosii Opera*. Pars I, ed. Carol Schenkl. CSEL edition. Vienna-Prague: Hoelder-Pichler-Tempsky, 1866.

Ammianus Marcellinus. *Rerum Gestarum Libri*. Trans. J.C. Rolfe. Loeb edition. Cambridge, MA: Harvard University Press, 1935.

Arnoldus Leodiensis. *Alphabetum narrationum*. Ed. B. Brilli. Turnhout: Brepols, 2015.

Augustine, Saint. *The City of God against the Pagans*. Trans. G.E. McCracken. Loeb edition. Cambridge, MA: Harvard University Press, 1957.

– *De genesi contra manichaeos*. Sancti Aurelii Augustini Hipponensis Episcopi *Opera Omnia*, vol. 3.1:173–220. *Patrologia Latina* series, vol. 34. Paris: J.-P. Migne, 1865.

– Sant'Agostino. *L'istruzione cristiana*. Ed. M. Simonetti. Lorenzo Valla series. Milan: Arnoldo Mondadori Editore, 1994.

Benjamin, Walter. "The Task of the Translator." In *Selected Writings*, ed. M.W. Jennings and M.P. Bullock. Vol. 1. Cambridge, MA: Belknap Press, 1996. 253–63.

Bible. *Biblia Sacra Iuxta Vulgatam Versionem*. Fourth edition. Ed. R. Weber. Stuttgart: Deutsche Bibelgesellschaft, 1994.

Boccaccio, Giovanni. *Decameron*. Ed. V. Branca. Turin: Einaudi, 1992.

– *The Decameron*. Trans. G.H. McWilliam. London: Penguin, 1995.

Brunetto Latini. *Tesoretto*. Ed. M. Ciccuto. Milan: Rizzoli, 1985.

Chaucer. Geoffrey. *The Canterbury Tales*. Text published through the Harvard Geoffrey Chaucer Website. https://chaucer.fas.harvard.edu/pages/literary-works.

– *Romaunt of the Rose; Minor Poems*. In *Chaucer's Works*, ed. W.W. Skeat. Oxford: Clarendon Press, 1899, volume 1. https://www.gutenberg.org/files/43089/43089-h/43089-h.htm.

Chrétien de Troyes. *Erec and Enide*. Ed. and trans. C.W. Carroll. New York: Garland, 1987.

220   Works Cited

– *Cligès*. Ed. and trans. I. Kasten. Berlin: De Gruyter, 2006.

Christine de Pizan et al. *Debate of the "Romance of the Rose."* Ed. and trans. D.F. Hult. Chicago: University of Chicago Press, 2010.

Claudian. Claudius Claudianus, *De raptu Proserpinae* in *Claudian*. Vol. 2. Trans. M. Platnauer. Loeb edition. Cambrdige, MA: Harvard University Press, 1922.

Dante Alighieri. *Commedia*. Ed. G. Petrocchi. Florence: Le Lettere, 1994.

– *Convivio. Dante's "Il Convivio."* Trans. R.H. Lansing. New York: Garland, 1990. https://dante.princeton.edu/pdp/convivio.htm.

– *De vulgari eloquentia*. Trans. S. Botterill. Cambridge: Cambridge University Press, 1996. https://dante.princeton.edu/pdp/vulgari.html.

– *Il Fiore*. Ed. G. Contini. Milan: Mondadori, 1984.

Epistle of Alexander the Great to Aristotle. In Zibaldone Laurenziano, BML Pluteo 29.8. http://mss.bmlonline.it.

Derrida, Jacques. "Roundtable on Translation." In *The Ear of the Other: Otobiography, Transference, Translation*. Ed. C.V McDonald; trans. P. Kamuf. New York: Shocken Books, 1988.

Guillaume de Lorris and Jean de Meun. *Le Roman de la Rose*. Ed. F. Lecoy. Paris: Champion, 1965–70.

Hrabanus Maurus. *In honorem sanctae crucis*. Ed. M. Perrin. Turnhout: Brepols, 1997.

Iacopo da Varazze. *Legenda Aurea*. Ed. G.P. Maggioni. Florence: Sismel – Edizioni del Galluzzo, 1999.

Isidore of Seville. Allegoriae quaedam Scripturae Sacrae. In *Opera Omnia*, vol. 5. *Patrologia Latina* vol. 83. Paris: J.-P. Migne, 1850.

– Isidori Hispalensis. Episcopi *Etymologiarum sive Originum Libri XX*. Ed. W.M. Lindsay. Oxford: Clarendon Press, 1985.

Jerome, Saint. Sancti Eusebii Hieronymi. *Commentaria in Evangelium Sancti Matthaei*. In *Opera Omnia*, vol. 4. Paris: J.-P. Migne, 1845: coll. 15–22.

Klemperer, Victor. *Lingua Tertii Imperii: A Philologist's Notebook*. Trans. M. Brady. New York: Continuum, 2006.

Levi, Primo. *Opere*. Ed. M. Belpoliti. 2 vols. Turin: Einaudi, 1997.

Magister Matthias. *Copia Exemplorum*. Ed. Lars Wåhlin. Uppsala: Institut für Klassische Philologie, 1990.

Marie de France. *The Fables of Marie de France: An English Translation*. Ed. and trans. M.L. Martin. Birmingham, AL: Summa Publications, 1984.

– *The "Lais" of Marie de France*. Ed. and trans. C.M. Waters. Peterborough, ON: Broadview Editions, 2018.

Ovid. *Heroides. Amores*. Trans. G. Showerman; ed. G.P. Goold. Loeb edition. Cambridge, MA: Harvard University Press, 1914.

– P. Ovidius Naso, *Tristium Libri V – Ibis – Ex Ponto Libri IV*, vol. 3.1. Ed. R. Ehwald and F.W. Levy. Leipzig: Teubner, 1922.

Persius. *Juvenal and Persius*. Ed. and trans. S. Morton Braund. Loeb edition. Cambridge, MA: Harvard University Press, 2004.

Petrarca, Francesco. *Le familiari*. Ed. Ugo Dotti. Urbino: Argalìa, 1974.

– *Res Seniles* Libri XIII–XVII. Ed. Silvia Rizzo and Monica Berté. Florence: Le Lettere, 2017.

Pliny the Younger. *C. Plini Caecili Secundi Epistularum Libri Decem*. Ed. R.A.B. Mynors. Oxford: Clarendon Press, 1963.

Priscian. *Institutionum Grammaticarum Libri I–XII*. Ed. M. Hertz. In *Grammatici Latini ex Recensione Henrici Keilii*, vol. 2. Lepizig: Teubner, 1855.

Vie de Saint Alexis. Ed. J.M. Meunier. Paris: Droz, 1933.

Virgil. *P. Vergili Maronis, Opera*. Ed. R.A.B. Mynors. Oxford: Clarendon Press, 1969.

Secondary Literature

Adams, Tracy. "*Arte Regendus Amor*: Suffering and Sexuality in Marie de France's Lai *Guigemar*." *Exemplaria* 17 (2005): 285–315.

Agamben, Giorgio. *The Kingdom and the Garden*. London-New York: Seagull Books, 2020.

Albanese, Gabriella. "La novella di Griselda." In *Petrarca e il Petrarchismo. Un'ideologia della letteratura*, ed. M. Guglielminetti, xix–xlix. Alessandria: Edizioni dell'Orso, 1994.

Alexander, Zaia. "Primo Levi and Translation." In *The Cambridge Companion to Primo Levi*, ed. R.S.C. Gordon, 155–69. Cambridge: Cambridge University Press, 2007.

Almansi, Guido. *The Writer as Liar: Narrative Technique in the "Decameron."* London: Routledge & Kegan Paul, 1975.

Ardizzone, M.L., ed. *Dante and Heterodoxy: The Temptations of 13th-Century Radical Thought*. Cambridge: Cambridge Scholars Publishing, 2014.

Armour, Peter. "The *Roman de la Rose* and the *Fiore*: Aspects of a Literary Transplantation." *Journal of the Institute of Romance Studies* 2 (1993): 63–81.

Arnds, Peter. "Translating Survival: Translation as Survival in Primo Levi's *Se questo è un uomo*." *Translation and Literature* 21 (2012): 162–74.

Artin, Tom. "Sowers of the Word." In *The Allegory of Adventure: Reading Chrétien's "Erec" and "Yvain*," 31–54. Cranbury, NJ: Associated University Presses, 1974.

Ascoli, Albert Russell. "Boccaccio's Auerbach: Holding the Mirror Up to *Mimesis*." *Studi sul Boccaccio* 20 (1991–2): 377–97.

– "Language: *Neminem ante nos*." In *Dante and the Making of a Modern Author*, 130–74. Cambridge: Cambridge University Press, 2008.

– "Petrarch's Middle Age: Memory, Imagination, History and the *Ascent of Mount Ventoux*." *Stanford Italian Review* 10 (1991): 5–43.

Barański, Zygmunt G. "Dante's Biblical Linguistics." *Lectura Dantis* 5 (1989): 105–43.

– "Latin Literature." In *"Now Feed Yourself": Themes, Traditions, and Cultures in Dante's Works*, ed. Z. Barański, T. Cachey, and A. Pegoretti. Oxford: Legenda, forthcoming.

Barański, Z.G., and P. Boyde, eds. *The "Fiore" in Context: Dante, France, Tuscany*. Notre Dame: Notre Dame University Press, 1997.

Barański, Z.G., and T.J. Cachey, eds. *Dante's "Other Works": Assessments and Interpretations*. Notre Dame: Notre Dame University Press, 2022.

Barolini, Teodolinda. *Dante's Poets: Textuality and Truth in the "Comedy."* Princeton: Princeton University Press, 1984.

– "Difference as Punishment and Difference as Pleasure: From the Tower of Babel in *De vulgari eloquentia* to the Death of Babel in *Paradiso* 26." *Textual Cultures* 12 (2019): 137–54.

– *The Undivine Comedy: Detheologizing Dante.* Princeton: Princeton University Press, 1992.

Battaglia Ricci, Lucia. *Ragionare nel giardino: Boccaccio e i cicli pittorici del "Trionfo della Morte."* Rome: Salerno, 1987.

Baumgartner, Emmanuèle. "The Play of Temporalities; Or, The Reported Dream of Guillaume de Lorris." In *Rethinking the "Romance of the Rose": Text, Image, Reception*, ed. K. Brownlee and S. Huot, 21–38. Philadelphia: University of Pennsylvania Press, 1992.

Beer, J., ed. *A Companion to Medieval Translation.* Amsterdam: Arc Humanities Press, 2019.

Beidler, Peter G. "Chaucer's *Merchant's Tale* and the *Decameron*." *Italica* 50 (1973): 266–84.

Benson, Larry D. "The Merchant's Tale and Its Analogues." In *The Literary Context of Chaucer's Fabliaux*, ed. Larry D. Benson and Theodore M. Andersson, 203–73. New York: Bobbs-Merrill, 1971.

Bettini, Maurizio. Vertere: *Un'Antropologia della traduzione nella cultura antica.* Turin: Einaudi, 2012.

Billanovich, G. "Petrarca e il Ventoso." *Italia Medievale e Umanistica* 9 (1966): 389–401.

– "Petrarch and the Textual Tradition of Livy." *Journal of the Warburg Institute* 14 (1951): 137–208.

Black, Robert. "Classical Antiquity." In *Dante in Context*, ed. Z.G. Barański and L. Pertile, 297–318. Cambridge: Cambridge University Press, 2015.

– "Ovid in Medieval Italy." In *Ovid in the Middle Ages*, ed. J.G. Clark, F.T. Coulson, and K.L. McKinley, 123–42. Cambridge: Cambridge University Press, 2011.

Blamires, Alcuin. *Chaucer, Ethics and Gender.* Oxford: Oxford University Press, 2006.

Bleeth, Kenneth A. "The Image of Paradise in the *Merchant's Tale*." In *The Learned and the Lewed: Studies in Chaucer and Medieval Literature*, ed. L.D. Benson, 45–60. Cambridge, MA: Harvard University Press, 1974.

Blumenfeld, Renate. "Remarques sur *songe/mensonge*." *Romania* 101 (1980): 385–90.

Blumenfeld-Kosinski, Renate. *Reading Myth: Classical Mythology and Its Interpretations in Medieval French Literature.* Stanford: Stanford University Press, 1997.

Boehrer, Bruce Thomas. *Parrot Culture: Our 2500-Year-Long Fascination with the World's Most Talkative Bird.* Philadelphia: University of Pennsylvania Press, 2004.

Bolduc, Michelle. *Translation and the Rediscovery of Rhetoric.* Toronto: Pontifical Institute of Mediaeval Studies, 2020.

Braida, Antonella. "Dante and Translation: An Approach to Untranslatability in the Poet's Work." In *Language and Style in Dante: Seven Essays*, ed. J.C. Barnes and M. Zaccarello, 63–83. Dublin: Four Court Press, 2012.

Brightenback, Kristine. "Remarks on the *Prologue* to Marie de France's *Lais*." *Romance Philology* 30 (1976): 168–77.

Brownlee, Kevin. "The Practice of Cultural Authority: Italian Responses to the French Cultural Dominance in *Il Tesoretto*, *Il Fiore*, and the *Commedia*." *Forum for Modern Languages* 33 (1997): 258–69.

– "The Problem of Faux Semblant: Language, History, and Truth in the *Roman de la Rose*." In *The New Medievalism*, ed. M.S. Brownlee, K. Brownlee, and S.G. Nichols, 253–71. Baltimore: Johns Hopkins University Press, 1991.

– "Pygmalion, Mimesis, and Multiple Endings of the Roman de la Rose." *Yale French Studies* 95 (1999): 193–211.

– "Why the Angels Speak Italian: Dante as Vernacular Poeta in *Paradiso* XXV." *Poetics Today* 5 (1984): 597–610.

Brzezinski Potkay, Monica. "The Parable of the Sower and Obscurity in the Prologue to Marie de France's *Lais*." *Christianity and Literature* 57 (2008): 355–78.

Butterfield, Ardis. "The English Subject." In *The Familiar Enemy: Chaucer, Language and Nation in the Hundred Years War*, 269–307. Oxford: Oxford University Press, 2009.

Cabrini, Anna Maria. "Piume d'angelo, penne di pappagallo." In *Boccaccio: Gli Antichi e i Moderni*, ed. A.M. Cabrini and A. D'Agostino, 179–95. Milan: LediPublishing, 2018.

Calderini, Sara, and Marina Riccucci. "L'ineffabilità della nefandezza: Dante 'per dire' il Lager: un sondaggio preliminare nelle testimonianze non letterarie." *Italianistica* 49 (2020): 213–28.

Campbell, Emma. *Reinventing Babel in Medieval French: Translation and Untranslatability (c. 1120–c. 1250)*. Oxford: Oxford University Press, 2023.

– "Sexual Poetics and the Politics of Translation in the Tale of Griselda." *Comparative Literature* 55.3 (2003): 191–216.

Campbell, E., and R. Mills, eds. *Rethinking Medieval Translation: Ethics, Politics, Theory*. Cambridge: D.S. Brewer, 2012.

Cardini, F., and Massimo Miglio, eds. *Nostalgia del paradiso: Il Giardino medievale*. Rome: Laterza, 2002.

Cestaro, Gary. "Reconstructing Subjectivity in *Purgatorio* and *Paradiso*." In *Dante and the Grammar of the Nursing Body*, 135–66. Notre Dame: University of Notre Dame Press, 2003.

Chiamenti, Massimiliano. *Dante Traduttore*. Florence: Le Lettere, 1995.

Ciavolella, Massimo. "The Tale of Masetto da Lamporecchio." In *The Decameron Third Day in Perspective*, ed. F. Ciabattoni and P.M. Forni, 9–21. Toronto: University of Toronto Press, 2014.

Cicioni, Mirna. "*Labour of Civilization and Peace*: Primo Levi Looks at Interpreters and Interpreting." In *Interpreting Primo Levi: Interdisciplinary Perspectives*, ed. M. Vuohelainen and A. Chapman, 37–49. London: Palgrave Macmillan, 2016.

Clarke, Kenneth P. "On Copying or Not Copying *Griselda*: Petrarch and Boccaccio." In *Boccaccio and the European Literary Tradition*, ed. P. Boitani and E. Di Rocco, 57–71. Rome: Edizioni di Storia e Letteratura, 2014.

– "Reading/Writing Griselda: A Fourteenth-Century Response." In *On Allegory: Some Medieval Aspects and Approaches*, ed. M. Carr, K.P. Clarke, and M. Nievergelt, 183–208. Cambridge: Cambridge Scholars Publishing, 2008.

Conklin Akbari, Suzanne. *Seeing through the Veil: Optical Theory and Medieval Allegory*. Toronto: University of Toronto Press, 2004.

Copeland, Rita. "Rhetoric and Vernacular Translation in the Middle Ages." *Studies in the Age of Chaucer* 9 (1987): 41–75.

Cornish, Alison. *Vernacular Translation in Dante's Italy: Illiterate Literature*. Cambridge: Cambridge University Press, 2010.

Corti, Maria. *Dante a un nuovo crocevia*. Florence: Sansoni, 1981.

Cottino-Jones, Marga. "Desire and the Fantastic in the *Decameron*: The Third Day." *Italica* 70 (1993): 1–18.

Courcelle, Pierre. "Pétrarque entre Saint Augustine et le Augustiniennes." *Studi Petrarcheschi* 7 (1961): 51–71.

Cox, Catherine S. "The Jewish Pardoner and Chaucer's *Canterbury Tales*." In *The Judaic Other in Dante, the "Gawain" Poet, and Chaucer*, 111–44. Gainesville: University Press of Florida, 2005.

Deen Schildgen, Brenda. "Dante's Utopian Landscape: The Garden of God." In *The Medieval World of Nature: A Book of Essays*, ed. J.E. Salisbury, 201–19. New York: Garland, 1993.

Delumeau, Jean. *The History of Paradise: The Garden of Eden in Myth and Tradition*. Trans. M. O'Connell. New York: Continuum, 1995.

Diggelmann, Lindsay. "Gardens as 'Emotional Communities': Three Medieval French Examples." *Digital Philology* 1 (2012): 253–67.

Di Scipio, Giuseppe C. "The Hebrew Women in Dante's Symbolic Rose." *Dante Studies* 101 (1983): 111–21.

Durling, Robert. "Il Petrarca, il Ventoso e la possibilità dell'allegoria." *Revue des Études Augustiniennes* 23 (1977): 304–23.

Eckhardt, Caroline D. "The Art of Translation in *The Romaunt of the Rose*." *Studies in the Age of Chaucer* 6 (1984.): 41–63.

Eco, Umberto. "Dante between Modistae and Kabbalah." In *From the Three to the Labyrinth: Historical Studies on the Sign and Interpretation*, trans. A. Oldocorn, 286–308. Cambridge, MA: Harvard University Press, 2014.

– "The Perfect Language for Dante." In *The Search for the Perfect Language*, 34–52. Oxford: Blackwell, 1995.

Eisner, Martin. "Dante and the Author of the *Decameron*: Love, Literature, and Authority in Boccaccio." In *The Oxford Handbook of Chaucer*, ed. S. Conklin Akbari and J. Simpson, 286–97. Oxford: Oxford University Press, 2020.

Fido, Franco. "Dante personaggio mancato nel *Decameron*." In *Boccaccio: Secoli di Vita*, ed. M. Cottino-Jones and E.F. Tuttle, 177–89. Ravenna: Longo, 1977.

Fioravanti, Gianfranco. Commentary on *Convivio* in Dante Alighieri, *Opere*, vol. 2: 3–805. Milan: Mondadori, 2011.

Fleming, John V. "The Garden of the *Roman de la Rose*: Vision of Landscape or Landscape of Vision?" In *Medieval Gardens*, ed. E.B. MacDougall, 201–34. Washington, DC: Dumbarton Oaks, 1986.

– "Jean de Meun and the Ancient Poets." In *Rethinking the Romance of the Rose: Text, Image, Reception*, ed. K. Brownlee and S. Huot, 81–100. Philadelphia: University of Pennsylvania Press, 1992.

– *The Roman de la Rose: A Study in Allegory and Iconography*. Princeton: Princeton University Press, 1969.

Folena, Gianfranco. *Volgarizzare e tradurre*. Turin: Einaudi, 1991.

Foster Gittes, Tobias. "*Nel Cospetto degli Uomini*: The Prophylactic Peep-Show of *Decameron* VI." In *Boccaccio's Naked Muse: Eros, Culture, and the Mythopoeic Imagination*, 181–209 and 309–16. Toronto: University of Toronto Press, 2008.

Foulet, Alfred, and Karl D. Uitti. "The Prologue to the *Lais* of Marie de France: A Reconsideration." *Romance Philology* 35 (1981–2): 242–9.

Franceschini, Fabrizio. "La Babele del Lager e le serie multilingui." In *Il chimico libertino: Primo Levi e la Babele del Lager*, 19–44. Rome: Carocci, 2022.

Frassica, Pietro. "At Loggerheads with *Lager* Jargon: The Untranslatable in Levi." In *Approaches to Teaching Primo Levi*, ed. N. Patruno and R. Ricci, 68–79. New York: MLA, 2014.

Freccero, John. "The Fig Tree and the Laurel: Petrarch's Poetics." *Diacritics* 5 (1975): 35–40.

Freeman, Michelle A. "The Prologue." In *The Poetics of "Translatio studii" and "Conjointure": Chrétien de Troyes' "Cligès,"* 21–44. Lexington, KY: French Forum, 1979.

Fumo, Jamie C. "An Interpretive Crux in Januarie's Garden: Chaucer's *Merchant's Tale* and the Crucifixion." *Mediaevalia* 23 (2002): 1–37.

– "Romancing the Rose: Apuleius, Guillaume de Lorris, and Moral Horticulture." *Modern Philology* 107 (2010): 343–79.

Fyler, John M. "Dante's *Logos*, Chaucer's Words." In *Language and the Declining World in Chaucer, Dante, and Jean de Meun*, 127–39. Cambridge: Cambridge University Press, 2007.

Gansel, Mireille. *Translation as Transhumance*. Trans. R. Schwartz. New York: Feminist Press at CUNY, 2017.

Geri, Lorenzo. "Una *nuova veste* per una fabella che commuove i dotti: Petrarca, il volgare e la traduzione di *Dec.* X 10." In *Toscana bilingue (1260 ca.–1430 ca.): Per una storia sociale del tradurre medievale*, ed. S. Bischetti, M. Lodone, C. Lorenzi, and A. Montefusco, 333–53. Berlin/Boston: De Gruyter, 2021.

Giamatti, A. Bartlett. *The Earthly Paradise and Renaissance Epic*. Princeton: Princeton University Press, 1966.

Gianferrari, Filippo. *Training the Reader: Dante and the Rise of Vernacular Literacy*. Cambridge: Cambridge University Press, 2024.

Gieseler, John C.L. *A Compendium of Ecclesiastical History*. Edinburgh: T. &. T. Clark, 1853.

Gousset, Marie-Thérèse. *Eden: Le Jardin médiéval à travers l'enluminure*. Paris: Albin Michel, 2001.

Greene, Thomas. *The Light in Troy*. New Haven: Yale University Press, 1982.

Grossman, Edith. *Why Translation Matters*. New Haven: Yale University Press, 2010.

Guadagnini, Elisa. "Les *Métamorphose* d'Ovide dans le Moyen Age Italien." In *Traire de Latin et Espondre: Études sur la Réception Médiévale d'Ovide*, 209–36. Paris: Classiques Garnier, 2021.

Hanning, Robert. "Courtly Contexts for Urban Cultus: Responses to Ovid in Chrétien's *Cligès* and Marie's *Guigemar*." *Symposium* 35 (1981): 35–56.

Harkins, Jessica. "Chaucer's Clerk's Tale and Boccaccio's *Decameron* X.10." *Chaucer Review* 47 (2013): 247–73.

Harrison, Robert Pogue. *Gardens: An Essay on the Human Condition*. Chicago: University of Chicago Press, 2008.

Heffernan, Carol Falvo. "Two 'English Fabliaux': Chaucer's *Merchant's Tale* and *Shipman's Tale* and Italian Novelle." *Neophilologus* 90 (2006): 333–49.

Heller-Roazen, Daniel. *Fortune's Faces: The "Roman de la Rose" and the Poetics of Contingency*. Baltimore: Johns Hopkins University Press, 2003.

Herzman, Ronald B., and Gary W. Towsley. "Squaring the Circle: *Paradiso* 33 and the Poetics of Geometry." *Traditio* 49 (1994): 95–125.

Hollander, Robert. *Boccaccio's Dante and the Shaping Force of Satire*. Ann Arbor: University of Michigan Press, 1997.

– "The Sibyl in Paradiso 33.66 and in De civitate Dei 18.23." *Electronic Bulletin of the Dante Society of America* (4 October 2007): online.

Howes, Laura. *Chaucer's Garden and the Language of Convention*. Gainesville: University Press of Florida, 1997.

Hult, David. *Self-Fulfilling Prophecies: Readership and Authority in the First Roman de la Rose*. Cambridge: Cambridge University Press, 1986.

Hunt, Tony. "Glossing Marie de France." *Romanische Forschungen* 86 (1974): 396–418.

Huot, Sylvia. "The Desire for Knowledge and the Knowledge of Desire." In *Dreams of Lovers and Lies of Poets: Poetry, Knowledge, and Desire in the "Roman de la Rose,"* 10–30. London: Legenda, 2010.

– *The "Romance of the Rose" and Its Medieval Readers: Interpretations, Receptions, Manuscript Transmission*. Cambridge: Cambridge University Press, 1993.

Insana, Lina N. *Arduous Tasks: Primo Levi, Translation, and the Testimony of Holocaust Testimony*. Toronto: University of Toronto Press, 2009.

– "Translation Matters: Levi, Translation, and Holocaust Testimony." In *Approaches to Teaching Primo Levi*, ed. N. Patruno and R. Ricci, 87–104. New York: MLA, 2014.

Jullien, Dominique. "Multilingual Maelstrom: Re-reading Primo Levi's *Canto of Ulysses*." In *Multilingual Literature as World Literature*, ed. J. Hiddleston and W.-C. Ouyang, 145–63. New York: Bloomsbury Academic, 2021.

Kay, Sarah. "Dante's Ex-Appropriation of the Troubadours in *De vulgari eloquentia* and the *Divina commedia*." In *Parrots and Nightingales: Troubadour Quotations and the Development of European Poetry*, 159–75. Philadelphia: University of Pennsylvania Press, 2013.

Kay, Tristan. "Primo Levi, Dante, and the Language in Auschwitz." *Modern Language Review* 117 (2022): 65–100.

Kelly, Douglas. *Internal Difference and Meanings in the Roman de la Rose*. Madison: University of Wisconsin Press, 1995.

– "*Translatio Studii*: Translation, Adaptation, and Allegory in Medieval French Literature." *Philological Quarterly* 57 (1978): 287–310.

Kern, Edith G. "The Gardens in the *Decameron* Cornice." *PMLA* 66 (1951): 505–23.

Kinoshita, Sharon, and Peggy McCracken. "Communication, Transmission, and Interpretation: Literary History." In *Marie de France: A Critical Companion*, ed. S. Kinoshita and P. McCracken, 17–49. Woodbridge, UK: D.S. Brewer, 2012.

Kirkham, Victoria. *Fabulous Vernacular: Boccaccio's "Filocolo" and the Art of Medieval Fiction*. Ann Arbor: University of Michigan Press, 2001.

Kirkpatrick, Robin. "The Griselda Story in Boccaccio, Petrarch and Chaucer." In *Chaucer and the Italian Trecento*, ed. P. Boitani, 231–48. Cambridge: Cambridge University Press, 1983.

Klerks, Suzanne. "The Pain of Reading Female Bodies in Marie de France's *Guigemar*." *Dalhousie French Studies* 33 (1995): 1–14.

Kochanske Stock, Lorrain. "Making It in the *Merchant's Tale*: Chaucer's Signs of January's Fall." *Seimotica* 63 (1987): 171–83.

Koff, Leonard Michael. "Imagining Absence: Chaucer's Griselda *and* Walter *without* Petrarch." In *The "Decameron" and the "Canterbury Tales": New Essays on an Old Question*, ed. L.M. Koff and B. Deen Schildgen, 278–316. Madison: Fairleigh Dickinson University Press, 2000.

Kraus, Henry. "Eve and Mary: Conflicting Images of Medieval Woman" and "Anti-Semitism in Medieval Art." In *The Living Theatre of Medieval Art*, 41–62 and 139–62. Philadelphia: University of Pennsylvania Press, 1967.

Lahiri, Jhumpa. *Translating Myself and Others*. Princeton: Princeton University Press, 2023.

Landsberg, Sylvia. *The Medieval Garden*. Toronto: University of Toronto Press, 2003.

Lange, Lawrence. "The Survivor as Author: Primo Levi's Literary Vision of Auschwitz." In *New Reflections on Primo Levi*, ed. R. Sodi and M. Marcus, 133–47. London: Palgrave Macmillan 2011.

Laurie, Helen C.R. "From *Erec* to *Cligès*." In *Two Studies in Chrétien de Troyes*, 11–138. Paris: Droz, 1972.

Leach, Elizabeth. *Sung Birds: Music, Nature, and Poetry in the Later Middle Ages*. Ithaca and London: Cornell University Press, 2007.

Lombardi, Elena. "Plurilingualism *sub specie aeternitatis*: Language/s in Dante's *Commedia*." In *Dante's Plurilingualism: Authority, Knowledge, Subjectivity*, ed. S. Fortuna, M. Gragnolati, and J. Trabant, 133–147. London: Routledge, 2010.

– "The Poetics of Trespassing." In *Vertical Readings in Dante's "Comedy,"* ed. G. Corbett and H. Webb, vol. 3: 71–88. Cambridge: Open Book Publishers, 2017.

– *The Syntax of Desire: Language and Love in Augustine, the Modistae, Dante*. Toronto: University of Toronto Press, 2007.

Lorenzini, Simona. "Petrarch and Boccaccio: The Rewriting of Griselda's Tale. A Rhetorical Debate on Latin and Vernacular Languages." *Heliotropia* 16–17 (2019–20): 205–27.

Luciani, Évelyne. *Les Confessions de Saint Augustine dans les lettres de Pétrarque.* Paris: Études Augustiniennes, 1982.

MacDougall, E.B., ed. *Medieval Gardens.* Washington, DC: Dumbarton Oaks, 1986.

Machan, Tim William. "Chaucer as Translator." In *The Medieval Translator: The Theory and Practice of Translation in the Middle Ages*, ed. Roger Ellis, 55–67. Cambridge: D.S. Brewer, 1989.

Marchesi, Simone. "Classical Culture." In *The Cambridge Companion to Dante's "Commedia,"* ed. Z.G. Barański and S. Gilson, 127–39. Cambridge: Cambridge University Press, 2019.

– *Dante and Augustine: Linguistics, Poetics, Hermeneutics.* Toronto: University of Toronto Press, 2011.

– *Stratigrafie Decameroniane.* Florence: Olschki, 2004.

Marcozzi, Luca. "Raccontare il Viaggio: Tra *Itineraria ultramarina* e dimensione dell'immaginario." In *Boccaccio Geografo*, ed. R. Morosini, 159–77. Florence: Pagliai, 2010.

Marcus, Millicent Joy. "Boccaccio's Singular Cicero." In *An Allegory of Form: Literary Self-Consciousness in the "Decameron,"* 64–78. New York: Anma Libri, 1979.

– "Seduction by Silence: A Gloss on the Tales of Masetto and Alatiel." *Philological Quarterly* 58 (1979): 1–15.

Marenbon, John. "Jean de Meun, Boethius, and Thirteenth-Century Philosophy." In *The "Roman de la Rose" and Thirteenth-Century Thought*, ed. J. Morton and M. Nivergelt, 173–93. Cambridge: Cambridge University Press, 2020.

Mazzocco, Angelo. *Linguistic Theories in Dante and the Humanists: Studies of Language and Intellectual History in Late Medieval and Early Renaissance Italy.* Leiden: Brill, 1993.

Mazzoni, Francesco. "Per il *topos* della gazza e del pappagallo (*Convivio* III vii 9 – *De Vulgari Eloquentia* I ii 7)." *Italia medioevale e umanistica* 2 (1959): 443–4.

Mazzotta, Giuseppe. "Allegory and the Pornographic Imagination." In *The World at Play in Boccaccio's "Decameron,"* 105–30. Princeton: Princeton University Press, 1986.

– "Rhetoric and History." In *Dante: Poet of the Desert*, 66–106. Princeton: Princeton University Press, 1979.

McWebb, Christine, ed. *Debating the Roman de la Rose: A Critical Anthology.* London: Routledge, 2011.

Mengaldo, Pier Vincenzo. "Preistoria e componenti di una tesi dantesca." In *Linguistica e Retorica in Dante*, 162–99. Pisa: Nistri-Lischi, 1978.

Mickel, Emanuel J. "Marie de France and the Learned Tradition." In *A Companion to Marie de France*, ed. L.E. Whalen, 31–54. Leiden: Brill, 2011.

Migiel, Marilyn. *The Ethical Dimension of the "Decameron."* Toronto: University of Toronto Press, 2015.

Miller, Anne-Hélène. "Nature and Authorship in Brunetto Latini and Guillaume de Machaut." *Nottingham Medieval Studies* 54 (2010): 93–112.

Minnis, Alastair. *From Eden to Eternity: Creations of Paradise in the Later Middle Ages.* Philadelphia: University of Pennsylvania Press, 2016.

– "Lifting the Veil: Sexual/Textual Nakedness in the *Roman de la Rose.*" In *Magister Amoris: The "Roman de la Rose" and Vernacular Hermeneutics*, 82–118. Oxford: Oxford University Press, 2001.

Montefusco, Antonio. "*Roman de la Rose.*" In *The Oxford Handbook of Dante*, ed. M. Gragnolati, E. Lombardi, and F. Southerden, 127–41. Oxford: Oxford University Press, 2021.

Nichols, Stephen. "Global Language or Universal Language? From Babel to the Illustrious Vernacular." *Digital Philology* 1 (2012): 73–109.

ó Cuilleanáin, Cormac. "The Tale of Frate Cipolla." In *The Decameron Sixth Day in Perspective*, ed. D. Lummus, 226–46. Toronto: University of Toronto Press, 2021.

Pearsall, Derek. "Gardens as Symbol and Setting in Medieval Poetry." In *Medieval Gardens*, ed. E.B. MacDougall, 237–51. Washington, DC: Dumbarton Oaks, 1986.

Pertile, Lino. "Dante, Agostino e i pesci di Mercurio (*Par.,* V 85–114)." In *"Tutto il lume de la spera nostra": Studi per Marco Ariani*, ed. G. Crimi and L. Marcozzi, 137–51. Rome: Salerno, 2018.

– "Dante and the Shoah." In *The Oxford Handbook of Dante*, ed. M. Gragnolati, E. Lombardi, and F. Southerden, 651–67. Oxford: Oxford University Press, 2021.

Pietropaolo, Domenico. "Dante on Translation." In *Lost in Translation?*, ed. D. Renevey and C. Whitehead, 87–92. Turnhout: Brepols, 2009.

Portnoff, Sharon. "Levi's Auschwitz and Dante's Hell." *Culture and Society* 46 (2009): 76–84.

Potter, Joy Hambuchen. *Five Frames for the "Decameron."* Princeton: Princeton University Press, 1982.

Powell Harely, Marta. "Narcissus, Hermaphroditus, and Attis: Ovidian Lovers at the Fontaine d'Amors in Guillaume de Lorris's *Roman de la Rose.*" *PMLA* 101 (1986): 324–37.

Ralph Hanna, T., R.G. Keightley, Alastair Minnis, and Nigel F. Palmer. "Latin Commentary Tradition and Vernacular Literature." In *The Cambridge History of Literary Criticism.* Vol. 2: *The Middle Ages*, ed. A. Minnis and I. Johnson, 363–421. Cambridge: Cambridge University Press, 2005.

Reeves, Marjorie. "The Scandal of the Eternal Evangel." In *The Influence of Prophecy in the Later Middle Ages*, 59–70. Oxford: Clarendon Press, 1969.

Reynolds, L.D., and N.G. Wilson, eds. *Texts and Transmission: A Survey of the Latin Classics.* Oxford: Oxford University Press, 1984.

Richards, Earl Jeffrey. "The *Fiore* and the *Roman de la Rose.*" In *Medieval Translators and Their Craft*, ed. J. Beer, 265–83. Kalamazoo, MI: Medieval Institute Publications, 1989.

– "The Translatio Topos and Dante." In *Dante and the "Roman de la Rose": An Investigation into the Vernacular Narrative Context of the "Commedia,"* 42–70. Tübingen: Niemeyer, 1981.

Robbins, Jill. "Petrarch Reading Augustine: *The Ascent of Mont Ventoux*." *Philological Quarterly* 64 (1985): 533–53.

Robertson, D.W. "The Doctrine of Charity in Mediaeval Literary Gardens: A Topical Approach through Symbolism and Allegory." *Speculum* 26 (1951): 24–49.

– "Marie de France, *Lais*, Prologue, 13–16." *Modern Language Notes* 64 (1949): 336–8.

– A Preface to Chaucer: Studies in Medieval Perspectives. Princeton: Princeton University Press, 1963.

Rorty, Richard. *Contingency, Irony, and Solidarity*. Cambridge: Cambridge University Press, 1989.

Rose, Christine M. "The Jewish Mother-in-Law: Synagoga and the Man of Law's Tale." In *Chaucer and the Jews: Sources, Contexts, Meanings*, ed. Sheila Delany, 3–23. London: Routledge, 2002.

Rosier-Catach, Irène. "Man as a Speaking and Political Animal: A Political Reading of Dante's *De vulgari eloquentia*." In *Dante's Plurilingualism: Authority, Knowledge, Subjectivity*, ed. S. Fortuna, M. Gragnolati, and J. Trabant, 34–51. London: Routledge, 2010.

Rossi, Luca Carlo. *Griselda*. Palermo: Sellerio, 1991.

Rossi, Luciano. "Metalepsis and Allegory: The Unity of the *Roman de la Rose*." In *The "Roman de la Rose" and Thirteenth-Century Thought*, ed. J. Morton and M. Nivergelt, 210–32. Cambridge: Cambridge University Press, 2020.

Rossiter, William. "Translation of Allegory or Allegory of Translation? Petrarch's Redressing of Boccaccio's *Griselda*." In *On Allegory: Some Medieval Aspects and Approaches*, ed. M. Carr, K.P. Clarke, and M. Nievergelt, 156–82. Cambridge: Cambridge Scholars Publishing, 2008.

Rowe, Nina. "Rethinking Ecclesia and Synagoga in the Thirteenth Century." In *Gothic Art and Thought in the Later Medieval Period*, ed. Colum Hourihane, 265–91. Princeton: Index of Christian Art, 2011.

Scafi, Alessandro. *Mapping Paradise: A History of Heaven on Earth*. Chicago: University of Chicago Press, 2006.

Schauch, Margaret. "The Allegory of Church and Synagogue." *Speculum* 14 (1939): 448–64.

Scott, John A. "Dante and Classical Antiquity." In *Understanding Dante*, 231–60. Notre Dame: Notre Dame University Press, 2003.

Segre, Cesare. "Primo Levi nella Torre di Babele." In *Primo Levi as Witness*, ed. P. Frassica, 86–97. Florence: Casalini, 1990.

Selenu, Stefano. "Nella caccia della lingua: La gioia di Dante e lo spettro di Babele tra volgare, vita e arti meccaniche." *Dante Studies* 132 (2014): 59–85.

Shaw, Prue. "A Reading of *Purgatory* XXVI." In *Dante and His Literary Precursors: Twelve Essays*, ed. J.C. Barnes and J. Petrie, 235–59. Dublin: Four Courts Press, 2007.

Smarr, Janet L. "*Mercury* in the Garden: Mythological Methods in the *Merchant's Tale* and in *Decameron* VII.9." In *The Mythographic Art: Classical Fable and the Rise of the Vernacular in Early France and England*, ed. J. Chance, 192–212. Gainesville: University of Florida Press, 1990.

Smith, Nathaniel B. "In Search of the Ideal Landscape: From *Locus Amoenus* to *Parc du Champ Joli* in the *Roman de la Rose*," *Viator* 11 (1980): 225–43.

Soro, Antonio. "*PESCE* in *Par.* V, 97–109: Un acrostico inverso." *Electronic Bulletin of the Dante Society of America* (February 15, 2009): online.

Spearing, A.C. *Medieval Dream-Poetry*. Cambridge: Cambridge University Press, 1976.

Spitzer, Leo. "The Prologue to the *Lais* of Marie de France and Medieval Poetics." *Modern Philology* 41 (1943): 96–102.

Spivak, Gayatri Chakravorty. "Translation as Culture." *Parallax* 6 (2000): 13–24.

Steinberg, Justin. "Arbitrium and Poetic License in *De vulgari eloquentia*." In *Dante and the Limits of the Law*, 63–71. Chicago: University of Chicago Press, 2013.

Stillinger, Thomas C. "The Language of Gardens: Boccaccio's *Valle delle Donne*." *Traditio* 39 (1983): 301–21.

Tavoni, Mirko. "Che cosa erano il volgare e il latino per Dante." *Letture Classensi* 41 (2013): 9–27.

– Commentary on *De vulgari eloquentia*. In Dante Alighieri, *Opere*, vol. 1:1066–1547. Milan: Mondadori, 2011.

– "Language and Style." In *The Cambridge Companion to Dante's "Commedia,"* ed. Z.G. Barański and S. Gilson, 95–109. Cambridge: Cambridge University Press, 2018.

Thompson, N.S. *Chaucer, Boccaccio, and the Debate of Love: A Comparative Study of "The Decameron" and "The Canterbury Tales."* Oxford: Clarendon Press, 1996.

Tufano, Ilaria. "Nel giardino di Boccaccio." In *"Prati, verzieri e Pomieri": Il giardino medievale. Culture, ideali, società*, ed. P. Caraffi and P. Pirillo, 59–73. Florence: Edifir, 2017.

Turner, Joseph. "Rhetoric and Performing Anger: Proserpina's Gift and Chaucer's *Merchant's Tale*." *Rhetorica* 34 (2016): 427–54.

Tylus, Jane. "Petrarch's Griselda and the Sense of an Ending." *Nottingham Medieval Studies* 56 (2012): 421–45.

Uitti, Karl D. "*Érec et Énide* and *Cligés*: Conjointure, Clergie and Translatio." *In Chrétien de Troyes Revisited*, 35–58. New York: Twayne Publishers, 1995.

Usher, Jonathan. "Frame and Novella Gardens in the *Decameron*." *Medium Aevum* 58 (1989): 274–85.

– "Frate Cipolla's *Ars Praedicandi*: Or a *Récit du Discourse* in Boccaccio." *Modern Language Review* 88 (1993): 321–36.

– "Pieces of Dante among Cipolla's Relics." *Lectura Dantis* 13 (1993): 22–31.

van Peteghem, Julie. *Italian Readers of Ovid from the Origins to Petrarch: Responding to a Versatile Muse*. Leiden: Brill, 2020.

Verdicchio, Massimo. "Griselda between Boccaccio and Petrarch." *Italica* 97.1 (2020): 5–31.

Victor, Jacqueline. "Time and the Reader of the *Roman de la Rose*." *Exemplaria* 32 (2020): 145–66.

Walker-Meikle, Kathleen. "Pets in Literature." In *Medieval Pets*, 90–107. Woodbridge, UK: Boydell Press, 2012.

Wallace, David. "'Whan She Translated Was': A Chaucerian Critique of the Petrarchan Academy." In *Literary Practice and Social Change in Britain, 1380–1530*, ed. Lee Patterson, 156–215. Berkeley, University of California Press, 1990.

Webb, Heather. "Language." In *The Oxford Handbook of Dante*, ed. M. Gragnolati, E. Lombardi, and F. Southerden, 464–79. Oxford: Oxford University Press, 2021.

Weiss, Roberto. "The Forerunners of Petrarch." In *The Renaissance Discovery of Classical Antiquity*, 16–29. Oxford: Blackwell, 1969.

Whalen, Logan E. "A Medieval Book-Burning: *Objet d'Art* as Narrative Device in the *Lai of Guigemar*." *Neophilologus* 80 (1996): 205–11.

– "The Prologues and Epilogues of Marie de France." In *A Companion to Marie de France*, ed. L.E. Whalen, 1–30. Leiden: Brill, 2011.

Wicher, Andrzej. "Geoffrey Chaucer's *The Merchant's Tale*, Giovanni Boccaccio's *The Tale of the Enchanted Pear-Tree*, and *Sir Orfeo*." *Text Matters* 3.3 (2013): 43–57.

Wimsatt, James I. "Chaucer and the Canticle of Canticles." In *Chaucer the Love Poet*, ed. J. Mitchell and W. Provost, 66–90. Athens: University of Georgia Press, 1973.

Wittig, Joseph S. "The Aeneas-Dido Allusion in Chrétien's *Erec et Enide*." *Comparative Literature* 22 (1970): 237–53.

Zak, Gur. "Petrarch's Griselda and the End of Humanism." *Le Tre Corone* II (2015): 173–91.

Zanoni, Marie-Louise. "Ceo Testimoine Precïens: Priscian and the Prologue to the *Lais* of Marie de France." *Traditio* 36 (1980): 407–15.

Zedolik, John. "*The gardyn is enclosed al aboute*: The Inversion of Exclusivity in the *Merchant's Tale*." *Studies in Philology* 112 (2015): 490–503.

Index